European Socialists Across Borders

European Socialists Across Borders

Transnational Cooperation and Alternative
Visions of Europe After 1945

Edited by Mélanie Torrent
and Andrew J. Williams

Available to purchase in print or download
for free at https://uolpress.co.uk

First published 2025 by
University of London Press
Senate House, Malet St, London WC1E 7HU

© the Authors 2025

The right of the authors to be identified as authors of this Work has been asserted by them in accordance with sections 77 and 78 of the Copyright, Designs and Patents Act 1988.

This book is published under a Creative Commons Attribution-NonCommercial-NoDerivatives 4.0 International (CC BY-NC-ND 4.0) license.

Please note that third-party material reproduced here may not be published under the same license as the rest of this book. If you would like to reuse any third-party material not covered by the book's Creative Commons license, you will need to obtain permission from the copyright holder.

A CIP catalogue record for this book is
available from The British Library.

ISBN 978-1-908590-82-4 (hardback)
ISBN 978-1-915249-71-5 (paperback)
ISBN 978-1-915249-74-6 (.epub)
ISBN 978-1-915249-73-9 (.pdf)
ISBN 978-1-915249-72-2 (.html)

DOI https://doi.org/10.14296/vjit1721

Cover image: XVIII Congress of the Socialist International, Stockholm, 20–22 June 1989. Socialist International Photo Archives.

Cover design for University of London Press by Nicky Borowiec.
Series design by Nicky Borowiec.
Book design by Nigel French.
Text set by Westchester Publishing Services UK in Meta Serif and Meta, designed by Erik Spiekermann.

Contents

Notes on contributors	vii
Acknowledgements	ix
List of abbreviations	xi
Introduction Mélanie Torrent and Andrew J. Williams	1

Part I. European socialism in war and peace

1. The Labour Party and its relations with the SFIO in London, 1940–44   33
   Andrew J. Williams

2. Trans-war continuities: the *Mouvement Socialiste pour les États-Unis d'Europe* (MSEUE) and socialist networks in the early Cold War   59
   Ben Heckscher and Tommaso Milani

Part II. Paths not taken? European socialists and the politics of worldmaking at the end of empire

3. Europe re-imagined? Claude Bourdet, *France-Observateur* and British critics of the Algerian war   91
   Mélanie Torrent

4. Social activism in the age of decolonisation: Basil Davidson and the liberation struggles in Lusophone Africa, c. 1954–75   127
   Pedro Aires Oliveira

5. Olof Palme, Sweden and the Vietnam War: An outspoken socialist among European socialists   157
   Lubna Z. Qureshi

Part III. Redefining Europe and reassessing Europeanisation: socialist readings of internationalism and liberalism

6. European socialists and international solidarity with Palestine: towards a socialist European network of solidarity in the 1970s and 1980s?   183
   Thomas Maineult

7. Black British Labour leaders and the Europeanisation of
   antiracism, 1986–93   201
   Pamela Ohene-Nyako

8. From dark to light: the fate of two European socialist
   employment initiatives in an age of austerity   223
   Mathieu Fulla

   Index   249

Notes on contributors

Mathieu Fulla is Research Fellow at the Sciences Po Centre for History in Paris. He has recently co-edited with Michele Di Donato *Leftist Internationalisms: A Transnational Political History* (Bloomsbury, 2023). He is currently working on a new book dealing with the relationship between West European Socialists and the 'neoliberal paradigm' from the late 1960s to Blairism.

Ben Heckscher teaches at the International School of Estonia, following a master's degree in world history and a PhD in European integration at the London School of Economics.

Thomas Maineult teaches history and is completing a doctoral thesis at the Sciences Po Centre for History in Paris. His main research focus is on movements that support the Palestinian cause in France between 1967 and the end of the 1980s. He has published several articles on the French left and on the Israeli–Palestinian conflict.

Tommaso Milani is a postdoctoral researcher (Wissenschaftlicher Mitarbeiter) at the Institut für soziale Bewegungen, Ruhr-Universität Bochum. A former Max Weber Fellow at the European University Institute (EUI), he taught at Balliol College, University of Oxford, and Sciences Po, Paris. His first monograph, *Hendrik de Man and Social Democracy: The Idea of Planning in Western Europe, 1914–1940*, was published in 2020 (Palgrave Macmillan).

Pamela Ohene-Nyako is a PhD candidate and teaching assistant in modern European history at the University of Geneva. Her research focuses on Black European women's internationalism and intersectional thought from the 1960s to the 2000s. Her interests are in transnational history, Black intellectual thought, and modern Black and women's history. She has recently published a peer-reviewed article on the transnational activism of French-Cameroonian feminist Lydie-Dood-Bunya (*Journal of Women's History*, Fall, 2023).

Pedro Aires Oliveira is Associate Professor at NOVA University of Lisbon – School of Social Sciences and Humanities (NOVA-FCSH) and an integrated researcher at the IHC. His main research topics are diplomatic history, colonialism and decolonisation, on which he has published extensively, either in book format or in scholarly journals. His latest publication is *Empires and Colonial Incarceration in the Twentieth Century* (co-edited with Philip J. Havik, Helena Pinto Janeiro and Irene Flunser Pimentel; Routledge, 2022).

Lubna Z. Qureshi is the author of *Olof Palme, Sweden, and the Vietnam War: A Diplomatic History* (Lexington Books, 2023) and *Nixon, Kissinger, and Allende: U.S. Involvement in the 1973 Coup in Chile* (Lexington Books, 2008). She holds a doctorate in American history, with an emphasis on US foreign policy, from the University of California, Berkeley.

Mélanie Torrent is Professor of British and Commonwealth history at the Université de Picardie Jules Verne (Amiens) and Senior Research Fellow at the Institute of Commonwealth Studies (London). She became a junior member of the Institut universitaire de France (IUF) in 2016. Her most recent book, resulting from her research with the IUF, is *Algerian Independence and the British Left: Solidarities and Resistance in a Decolonizing World* (Bloomsbury, 2024).

Andrew J. Williams is Emeritus Professor of International Relations at the University of St Andrews. His most recent books include *France, Britain and the United States in the Twentieth Century: 1900–1940* (Palgrave Macmillan, 2014) and a second volume, *1940–1961* (Palgrave Macmillan, 2020); a third volume is in progress, covering 1961–1970. He is also planning a new book on 'France and the International', which will be a 'history of ideas'.

Acknowledgements

The chapters assembled in this volume were first discussed at a conference held in November 2019 at the Institute of Commonwealth Studies, in London. The editors extend their warmest thanks to the team in place at the time – Philip Murphy, its director, Chloe Pieters, its administrative manager, and Olga Jimenez, its events manager. They ensured we had a relaxed, friendly and stimulating two days, and it was a fond memory for us to cherish during the times of COVID-19, lockdown and the restrictions of virtual conferences that hit us so soon afterwards.

Acknowledgements are also due to the Institut universitaire de France (IUF), the Université de Picardie Jules Verne (and the research unit CORPUS UR 4295) and the University of St Andrews, for providing material support for this project, both in London and since then; and to our anonymous reviewers as well as Emma Gallon at the University of London Press, for extremely useful and constructive recommendations and suggestions.

Last, but certainly not least, we would also like to express our profound thanks to all of our contributors for their patience, good humour and support as this volume took shape. In what were sometimes difficult circumstances, it has been a pleasure working with such an excellent team of colleagues.

Abbreviations

AES	Alternative Economic Strategy
ASFA	*Association de solidarité franco-arabe*
BWEN	Black Women and Europe Network
CAP	Common Agricultural Policy
CDU	*Christlich Demokratische Union Deutschlands*
CEPG	Cambridge Economic Policy Group
CERES	*Centre d'études, de recherches et d'éducation socialiste*
CFMAG	Committee for Freedom in Mozambique, Angola and Guinea
CIR	*Convention des institutions républicaines*
CND	Campaign for Nuclear Disarmament
CNF	*Comité national français*
CPGB	Communist Party of Great Britain
CSPEC	Confederation of the Socialist Parties of the European Community
ECOSOC	Economic and Social Council of the United Nations
EDC	European Defence Community
EEC	European Economic Community
EEI	European Employment Initiative
EFTA	European Free Trade Association
EM	European Movement
EMS	European Monetary System
EMU	Economic and Monetary Union
EU	European Union
FAO	Food and Agriculture Organisation of the United Nations
FCB	Fabian Colonial Bureau
FDP	*Freie Demokratische Partei*
FERE	*Fédération européenne de recherches économiques*
FIDH	*Fédération internationale pour les droits humains*
FLN	*Front de libération nationale*
FRELIMO	*Frente de Libertação de Moçambique*
GJJ	*Groupe Jean Jaurès*
GPRF	*Gouvernement provisoire de la République française*
GRAPP	*Groupe de recherche et d'action pour le règlement du problème palestinien*
ILP	Independent Labour Party
IMF	International Monetary Fund
IRR	Institute of Race Relations
ISD	*Initiativ Schwarze Deutsche*

LSI	Labour and Socialist International
MAPAÏ	*Mifléguet Poalei Eretz Israel*
MAPAM	*Mifleget HaPoalim HaMeuhedet*
MCF	Movement for Colonial Freedom
MEP	Member of the European Parliament
MP	Member of (the British) Parliament
MPLA	*Movimento Popular de Libertação de Angola*
MSEUE	*Mouvement socialiste pour les États-Unis d'Europe*
MUSSE	Movement for the United Socialist States of Europe
NATO	North Atlantic Treaty Organisation
NLR	*New Left Review*
OAS	*Organisation armée secrète*
OURS	*Office universitaire de rercherche socialiste*
PAIGC	*Partido Africano da Independência da Guiné e Cabo Verde*
PCF	*Parti communiste français*
PES	Party of European Socialists
PLO	Palestine Liberation Organisation
POUM	*Partido Obrero de Unificación Marxista*
PS	*Parti socialiste*
PSI	*Partito socialista italiano*
PSU	*Parti socialist unifié*
PWW	Post-War Planning
QIAR	Quaker International Affairs Representative
RAP	Rock Against Police
SAMAK	Co-operation Committee of the Nordic Social Democratic Parties and Trade Union Labour Organisations
SAP	*Sveriges Socialdemokratiska Arbetarepartiet*
SCORE	Standing Conference for Racial Equality in Europe
SEA	Single European Act
SFIO	*Section française de l'internationale ouvrière*
SGEP	Socialist Group in the European Parliament
SOE	Special Operations Executive
SPD	*Sozialdemokratische Partei Deutschlands*
UDC	Union of Democratic Control
UEF	*Union européenne des fédéralistes*
UGS	*Union de la gauche socialiste*
ULR	*Universities and Left Review*
UNESCO	United Nations Educational, Scientific and Cultural Organisation
UNITA	*União Nacional para a Independência Total de Angola*
UPA	*União das Populações de Angola*
USA	United States of America
USSR	Union of Soviet Socialist Republics

Introduction

Mélanie Torrent and Andrew J. Williams

From the post-war debates on institutionalised cooperation in Western Europe to the more recent dynamics of the European Union, this volume investigates the impact of socialist cooperation across borders on European construction and integration, as well as how various European socialists analysed international (dis-)orders and envisioned alternatives. Focusing on the interplay between policy making and international theory, the chapters assess how various socialist networks in Western Europe were influenced by relations with socialist parties and groups outside Europe, and how they navigated local, national and global politics. The scholars whose contributions are gathered here are interested in – and for some, have dedicated a good portion of their careers to – the untangling of a series of *conundra* that are crucial for understanding not only the development of European socialism after the Second World War but also how different socialist movements interacted with each other and what the longer-term results of that interaction can be said to have been. Believing with Daniel Gorman that '[t]ransnational personal relationships were a defining feature of post-war internationalism in Britain',[1] our common interest lies in how those who defined themselves as democratic socialists (as opposed to communists) in Europe talked to each other after 1945, and to a certain extent before and during the Second World War. What influenced them, how and why did they communicate? What were the vectors of that communication? How effective were they in ironing out the inevitable differences that existed between them, and how desirous were they of actually doing so? What influence did the long endings of the European colonial empires have on relations between socialist individuals and groups? And what role did the very experience of empire, post-empire and structures of exploitation and domination have on the decision of some individuals to embrace, critique and redefine socialism, specifically in Western Europe?

There were obvious shared concerns between European socialist parties at the end of the Second World War. How should the 'vanquished' be treated in such a way that a possible future together could be envisioned?[2] How could Europe be reconstructed, avoiding the problems that had arisen after 1919? Who or what could act as inspiration for re-growth, and what policies could be developed either separately or together? More widely, how could advice from foreign comrades help the domestic cause of socialism in countries, like Portugal and Spain, that were still ruled by fascist dictators? Were the ideological priorities of the different parties compatible, especially given their very different historical trajectories and experiences of power (or lack of it)? What inspiration could be drawn from the struggles of peoples still dominated by Western powers in Algeria, Vietnam, Angola and elsewhere? On a more individual note, who could be trusted to cooperate without taking advantage of real or perceived weaknesses in the interlocutor? What the answers could or should be, and how to translate them into policies also generated fierce divisions among socialists across and within their nations.

Europe(s) since 1945

In 1945, there was no pre-determined path to the kind of Europe(s) that can be said to exist today. Even now, as Boaventura de Sousa Santos notes, it is essential to stress that 'there is not "one Europe"', but 'rival and contrasting European identities, depending on where the boundaries of Europe are drawn and how the nature of "European-ness" is perceived'.[3] Such diversity, resulting in tensions and competing narratives, is something that the contributors to this volume are very alert to, as were several of the individuals whose engagement for social democracy they trace. While the 'new cartography of Europe' de Sousa Santos calls for is undoubtedly limited here by the focus on European archival material, several of the contributions investigate the ways in which 'the colonial world [as] a multifaceted site of resistance and survival ingenuity'[4] was taken into account – to what extent and with what intellectual and practical consequences – by the individuals and groups that sought to build a more open Europe. The various 'Europes' which they dreamed of and tried to establish, and those which eventually prevailed, need to be situated within the broader political spectrum of post-war politics.

The conservative right of European politics, especially that associated with the ideas generally known as 'Christian Democratic', and even much more overtly nationalist parties, were massively backed by US think tanks and wealthy organisations well versed in the wiles of Madison Avenue.[5] Parties started by liberals were built on pre-existing democratic foundations, ones that had often succumbed to Adolf Hitler's *Neuordnung* or, as with the communists, the allure of the Soviet Union.[6] The Gaullists in France, who captured large portions of the vote, had their counterparts in most European countries. De Gaulle needs no introduction of course, but his ideas and personality towered above every party in France, with the exception of the *Parti Communiste Français* (PCF), who called itself 'le parti des fusillés'. These two major contributors to the Resistance thus partially squeezed out the French socialists, who did make a significant contribution in spite of the overwhelming noise emanating from the Gaullists and the PCF. Notwithstanding their 'past imperfect', as Tony Judt put it,[7] the PCF managed to dominate much of the discourse of what Europe (as well as France) should aspire to, often in direct challenge to the more liberal desire to stay close to the United States and Britain. As a similar pattern was played out in other parts of Europe, how could socialists make their voice heard?

An important part of post-1945 Europe that needs to be mentioned here, but that space and the logic of this book rather excludes, is the role that has been increasingly played by liberal thinking about Europe in competition with socialist thought. In 1945, as we show in this volume, socialist and broader state interventionist thinking dominated the debate about how a future Europe should evolve. This was termed 'Keynesianism' across Europe and denoted the broad consensus that the 'planning' that had dominated state thinking during the war should be continued into the peace. Hence in France *le commissariat général du Plan* established under Charles de Gaulle's presidency (1944–46) was embellished and extended under subsequent governments of the Fourth and Fifth Republics. In Britain the term 'Butskellism' was used to denote a consensus – albeit an incomplete and contested one[8] – between the Labour Party of the 1950s (under Hugh Gaitskell) and the Conservative Party of 'Rab' Butler on how to best reconstruct the British economy. This was not seriously challenged across Europe until the advent of 'Thatcherism' in Britain in 1979 where Prime Minister Margaret Thatcher ditched Keynes in favour of what are now termed 'neoliberal' free-market policies. These were in turn adopted across Western Europe, even by most socialist parties, and certainly by the Labour Party after Tony Blair became leader in 1994. But neoliberalism had been touted by thinkers like Friedrich Hayek at the London School of Economics from the publication of his book, *The Road to Serfdom*, in 1944.[9] Hayek, Ludwig van Mises and the majority of the 'neoliberal' 'Mont Pelerin' group were nostalgic for their native Austro-Hungarian Empire, an entity which had been multi-ethnic with fully open internal borders, a model which can be said to characterise – up to a point – the present-day European Union.[10] This process, aided by the conversion of the United States under Ronald Reagan in the 1980s has been examined by authors such as Alain Laurent with some distaste.[11] Sidelined by most states and in international organisations until the 1980s, neoliberalism thus emerged as a direct counter to socialist ideas about planning and has been dominant in Europe ever since at least the Treaty of Maastricht which came into effect in 1993. Thus, while socialism was dominant as one form of 'globalism' until the 1970s, this has been on contested ground since the 1940s, and still is today.

During the period covered by this book, outside France and Western Europe as a whole, the siren drums of collectivist communism and individualist capitalism were amplified by expert propaganda disseminated by entities in Washington and Moscow, both proposing an opposing and compelling set of arguments. European intellectuals and diplomats were not alone in being impressed by the astonishing material progress of the United States and the heroic defence of both Stalingrad and the former European colonies by the Soviet Union, the 'homeland of the proletariat'. De Gaulle himself went to Moscow in his first foreign foray as head of the *Gouvernement Provisoire de la République française* in late 1944, an initiative that impressed neither Franklin Delano Roosevelt nor Josef Stalin.[12] Others looked to a partly functional, and partly mythical Europe based on liberal democratic principles – what we now call 'neoliberalism' originated in dreams of a borderless Europe where the realities of the market would eventually overcome nationalist fervour, as mentioned above.[13]

Trans-nationalising international policy making

In considering why thinking and acting across borders mattered to a number of European socialists, and how socialism was embedded – only partly, or fully – in their initiatives for international policy in Europe, this volume takes stock of the fact that in recent years, the study of international policy has largely been renewed in four ways.

First, scholars have turned their attention to the connected evaluation of the decolonisation and globalisation processes, the internationalisation of colonial issues and transnational anti-colonial mobilisation, and the expansion of new international norms during colonial retreat.[14] Historians of European integration and global financial networks have demonstrated that the history of the European Union is intrinsically linked to decolonisation processes,[15] and that the ends of the colonial empires have had a tangible impact on the former imperial powers of the EU.[16] The history of Europe more broadly has also benefited from the study of migration, diaspora and struggles for equality and liberation in challenging and redefining cosmopolitanism, which resonates with some of the aspirations and issues in this volume. 'European cosmopolitanism', as Gurminder Bhambra and John Narayan note, can only be properly understood if 'those multicultural others who come to constitute European polities through imperial endeavours' are considered.[17] Even then, the very concept of cosmopolitanism, as underlined by Stefan Berger and Sean Scalmer, is so strongly 'connected in European intellectual traditions with humanism and the Enlightenment that it seems to suggest an open, tolerant and intercultural approach to transnationalism' that risks obscuring others.[18] It is therefore important to state that the following chapters, despite their primary reliance on Western and Northern European sources, take full stock of the criticism that European socialists, including those who sought to work across borders and imagine an alternative Europe and fairer world order, faced from within the empires and ex-empires. As two Algerian members of the new independent assembly told their Italian hosts in Milan in 1962: 'A shared future for Africa and the European left was only possible under the banner of an "unconditional anticolonialism". [...] The problem is therefore whether the European Left is hereafter truly determined to understand our reality'. What for an Italian delegate was merely 'the myth of Bandung' was to the Algerians 'not a myth [but] the crystallisation of the efforts of Africa and Asia in the struggle against colonialism', which had given the Algerian movement for liberation material assistance and a diplomatic platform.[19] We also acknowledge the pitfalls associated with 'the Anglicising of intellectual lives around the world' and the dangers of narratives of 'encounters' being reduced to 'Westerners and Resterners', in the words of Jeremy Adelman. By being critically aware of the sources used in this volume – in a range of languages and locations, but European ones – the contributors try to take fully into account Adelman's suggestion that 'understanding inter-dependence means seeing how it expands personal and social horizons for some, but also thins bonds with others'.[20]

Such debates also point to the need to unpack forms and meanings of 'internationalisation', which, as Rob Skinner has shown in his recent study of peace networks, has often 'in the context of post-war peace movements tended to mean transatlantic cooperation and communication rather than a form of globalization'.[21] It is at the very least, as suggested by Jessica Reinisch and David Brydan, 'the search for intergovernmental agreements and conventions; the practice of international assembly; the projection of national agendas across the globe; or the transfer of ideas, objects or people across national boundaries', as well as 'the shared agendas of particular international movements or organizations – both as an aspiration to universalism and as a much more limited, less ambitious attempts at cooperation'.[22] What we are particularly interested in, in socialist circles of various sizes and shapes, is the extent to which these forms of internationalism intersected, and how the practice of cooperation across borders resulted in transnational projects. Several of our contributors thus trace transnational actions and narratives as means of 'reveal[ing] the ways in which processes of modernity, including decolonization "occur in varied and often unpredictable ways"'.[23] While it is not always possible to determine exactly how transnational endeavours were 'adopted, adapted and reinterpreted in particular national and local contexts',[24] the chapters show instances in which for individuals, groups or networks, earlier encounters, debates and trips across borders influenced specific policy decisions or understandings of what European socialism could or should be. Some of the contributors also take inspiration from a series of studies that have emphasised the porosity of cooperation across Cold War borders in Europe. This would include alternative agencies such as the United Nations Economic Commission for Europe (1947–64), whose first secretary, Swedish economist Gunnar Myrdal – who surfaces in Lubna Qureshi's chapter – 'refused to accept Europe's split into East and West as a lasting geopolitical reality';[25] cultural forums such as the European Society of Culture, formed in 1950 as part of a wider 'powerful, if generally overlooked, international response from intellectuals because of the global challenge [the Cold War] presented to peace';[26] and less organised forms of intellectual solidarity which covered a wide range of political sensibilities.[27]

Second, histories of European socialist parties have been revised by scholars locating their analysis in alternative spaces (such as Neville Kirk's work on labour movements in the British world[28] or Claire Marynower's study of French socialism – the *Section française de l'Internationale ouvrière*, SFIO – in Algeria[29]), in multilateral bodies such as the Socialist International,[30] and by connecting anti-colonial activity across the empires and ex-empires.[31] Equally important has been the mapping out of socialist activism in Africa after empire and in Latin America, with the actions of individuals and non-governmental groups shedding light on the shifting conceptions of social democracy and democratic socialism, fairness and equality, as well as reform and revolution as a means to achieve individual and collective emancipation and freedom.[32] Part of this renewal has focused on a broad conception of socialism, encompassing both democratic socialism and communism.[33] New studies of the global socialism of the Soviet Union, for instance, also bear on the reading of the contributions in this volume. As the team around James Mark and Paul Betts has shown, in the period after 1945, 'socialism's importance as a globalizing force accelerated and drew together what contemporaries called the "Second" and "Third Worlds"; and the processes of European integration and enlargement from 1989 'brought an end to many internationalist paradigms and linkages', resulting in Eastern Europe in 'a process of de-internationalization from a world which had opened up through the decolonization of Western European empires'.[34] As Françoise Blum and the authors of *Socialisms in Africa* have recently argued: 'The history of socialism is also the history of travel and circulations across the globe: the travel of practices and concepts, the travel of a word across the languages of the world'.[35] Taking stock of the wide remit and uses of 'socialism', Blum and her co-authors suggest that socialism is at times perhaps best defined in the negative, as 'any doctrine which is not animated by a quest for social justice or does not promote an emancipation project for the human race', they argue, 'is not socialist'; and the 'socialists' who inhabit their volume are those who 'used the term themselves to identify their practice or the ideologies in which it was rooted'.[36] This applies to some extent to the European socialists of this volume, who all shared membership of, or a willingness to join, the Socialist International as the embodiment of a democratic, parliamentary version of socialism *and* a socialism experienced across borders. This does not imply idealising intentions or processes.

As the contributions show, the 'emancipation project', particularly in its colonial sense, was deeply contested and not collectively embraced. Where French socialism is concerned, and for a time at least, '[a] marginalization of socialist internationalism was part of the "remaking of France" during the "invention of decolonization"', with the conflict between an older, SFIO Europeanism and the more recent 'Third Worldism' ultimately resulting in 'internationalism largely vanish[ing] as a guiding principle of French socialism'.[37] Such debates were not confined to the French. At the level of both European institutions (EEC/EU) and wider (but still largely European) networks such as the Socialist International, European socialists grappled with the critique formulated by other socialists like the Jamaican Michael Manley, for whom the world was divided along a North–South, rather than an East–West divide: 'When viewed from the "tropics"', as Adom Getachew has put it, 'the world was not bifurcated by ideology, but by a global economy whose origins lay in the project of European imperial expansion'.[38] Following the call for a New International Economic Order, the 'Programme for Survival' issued by the Independent Commission on International Development chaired by Germany's *Sozialdemokratische Partei Deutschlands* (SPD) leader Willy

Brandt – a recurring figure in this volume – was one response. It 'fused the hope for global redistribution with a dream of global peace and disarmament', in the words of Gyan Prakash and Jeremy Adelman,[39] but it also, as Mathieu Fulla's chapter shows, led to significant discussions – albeit not straightforward or necessarily conclusive ones – among European socialists on 'common security, North–South dialogue and human rights'.

For Blum and her co-authors, it is particularly worthwhile for historians to focus on 'how ideas circulate (materially and symbolically)', and on 'the lived experience, the ways of being and thinking of oneself as "socialist" depending on spaces and historical periods'.[40] This is particularly fruitful, in fact, when thinking of socialism in connection with other '-isms', notably, for this volume, transnationalism and internationalism, and when considering the importance of emotions – including trust. A remarkable demonstration of this in recent months is Su Lin Lewis's study of hospitality in women's international socialist networks across Europe and Asia, which also – incidentally – notes that Northern Europe (not Britain) dominated as a possible model of welfare and socialist equality in many of the discussions held in Asian socialist circles in the 1950s.[41] These concerns, which prompt historians to think 'against the grain' more decidedly, are also evident in a renewed attention given to space, which is our third area of inspiration.

It is the primacy of 'place' that has led us to focus on European socialists 'across borders'. In many ways, 'across borders' encompasses the wide range of meanings that Michele Di Donato and Mathieu Fulla have given in their recent book to 'internationalism', as 'a functional umbrella definition for a vast array of practices of transnational political organizing, cooperation and solidarity; cross-border circulation of political actors, information, ideas and experiences; engagement with international organizations and internationalizing initiatives'.[42] We concur with them – and Mathieu Fulla is one of the contributors to this volume – on the importance of 'interactions and hybridizations', and on the fact that for many of the socialist individuals studied here, 'these practices also involve significant symbolic dimension, epitomizing allegiance to specific political cultures and transnational "imagined communities"'.[43] Taken together, the contributions in this volume also speak to the role of individual men and (to a lesser extent in our case studies) women for whom crossing borders was an essential, fundamental part of identifying as socialists. This means crossing both physical borders (going into exile, networking across Europe, travelling to Africa in support of liberation movements, serving as diplomats abroad) and symbolic borders (crossing the line in a sense, by speaking out, or writing against, torture in

Algeria, challenging Eurocentric and racially restrictive visions of European construction, identity and mobility, or contesting the domination of English and 'Anglo-Saxon' tropes in world politics). But the contributions also consider the practice of crossing borders in the form of 'transnational social democratic politics' discussed by Di Donato, or the organised transnational networks analysed by Christian Salm,[44] with both scholars focusing on the Socialist International, its contribution to European construction and Europeanisation – and it remained, after all, as Di Donato notes, despite 'efforts to overcome Eurocentrism [. . .] a predominantly European organization'.[45]

The importance of place in the act of crossing borders or acting across borders is also brought to light by the work of historical geographers on international conferences and the 'placing' of internationalism. Stephen Legg, Mike Heffernan, Jake Hodder and Benjamin Thorpe show that 'internationalism and the international conference were co-constitutive' and that 'modern internationalism reflects the ephemeral, messy and unpredictable nature of international conferences'.[46] Likewise, tracing shifts in cooperation between European socialists means reflecting on 'physical locations'; on 'the cultural and social content' of meetings; and on meetings as 'nodes' of networking,[47] which also implies focusing on mundane but vital considerations of transport and language, and – as several of the contributions show – on what people read or listened to. This also helps us as scholars 'to consider carefully the kinds of global stories, mobilities, and networks we choose to foreground', partly because 'the choice to emphasize connection and mobilities can have distorting effects on the way we understand the world of the unconnected and the immobile', in the words of Kristin Roth-Ey.[48]

Fourth, the study of European integration itself has benefited from a wide range of studies into these processes of cross-border and transnational socialisation, focusing on non-state actors with diverse humanitarian, business and other motives,[49] and internationalisms.[50] It has also been served by new studies of the transnational relations of European socialist parties since the Second World War[51] and of the intellectual history of European relations and planning,[52] reflecting on the interplay between international relations theory, history and political thought.[53] The last two chapters, in particular, provide important contributions to the research questions posed by Christian Salm in his work on transnational Europeanisation: 'firstly, what transnational political networks including other societal actors such as experts and non-governmental organizations (NGOs) did the socialists establish and use? Secondly, to what extent was the ongoing debate on the future of EC development policy shaped by the transnational cooperation of the

European socialists?'[54] The volume also contributes to the debate on 'polity-building', defined by Wolfram Kaiser and Jan-Henrik Meyer as 'the creation of institutions, procedures and institutional working patterns, and on policy making'.[55] Several of the chapters also show that for a number of European socialists, cooperation across borders was a means to critique, and hopefully ultimately prevent, processes of supranationalisation within a restricted Western European framework. Even if results fell below expectations, this did not stop transnational networks, even in fairly loose forms in the post-war years, from seeking, and achieving on occasion, 'an important, pro-active agenda-setting role'.[56] All chapters shed light on the functional role of those European socialists for whom the remaking of international policy after the Second World War, during the Cold War and decolonisation, necessarily entailed crossing borders. As European construction generated a greater number of formal institutions working at the supranational and infranational levels, European socialists also acted via 'epistemic communities', defined as 'a network of experts who share a common understanding of the scientific and political nature of a particular problem', and advocacy coalitions, whereby those 'who share a similar perspective will forge coalition type relationships with each other'.[57] Taken together, the contributions gathered here assess, in different ways, how the successes and failures of socialist endeavours resulted from the feasibility of networking, i.e. 'a degree of geographical or communicative proximity [. . .] a degree of shared cultural norms and values and the availability and/or willingness of organizations to devote sufficient time, capital and personnel resources to the network'.[58] The multiple circles in which the European socialists studied in the chapters lived, militated and made policy, could therefore turn out to be, as the chapters show, a strength or a hindrance depending on structural factors, ideological preferences and personal choices.

Europeanisation, globalisation and decolonisation, from the travails of the Second World War to the grey areas of the Single European Act

While the title of this volume focuses on the post-1945 period, we do not suggest that the end of the Second World War was a hard turning point. In many ways, the contributors seek to trace longer-term trends, in the memory and practice of democratic socialism. As recent research has emphasised, for instance, the Spanish civil war was key in shaping 'an anti-fascist public sphere that momentarily served, with all its contradictions, as a functional equivalent of a global left', but one which also suffered from many illusions, in 'hyper-fragmented political environments and a deeply unequal state system', and left divisions, between European socialists, and between them and anti-colonial activists on account of Spain's colonial possessions.[59] Conversely, in the post-war world, cooperation across borders was significantly hindered from 1947, as shown for instance by the experience of transnational resistance fighters in Europe, whose travels were now impeded and whose allegiances became suspect.[60] It should also be noted that not all of the actors considered in this volume (far from it) come under the label of the 'activist', defined by Stefan Berger and Holger Nehring as 'a social figure that was loaded with symbolic meanings that reflected and refracted struggles over power and other political contestations'.[61] But the five areas of debate and interest listed by Berger and Sean Scalmer in their study of 'the transnational activist' are all heeded, in different ways, by the contributors: 'periodisation, context, action, form, and dynamics'.[62]

By focusing on relations between European socialist parties and groups in an international context and tracing the impact of these connections on political thought and on policy practices, this volume reflects on the successes and failures of trans-border and transnational processes of socialisation. Authors pay particular attention to connections beyond the state, both above (through supranational, transnational and global frameworks) and below (with grassroots movements acting in parallel to, support or defiance of official institutions), to analyse the drivers and limits of socialist and European identities. The contributions presented here investigate four main areas. First, the extent to which ideals of European cooperation have trickled down into more daily, routine and domestic politics and, in turn, the extent to which power, welfare and employment politics at home have shaped European policies among socialists. Second, the shifting definitions of political elites and popular understandings of Europe, including the influence of people of African, Caribbean and Asian descent on the transformation of socialist thought, policies and practices in the European (ex-)imperial powers and their agency in connecting socialist groups across national boundaries. Third, the extent to which European socialists attempted to propose a post-colonial, post-imperial agenda for Europe and to grasp the nexus between ends of empire and new international orders, through campaigns of international solidarity, and reflecting on the ways in which the later ends of the European colonial empires affected both socialist and European identities and politics. Finally, some of the contributions consider the extent to which European institutions were used, with what ends and with what results, by European socialists and their contacts. All four areas also shed light on how the material and symbolic resources available to individuals and groups mattered, and on the extent to which interdependence was both a constraint and a vector of socialist activity.

The first section of this volume examines the attitudes and actions of various European socialist parties during the war and immediately after it, reconsidering its historical significance. Andrew J. Williams looks at the Labour Party and the SFIO, a significant section of whose leadership found itself in London in the 1940s in what was on occasion a difficult relationship with the British Labour Party. This 'uncomfortable' situation arose because the British government was one which saw the Labour Party as an equal partner with Winston Churchill's Conservatives and as one of the key Allied Powers of the war. Churchill spent most of his energy as it concerned France, already a much-diminished force, in a difficult relationship with de Gaulle. The SFIO was divided between those who had decided to follow de Gaulle's line in all (or most) things and those who saw him as a *boulangiste*, a dangerous proto-dictator. The chapter traces the course of the socialist *Groupe Jean Jaurès*, a colourful collection of what were often seen by their Labour counterparts as Gallic misfits whose views could be either ignored or condescended to. They had lost their country and were subject to the same humiliation as that experienced by other French exiles, notably de Gaulle. The *Groupe*, and many in de Gaulle's orbit, were nonetheless very drawn to Labour's ideas about welfareism (reforms of education, health, and planning) and carried out extensive research into how these ideas might translate to a post-war France and Europe. Building on the pre-existing ideas inherited by both Labour and the SFIO from the pre-war period, the experiences of wartime gave rise to many personal relationships that persisted long after the war ended. Personal relations could be difficult, as when André Philip was scathing about French alternatives to Gaullism (a position he later modified). Labour Party members were often equally ambivalent about some of their new French comrades. Britain's generally ambiguous relationship with both the European project and its colonial past was mirrored with mixed feelings about both subjects *outre-Manche*. The Labour Party, then as now a 'broad church', had members who spanned a number of factions, some of them more pro-European than others. This experience laid the groundwork for what was to be a post-war (mostly) friendly rivalry that still exists today.

Ben Heckscher and Tommaso Milani's chapter on the *Mouvement Socialiste pour les États-Unis d'Europe* (MSEUE, and its predecessor the Movement for the Socialist States of Europe, MUSSE) explores the socialist networks that emerged after 1945 to promote European integration in the light of the developing Cold War. A study of 'a pro-federalist, left-wing, anti-Stalinist organisation', so very different from the aims and ambitions of Stalin's *Comintern*, the chapter shows very clearly the continuities in contacts between socialist parties, as explored in the previous chapter, as well as the ways in which pre-war debates informed post-war thinking about Europe. It examines how and why the path to cooperation did not always run smoothly, and traces how many avenues for cooperation came through London during the war, in the aptly named 'London Bureau', in which André Philip played a key role. It also highlights the importance of British socialists, like Fenner Brockway of the Independent Labour Party (ILP), who were leftist socialists, outside the mainstream but very vocal critics of both colonialism – intersecting with platforms and individuals whose main engagement lay in overthrowing empires – and any hint of Stalinism, and who flirted with the Soviet alternative of Trotskyism. This criticism was vitally important in the anti-fascist movements of the 1930s, in Spain for example, and it provided a left alternative after the war. The MSEUE is presented as a bridge towards a new kind of socialist Europe. It collided with the realities of the Cold War, with the Labour Party taking a generally very pro-American attitude and the MSEUE was itself eventually forced to take sides, again against Stalinism in uneasy cooperation with the United States. The organisation provided a vital part of what became the ideas that emerged in the European Economic Community, one that this chapter explores in some detail.

The next three chapters examine European socialist attitudes to the question of the end of empire, a development that happened in some areas very rapidly and to some extent unexpectedly in the late 1940s and 1950s, but also protractedly in many others. The violence of imperial and colonial domination, as well as the need to resort to armed force to overthrow the occupying European power, gave rise to many debates among socialists, and generated comparisons across the empires. Also at stake were major questions of international order and diplomacy. What kind of world would emerge from an international system and society that had lost one of its most hitherto enduring aspects? Again, the re-imagining of that system and society passed through and with the emergence of an equally new idea, that of Europe, approached from very different perspectives among European socialists.

In the first chapter of the three, Mélanie Torrent examines the role of Claude Bourdet in the re-imagination of Europe in the context of the war of Algerian independence. His influence among anti-colonial British socialists, with many of them again coming from the diminished ranks of the ILP like Brockway, lay in his wartime role in the Resistance and in his reputation as a journalist and co-founder of *France-Observateur*, as well as his broader political activities. Acting as a broker across the Channel, aided by his good command of English, Bourdet had hoped that the Labour Party would play an important role in world peace and in pan-European dialogue after the war, and in the withdrawal of Britain and France from their colonial possessions. Tracing the use of trans-Channel cooperation to counter press censorship in France, and various intellectual and practical attempts to stimulate a new socialism against empires and against a 'neo-colonial' integration process in Europe, the chapter shows that Bourdet played a vital role in circulating and mediating information. It argues that he was able to do so because he acted in several networks and entertained friendships in and beyond socialist circles, such as within the Society of Friends. Ultimately, the alternative Europe that was imagined in opposition to the war in Algeria did not lead to effective, alternative, pan-European structures. But the debate over solidarity did challenge Western European interpretations of what being European and being socialist meant, and what European socialists should practice.

Another important expression of solidarity in another part of Europe is explored in the next chapter by Pedro Aires Oliveira. The focus of Oliveira is the activities of British historian and journalist Basil Davidson and his support for the liberation struggles in Lusophone Africa. Davidson brought to a much wider section of European public opinion the full horrors of what the Portuguese fascist regime of Antonio de Oliveira Salazar was doing in Africa. Davidson acted as a standard bearer for European socialist opinion and was able to influence the Labour Party's policies in important ways until independence was achieved in 1975. His intimate knowledge of Africa and his linguistic competence allowed him to act as 'a cultural intermediary' between British socialists and local revolutionaries. He was also able to explain in London why support for Salazar's Portugal, which was a member of NATO, was not in the interests of Britain given that Salazar was anti-democratic in the extreme and not likely to survive. Davidson straddled a number of networks, socialist and even military (he was a former member of the Special Operations Executive and achieved the rank of Lieutenant-Colonel) as well as being a valued correspondent for the *Economist* and other prominent publications of continental reach, notably the *New Statesman and Nation*, then as now the principal authoritative voice for the British left. His denunciation of both the apartheid regime in South Africa and the Soviet invasion of Hungary in 1956 showed him to be a democratic socialist, and one who could 'sens[e] a sea-change in the political situation of the continent'. Tracing Davidson's activities before and after the transfer of power agreements, the chapter shows the complexities of his relations with, and analysis of, the new regimes of Lusophone Africa, at a time when the political fractures of the Cold War were exacerbating the difficulties which the new states were starting to face while engaging with top-down nation-building processes.

Nowhere was a sense of 'sea change' so evident as in the case of Sweden. As Lubna Z. Qureshi shows in her chapter, Swedish socialist Prime Minister Olof Palme went further than any other European politician to disavow any 'neo-colonial' actions, notably those of the United States in Vietnam. Qureshi provides a rich analysis of Palme's political views and shows how Palme often made statements that were seen with great hostility in Washington. His moral stand was courageous in the extreme, which explains that he is a hero of the European left, and beyond, to this day. The Swedish Foreign Minister, Krister Wickman, also made speeches denouncing US actions such as the bombing of the North when British Labour Prime Minister Harold Wilson was far more circumspect. Palme had close personal relations with Austrian socialist Chancellor Bruno Kreisky and German Chancellor Willi Brandt, dating back to the period when they had lived in exile in Sweden during the war. Kreisky and Palme were both leaders of neutral countries while Germany was occupied in the 1960s by nearly half a million US troops, a situation that limited German and Austrian room for foreign policy manoeuvre. Palme's friendship with the two men meant he was able to voice a non-aligned but morally important view on the Vietnam War, which gave an important impetus to the European, and American, anti-war movement and through that to other struggles against neo-colonialism.

The last section of the volume has three chapters which deal with issues of intense contemporary, as well as historical significance. They all raise questions about what Europe means in terms of its international identity, reflected to some extent in the literature on 'normative Europe'.[63] They examine the questions of cultural, racial/ethnic, gender and national identity that are constantly in the headlines as this book goes to print. The first of these contributions is by Thomas Maineult on how European socialists came to increasingly stress international solidarity with Palestine, in particular in the 1970s and 1980s. From the vantage point of the French case, Maineult traces the socialist parties of Europe from their initial enthusiastic support of the new state of Israel after 1948 to the growing disillusion that followed the realisation that the democratic socialist entity they had all applauded seemed to deny that to the Palestinian populations who had left after Israel's creation. The change of heart was not sudden or complete. There are still supporters of Israel in all socialist parties in Europe, and all these parties are sensitive to any claim that criticism of Israel is in any way antisemitic, as has been demonstrated in Britain in recent years and which the situation in Gaza, as we write this introduction, is putting to the test. Mollet's support for the Suez invasion in Egypt was partly due to his support for Israel. French socialists like Robert Pontillon were great supporters of Israel throughout the 1970s. The Labour Party of Harold Wilson was largely in step with this sentiment. Again, the wartime experience in the Resistance and in London dictated a strong vein of personal support for Israel. A change in emphasis was noted in the late 1960s in both France and Germany, especially with Willi Brandt's 'policy of even-handedness (*Ausgewogenheit*)' towards Israel and the Arab states. As the leader of the new French Socialist Party (*Parti socialiste*, PS) François Mitterrand declared support for both Israel and the 'Palestinian national fact'. The plight of the ordinary Palestinian people became more evident as the 1970s wore on, and Mitterrand's perspective evolved after his visit to Gaza in 1972, and again after meeting Yasser Arafat in 1974 and 1976. Overt support for a Palestinian state increased over the next ten years and has continued to do so, in the event marginalising Pontillon's pro-Israeli policy. European social democracy became ever more pro-integration and *tiermondiste* in the 1980s, and the Palestinian question grew in salience. Maineult's chapter shows that, here again, Bruno Kreisky in Austria and Olof Palme in Sweden were opinion leaders, and ultimately reflects on the division of opinions across party lines in European socialist politics.

Turning to the issue of racism and antiracism in Europe in the 1980s and 1990s, Pamela Ohene-Nyako examines the activities of Black British Labour leaders and their role in helping to formulate policies and practices that have since become much more mainstream within European socialist circles. She identifies the recent and ongoing change of tone in Europe thus: 'In 1986, the announcement of a Single European market to be implemented by 1992 led to the formation of a number of local and transnational initiatives for social justice led by people of colour in Europe.' This seminal development for European integration was thus the trigger for a concerted push among, particularly, British Labour leaders for a much more antiracist Europe. Ohene-Nyako concentrates her analysis on the activities of a number of key activists, among whom Labour MP Bernie Grant and Labour councillor and campaigner Martha Osamor (now Baroness Osamor). Their focus was on the emerging legislation being created by governments and EU institutions on migration, asylum and equality. She looks at how the Single European Act became a focus for their attempts towards a transnational antiracism and how they organised these efforts. Would the Single Market create an exclusionary 'Fortress Europe' or one of much more humanity? The period since 1986 seems to indicate the former rather than the latter. In Britain itself, Commonwealth but also British citizens have found themselves in dire situations, as in the notorious 'Windrush' scandal and the subsequent deportations that have still not all been resolved – to say nothing of the controversial 'Migration and Economic Partnership' signed by the former Conservative government with Rwanda; that Labour scrapped it on returning to power in July 2024 is a hopeful sign, but much remains to be done. Several high-profile movements were created thanks to Grant, Osamor and others, continuing the fight for equality. The chapter provides a detailed examination of the discussions of these groups and shows that the existence of pan-European networks has been of great utility in this struggle, damaged to some extent by Brexit in 2016.

Lastly Mathieu Fulla addresses the problem with which Europe as a whole has been grappling for many years, possibly dating back to 1975 and the end of *les trente glorieuses*, that of unemployment. He outlines two European socialist employment initiatives, established to try and cope with the results of neoliberal policies, that have outsourced employment and production and are now showing the limits of globalisation. Fulla takes as his starting point the Confederation of the Socialist Parties of the European Community (CSPEC), established in 1983 and which first rang the alarm on the de-industrialisation of Europe and its consequences for traditional working-class communities and jobs. This was followed by a European Employment Initiative in 1993, while the issue of the end of the Cold War and the arrival of a potentially huge number of new workers from Eastern Europe rang more alarm bells. There is clear evidence that the neoliberal elites in Western Europe either downplayed the risks presented by this development and the emergence of more 'offshoring' in an increasingly globalised world or ignored them. Even French socialist Jacques Delors, then Head of the European Commission, downplayed the risks but still inserted a clause in the 1997 Amsterdam Treaty to give the issue some prominence, in theory at least. The chapter analyses in much detail why European socialists were so wrong-footed by the employment implications of the post-Cold War era. Fulla uses a wealth of archival material to show how this process evolved in an atmosphere which 'was one of resignation rather than enthusiasm'. The chapter ultimately reflects on the role of economic policy and economic thinking, and on the interplay between the domestic and international changes of the early 1990s in the redefinitions of European socialism.

Cultural intermediaries, bridge-builders – and stock-takers?

By way of conclusion, we can point to a number of perspectives that we think contributors have helped refine. The first relates to the very meaning of 'socialism' and its conceptions: is it contingent on the challenges it faces and the agendas it espouses? The challenges of the pre-war Depression were maybe quite different from the wartime burdens and those of the period of reconstruction after it, in Europe and internationally. The case studies reflect on the extent to which physical and intellectual circulations generated a certain memory of socialist achievements, failures and duties, and informed plans for the future. Individual connections – between Philip and Labour leaders, between Bourdet and Brockway or Davidson, between Brandt and Kreisky – certainly stimulated a socialist imaginary, 'a politics of network-making' to borrow Rob Skinner's words, which resulted (although not systematically, as shown) in 'a collective enterprise'.[64] They acted as 'transnationally networked "cultural brokers" who are culturally and linguistically versatile'; and while linguistic ability varied, even within already small groups, they did provide 'translation between different socio-economic, political and cultural contexts'.[65] Such activities were intimately tied to their socialist beliefs but not dependent on it. As the case of Olof Palme shows, the practice of diplomacy (if not foreign policy) was distinctly shaped by a Swedish tradition of neutralism, informed but not entirely guided by socialist connections and sentiments, while North Vietnamese perspectives on the Swedish prime minister suggest he was primarily identified as *European*, and compared to other *European* rather than *socialist* leaders. Influence also came from those who moved across several transnational circles, either within socialist groupings (the Socialist International and the MSEUE, or Keep Left, or the Party of European Socialists), across party affiliations (Labour and the European Greens, as shown by Osamor and French Member of the European Parliament Djida Tazdaït), or outside party affiliations (with connections with, for instance, the Society of Friends, the World Council of Churches and, in Britain, the Commission for Racial Equality). As Kiran Klaus Patel has recently argued, there was and is 'a multiplicity of internationalisms in Europe', which cooperated but also 'compet[ed] with each other over which vision would dominate and consequently be identified as "European" within and beyond its shores'.[66] Navigating a diversity of networks was therefore also important for those kept out of the Socialist International – like the PSU in France – by the politics of the left in their home nation, or for those who militated at transnational local levels.

The second broad question addresses whether socialist dilemmas all have a common thread, that of finding pragmatic and moral solutions for pressing continental and global problems. Whereas 'planning' and welfare policies started the period of this book in having precedence by the 1950s, it was evident that the collapse of the European empires necessitated a change of focus for the whole continent. Several of the contributors reflect, in the words of Milani and Heckscher, on the 'blueprints' of both European unity and European socialism, changing readings and understandings of old ones, and the ideological and practical obstacles in defining new versions. While they offer insights into how international questions influenced conceptions of socialism, or led to divisions between generations along national or transnational lines, they also suggest that the heterogeneity of European socialists – *socialistes*, social democrats, Labour Party members and others – requires further collective study. So does the practice of socialism in Europe and of European socialists anywhere, if one follows Christoph Kalter's interest in 'globality', which he defines as 'the relationships – extending across great distances – of certain actors to other people, spaces, institutions, and things, as well as the awareness of these relationships and their intellectual localization within a picture of the world as a whole'.[67] While the selected chapters cannot embrace such a vast horizon, what they delve into and confirm is the value of assessing 'the transformative dimension of translocal encounters (and clashes)', as noted by Andrea Brazzoduro.[68]

The geographical limits of 'Europe' were themselves the subject of intense debates, as was the redefinition of metropolitan identity/identities after the formal end of empire, with no agreement on what policy to pursue as 'Europeans' within the EEC and the EU. One recurring, if not dominant actor, in this volume is Britain – its governments, its Labour Party and various promoters of peace and cooperation in and out of Labour circles. While there has been no lack of studies on Britain, contributors shed here additional light on at least two aspects of the complicated relationship between Britain, Europe and the wider world: a certain (albeit fluctuating) sense of superiority – including Labour superiority – that came with the rising expansion of English, as shown for instance by Fulla in the tensions with the Dutch and the Portuguese socialists; and the importance for historians of centring on the British context if the complex Europeanisation of 'political blackness [as] a concept and strategy', as Ohene-Nyako shows, is to be properly understood. Several of the British socialist activists discussed here thus denounced what Patricia Clavin has called the 'processes of delimitation and "othering", fragmentation and conflict' inherent in European integration and 'Europeanisation'.[69] A common thread in the volume is the socialist critique of the European project that gave birth to the current EU. The contributions show that in this sense, cooperation across Europe's borders, and with a view to fostering closer relations among those living in Europe/the EEC/EU, was also intended to reform, or even alter altogether, European integration as it had been conceived. A wealth of knowledge was produced in the process, but not always – and this in itself requires further collective forays into the fabric of policy making – acted on.

Such processes of redefinition and adaptation are still not complete, and may indeed never be, given the plethora of ideological and contending pressures encompassed in Europe. With the rise since 1945 of new ways of thinking about who we are as human beings and how we relate to the state and each other, the agenda often called 'human rights' has emerged as a vital component of European identity, especially given Europe's troubled relations with its former colonies and the racial tensions and exclusions that have accompanied and resulted from that relationship. As Wolfram Kaiser wrote almost twenty years ago of transnational Western Europe since 1945, '"Europe" was neither made then nor is now by governments alone'.[70] Looking in turn at successes and failures, at the role of cultural intermediaries and bridge-builders, and at the reasons behind misunderstandings, failed projects and missed opportunities for peace and equality, the chapters that follow examine how socialist politicians and activists conceived of Europe's role in worldmaking in the transition out of, and after, conflict and empire. In doing so, this volume will have contributed, we hope, to a better understanding of, and support for, cooperation across borders.

Notes

1. Daniel Gorman, *Uniting the Nations* (Cambridge: Cambridge University Press, 2022), 185, quoted here in Mélanie Torrent's contribution to this volume.

2. One excellent study of the issue of retribution is István Deák, Jan T. Gross and Tony Judt, eds. *The Politics of Retribution in Europe: World War II and Its Aftermath* (Princeton: Princeton University Press, 2000). On France, see Bénédicte Vergez-Chaignon, *Vichy en prison: Les épurés à Fresnes après la Libération* (Paris: Gallimard, 2006). On reconstruction see David A. Mayers, *America and the Postwar World: Remaking International Society, 1945–1956* (London: Routledge, 2018); Andrew J. Williams, *Liberalism and War* (London: Routledge, 2024, 2nd edition, forthcoming), especially Chapter 4, 'Reconstruction until the Marshall Plan'.

3. Boaventura de Sousa Santos, 'Epilogue. A New Vision of Europe: Learning from the South', in *European Cosmopolitanism. Colonial Histories and Postcolonial Societies*, ed. Gurminder Bhambra and John Narayan (London: Routledge, 2016), 175.

4. De Sousa Santos, 'Epilogue', 175.

5. Inderjeet Parmar, *Think Tanks and Power in Foreign Policy* (London: Palgrave, 2004).

6. The father of one of the editors of this volume was a junior member of the Communist Party of Great Britain (he defected after the Soviet invasion of Finland in 1939). For John Williams, there was no choice – he had to wear a red or a black shirt. Andrew Williams never wore a black one in his presence.

7. Tony Judt, *Past Imperfect: French Intellectuals, 1944–1956* (New York: New York University Press, 2011); see also his *The Burden of Responsibility: Blum, Camus, Aron and the French Twentieth Century* (Chicago: Chicago University Press, 1998).

8. Richard Toye, 'From "Consensus" to "Common Ground": The Rhetoric of the Postwar Settlement and its Collapse', *Journal of Contemporary History* 48, no. 1 (2013): 3–23.

9. Friedrich Hayek, *The Road to Serfdom* (London: Routledge, 2001 [1994]); Nicholas Wapshott, *Keynes Hayek: The Clash That Defined Modern Economics* (London: W.W. Norton, 2011).

10. Quinn Slobodian, *Globalists: The End of Empire and the Birth of Neoliberalism* (Cambridge, MA: Harvard University Press, 2018); Or Rosenboim, *The Emergence of Globalism: Visions of World Order in Britain and the United States, 1939–1950* (Princeton: Princeton University Press, 2017).

11. Alain Laurent, *Le libéralisme américain: Histoire d'un détournement* (Paris: Les Belles Lettres, 2006).

12. Andrew J. Williams, 'France and the Origins of the United Nations, 1944–1945: "Si La France ne compte plus, qu'on nous le dise"', *Diplomacy and Statecraft* 28, no. 2 (2017): 215–34.

13. One advocate of a Christian Democratic Europe was the Franco-Swiss philosopher Denis de Rougemont, whose writings were deeply embedded in the thinking of the 1930s and his experiences of Swiss Confederation: Denis de Rougemont, *Amour et Occident* (Paris: 10/18, 2001 [1938]), and Nicolas Stenger, *Denis de Rougemont: Les intellectuels et l'Europe au XXe siècle* (Rennes: Presses universitaires de Rennes, 2015). The most celebrated liberal of all can be said to have been Jean Monnet, widely seen as the architect of the EEC and the Treaty of Rome: Sherrill Brown Wells, *Jean Monnet: Unconventional Statesman* (Boulder, CO: Lynne Rienner Publishers, 2011). On neoliberalism see Slobodian, *Globalists*.

14. Martin Thomas and Andrew Thompson, 'Empire and Globalisation: from "High Imperialism" to Decolonisation', *The International History Review* 36, no. 1 (2014).

15. Marie-Thérèse Bitsch and Gérard Bossuat, eds. *L'Europe unie et l'Afrique: de l'idée d'Eurafrique à la convention de Lomé 1* (Brussels: Bruylant, 2005); Véronique Dimier, *The Invention of a European Development Aid Bureaucracy: Recycling Empire* (Basingstoke: Palgrave Macmillan, 2014); Peo Hansen and Stefan Jonsson, *Eurafrica: The Untold History of European Integration and Colonialism* (London: Bloomsbury Academic, 2014).

16. Elizabeth Buettner, *Europe after Empire: Decolonization, Society and Culture* (Cambridge: Cambridge University Press, 2016); Sarah Stockwell, *The British End of the British Empire* (Cambridge: Cambridge University Press, 2018); Berny Sebe and Matthew G. Stanard, eds. *Decolonising Europe? Popular Responses to the End of Empire* (London: Routledge, 2020).

17. Gurminder Bhambra and John Narayan, eds. *European Cosmopolitanism. Colonial Histories and Postcolonial Societies* (London: Routledge, 2016), 2.

18. Stefan Berger and Sean Scalmer, 'The Transnational Activist: An Introduction', in *The Transnational Activist: Transformations and Comparisons from the Anglo-World since the Nineteenth Century*, ed. Stefan Berger and Sean Scalmer (Cham: Palgrave Macmillan, 2018), 6.

19. Christoph Kalter, *The Discovery of the Third World: Decolonization and the Rise of the New Left in France, c. 1950–1976* (Cambridge: Cambridge University Press, 2016), 254–5.

20. Jeremy Adelman, 'What is global history now?', *Aeon*, 2 March 2017 [accessed 21 July 2024], https://aeon.co/essays/is-global-history-still-possible-or-has-it-had-its-moment.

21. Rob Skinner, *Peace, Decolonization, and the Practice of Solidarity* (London: Bloomsbury, 2023), 27.

22. Jessica Reinisch and David Brydan, eds. *Internationalists in European History: Rethinking the Twentieth Century* (London: Bloomsbury, 2021).

23. Skinner, *Peace*, 212.

24. Skinner, *Peace*, 212.

25. Daniel Stinsky, *International Cooperation in Cold War Europe: The United Nations Economic Commission, 1947–64* (London: Bloomsbury, 2021).

26. Nancy Jachec, *Europe's Intellectuals and the Cold War: The European Society of Culture, Post-War Politics and International Relations* (London: Bloomsbury, 2020 [2015]).

27. See for instance Laurence Cossu-Beaumont, 'Race across the Atlantic: Jean-Paul Sartre and Richard Wright's Transatlantic Network in 1940s Paris', in *Transatlantic Intellectual Networks 1914–1964*, ed. Hans Bak and Céline Mansanti (Newcastle-upon-Tyne: Cambridge Scholars Publishing, 2019).

28. Neville Kirk, *Labour and the Politics of Empire: Britain and Australia, 1900 to the Present* (Manchester: Manchester University Press, 2017).

29. Claire Marynower, *L'Algérie à gauche, 1900–1962. Socialistes à l'époque coloniale* (Paris: Presses universitaires de France, 2018).

30. Guillaume Devin, *L'internationale socialiste: histoire et sociologie du socialisme international, 1945–1990* (Paris: Presses de la Fondation nationale des sciences politiques, 1993); Talbot Imlay, *The Practice of Socialist Internationalism: European Socialists and International Politics, 1914–1960* (Oxford: Oxford University Press, 2018).

31. Pedro Aires Oliveira, *Os Despojos da Aliança: A Grã-Bretanha e a Questão Colonial Portuguesa, 1945–1975* (Lisbon: Tinta da China, 2007); Miguel Bandeira Jerónimo and José Pedro Monteiro, eds. *Internationalism, Imperialism and the Formation of the Contemporary World: The Pasts of the Present* (Basingstoke: Palgrave Macmillan, 2017); Yann Béliard and Neville Kirk, eds. *Workers of the Empire, Unite: Radical and Popular Challenges to British Imperialism, 1910s–1960s* (Liverpool: Liverpool University Press, 2021).

32. See for instance Catherine Simon, *Algérie, les années pieds-rouges: des rêves de l'indépendance au désenchantement, 1962–1969* (Paris: La Découverte, 2009); and George Roberts, *Revolutionary State-Making in Dar es Salaam: African Liberation and the Global Cold War, 1961–1974* (Cambridge: Cambridge University Press, 2021).

33. Constantin Katsakioris and Alexander Stroh, 'Africa and the Crisis of Socialism: Postsocialism and the Left', Special Issue: 'Africa and the Crisis of Socialism', *Canadian Journal of African Studies / Revue canadienne des études africaines* 55, no. 2 (2021).

34. James Mark and Paul Betts, 'Introduction', in *Socialism Goes Global: The Soviet Union and Eastern Europe in the Age of Decolonisation*, ed. James Mark and Paul Betts (Oxford: Oxford University Press, 2022), 4, 24.

35. Françoise Blum, Héloïse Kiriakou, Martin Mourre et al., 'Introduction. Pour une histoire des socialismes en Afrique', in *Socialismes en Afrique. Socialisms in Africa*, ed. Françoise Blum et al. (Paris: Éditeur de la Maison des sciences de l'homme, 2021), online edn.

36. Blum, Kiriakou, Mourre et al., 'Introduction'.

37. Brian Shaev, 'The Algerian War, European Integration, and the Decolonization of French Socialism', *French Historical Studies* 41, no. 1 (2019), 90.

38. Adom Getachew, 'When Jamaica Led the Postcolonial Fight Against Exploitation', *Boston Review*, 5 February 2019. See also Adom Getachew,

Worldmaking after Empire: The Rise and Fall of Self-Determination (Princeton: Princeton University Press, 2019).

39. Gyan Prakash and Jeremy Adelman, 'Introduction: Imagining the Third World: Genealogies of Alternative Global Histories', in *Inventing the Third World: In Search of Freedom for the Postwar Global South*, ed. Gyan Prakash and Jeremy Adelman (London: Bloomsbury, 2023), 21.

40. Blum, Kiriakou, Mourre et al., 'Introduction'.

41. Su Lin Lewis, 'Women, Hospitality and the Intimate Politics of International Socialism', *Past & Present* 262, no. 1 (2023).

42. Michele Di Donato and Mathieu Fulla, 'Introduction: Leftist Internationalisms in the History of the Twentieth Century', in *Leftist Internationalisms: A Transnational Political History*, ed. Michele Di Donato and Mathieu Fulla (London: Bloomsbury 2023), 6.

43. Di Donato and Fulla, 'Introduction', 6.

44. Christian Salm, 'Shaping European Development Policy? Socialist Parties as Mediators from the International to the European Level', in *Societal Actors in European Integration: Polity-Building and Policy-Making, 1958–1992*, ed. Wolfram Kaiser and Jan-Henrik Meyer (Basingstoke/New York: Palgrave Macmillan, 2013).

45. Michele Di Donato, 'The Socialist International and Human Rights', in *Leftist Internationalisms*, ed. Di Donato and Fulla, 171.

46. Stephen Legg, Mike Heffernan, Jake Hodder and Benjamin Thorpe, 'Introduction' in *Placing Internationalism: International Conferences and the Making of the Modern World*, ed. Stephen Legg, Mike Heffernan, Jake Hodder and Benjamin Thorpe (London, Bloomsbury, 2022), 4.

47. Legg, Heffernan, Hodder and Thorpe, 'Introduction', 4 .

48. Kristin Roth-Ey, 'Introduction', in *Socialist Internationalism and the Gritty Politics of the Particular: Second-Third World Spaces in the Cold War*, ed. Kristin Roth-Ey (London: Bloomsbury, 2023), 9, 6.

49. Wolfram Kaiser, Brigitte Leucht and Michael Gehler, eds. *Transnational Networks in Regional Integration: Governing Europe, 1945–83* (Basingstoke: Palgrave Macmillan, 2010); Wolfram Kaiser and Jan-Henrik Meyer, eds. *Societal Actors in European Integration: Polity-Building and Policy-Making, 1958–1992* (Basingstoke: Palgrave Macmillan, 2013); and Christian Salm, *Transnational Socialist Networks in the 1970s: European Community Development Aid and Southern Enlargement* (Basingstoke: Palgrave Macmillan, 2016).

50. Glenda Sluga and Patricia Clavin, eds. *Internationalisms: A Twentieth-Century History* (Cambridge: Cambridge University Press, 2017).

51. See for instance Noëlline Castagnez et al., eds. *Les socialistes français à l'heure de la libération: perspectives française et européenne, 1943–1947* (Paris: L'OURS, 2016); and Mathieu Fulla and Marc Lazar, eds. *European Socialists and the State in the Twentieth and Twenty-First Centuries* (Cham: Palgrave Macmillan, 2020).

52. Tommaso Milani, *Hendrik de Man and Social Democracy: The Idea of Planning in Western Europe, 1914–1940* (Basingstoke: Palgrave Macmillan, 2020).

53. Ian Hall, ed., *Radicals and Reactionaries in Twentieth Century International Thought* (London: Palgrave Macmillan, 2015).

54. Salm, 'Shaping European Development Policy', 40.

55. Kaiser and Meyer, 'Beyond Governments and Supranational Institutions', 2.

56. Wolfram Kaiser and Peter Starie, 'Introduction: The European Union as a Transnational Political Space', in *Transnational European Union: Towards a Common Political Space*, ed. Wolfram Kaiser and Peter Starie (Abingdon: Routledge, 2005), 2.

57. Karen Heard-Lauréote, 'Transnational Networks: Informal Governance in the European Political Space?' in *Transnational European Union: Towards a Common Political Space*, ed. Wolfram Kaiser and Peter Starie (Abingdon: Routledge, 2005), 41, 43.

58. Heard-Lauréote, 'Transnational Networks', 46.

59. Hugo García, '"World Capital of Anti-Fascism"? The Making – and Breaking – of a Global Left in Spain, 1936–1939', in *Anti-Fascism in a Global Perspective: Transnational Networks, Exile Communities and Radical Internationalism*, ed. Kasper Braskén, Nigel Copsey and David Featherstone (Abingdon: Routledge, 2021), 242, 247. See also Robert Shilliam, "Ah, We Have Not Forgotten Ethiopia": Anti-Colonial Sentiment for Spain in a Fascist Era', in *European Cosmopolitanism*, ed. Bhambra and Narayan, 33.

60. Robert Gildea and Olga Manojlović Pintar with Mercedes Yusta Rodrigo et al. 'Afterlives and Memories', in *Fighters across Frontiers: Transnational Resistance in Europe, 1936–48*, ed. Robert Gildea and Ismee Tames (Manchester: Manchester University Press, 2020).

61. Stefan Berger and Holger Nehring, 'Series Editors' Preface', in *Transnational Activist*, ed. Berger and Scalmer, viii.

62. Berger and Scalmer, eds. *Transnational Activist*, 7.

63. See for instance Zaki Laïdi, *La norme sans la force: L'énigme de la puissance européenne* (Paris: Presses de Sciences Po, 2008); Ian Manners, 'Normative Power Europe: A Contradiction in Terms?', *JCMS: Journal of Common Market Studies* 40, no. 2 (2002), and Ian Manners, 'Normative Power Approach to European Union External Action', in *The External Action of the European Union: Concepts, Approaches, Theories*, ed. Sieglinde Gstöhl and Simon Schunz (London: Bloomsbury, 2021); and Laurence Badel, *Diplomaties européennes, XIXè-XXIè siècles* (Paris: Presses de Sciences Po, 2021).

64. Skinner, *Peace*, 53.

65. Wolfram Kaiser, 'Transnational Networks in European Governance', in *The History of the European Union: Origins of a Trans- and Supranational Polity 1950–72*, ed. Wolfram Kaiser, Brigitte Leucht and Morten Rasmussen (Abingdon: Routledge, 2009), 18.

66. Kiran Klaus Patel, 'Afterword: On the Chances and Challenges of Populating Internationalism', in *Internationalists in European History: Rethinking the Twentieth Century*, ed. David Brydan and Jessica Reinisch (London: Bloomsbury, 2021), 267, 265.

67. Kalter, *The Discovery of the Third World*, 419–20.

68. Andrea Brazzoduro, 'Algeria, Antifascism, and Third Worldism: An Anticolonial Genealogy of the Western European New Left (Algeria, France, Italy, 1957–1975)', *The Journal of Imperial and Commonwealth History* 48, no. 5 (2020), 964.

69. Patricia Clavin, 'Time, Manner, Place: Writing Modern European History in Global, Transnational and International Contexts', *European History Quarterly* 40, no. 4 (2010), 631.

70. Wolfram Kaiser, 'Transnational Western Europe since 1945: Integration as Political Society Formation', in *Transnational European Union*, ed. Kaiser and Starie, 32.

Bibliography

Adelman, Jeremy. 'What is global history now?' *Aeon*, 2 March 2017. https://aeon.co/essays/is-global-history-still-possible-or-has-it-had-its-moment [accessed 21 July 2024].

Badel, Laurence. *Diplomaties européennes, XIXè-XXIè siècles*. Paris: Presses de Sciences Po, 2021.

Bandeira Jerónimo, Miguel and José Pedro Monteiro, eds. *Internationalism, Imperialism and the Formation of the Contemporary World: The Pasts of the Present* (Basingstoke: Palgrave Macmillan, 2017).

Béliard, Yann and Neville Kirk, eds. *Workers of the Empire, Unite: Radical and Popular Challenges to British Imperialism, 1910s–1960s*. Liverpool: Liverpool University Press, 2021.

Berger, Stefan and Sean Scalmer. 'The Transnational Activist: An Introduction'. In *The Transnational Activist: Transformations and Comparisons from the Anglo-World since the Nineteenth Century*, edited by Stefan Berger and Sean Scalmer, 1–30. Cham: Palgrave Macmillan, 2018.

Berger, Stefan and Holger Nehring. 'Series Editors' Preface'. In *The Transnational Activist: Transformations and Comparisons from the Anglo-World since the Nineteenth Century*, edited by Stefan Berger and Sean Scalmer, v–viii. Cham: Palgrave Macmillan, 2018.

Bhambra, Gurminder and John Narayan, eds. *European Cosmopolitanism: Colonial Histories and Postcolonial Societies*. London: Routledge, 2016.

Bitsch, Marie-Thérèse and Gérard Bossuat, eds. *L'Europe unie et l'Afrique: de l'idée d'Eurafrique à la convention de Lomé 1*. Brussels: Bruylant, 2005.

Blum, Françoise, Héloïse Kiriakou, Martin Mourre et al. 'Introduction. Pour une histoire des socialismes en Afrique'. In *Socialismes en Afrique. Socialisms in Africa*, edited by Françoise Blum et al., 1–25. Paris: Éditeur de la Maison des sciences de l'homme, 2021.

Brazzoduro, Andrea. 'Algeria, Antifascism, and Third Worldism: An Anticolonial Genealogy of the Western European New Left (Algeria, France, Italy, 1957–1975)', *The Journal of Imperial and Commonwealth History* 48, no. 5 (2020): 958–78.

Brown Wells, Sherrill. *Jean Monnet: Unconventional Statesman*. Boulder, CO: Lynne Rienner Publishers, 2011.

Buettner, Elizabeth. *Europe after Empire: Decolonization, Society and Culture*. Cambridge: Cambridge University Press, 2016.

Castagnez, Noëlline et al., eds. *Les socialistes français à l'heure de la libération: perspectives française et européenne, 1943–1947*. Paris: L'OURS, 2016.

Clavin, Patricia. 'Time, Manner, Place: Writing Modern European History in Global, Transnational and International Contexts', *European History Quarterly* 40, no. 4 (2010): 624–40.

Cossu-Beaumont, Laurence. 'Race across the Atlantic: Jean-Paul Sartre and Richard Wright's Transatlantic Network in 1940s Paris'. In *Transatlantic Intellectual Networks 1914–1964*, edited by Hans Bak and Céline Mansanti, 192–211. Newcastle-upon-Tyne: Cambridge Scholars Publishing, 2019.

De Sousa Santos, Boaventura. 'Epilogue. A New Vision of Europe: Learning from the South'. In *European Cosmopolitanism. Colonial Histories and Postcolonial Societies*, edited by Gurminder Bhambra and John Narayan, 172–84. London: Routledge, 2016.

Deák, István, Jan T. Gross and Tony Judt, eds. *The Politics of Retribution in Europe: World War II and Its Aftermath*. Princeton: Princeton University Press, 2000.

Devin, Guillaume. *L'internationale socialiste: histoire et sociologie du socialisme international, 1945–1990*. Paris: Presses de la Fondation nationale des sciences politiques, 1993.

Di Donato, Michele. 'The Socialist International and Human Rights'. In *Leftist Internationalisms: A Transnational Political History*, edited by Michele Di Donato and Mathieu Fulla, 159–71. London: Bloomsbury, 2023.

Di Donato, Michele and Mathieu Fulla. 'Introduction: Leftist Internationalisms in the History of the Twentieth Century'. In *Leftist Internationalisms: A Transnational Political History*, edited by Michele Di Donato and Mathieu Fulla, 1–21. London: Bloomsbury, 2023.

Dimier, Véronique. *The Invention of a European Development Aid Bureaucracy: Recycling Empire*. Basingstoke: Palgrave Macmillan, 2014.

Fulla, Mathieu and Marc Lazar. eds. *European Socialists and the State in the Twentieth and Twenty-First Centuries*. Cham: Palgrave Macmillan, 2020.

García, Hugo. '"World Capital of Anti-Fascism"? The Making – and Breaking – of a Global Left in Spain, 1936–1939'. In *Anti-Fascism in a Global Perspective: Transnational Networks, Exile Communities and Radical Internationalism*, edited by Kasper Braskén, Nigel Copsey and David Featherstone, 234–53. Abingdon: Routledge, 2021.

Getachew, Adom. 'When Jamaica Led the Postcolonial Fight Against Exploitation', *Boston Review*, 5 February 2019.

Getachew, Adom. *Worldmaking after Empire: The Rise and Fall of Self-Determination*. Princeton: Princeton University Press, 2019.

Gildea, Robert and Olga Manojlović Pintar with Mercedes Yusta Rodrigo et al. 'Afterlives and Memories'. In *Fighters across Frontiers: Transnational Resistance in Europe, 1936–48*, edited by Robert Gildea and Ismee Tames, 214–39. Manchester: Manchester University Press, 2020.

Gorman, Daniel. *Uniting the Nations*. Cambridge: Cambridge University Press, 2022.

Hall, Ian, ed. *Radicals and Reactionaries in Twentieth Century International Thought*. London: Palgrave Macmillan, 2015.

Hansen, Peo and Stefan Jonsson. *Eurafrica: The Untold History of European Integration and Colonialism*. London: Bloomsbury Academic, 2014.

Hayek, Friedrich. *The Road to Serfdom*. London: Routledge, 2001 [1994].

Heard-Lauréote, Karen. 'Transnational Networks: Informal Governance in the European Political Space?' In *Transnational European Union: Towards a Common Political Space*, edited by Wolfram Kaiser and Peter Starie, 36–60. Abingdon: Routledge, 2005.

Imlay, Talbot. *The Practice of Socialist Internationalism: European Socialists and International Politics, 1914–1960*. Oxford: Oxford University Press, 2018.

Jachec, Nancy. *Europe's Intellectuals and the Cold War: The European Society of Culture, Post-War Politics and International Relations*. London: Bloomsbury, 2020 [2015].

Judt, Tony. *The Burden of Responsibility: Blum, Camus, Aron and the French Twentieth Century*. Chicago: Chicago University Press, 1998.

Judt, Tony. *Past Imperfect: French Intellectuals, 1944–1956*. New York: New York University Press, 2011.

Kaiser, Wolfram and Peter Starie. 'Introduction: The European Union as a Transnational Political Space'. In *Transnational European Union: Towards a Common Political Space*, edited by Wolfram Kaiser and Peter Starie, 1–14. Abingdon: Routledge, 2005.

Kaiser, Wolfram. 'Transnational Western Europe since 1945: Integration as Political Society Formation'. In *Transnational European Union: Towards a Common Political Space*, edited by Wolfram Kaiser and Peter Starie, 17–35. Abingdon: Routledge, 2005.

Kaiser, Wolfram. 'Transnational Networks in European Governance'. In *The History of the European Union: Origins of a Trans- and Supranational Polity 1950–72*, edited by Wolfram Kaiser, Brigitte Leucht and Morten Rasmussen, 12–33. Abingdon: Routledge, 2009.

Kaiser, Wolfram, Brigitte Leucht and Michael Gehler, eds. *Transnational Networks in Regional Integration: Governing Europe, 1945–83*. Basingstoke: Palgrave Macmillan, 2010.

Kaiser, Wolfram and Jan-Henrik Meyer. 'Beyond Governments and Supranational Institutions: Societal Actors in European Integration'. In *Societal Actors in European Integration: Polity-Building and Policy-Making, 1958–1992*, edited by Wolfram Kaiser and Jan-Henrik Meyer, 1–14. Basingstoke: Palgrave Macmillan, 2013.

Kaiser, Wolfram and Jan-Henrik Meyer, eds. *Societal Actors in European Integration: Polity-Building and Policy-Making, 1958–1992*. Basingstoke: Palgrave Macmillan, 2013.

Kalter, Christoph. *The Discovery of the Third World: Decolonization and the Rise of the New Left in France, c. 1950–1976*. Cambridge: Cambridge University Press, 2016.

Katsakioris, Constantin and Alexander Stroh. 'Africa and the Crisis of Socialism: Postsocialism and the Left'. Special Issue: 'Africa and the Crisis of Socialism', *Canadian Journal of African Studies / Revue canadienne des études africaines* 55, no. 2 (2021): 241–9.

Kirk, Neville. *Labour and the Politics of Empire: Britain and Australia, 1900 to the Present*. Manchester: Manchester University Press, 2017.

Laïdi, Zaki. *La norme sans la force: L'énigme de la puissance européenne*. Paris: Presses de Sciences Po, 2008.

Laurent, Alain. *Le libéralisme américain: Histoire d'un détournement*. Paris: Les Belles Lettres, 2006.

Legg, Stephen, Mike Heffernan, Jake Hodder and Benjamin Thorpe, 'Introduction'. In *Placing Internationalism: International Conferences and the Making of the Modern World*, edited by Stephen Legg, Mike Heffernan, Jake Hodder and Benjamin Thorpe, 1–10. London, Bloomsbury, 2022.

Lin Lewis, Su. 'Women, Hospitality and the Intimate Politics of International Socialism'. *Past & Present* 262, no. 1 (2023): 242–80.

Manners, Ian. 'Normative Power Europe: A Contradiction in Terms?' *JCMS: Journal of Common Market Studies* 40, no. 2 (2002): 235–58.

Manners, Ian. 'Normative Power Approach to European Union External Action'. In *The External Action of the European Union: Concepts, Approaches, Theories*, edited by Sieglinde Gstöhl and Simon Schunz, 61–76. London: Bloomsbury, 2021.

Mark, James and Paul Betts. 'Introduction'. In *Socialism Goes Global: The Soviet Union and Eastern Europe in the Age of Decolonisation*, edited by James Mark and Paul Betts, 1–24. Oxford: Oxford University Press, 2022.

Marynower, Claire. *L'Algérie à gauche, 1900–1962. Socialistes à l'époque coloniale*. Paris: Presses universitaires de France, 2018.

Mayers, David A. *America and the Postwar World: Remaking International Society, 1945–1956*. London: Routledge, 2018.

Milani, Tommaso. *Hendrik de Man and Social Democracy: The Idea of Planning in Western Europe, 1914–1940*. Basingstoke: Palgrave Macmillan, 2020.

Oliveira, Pedro Aires. *Os Despojos da Aliança: A Grã-Bretanha e a Questão Colonial Portuguesa, 1945–1975*. Lisbon: Tinta da China, 2007.

Parmar, Inderjeet. *Think Tanks and Power in Foreign Policy*. London: Palgrave, 2004.

Patel, Kiran Klaus. 'Afterword: On the Chances and Challenges of Populating Internationalism'. In *Internationalists in European History: Rethinking the Twentieth Century*, edited by David Brydan and Jessica Reinisch, 263–80. London: Bloomsbury, 2021.

Prakash, Gyan and Jeremy Adelman. 'Introduction: Imagining the Third World: Genealogies of Alternative Global Histories'. In *Inventing the Third World: In Search of Freedom for the Postwar Global South*, edited by Gyan Prakash and Jeremy Adelman, 7–27. London: Bloomsbury, 2023.

Reinisch, Jessica and David Brydan, eds. *Internationalists in European History: Rethinking the Twentieth Century*. London: Bloomsbury, 2021.

Roberts, George. *Revolutionary State-Making in Dar es Salaam: African Liberation and the Global Cold War, 1961–1974*. Cambridge: Cambridge University Press, 2021.

Rosenboim, Or. *The Emergence of Globalism: Visions of World Order in Britain and the United States, 1939–1950*. Princeton: Princeton University Press, 2017.

Roth-Ey, Kristin. 'Introduction'. In *Socialist Internationalism and the Gritty Politics of the Particular: Second-Third World Spaces in the Cold War*, edited by Kristin Roth-Ey, 1–18. London: Bloomsbury, 2023.

Salm, Christian. 'Shaping European Development Policy? Socialist Parties as Mediators from the International to the European Level'. In *Societal Actors in European Integration: Polity-Building and Policy-Making, 1958–1992*, edited by Wolfram Kaiser and Jan-Henrik Meyer, 38–58. Basingstoke: Palgrave Macmillan, 2013.

Salm, Christian. *Transnational Socialist Networks in the 1970s: European Community Development Aid and Southern Enlargement*. Basingstoke: Palgrave Macmillan, 2016.

Sebe, Berny and Matthew G. Stanard, eds. *Decolonising Europe? Popular Responses to the End of Empire*. London: Routledge, 2020.

Shaev, Brian. 'The Algerian War, European Integration, and the Decolonization of French Socialism'. *French Historical Studies* 41, no. 1 (2019):63–94.

Shilliam, Robert. '"Ah, We Have Not Forgotten Ethiopia": Anti-Colonial Sentiment for Spain in a Fascist Era'. In *European Cosmopolitanism. Colonial Histories and Postcolonial Societies*, edited by Gurminder Bhambra and John Narayan, 31–46. London: Routledge, 2016.

Simon, Catherine. *Algérie, les années pieds-rouges: des rêves de l'indépendance au désenchantement, 1962–1969*. Paris: La Découverte, 2009.

Skinner, Rob. *Peace, Decolonization, and the Practice of Solidarity*. London: Bloomsbury, 2023.

Slobodian, Quinn. *Globalists: The End of Empire and the Birth of Neoliberalism*. Cambridge, MA: Harvard University Press, 2018.

Sluga, Glenda and Patricia Clavin, eds. *Internationalisms: A Twentieth-Century History*. Cambridge: Cambridge University Press, 2017.

Stenger, Nicolas. *Denis de Rougemont: Les intellectuels et l'Europe au XXe siècle*. Rennes: Presses universitaires de Rennes, 2015.

Stinsky, Daniel. *International Cooperation in Cold War Europe: The United Nations Economic Commission, 1947–64*. London: Bloomsbury, 2021.

Stockwell, Sarah. *The British End of the British Empire*. Cambridge: Cambridge University Press, 2018.

Thomas, Martin and Andrew Thompson. 'Empire and Globalisation: From "High Imperialism" to Decolonisation'. *The International History Review* 36, no. 1 (2014): 142–70.

Toye, Richard. 'From "Consensus" to "Common Ground": The Rhetoric of the Postwar Settlement and its Collapse'. *Journal of Contemporary History* 48, no. 1 (2013) : 3–23.

Vergez-Chaignon, Bénédicte. *Vichy en prison: Les épurés à Fresnes après la Libération*. Paris: Gallimard, 2006.

Wapshott, Nicholas. *Keynes Hayek: The Clash That Defined Modern Economics*. London: W.W. Norton, 2011.

Williams, Andrew J. 'France and the Origins of the United Nations, 1944–1945: "Si La France ne compte plus, qu'on nous le dise"'. *Diplomacy and Statecraft* 28, no. 2 (2017): 215–34.

Williams, Andrew J. *Liberalism and War*. London: Routledge, 2025 (2nd edition, forthcoming).

Part I

EUROPEAN SOCIALISM IN WAR AND PEACE

Chapter 1

The Labour Party and its relations with the SFIO in London, 1940–44

Andrew J. Williams

Introduction

France's defeat in 1940, *la débâcle*, and its surrender on 22 June, while Britain fought on to ultimate victory, set the stage for a very changed relationship between the political elites in France and Britain. This chapter is about the relations that developed between the British Labour Party and the *Section française de l'International Ouvrière* (SFIO) in exile in London, after mid-1940. This chapter will examine that relationship in tandem with a, less detailed, analysis of how the wider debate within the French Resistance in exile related to the British government and to that in Washington. In particular it will examine the activities of the SFIO's *Groupe Jean Jaurès*, which has left us a detailed account of its activities in London between 1940 and 1944. There is not space to explore the wider context of Charles de Gaulle's *Comité national français* (CNF) which was based in London until 1943 and coordinated what became known as *La France Libre* (or 'The Free French'), when it transferred to Algiers, but it will make some remarks on how that organisation's reputation affected that of the SFIO in exile. It also aims to highlight that the mutual suspicion that existed between the two socialist parties on occasion led to real cooperation and even mutual respect, particularly in the context of planning for post-war societal change. The result of these relationships during wartime was to have a lasting effect on the subsequent unfolding of Anglo-French relations during the Fourth Republic and beyond.

After 1940 the Labour Party came to be a central part of both the British government, and of the alliance that developed between Britain, the United States, the Soviet Union and other Allies. This meant that the Party now had the potential to influence British domestic and foreign policy in a way that it had not since at least its brief and tumultuous period in power between 1929 and 1931, after which it had descended into factional infighting and near political irrelevance until the Second World War. During the war it had a major revival electorally, most notably in its influence over the emerging consensus in British politics that the war had to mark the start of a new relationship between the people and the state. This was stimulated by the publication of a series of reports by William Beveridge, the 'Beveridge Report', on topics ranging from the need for full employment to one which became known as the 'Welfare State', accompanied during two Labour governments after 1945 with widespread nationalisations and the establishment of the National Health Service.[1]

The Labour Party and the SFIO before 1940

In contrast to the relative impotence of the Labour Party before 1940, during the 1930s the SFIO had been influential in French politics as never before, with its crowning achievement in Prime Minister Léon Blum's *Front Populaire* of 1936. By mid-1940, unlike the Labour Party, it was dispersed, with many of its members under arrest or in exile. So an essential starting point for thinking about how the British and French socialists prepared for the post-1945 relationship is to look at how they interacted before and during the Second World War – a war that was to prove a vital watershed for both societies and their respective major socialist parties.

The two parties came from different traditions of political thought and struggle. The British Labour Party was a party of less than burnished internationalist credentials and largely eschewed Marxist thinking. The SFIO's ideological position reflected its rather different background, which had more than a dash of revolutionary and syndicalist fervour.[2] The Labour Party's belief system was embedded in forms of Christian Socialism and the ideas of Robert Blatchford's 1894 *Merrie England* which appealed for a 'Socialism [that was] a profound and noble religion possessing a definitely practical and economic aspect' and shunned too much serious philosophical discourse. Blatchford's contemporary Neil Lyons was correct in saying that 'Merrie England alone has attracted more followers to the standard of English socialism than all or any of the other books contained in the library of the London School of Economics'.[3] French socialists were much more likely to evoke books like those of Georges Sorel, who in 1908 denounced '[t]he optimist in politics [as] an inconstant and even dangerous man, because he takes no account of the great difficulties presented by his projects . . . Liberal political economy is one of the best examples of a Utopia that could be given'.[4] Labour Party politicians on the whole dreamt of such utopias and considered 'continental' socialists as dangerous extremists. With such divergent traditions it is not surprising that misunderstandings might arise.

The SFIO and Labour had shared membership of the Labour and Socialist International (LSI) from 1923 to 1940, succeeding the so-called 'Second and a Half International' of 1920–22. The rump of the LSI was based in London during the war and dominated by Belgian Socialists like Louis de Brouckère and Camille Huysmans, now exiles. Belgian and French socialists had had an uneasy relationship with their respective Communist parties, in the French case the *Parti Communiste Français* (PCF) since the PCF's founding *Congrès de Tours* in 1920.[5] The Labour Party's ideological and personal difficulties with the British Communist Party (CPGB) were never quite so fraught, mainly because Labour was such a mainstream party by the 1930s and the CPGB had very few MPs to give it a public platform or much of a membership total. CPGB membership was possibly 60,000 at its peak in 1945; the Labour Party had over a million members and won over 47 per cent of the total vote in the same year, nearly 12 million people.[6] The lack of common purpose with their Communist parties within both the SFIO and Labour Party was reflected in the gyrations of the CPGB and PCF about the USSR during the period before the German invasion of June 1941 and towards the USA after the Atlantic Charter of August 1941. The SFIO members brought their memories of past combat with them to London, often mystifying their British Labour hosts, who had not experienced the same internecine hatred in its struggles with the CPGB, even though there was much mutual hostility, not least over the importance of the USSR in the fight for socialism.

Neither had the Labour Party experienced exile and humiliation on the scale of that experienced by the SFIO after 1940. Both parties had certainly lived through turbulent 1930s with periods in government, in Labour's case in 1929–31, and in the SFIO's the *Front Populaire* of 1936–37.[7] Both had also experienced periods in the political wilderness, with Labour at one point being reduced to fifty-five MPs after the formation of the National Government by James Ramsay MacDonald in 1931 in what has for ever more been referred to as the 'Great Betrayal'.[8] And by 1940 both had lost their faith in the peace-keeping strengths of the League of

Nations, whose last Secretary General, former French diplomat Joseph Avenol, wrote to Blum in December 1945: 'The League of Nations has become the collective alibi of those whose weakness allowed Hitler to come to power', adding that 'I humbly share in that disgrace'.[9] He had pledged allegiance to Marshall Philippe Pétain's Vichy Government in 1940 and died in disgrace in Switzerland in 1952. The Beveridge publication *The Price of Peace* summed up the League as being 'inadequate for its purpose'.[10]

The Labour Party in government, 1940

During the war itself the Labour Party's fortunes improved considerably, with party leader Clement Attlee being made Deputy Prime Minister in the Churchill Cabinet of April 1940.[11] After a few years of inconclusive direction from the veteran George Lansbury, from 1935 Attlee had gradually established Labour as an effective Opposition to a Conservative Government that was increasingly divided about how to respond to the threat posed by Hitler. Attlee was no socialist firebrand, retaining an affection for the British Empire, if not for all aspects of imperialism, and was a great admirer of the United States. If he can be characterised as such he was in effect a British 'New Dealer'.[12] Labour became the main, but not sole, voice of anti-appeasement (which included Conservatives like Winston Churchill, Anthony Eden and Bob Boothby), emerging as a leader in debates criticising the military incompetence of the Conservative government, especially in the aftermath of the fiasco of the Norwegian campaign of May 1940. After the defeat of the expeditionary force to Narvik in Norway a bitter and splendid debate led to a second National Government under Winston Churchill. It was one that gave Labour effective control over much of Britain's domestic wartime policy and a significant role in foreign policy,[13] with over twenty ministerial level positions and a significant role in the War Cabinet.[14] This laid an effective basis for Labour's landslide election victory in 1945 and a spell in government until October 1951.

The SFIO meanwhile was itself forced into an electoral pact from 1944 to 1947 in spite of having had a difficult relationship with the PCF in the Resistance. Claiming they were the 'meilleurs soldats de la Libération et de la République [the best soldiers to have liberated the Republic]' the SFIO could not hide their disquiet in being forced into such a partnership only agreed by the PCF (who 'hadn't the time or the leisure to indulge in polemic') so they could push the interests of the USSR within France.[15] The disparity between the Labour Party and the SFIO was clear.

The SFIO in exile

After the humiliation of the French surrender in May 1940 – *la débâcle* – many exiles, including a number of SFIO politicians, arrived in London. This was in addition to many others who were not directly or indirectly linked to the party, like de Gaulle, who managed nonetheless to attract a number of SFIO figures to his cause, as we will see. Notable initial exiles included the philosopher Simone Weil, whose appeal to be allowed to cooperate with the Free French was rejected by de Gaulle, very possibly leading to her subsequent death in Ashford in 1943.[16] SFIO exiles notably included the leader of the French socialists in exile, Vincent Auriol, who was to become the second President of the Fourth Republic after 1947.

Léon Blum, the former Prime Minister of the *Front Populaire* of 1936–7, remained the best known leader of the SFIO, but he was in detention in France. Between 1943 and 1946 his place was taken by the lesser known *résistant* Daniel Mayer, who periodically appeared in London with news of the struggle in France itself. Also a notable figure in the *Front Populaire*, Auriol was imprisoned for his anti-Vichy views (he was one of the eighty *députés* who voted not to make Pétain Head of State in July 1940) and subsequently joined the Resistance. He arrived in London in October 1943, and then went to Algiers with de Gaulle, where he represented the SFIO in the Free French Consultative Assembly in later 1943, and France at the Bretton Woods Conferences in July 1944 (as did de Gaulle loyalist René Pleven) and then at the San Francisco Conference in June 1945.[17] He was thus quite unlike some of the SFIO whom we will encounter in this chapter, some of whom have been described as 'dissiden[ts] within the dissidence'.[18]

Blum meanwhile found himself in a Vichy gaol after the French defeat of June 1940, blamed, along with French military commander Maurice Gamelin and other generals and politicians, for their pre-war policies and wartime actions, which allegedly bore a massive responsibility for the weakening of French prowess, events and accusations recounted by Blum in a post-war volume, *L'histoire jugera*.[19] After a show trial in Riom, where Blum's eloquent testimony embarrassed Vichy far more than had been expected, he and the other accused were imprisoned in France and then in Germany,[20] from whence most of them miraculously returned after the German defeat. French socialists continued to recognise Blum's moral leadership even from his prison cell, but of course he could not play an active part in the war effort. We can add that Blum's reputation in the United States also continued to be high, and certainly better than that of de Gaulle, famously distrusted by Franklin Delano Roosevelt.[21] Auriol even quoted Blum's endorsement (smuggled out of prison) of de Gaulle as leader of the Free French in an attempt to soften Roosevelt's views on de Gaulle, as early as December 1942.[22] Others also quoted his example as everything that was good about France. The American Ambassador in Paris in 1940, William Bullitt, wrote a glowing elegy to Blum in the *Préface* to *L'histoire jugera*. Unfortunately Bullitt and FDR were to seriously fall out later in the war. His successor, Ambassador to Vichy, Admiral William Leahy, was also dismissive about de Gaulle, and had an undoubted influence on Roosevelt's feelings.[23] Blum's absence in London certainly reduced the potential weight of the SFIO in both official British and American thinking.

The reception of the French exiles in London and New York was not unequivocally warm. The ground had been set by a period when Britain, and the United States, watched as France seemingly auto-destructed under the Third Republic. The celebrated British sociologist and Labour Party intellectual R. H. Tawney, in an article about Arnold Toynbee's latest volumes on the collapse of civilisations, might well have had France in mind when he wrote: 'The secret of vitality [in a civilisation] is perpetual adaptation in response to new emergencies; but the effort, once made, is not easily repeated . . . It perpetuates itself, long after a changing environment has turned its virtues into vices, so that victory at one stage spells defeat at the next.'[24] That was in December 1939. By late 1940 the tone was even stronger, as we shall see below. Equally, in line with Tawney's jibe about 'victory at one stage spells defeat at the next' the French were being partly blamed for the mistakes of the Treaty of Versailles. President Wilson was quoted with approval by Beveridge when he had said in 1918 that 'I know that Europe is still governed by the same reactionary forces which controlled this country until a few years ago [the reference is to his 'progressive' reform policies] . . . too much success or security on the part of the Allies will make a genuine peace settlement exceedingly difficult if not impossible . . . They need to be coerced'.[25] This was now a message that was received with some agreement in London, and it is highly unlikely that de Gaulle would have accepted it, or the SFIO for that matter. But the Labour Party saw itself as the embodiment of the new broom that would sweep aside the 'reactionary' forces of the past twenty years.

This was a view held across the political spectrum in Britain, one major milestone being Foreign Secretary Anthony Eden's Mansion House speech of 29 May 1941, duly noted by the Labour Party's Undersecretary of State for Foreign Affairs, and a major link to the Free French in London, Philip Noel-Baker. Eden proclaimed that 'we have declared that social security must be the first objective of our domestic policy after the war'. The League of Nations produced a report in the same year that explicitly linked 'social and economic reconstruction' to the 'post-war settlement' and quoted Eden in its defence. The link was explicitly made between the need to reduce unemployment through 'international control', while defending the 'freedom of the individual'. An approbatory appendix by Oxford Labour Party supporting economist Thomas Balogh is almost as long as the report itself. And other economists like A. C. Pigou, who had been crucial in the 1914–18 debate on the same topic, contributed very similar views. The 'transition from war to peace' had to be socially as well as economically uplifting.[26]

A new peace thus had a 'price' and one that the Labour Party and a powerful coalition of foreign policy thinkers on both sides of the Atlantic were prepared to accept. The British and Americans' distrust of the old French elites often meant that they saw exiled French generals like de Gaulle as those who had not appreciated the new realities and who lacked determination to break with the past. Such ideas were being mapped out by the Anglo-American axis, not side by side with the French. The Chatham House link with the Council on Foreign Relations was in particular vital. While de Gaulle was to spend much of the war demanding that France's *security* aims be understood and respected, for the Americans and the British the key intellectual link was one that recognised the *economic* causes of war, and their solution to it. As Beveridge put it in *The Price of Peace*, the 'target' of British policy was the abolition of the 'international anarchy', which not only required robust international dispute mechanisms and a respect for the 'rule of law' but also an understanding of what underpinned the 'seed of fear' from which war grew.[27]

That 'seed' had to be recognised as at least partly economic rivalry, and that required international cooperation on a vast scale, what the United States administration saw as promoting 'freedom from fear' at the same time as 'freedom from want'. In Britain this manifested itself in the influence of progressive thinkers like Toynbee, eventually institutionalised in a 'Reconstruction Committee' set up in Chatham House and a 'Reconstruction Ministry' in Whitehall. Again the economic and the security elements of the coming war were explicitly linked. The impetus in Chatham House started well before the war began in Anglo-American meetings of Chatham House and the Council on Foreign Relations.[28] There was no place in this vision for the narrow-minded nationalism of the past, one that was embodied for some in the figure of de Gaulle.

De Gaulle was hard pressed to believe in the supposedly idealistic aims of his new 'Allies'. His advisors said this made it very difficult to 'synchronise [France's] policy with that of the Allies' [*synchroniser sa politique sur celle des Alliés*]. The Atlantic Charter of August 1941 was dismissed as 'nothing but theories and even more vague ideals' [*que des théories et des ideaux plus vagues encores]*, a trait not unreasonably ascribed to the 'idealist' Roosevelt. But in an analysis as late as April 1943 it was felt that Britain *had* a foreign policy, the USA *did not*. Britain and the USSR were 'realist', they could do a deal involving territorial and other demands, especially in North Africa and Britain 'might even envisage an economic union with France' [*viserait même à la constitution d'une union économique avec la France*].[29] This showed a clear misunderstanding of the changed atmosphere on both sides of the Atlantic. Neither the British nor the American 'Post-War Planning' teams wanted a return to the problems after Versailles. That, said Beveridge among others, had been caused by the 'disunity of [the] victors'; there would be no more talk of 'security', but rather of the need for 'democracy', in which both the Americans and British put their faith.

It was not entirely a wrong-headed analysis. A 'union' had indeed been mooted at the time of the French surrender in 1940, and de Gaulle had been in reluctant agreement with the idea as Prime Minister Paul Reynaud's military envoy in London and in accord with Jean Monnet who held the same position as the French economic representative.[30] Where the analysis was wrong was in assuming that Sumner Welles and others were indulging in mere humbug when they asserted, in line with the Atlantic Charter, that the United States wanted 'a system of international economic collaboration' [*un système de collaboration internationale économique*].[31] The Free French were not being made privy to whatever planning for the post-war period was being decided upon. And the main reason for worry among French exiles in both London and Washington until the end of 1942 was that the Vichy Government remained the principal channel of communication between the Allies and France (largely through the American Ambassador to Vichy Admiral William Leahy, a close associate of Roosevelt). As the French diplomat in Washington Jean-Marc Boegner had told de Gaulle in early December 1941, Welles considered the Free French were putting up 'no resistance', and 'he had a very pessimistic view of the situation in France' [*il regardait la situation en France avec un très grand pessimisme*]. He even 'considered the game to be up in France' [*considérait le jeu comme perdu en France*]. Boegner continued with the same theme in later December, there had been 'no significant change in relations between Vichy and Washington' [*aucun changement important dans les relations entre Washington et Vichy*]. Moreover Welles doubted that the Free French could ever move beyond being a 'militant' organisation 'in order to become a properly democratic entity'. There was even doubt that they *could* 'unite a majority of the French, even those outside the country' [*rallier une majorité de Français, même en dehors de la France*].[32] This was not a promising background for the SFIO to hope to make a positive impact on the Labour Party or indeed anyone else in London. Whether they liked it or not, their standing was linked to that of de Gaulle, himself not given a place at the top table or even given much credibility of being the leader of a new France. As we shall see, many within the SFIO exiles tried to distance themselves from de Gaulle, with not much success, even if key members of the Labour Party did slowly warm to them.

The SFIO in exile and the Labour Party

Relations with the Free French in exile in London were largely a Labour Party preserve. It is important to note that this extended to cooperation with the Free French in France itself. Labour's Hugh Dalton was appointed as Minister of Economic Warfare (1940–42) and given the vital task of starting a secret war to 'set Europe alight' with the Special Operations Executive (SOE). SOE played a huge role in France supplying the French Resistance with munitions, arms and agents to fight the Germans, though some French historians have accused SOE of never providing what the *Maquis* most wanted, effective light arms, as well as the freely provided explosives.[33] The Foreign Office, directed by Conservative Anthony Eden, also contained another important Labour Junior Minister, Philip Noel-Baker, who was the main point of contact between the Foreign Office and the exiled French groups in London, both Gaullist and those of the SFIO. Noel-Baker and other British officials found they often had to deal with the competing claims and egos of a very disparate French diaspora, one that often disagreed about its wartime and post-war policies, and in particular the relative weight that General de Gaulle should have in those policies.

Initial Labour Party reticence about the SFIO in London

Noel-Baker was thus the main link with the French Committee of National Liberation (*Conseil National Français* – CNF – established on 3 June 1940) and was an initial sceptic. He told Dalton and Attlee in June 1940 that trusting any French leader at that stage was problematic: 'The more I think of it, the more I am sure it would be a fatal mistake to make – or even allow these Frenchmen to come to London'. He thought the best place for them to go was to 'Morocco or Algeria, it will seem thoroughly independent and real to every Frenchman, and more and more so as it becomes quite plain that it is the Two Hundred Families who have betrayed the country'.[34] Given that this conspiracy theory was current among French people who had accepted their defeat, this was not a good start.[35] In support of his view he cited Jean Monnet, also stranded in London as part of the Allied joint commissioning programme, and a recent advocate of an Anglo-French Union. He was also influenced by his old friend, the sometime French Independent Socialist Pierre Cot, Air Minister in the *Front Populaire*, one of those trying to negotiate the purchase of aircraft from the United States in the latter part of the peace.[36]

Cot, who had worked with and remained close to Noel-Baker since their days together in the League of Nations, was a great sceptic of de Gaulle's true intentions, a trait he shared with many other French exiles. Both Cot and Noel-Baker feared that de Gaulle might prove to be a 'Boulangist', a dictator in uniform. When Cot asked de Gaulle to give him a job in the Free French hierarchy he was rebuffed in no uncertain terms.[37] But de Gaulle did his best to disabuse Noel-Baker of his fears, writing to him in the warmest terms and even inviting him to be a member of the *Association des Amis des Volontaires Français*. As late as February 1941 Noel-Baker was apologising to de Gaulle that then Minister of Information Duff Cooper had tried to stop him broadcasting in June 1940, testimony to de Gaulle's powers of charm and flattery when he chose to exercise them.

Later Duff Cooper was a key liaison between Churchill and de Gaulle (1943–44), and Ambassador to France, 1944–48.[38] Noel-Baker also spoke warmly of de Gaulle in the House of Commons in early 1941 when de Gaulle was being seen as a troublemaker after the St Pierre et Miquelon affair.[39] His appreciation of Blum was also evident in his defence of other French exiles, notably André Blumel, Blum's former Chief of Staff in the Front Populaire of 1936–37.[40] As for Noel-Baker, in 1946 Harold Laski told Blum (by now released from his prison) that Noel-Baker was a 'charming liberal but with no capacity for decisive action'.[41] This unfortunately was but one explanation of other SFIO disappointments with the Labour Party that were to follow well before Blum was freed.

The *Groupe Jean Jaurès* [42]

A lively counter-point to the Gaullists in London was the *Comité de liaison des socialistes français en Grande Bretagne*, usually known as the *Groupe Jean Jaurès* (GJJ), described by its most complete *historienne*, Fanny Emmanuelle Rey, as a 'dissidence within the dissidence'.[43] Rey points out that initially SFIO members in exile were split 'unequally ... between the Resistance and collaboration'. Those who made a key input into wider

Free French activities were Auriol, André Tixier, André Philip, Henry Hauck and Georges Boris. Boris was de Gaulle's Commissioner for the Interior after 1942, and fell out with other socialists in London over his support for de Gaulle, notably with the GJJ's Georges Gombault, the socialist journalist and Vice President of the *Ligue des Droits de l'Homme*. During the war itself Henri Hauck advised de Gaulle about labour matters from 1940 onwards and Philip was de Gaulle's *Commissaire de l'Intérieur* (Minister of the Interior) from July 1942 to November 1943 in succession to René Cassin. There were attempts to set up a separate *Comité d'Action Socialiste* by Daniel Mayer (aka 'Villiers', leader of the SFIO in Blum's absence as we have noted, 1943–46), Albert Van Wolput (aka 'Bosman') and Henri Ribière, as a distinctive Resistance organisation, but such efforts tended to end up with local cooperation between Communists, Gaullists and other groups in particular areas, in this case calling itself *Libération Nord*.[44]

The GJJ was made up mainly of those exiled to London, and organised by Louis Lévy, a prominent journalist and Vice President of the LSI.[45] They met monthly from 19 August 1940 to 22 October 1944. The initial intention was to work with what remained of the LSI and the Labour Party with the somewhat grandiose aim (in 1940 at least) of 'promoting a popular revolution in Europe to liberate its peoples from foreign oppression and capitalist domination'.[46] The *Groupe* spent much of its time attending meetings of the rump of the LSI, by this period reduced to the exiled Belgian veteran socialists, notably Huysmans and the Austrian Emmanuel Adler. They also participated in a group that met at the St Ermin's Hotel in Westminster which seems to have been an occasion for an 'assembly of socialist allies' to complain about how they were being treated. The SOE was also based there, as was much of the British Security Service, MI6.

GJJ relations with the Labour Party

The direct relations of the GJJ with the Labour Party tended to be through William Gillies, the long-standing first International Secretary (1920–44) of the party, a man renowned for his no-nonsense rejection of any acceptance by Labour of the CPGB, which he had denounced as being part of a 'Communist Solar System'.[47] He can be seen as a fairly typical Labour Party apparatchik of the period, a dour Scot who was not particularly fond of 'foreigners', despite the international vocation of socialism, a trait noticed on more than one occasion by the GJJ. On one occasion Huysmans commented that 'it seems that the Secretary of the Labour

Party does not care for [*ne tient pas*] with international meetings [*manifestations internationales*]'. Gillies was also fond of sermonising to French socialists about how they should adopt the English 'model' of democracy which, if adopted across Europe, would eradicate fascism.[48] Members of the GJJ also contributed a number of articles to Labour Party publications like *Tribune*, and produced pamphlets with the Fabian international Bureau like *France and Britain*, and spoke at Labour Party annual conferences. Attlee also often spoke warmly about France at these conferences, as did Noel-Baker.

Relations of the GJJ with de Gaulle

Georges Boris, a regular attender at GJJ meetings, proposed that they should work with de Gaulle from the time of his arrival in Brazzaville in late 1940, an idea that was taken up with fervour by the trades unionist Hauck and Philip, economics professor and socialist *député* (for the Rhône) who was also one of the eighty who had voted not to accept Pétain in 1940. Philip in particular would have no truck with what he saw as the ideological purity of the GJJ, for him all that existed in France was 'a party of the Right and a party of the Left'. There were only three issues that mattered: no more 'personal power', no more corporative economy, and France having a future as a 'great industrial nation'. France therefore had to adapt, as all it had at present were '*paysans attardés*' [backward peasants]. So the Right wing of the Resistance wanted its nation back, and the Left wanted Socialism, which would require a major reorganisation of the peasantry. But nothing would happen until they had 'Liberation'.[49]

This split the French Left in exile in dangerous ways. Hauck, whom we will see was fully prepared to collaborate with de Gaulle on planning French social policy after the war (in the *Sous-Commission Sociale* – see below) found himself at odds with Levy and Félix Gouin (aka 'Henry' in the Resistance). De Gaulle's setting up of the CNF as an umbrella for *La France Libre* in September 1941 led to further complaints about dictatorial behaviour, and especially because the *Commissaires*, in effect Cabinet ministers of the Free French, would report directly to de Gaulle, *le chef des Français libres*, in his own formulation. It could never be 'an authentic and exact representation of France abroad', protested the GJJ.[50] Hauck believed that 'even the Labour Party has become Gaullist', for there was increasingly no alternative to his personal profile.[51] But before de Gaulle had really assumed a dominant presence as the symbol of Free France, so by about early 1942, the GJJ, even on occasion Hauck, and especially Gombault, were often very suspicious of de Gaulle, Gombault protesting that it would look as if they 'were marching behind a general'. Yet others saw in de Gaulle their only, if inadequate, hope. By the latter part of 1943, as 'Henry' (another SFIO operative still based in London) reported to Mayer, by then in Algiers, Gaullism was 'in full control' [*c'est le Gaullisme qui l'emporte*], though 'making progress towards democracy'; they should be 'prudent' and show 'patience'.[52]

These differences of view were more than a storm in an SFIO tea cup, as the disagreement affected the vital link with the British Left, upon whom the GJJ and to some extent the entire Free French operation in London relied for support. The Fabian Society at one point felt moved to downplay assertions in a lengthy pamphlet in the British press (all of the left, like the *News Chronicle*, the *Observer*, and even the *New Statesman and Nation*) that de Gaulle's operations in Brazzaville and Algiers had been using 'thumb screws' on trades unionists and had authors 'shot'. The pamphlet stated boldly that 'whether we like it or not . . . it is time that the Governments – and by extension, the peoples – of Great Britain and the United States hold in their hands the future of France' for they will ultimately decide

> whether the political evolution of post-war France shall be peaceful or bloodily violent. If we help them to find that Government [that they want] peacefully, they may or may not be grateful to us, but if we compel them to resort to civil war to get it, they will most certainly regard us as enemies.[53]

Gombault, ever keen on SFIO independence, also worried that the SFIO and the wider French labour movement might look like it was being 'directed' by the Labour Party, an interesting parallel with de Gaulle's worries about French independence from Britain more widely.[54] The broader complaint, also echoed in the British Labour Party's newspaper *Tribune* in April 1943 was that de Gaulle's slow development of military resistance, first in Brazzaville and later in North Africa, would create an army that was full of 'reactionary elements' behind a 'democratic façade'. There was, the writer agreed, a real need for 'unity' among the various Resistance factions, 'but unity itself is a snare and delusion . . . a reactionary unity will be worse than no unity'.[55]

Cooperation and inspiration: Beveridge and planning and the SFIO[56]

It is easy to see the ultimately somewhat futile machinations of the GJJ as typical of the SFIO's relations with the Labour Party. Probably far more important were the lessons learned by many in the Free French more broadly and the SFIO in particular about how France should be organised after the war, *Projets pour après la Libération*.[57] The admiration of many of the exiles for the Labour Party and other ideas of 'planning' was obvious, and it often chimed with pre-war French thinking along the same lines. As Philip Nord has shown, there is a clear continuity of thought between pre-war *planification*, even 'corporatism', and that of the post-war *Plan* devised by Jean Monnet, himself a prominent admirer of 'Anglo-Saxon' thinking in London and Washington, which made him a constant target for de Gaulle's suspicion.[58] Labour's domination of domestic policy in the wartime coalition worked very well on the whole and the Labour- (and Liberal-)inspired Beveridge Report defined much of what came to be known as the Welfare State. The SFIO and wider French input into this, and reaction to it, was therefore of crucial importance in a number of areas of international social policy.

One place where this took place within the Free French umbrella from January 1942 in London was the Commission for the study of post-war problems [*Commission pour l'étude des problèmes d'après-guerre*] which was chaired by the pre-war *Quai d'Orsay* senior diplomat Hervé Alphand, de Gaulle's National Commissioner for the Economy, Finance and the Colonies and Director of Economic Affairs. But it had a large SFIO contingent and its thinking was very much influenced by contemporary Labour Party thinking about the Beveridge Report, and especially influenced Boris and Hauck. There was also a *Sous-Commission Sociale*, which had many of the same members.[59] As the discussions developed during the war, the SFIO worked closely with William Jowitt, the Labour Party Solicitor General and Minister for Reconstruction within the British government, and later the main architect of National Insurance in 1944. Another important point of contact was with the 'London International Assembly', a body that met through most of the war and made a significant impact on thinking about the post-war organisation of the UN and about war crimes tribunals, as well as matters of social policy, again with the Beveridge Report figuring as a key point of departure.[60] So did the economic thinking of John Maynard Keynes, and his call for policies to ensure continued full employment after the war take pride of place in the *Commission* and *Sous-Commission*'s deliberations. 'England had shown the way' and Keynes's policies would stop 'the mechanism of crisis' [*le mécanisme des crises*].[61]

The main worry that comes through in the papers of the *Commission* and the *Sous-Commission Sociale* was how to avoid 'the economic quagmire into which France was progressively sinking' [*le marasme économique dans lequel le pays [France] s'enfermait de plus en plus*]. In a report that was produced in March 1943 by the *Institut de la Conjoncture* (1937–45, set up by the demographer and historian Alfred Sauvy), the competitive devaluations and the attendant deflation of the interwar period were identified as key problems. It was realised that this would mean a very different set of French macro-economic policies from now on. But they also rejected an overall 'autarkic' approach, as in the USSR. The future of France had to be 'international', for an autarkic system would put in danger 'the economic balance and peace of the world' [*l'équilibre économique et la paix du monde*]. Moreover this new system had to be based on free access to primary commodities, markets and, most of all, to 'the establishment of an international minimum level of living standards' [*l'établissement international d'un niveau de vie minimum*].[62] But there were evident fissures in the *Sous-Commission* when it came to putting some detail to these broad ideas.

Perhaps the most important document produced by the *Sous-Commission* that seemingly supported the American post-war planning (PWP) process came in September 1942 in a discussion of world orders. The view expressed there was that France had to face up to the fact that it had not escaped 'by the skin of its teeth' [*de justesse*] in 1918 and that it had gone on to 'lose the peace', even worse, 'it [France] had lost its soul. It must be refound' [*Elle avait perdu son âme. Elle doit la retrouver*]. The reason why Hitler had appealed to many in Europe was because he had given economic 'hope' with his *nouvel ordre (allemand)*, while the democracies had pursued economic nationalism, including in the United States, and in Britain (with the 1932 Ottawa Agreement). The Atlantic Charter gave hope that they had now put this behind them, but these proposals were still 'vague' and left the details '*dans l'ombre*'. But they liked Welles's initial ideas for 'international economic collaboration', guarantees for individual liberties and 'a well-planned economy' [*une économie bien dirigée*]. First there had to be (as Welles agreed) a 'recovery plan' [*plan de ravitaillement*] (as United Nations Relief and Rehabilitation Administration (UNRRA) was to become), then job security for all to counter Hitler's propaganda, then international solutions passing through a combination (initially) of regional arrangements and finally one that was 'universal' like the League had tried to do.[63]

Discussions within the various Free French organisations, and especially those dominated by the SFIO about the future of Germany and Europe proliferated in the twelve months before the Normandy landings of 6 June 1944. Could Germany be trusted and should it be accepted as a re-educated, demilitarised, democratic state? Not only the SFIO but also the PCF expressed these hopes. And most of all, could there be a 'socialist plan for Europe'? Could there even be a 'United States of the World' [*États-Unis du Monde*]?[64] These ideas had a remarkable symmetry with the other

Allies, and made the Labour Party link vital for the Free French to contribute indirectly to the process of PWP.

Such relative optimism was countered by others, like the prominent Socialist (and later a member of the French delegation to the Economic and Social Council of the United Nations (ECOSOC)) Boris, who expressed the fear in the *Commission* that the post-war world would be one where the 'new world would impose its will on the old' [*le nouveau monde sera en mesure d'imposer ses directives à l'ancien*]. The Americans must be distrusted, as they will not present this as 'imperialism' but as 'altruism'. But what they will really bring is not the 'New Deal' (which he agrees with), but 'risk and competition'. And once Roosevelt left the scene, as he must, Big Business will take over, and a Boom will be organised. In all of this Europe will be subjected to 'the panaceas of liberalism' [*les panacées du liberalisme*], free trade as described in the Atlantic Charter, but without much clarity as to whether this Anglo-American statement would be extended to Europe. He further speculated that the United States might 'experiment with monetary manipulation' [*tenter l'expérience de dirigisme monétaire*]. But how could there be 'free' trade when after the war the United States would have huge positive credit balances with all other countries? The inevitable result would be that Europeans would see any new system as 'purely provisional'.[65]

Boris had but one answer, and that was to turn to the British. His time in London had clearly impressed him that Britain was more and more interested in a 'planned economy'. Britain was showing that Europe could pursue a different, classless road, based on 'the principle of salvation, or even of the common good' [*le sentiment du salut ou simplement du bien commun*]. This would not be without problems, the USA and even the USSR would try and divide Europe, with the latter seen as being more of a friend, but one to keep at arm's length. For it was up to France to 'direct and represent this coalition of European interests' [*diriger et représenter cette coalition des intérêts européens*], with the British playing a role if possible. By this he meant that it depended on Britain remaining closer to Europe than to the United States. Europe should therefore be independent of the United States, for Europe had now 'arrived at a more advanced stage' [*parvenue à un stade plus avancé*] than the United States. And to make sure it stayed that way Europe must keep its own armaments.[66]

Auriol was a particularly important participant in French thinking and action for the future where economic matters were concerned. As we have noted he was the Head of the *Groupe Socialiste* in both London and Algiers, where he was from early 1944, as well as *Président de la Commission de l'Intérieur*, the equivalent of the British Home Office. He was also a French delegate to the Bretton Woods Conferences in July 1944[67] and later San Francisco in 1945. His papers nonetheless show a depth of bitterness about how France was being kept in the dark about post-war planning. On one occasion in July 1944 Auriol exploded to his London comrades from Algiers, with: 'If France no longer counts then tell us that' [*Si la France ne compte plus, qu'on nous le dise*]. It was important that Attlee and Gillis [sic] be told so.[68] There is no record in the Auriol Papers of a reply, the occasion of his above noted explosion about having been ignored.[69]

Conclusions: post-war SFIO–Labour Party cooperation?

The celebrated French literary collaborator Pierre Drieu la Rochelle is said to have dismissed the Germans as essentially stupid when accused of 'giving secrets to the enemy' [*intelligence avec l'ennemi*], the juridical term for collaboration.[70] The Resistance was just as divided on the point of what it was 'intelligent' to do with both Allies and enemies. The French Resistance in Algiers and London feared being left to deal with Germany again as it had been in 1919. Raymond Haas-Picard was quoted above complaining to 'Villiers' (socialist Daniel Mayer) about the 'dangerous perspectives' of a weakened Britain allying with France and the 'smaller democracies' against a resurgent Germany, and especially one that, as South African General Jan Smuts had said, was admired by the British.[71] But broadly the Socialist Resistance wanted to ally with Britain against both Germany and the United States.

Hence after the Liberation many French socialists continued to believe that an alliance with the British Labour Party, and not the United States, would help France to recover its equilibrium. Auriol had said in a lengthy speech in May 1944 that part of France's recovery depended on an 'essential European federalism' [*Féderalisme européen absolument nécessaire*]. Why should this not be as part of an Anglo-Franco-Soviet alliance, *une alliance naturelle*, as he had heard de Gaulle say recently, even if with an 'eastern' *groupe oriental* and a 'western' *groupe occidental*? Indeed one of de Gaulle's first important foreign policy actions in December 1944 as head of the *Gouvernement Provisoire* (GPRF) was to conclude a Treaty of Mutual Assistance with Moscow, one which unfortunately did not encourage Stalin to invite de Gaulle to Yalta.[72]

Also unfortunately for both the SFIO in particular and the GPRF and the subsequent Fourth Republic (1947–58), the Labour Party was largely powerless to support an Anglo-French entente to create a Europe in their own image. Warm words were spoken about France by Labour Party leaders at the First Socialist Party Conference on French soil in November 1944, attended by Gillies, Noel-Baker and Dalton among others. Equally warm words were exchanged in March 1945 at the International Conference in London, with the announcing of a *pacte franco-britannique* that endorsed the UN agreements of Dumbarton Oaks, the Franco-Soviet Treaty of 1944, and even *des bases possibles* to stabilise currencies, the subject of much French angst. But the United Nations horse had already fled the stable, the Dumbarton Oaks' decisions having been confirmed at Yalta without French agreement.[73] Later in the 1940s the policies of Labour Party Foreign Secretary Ernest Bevin for a 'third world power', a Franco-British condominium in Europe, came to nothing.[74] In 1945 the future of Europe was essentially in the hands of the United States and the Soviet Union.

Notes

1. William Beveridge, *Report on Social Insurance and Allied Services*, November 1942; William Beveridge, *Full Employment in a Free Society*, November 1944; William Beveridge, *The Price of Peace* (London: Pilot Press, 1945).

2. See Lucian Ashworth, *International Relations and the Labour Party: Intellectuals and Policy Making from 1918–1945* (London: Tauris, 2007). It is fair to say that the Labour Party was less impressed with the Soviet Union than the SFIO. On Labour's attitudes, see Ben Pimlott, *Labour and the Left in the 1930s* (Cambridge: Cambridge University Press, 1977), and Andrew J. Williams, *Labour and Russia: The Attitude of the British Labour Party to the USSR, 1924–1934* (Manchester: Manchester University Press, 1989).

3. A. N. Lyons, *Robert Blatchford: The Sketch of a Personality: An Estimate of Some Achievements* (London: Clarion Press, 1910), 97 and 107–8; R. Blatchford, *Merrie England*, (London: Clarion Press, 1894).

4. Georges Sorel, *Reflections on Violence* (New York: Peter Smith, 1941, 1st pub. 1908), 9 and 33.

5. Annie Kriegel, *Les Communistes français* (Paris: Seuil, 1968).

6. A. J. Davies, *To Build a New Jerusalem: The Labour Movement from the 1890s to the 1990s* (London: Abacus, 1996), 179; Henry Pelling, *The British Communist Party* (London: A. and C. Black, 1975); Francis Beckett, *The Enemy Within: The Rise and Fall of the British Communist Party* (London: John Murray, 1995).

7. Jean Lacouture, *Léon Blum* (Paris: Seuil, 1979).

8. David Marquand, *Ramsay MacDonald* (London: Jonathan Cape, 1977).

9. Avenol to Blum, 2 December 1945, Blum Papers, *Archives Nationales*, Paris, 4 BL 1.

10. Beveridge, *The Price of Peace*, 19.

11. John Bew, *Citizen Clem: A Biography of Attlee* (London: Quercus, 2016). Bew also stresses Attlee's moderate left-wing politics.

12. Bew, *Citizen Clem*, 44–5, 92 and 98.

13. Such as the sending of Labour firebrand Sir Stafford Cripps as Ambassador to Moscow until 1942: Gabriel Gorodetsky, *Stafford Cripps' Mission to Moscow, 1940–42* (Cambridge: Cambridge University Press, 2002).

14. Bew, *Citizen Clem*, 250.

15. 'Commissariat de l'Intérieur': Exchange of letters between the PCF and the SFIO 'Très Secret', March 1944: A[rchives] N[ationales], Paris, 552 AP 34, 3 AU 9 Dr 2, Auriol Papers.

16. Weil is widely believed to have starved herself to death out of sorrow that de Gaulle could find no place for her undoubted talents in the Free French organisation in London. See David McLellan, *Utopian Pessimist: The Life and Thought of Simone Weil* (London: Palgrave Macmillan, 1990); Simone Pétrement, *La vie de Simone Weil; Avec des lettres et d'autres textes inédits de Simone Weil* (Paris: Fayard, 1997).

17. For more on Auriol, see below. Pleven's files on Bretton Woods can be found in René Pleven, 'Bretton Woods: Notes, rapports, correspondence', 1 July 1944–28 December 1945; He also attended San Francisco with Auriol: both AN 560 AP 32.

18. Fanny Emmanuelle Rey, *La dissidence socialiste à Londres: Le groupe Jean Jaurès et la France (août 1940–août 1944)*, Mémoire de maitrise d'histoire, Université Paris 1, Panthéon-Sorbonne, 1997–8.

19. Blum's own account of this can be found in Léon Blum, *L'histoire jugera* (Paris: Editions de l'Arbre, 1945).

20. Also recounted in Blum *L'histoire jugera*, 249–332.

21. Andrew J. Williams, *France, Britain and the United States in the Twentieth Century, Volume 1: 1900–1940* (London and New York: Palgrave Macmillan, 2014), where I discuss FDR's liking for Blum in the 1930s, and Williams, *France, Britain and the United States in the Twentieth Century, Volume 2: 1940–61* (London and New York: Palgrave Macmillan, 2020), where I discuss his profound dislike for de Gaulle.

22. Auriol to Roosevelt, 12 May 1944, 'Groupe Socialiste/ Parti Socialiste' (in Algiers) 3 AU 9 DR 5, Auriol Papers.

23. Philips O'Brien, *The Second Most Powerful Man in the World, Fleet Admiral William D. Leahy, Chief of Staff* (London: Penguin, 2019); William D. Leahy, *I Was There* (London: Gollancz, 1950). See also Leahy's fellow diplomat in Vichy: Robert Murphy, *Diplomat Among Warriors* (Garden City, NY: Doubleday, 1964).

24. R. H. Tawney, 'Dr. Toynbee's Study of History', *International Affairs* 18, no. 6 (Nov.–Dec., 1939), 798–806.

25. Beveridge, *The Price of Peace*, 20.

26. A. C. Pigou, *The Transition from War to Peace* (Oxford: Oxford University Press, 1943); Anthony Eden, Mansion House speech of 29 May 1941; League of Nations Draft Report on Social and Economic Reconstruction in the Post-War Settlement', n.d., 1941; Noel-Baker (Philip) Papers, Churchill College, Cambridge NBKR 4/229.

27. Beveridge, *The Price of Peace*, 11–12.

28. Andrew J. Williams, 'Before the Special Relationship: The Council on Foreign Relations, The Carnegie Foundation and the Rumour of an Anglo-American War', *Journal of Transatlantic Studies* 1, no. 2 (Autumn 2003): 233–51.

29. 'Politique Extérieure des Etats-Unis', 'Note' of April 1943, no author, in Papiers de Gaulle, Dossier 1, France Libre de Gaulle: 1) Affaires étrangères – ETATS-UNIS, AN, AG/3(1)/256.

30. Andrea Bosco, *June 1940: Great Britain and the First Attempt to Build a European Union* (Newcastle upon Tyne: Cambridge Scholars Publishing, 2016).

31. Bosco, *June 1940*.

32. Boegner (Washington) to de Gaulle (Brazzaville, via Foreign Office), 1 and 24 December 1941, in Papiers de Gaulle, France Libre de Gaulle: 1a) Informations sur les ETATS-UNIS), AN, AG/3(1)/256.

33. Olivier Wieviorka, *The French Resistance* (Cambridge, MA: Harvard University Press, 2016), especially 335; Ben Pimlott, *Hugh Dalton* (London: HarperCollins,1995); Hugh Dalton and Ben Pimlott, *The Fateful Years: Memoirs, 1931–1945* (London: Jonathan Cape,1957); Ben Pimlott, ed., *Second World War Diary of Hugh Dalton, 1940–45* (London: Cape, 1986).

34. Noel-Baker to Dalton, 27 June 1940, and to Attlee, 28 June 1940: Noel-Baker Papers, NBKR 4/261.

35. This conspiracy theory had a long back-story, but was very widely believed in the 1930s: Malcolm Anderson, 'The Myth of the Two Hundred Families', *Political Studies*, 13, no. 2 (June 1965), 163–78.

36. For some of Noel-Baker's correspondence with Cot, see Noel-Baker Papers, NBKR 4/258.

37. Cot to Pleven, 13 September 1941, annotations by de Gaulle; de Gaulle to Pleven, 18 March 1942, Pleven Papers, AN, 550 AP 16.

38. Duff Cooper, *Old Men Forget* (London: Faber and Faber, 2011), first published 1953; J. J. Norwich, *The Duff Cooper Diaries 1915–1951* (London: Weidenfeld & Nicolson, 2005).

39. David Woolner, 'Canada, Mackenzie King and the St. Pierre and Miquelon Crisis of 1941', *London Journal of Canadian Studies*, 24, (2010).

40. De Gaulle to Noel-Baker, 10 July and 28 August 1940, Noel-Baker Papers, NBKR 4/261.

41. Laski to Blum 29 January 1946; notes of 19 October 1945, Blum Papers AN, 4 BL 1.

42. Some of the following builds on Williams, *France, Britain and the United States . . . , Volume 2: 1940–1961*, Chapter 2, 56–7.

43. The best account of this organisation is: Rey, *La dissidence socialiste à Londres*, 1. The files of the 'Comité de liaison des Socialistes français en Grande Bretagne (Groupe Jean Jaurès, *hereafter* 'GJJ') can be found in the Office Universitaire de Recherche Socialiste (OURS) in Paris, under 'Fonds Louis Levy', 95APO 1–26.

44. Rey, *La dissidence socialiste à Londres*, 1.

45. Lévy worked as a journalist, mainly, but not exclusively, on *l'Humanité*, then the *Petit-Provençal* and *Le Populaire* (including as its London correspondent, 1940–1952) and was a prominent member of the Executive of both the SFIO and the Labour and Socialist International.

46. Minutes of First Meeting of the GJJ, 19 August 1940, Fonds Louis Levy, OURS, 95APO 3.

47. See Williams, *Labour and Russia*, Chapter 16.

48. GJJ, Minutes of meeting of 27 April and 25 May 1941, Fonds Louis Levy, OURS, 95APO 3.

49. GJJ, Minutes of meeting of 3 October 1942, Fonds Louis Levy, OURS, 95APO 3.

50. GJJ, Minutes of meeting of 21 September 1941, Fonds Louis Levy, OURS, 95 APO 3.

51. GJJ, Minutes of meeting of 16 June 1942, Fonds Louis Levy, OURS, 95APO 3.

52. See, for example, Henry (London) to 'Villiers' (Daniel Mayer) (Algiers) 3 September 1943, OURS, Mollet Papers, AGM1.

53. 'France and Britain', 'Anglo-French Committee of the Fabian International Bureau, No. 6, vol. 2, April 1943, Fonds Louis Levy, OURS, 95APO 3.

54. GJJ, Minutes of meeting of 1 December 1940 and 30 March 1941, Fonds Louis Levy, OURS, 95APO 3.

55. 'The Future of France', *Tribune*, 2 April 1943, Fonds Louis Levy, OURS, 95APO 3.

56. Again, some of the below is taken from Williams, *France, Britain and the United States in the Twentieth Century, Vol. 2, 1940–61*, Chapter 3.

57. Henri Michel and Boris Mirkine-Guetzévitch, eds. *Les idées politiques de la Résistance (documents clandestins, 1940–1944)* (Paris: Presses universitaires de France, 1954). The file 'Projets pour après la Libération' can be found in AN, F^{1A}3734. This was also published in abbreviated form as a 'compte rendu' by Lucien Febvre, 'Henri Michel et Boris Mirkine-Guetzévitch, *Les idées politiques de la Résistance*', *Annales*, 9, no. 3 (1954): 413–16.

58. Philip Nord, *France's New Deal: From the Thirties to the Postwar Era* (Princeton, NJ: Princeton University Press, 2010).

59. The files of the Commission can also be found in the AN under 'France libre', F^{1A}3734. The 'Sous-Commission Sociale' is the first file.

60. The Minutes (1941–45) of the London International Assembly can be found in the Library of the London School of Economics, under LNU65-8.

61. 'Rapport sur les Problèmes Européens d'Après-Guerre (avant-projet de 20 mai 1942)' (author probably Boris), and (on Keynes among other matters), 'Rapport sur l'organisation de l'économie de Paris', 1 July 1944 (author F. Walters), AN, F^{1A}3734.

62. 'Commission pour l'étude des problèmes d'après-guerre' meetings of 10 February and 5 March 1942; 'L'Institut de la Conjoncture', 64-page report, 15 March 1943, AN, 'France Libre', F^{1A}3734

63. L. Jacquemin, 'Commission pour l'étude des problèmes d'après-guerre', 10 September 1942, AN, 'France Libre', F^{1A}3734. This paragraph was taken from Chapter 2 of Williams, *France, Britain and the United States*.

64. See, for example: GJJ discussions of 21 June 1943 and 13 May 1944, Fonds Louis Levy, OURS, 95 ARO 3.

65. Georges Boris, 'Politique Américaine – les données fondamentales du problème', July 1942, 'Commission pour l'étude des problèmes d'après guerre', AN, 'France Libre', F^{1A}3734.

66. Boris, 'Politique Américaine – les données fondamentales du problème'.

67. The file of Bretton Woods can be found in Auriol Papers, AN, AU 15 Dr 2. His notes from San Francisco (largely illegible, it has to be said) are in 3 AU 15 Dr 3sdrb.

68. Auriol to London (no name is mentioned but Attlee is addressed), 13 July 1944. The letters had been written on 12 May: Auriol Papers, AN, AU 10 Dr 5. My analysis of this can be found in: Andrew Williams, 'France and the Origins of the United Nations, 1944–1945: "Si La France ne compte plus, qu'on nous le dise"', *Diplomacy and Statecraft* 28, no. 2 (June 2017).

69. Auriol to Roosevelt, 12 May 1944, and also to Churchill and Attlee, same date, Auriol Papers, AN, 3 AU 9 Dr 5.

70. Pierre Drieu La Rochelle, *Récit secret*, quoted by Pascal Ory, *Les Collobarateurs* (Paris: Seuil, 1976), 269; here from: Bénédicte Vergez-Chaignon, *Vichy en Prison: Les épurés à Fresnes après la Libération* (Paris: Gallimard, 2006), 42. The practically untranslateable wordplay he used was to say: '*Oui, je suis un traître. Oui, j'ai été d'intelligence avec l'ennemi. J'ai apporté l'intelligence française. Ce n'est pas de ma faute si l'enemmi n'a pas été intelligent*'.

71. Raymond Haas-Picard (London) to 'Villiers' (Daniel Mayer), (Algiers) 3 December 1943 and end (n.d.) January 1944, OURS, Mollet Papers, AGM1.

72. Speech by Auriol, 12 May 1944, Auriol Papers, AN, 3 AU 9 Dr 6. For the relations of de Gaulle with the USSR, see Maurice Vaisse, *De Gaulle et la Russie* (Paris: CNRS, 2006).

73. 'Parti Socialiste, relations avec le PCF' (in which notes on the 1st Socialist Party Conference can be found), and International Conference of London (3–5 March 1945) Auriol Papers, AN, 3 AU 13 Dr 1 and Dr 2.

74. Anne Deighton, 'Entente Neo-Coloniale? Ernest Bevin and the Proposals for an Anglo-French Third World Power, 1945–1949', *Diplomacy and Statecraft* 17, no. 4 (2006): 835–52.

Bibliography

Anderson, Malcolm. 'The Myth of the Two Hundred Families', *Political Studies* 13, no. 2 (June 1965): 163–78.

Ashworth, Lucian. *International Relations and the Labour Party: Intellectuals and Policy Making from 1918–1945*. London: Tauris, 2007.

Beckett, Francis. *The Enemy Within: The Rise and Fall of the British Communist Party*. London: John Murray, 1995.

Beveridge, William. *Full Employment in a Free Society*. London: Pilot Press, 1944.

Beveridge, William. *The Price of Peace*. London: Pilot Press, 1945.

Beveridge, William. *Report on Social Insurance and Allied Services*. London: HMSO, 1942.

Bew, John. *Citizen Clem: A Biography of Attlee*. London: Quercus, 2016.

Blatchford, R. *Merrie England*. London: Clarion Press, 1894.

Blum, Léon. *L'histoire jugera*. Paris: Editions de l'Arbre, 1945.

Bosco, Andrea. *June 1940: Great Britain and the First Attempt to Build a European Union*. Newcastle upon Tyne: Cambridge Scholars Publishing, 2016.

Cooper, Duff. *Old Men Forget*. London: Faber and Faber, 2011.

Dalton, Hugh and Ben Pimlott. *The Fateful Years: Memoirs, 1931–1945*. London: Jonathan Cape, 1957.

Davies, A. J. *To Build a New Jerusalem: The Labour Movement from the 1890s to the 1990s*. London: Abacus, 1996.

Deighton, Anne. 'Entente Neo-Coloniale? Ernest Bevin and the Proposals for an Anglo-French Third World Power, 1945–1949', *Diplomacy and Statecraft* 17, no. 4 (2006): 835–52.

Febvre, Lucien, 'Henri Michel et Boris Mirkine-Guetzévitch, *Les idées politiques de la Résistance*', *Annales*, 9, no. 3 (1954): 413–16.

Gorodetsky, Gabriel. *Stafford Cripps' Mission to Moscow, 1940–42*. Cambridge: Cambridge University Press, 2002.

Kriegel, Annie. *Les Communistes français*. Paris: Seuil, 1968.

Lacouture, Jean. *Léon Blum*. Paris: Seuil, 1979.

Leahy, William D. *I Was There*. London: Gollancz, 1950.

Loyer, Emmanuelle. *Paris à New York: Intellectuels et artistes français en exil (1940–1947)*. Paris: Grasset et Fasquelle, 2005.

Lyons, A. N. *Robert Blatchford: The Sketch of a Personality: An Estimate of Some Achievements*. London: Clarion Press, 1910.

Marquand, David. *Ramsay MacDonald*. London: Jonathan Cape, 1977.

McLellan, David. *Utopian Pessimist: The Life and Thought of Simone Weil*. London: Palgrave Macmillan, 1990.

Michel, Henri and Mirkine-Guetzévitch, Boris, eds. *Les idées politiques et sociales de la Résistance (documents clandestins, 1940–1944)*. Paris: Presses Universitaires de France, 1954.
Murphy, Robert. *Diplomat Among Warriors*. Garden City, NY: Doubleday, 1964.
Nord, Philip. *France's New Deal: From the Thirties to the Postwar Era*. Princeton, NJ: Princeton University Press, 2010.
Norwich, J. J. *The Duff Cooper Diaries 1915–1951*. London: Weidenfeld & Nicolson, 2005.
O'Brien, Phillips. *The Second Most Powerful Man in the World, Fleet Admiral William D. Leahy, Chief of Staff*. London: Penguin, 2019.
Ory, Pascal *Les Collobarateurs*. Paris: Seuil, 1976.
Pelling, Henry. *The British Communist Party*. London: A. and C. Black, 1975.
Pétrement, Simone. *La vie de Simone Weil; Avec des lettres et d'autres textes inédits de Simone Weil*. Paris: Fayard, 1997.
Pigou, A. C. *The Transition from War to Peace*. Oxford: Oxford University Press, 1943.
Pimlott, Ben. *Labour and the Left in the 1930s*. Cambridge: Cambridge University Press, 1977.
Pimlott, Ben. *Hugh Dalton*. London: HarperCollins, 1995.
Pimlott, Ben, ed. *Second World War Diary of Hugh Dalton, 1940–45*. London: Cape, 1986.
Rey, Fanny Emmanuelle. *La dissidence socialiste à Londres: Le groupe Jean Jaurès et la France (août 1940–août 1944)*. Mémoire de maitrise d'histoire, Université Paris 1, Panthéon-Sorbonne, 1997–8.
Sorel, Georges, *Reflections on Violence*. New York: Peter Smith, 1941 [1908].
Tawney, R. H. 'Dr. Toynbee's Study of History', *International Affairs* 18, no. 6 (1939): 798–806.
Vaisse, Maurice. *De Gaulle et la Russie*. Paris: CNRS, 2006.
Vergez-Chaignon, Bénédicte. *Vichy en Prison: Les épurés à Fresnes après la Libération*. Paris: Gallimard, 2006.
Wieviorka, Olivier. *The French Resistance*. Cambridge, MA: Harvard University Press, 2016.
Williams, Andrew J. *Labour and Russia: The Attitude of the British Labour Party to the USSR, 1924–1934*. Manchester: Manchester University Press, 1989.
Williams, Andrew J. 'Before the Special Relationship: The Council on Foreign Relations, The Carnegie Foundation and the Rumour of an Anglo-American War', *Journal of Transatlantic Studies* 1, no. 2 (2003): 233–51.

Williams, Andrew J. *France, Britain and the United States in the Twentieth Century, Volume 1: 1900–1940*. London and New York: Palgrave Macmillan, 2014.
Williams, Andrew J. 'France and the Origins of the United Nations, 1944–1945: "Si La France ne compte plus, qu'on nous le dise"', *Diplomacy and Statecraft* 28, no. 2 (2017): 215–34.
Williams, Andrew J. *France, Britain and the United States in the Twentieth Century, Volume 2 1940–61*. London and New York: Palgrave Macmillan, 2020.
Woolner, David. 'Canada, Mackenzie King and the St. Pierre and Miquelon Crisis of 1941', *London Journal of Canadian Studies*, 24, (2010): 42–84.

Chapter 2

Trans-war continuities: the *Mouvement Socialiste pour les États-Unis d'Europe* (MSEUE) and socialist networks in the early Cold War

Ben Heckscher and Tommaso Milani

In recent years, scholars have been increasingly willing to question the orthodox periodisation of European integration, according to which the European Communities emerged out of the ashes of the Second World War. Rejecting the notion of *Stunde null*, historians now point to substantial continuities between the interwar and post-war periods in terms of personalities, institutions, practices and ideas.[1] In the same vein, this chapter sets out to investigate how connections, exchanges and debates dating back to the 1930s impacted upon the founding and early life of the *Mouvement Socialiste pour les États-Unis d'Europe* (henceforth MSEUE), a pro-federalist, left-wing, anti-Stalinist organisation which very few studies have covered in detail.[2] At first glance, the MSEUE's trajectory closely resembles that of other, better-known groupings committed to European unity in the mid- to late 1940s – and indeed, after an initial refusal, the MSEUE coalesced into the European Movement (henceforth EM) that aimed to reunite them.[3] A closer examination, however, reveals that the MSEUE was hardly immune from the legacies, animosities and divisions that characterised European socialism at large, further exacerbated by the need to redefine what 'European unity' concretely meant in the early Cold War. First, the chapter discusses how a cohort of far-left revolutionary socialists previously gathered in the so-called 'London Bureau' formed the bedrock of the MSEUE. Second, it shows how the MSEUE initially stuck to a wartime vision of socialist Europe as a Third Force that became increasingly far-fetched and almost untenable from mid-1947 onwards. Third, it highlights how the MSEUE's Europeanism could barely conceal other long-standing, and arguably more deep-seated, ideological differences about the nature of socialism among its members and sympathisers, some of which bore the mark of interwar controversies and splits. For all these reasons, and notwithstanding the emphasis it placed on the future in its own propaganda, the MSEUE had difficulties in cutting loose from its pre-war past.

The shadow of the London Bureau

The Paris-based MSEUE began its life as the Movement for the United Socialist States of Europe (henceforth MUSSE), in many respects a revival of the interwar London Bureau. It would take a few years to fully transition from the British-led movement to the better-known French-led MSEUE, and the process illustrates the evolution of a particular strand of socialist internationalism from the outbreak of the Second World War to the consolidation of the geopolitical landscape of the late 1940s.

Transnational left socialism has been often described as 'largely a marginal phenomenon, as its members found themselves squeezed between the two dominant leftist tendencies during the 1930s: reformist socialism and Soviet-dominated communism', and this perhaps helps explain the scant attention historians have paid to it.[4] Still, when scrutinised from the point of view of social network analysis and as a vehicle for ideas, even the smallest splinter group may be worthy of consideration.[5] This is certainly the case of the London Bureau, whose origins can be traced to 1933, when members of three non-communist, non-reformist fringe organisations – the so-called *Bureau de Paris*, the *Internationale Arbeitsgemeinschaft* and the Trotsky-led International Left Opposition – began to meet in a new forum bearing the unwieldy name of the 'International Revolutionary Marxist Centre'.[6] The Bureau was managed in London by the Independent Labour Party (ILP), hence the moniker, and was characterised by at least three main ideological tendencies. The first was towards a reconstituted global workers' movement in the social democratic vein, a position that implied the rejection of the Stalinist model and any sort of coercive unitary structure; the second, led by the ILP, envisioned an independent line with a possible future alignment with the Comintern; the third, largely inspired by Trotsky, strove for a new anti-Stalinist global unitary movement based on strict Marxist-Leninist theory.[7] Although Hitler's seizure of power in

1933 provided a strong rationale for increasing coordination, turning the fight against Fascism into the common denominator of this otherwise heterogeneous group, some members felt that an effective strategy required collaboration within the existing capitalist national structures, whereas others – who eventually prevailed – espoused a strictly anti-capitalist view and prioritised international engagement.[8] Another key ideological component was anti-colonialism, which dovetailed nicely with the widely held assumption that the class struggle had to be waged at a global, rather than national, level.[9] At this stage, collective security under capitalist governments was dismissed as a pipe dream and alternative forms of intra-European cooperation were glossed over.[10]

The Bureau was organised under the guidance of pacifist and then former MP Fenner Brockway; his colleagues Bob Edwards, Francis Ridley and John McNair were also leading members. Other parties included the Greek Archeio-Marxist Party, led by Dimitris Giotopoulos, alias Witte; French Socialist Marceau Pivert's leftist faction of the French *Section française de l'Internationale Ouvrière* (SFIO), *Gauche Révolutionnaire*, which joined the London Bureau in 1935; and the Spanish *Partido Obrero de Unificación Marxista* (POUM), also involved from 1935 onwards.[11] The presence of POUM delegates is especially significant, as a substantial amount of the London Bureau's resources in the late 1930s would be directed at supporting the POUM and affiliated anti-Francoist forces in Spain – thus providing a clear example of international solidarity cemented by a common anti-fascist cause.[12] To give a few examples: Bob Edwards drove an ambulance and helped assist British volunteers, Pivert organised transit through France, McNair was briefly arrested in June 1937 as he coordinated efforts in Spain, and Fenner Brockway made a trip in late 1937 to secure the release of some 15,000 prisoners, including 1,000 POUMistas.[13]

By 1938, the Bureau also included independent factions of the German, Italian and Polish socialist parties as well as a number of Eastern European parties, the American Socialist Party and several organisations from non-independent countries, such as Senegal, Indo-China and Madagascar, in an observer capacity.[14] The Paris Congress, held in February 1938, provided a platform to activists such as George Padmore, who – speaking on behalf of the pan-African group International African Service Bureau, which he had cofounded with C. L. R. James, Amy Ashwood Garvey, Jomo Kenyatta and other opponents of colonial rule – expressed his disenchantment with both the Labour and Socialist International (LSI) and the Comintern, claiming that only a bottom-up alliance between the working class of the capitalist world and the national liberation movements operating within colonies could end racial oppression.[15]

Yet the growing pressure under which the ILP found itself, also because of the highly contentious policy of rearmament, made its position as lynchpin of the network increasingly unsustainable.[16] The last London Bureau meeting was held in April 1939 as the next one, scheduled for September, was rendered impossible by the outbreak of the Second World War. Aside from interrupting the Bureau's activities, the war also scattered some of its members. Most notably, Pivert and POUMista Enric Adroher (*nom-de-plume* 'Gironella') ended up in Mexico. Gironella had been arrested in Spain and upon release had found passage to Mexico via Bordeaux. For Pivert, a conviction *in absentia* for inciting insubordination in French troops and a speech he gave at an American Socialist Party rally combined to maroon him in Mexico City. If he and Gironella had not known each other personally beforehand, they did by the war's end.[17]

The fragmentation and lack of operational capacity of the Bureau resulted in greater ideological suppleness and search for new paradigms – and it was in that context that the idea of a socialist united Europe begin to gain traction. In 1944, then-ILP members Francis A. Ridley and Bob Edwards penned a document that would have a huge and lasting impact on the MUSSE/MSEUE, a short pamphlet entitled *The United Socialist States of Europe*. Both men were deeply entangled with the British far left: Ridley, a Marxist who had ties with Trotsky before entering the ILP, would later become an outspoken critic of colonialism alongside the already mentioned Padmore; Edwards, a trade unionist who had visited the Soviet Union in 1926, would stand out as a pro-European member of the Labour Party, spending more than three decades in Westminster, but – according to Soviet double agent Oleg A. Gordievsky – he would also operate as a KGB informant and agent throughout the Cold War.[18] In Ridley's and Edwards's interpretation, the war reflected the inability of the nation-state system to handle the 'new technology of the Machine Age', and proved that if the anachronistic nation-state system was not done away with, 'the inexorable working-out of the laws of Capitalist-Imperialism' would bring about 'a Third World-War as much more terrible and total than this most terrible and total of all of wars as this one surpasses all its historic predecessors'.[19] They ridiculed the supposed righteousness of Allied forces, 'which include the two most ruthless dictatorships on earth, those of Stalin and Chiang Kai-Shek', calling the 'bluff' of framing the conflict as a 'war for "Freedom", or "Democracy", or the "Common Man", or some such high-sounding abstraction', pinning their hopes instead on 'the socialist unity of Europe', which would 'owe nothing to the criminal ambitions of either the European camps of world reaction, whether in its Fascist German or its plutocratic (pseudodemocratic) American form. The emancipation of the European peoples must be the work of the European people'.[20] Although the authors maintained that 'World-Socialism – the United States of the World –' was their 'majestic goal', the pamphlet emphatically stressed the benefits deriving from the 'intermediate, but, it would seem, indispensable stage of the United Socialist States of Europe', warning that 'should European civilisation die of blood-letting and exhaustion the road to World Socialism would be immeasurably lengthened: for then its attainment would be left to the nations of the East, who still, for the most part, lack its first prerequisites'.[21] The *socialist* character of European unity was also heavily underscored: since socialism was, and would continue to be, the only way to break down the dominance of Finance Capital over the international system, post-war European states would be united *and* socialist.[22] Besides, the pamphlet confidently asserted that 'a Socialist Europe would strike a death blow at world imperialism by proclaiming the independence of the colonial people', hence reviving the anti-imperialist tropes cherished by the London Bureau.[23] Around the same period, similar pro-European views were articulated by several ILP-affiliated activists and sympathisers, ranging from Brockway to Walter Padley, and fed into a wider discourse on European unity that sprang out of Marxist, left-wing revolutionary milieux, often directly or indirectly influenced by Trotsky's writings, in the late 1930s–40s.[24]

Ridley's and Edwards's views – popularised also through the ILP's mouthpiece *The New Leader* – tackled the fundamental issue of 'whether socialism could even be attained within the individual nation-state', reaching a negative conclusion, and thereby struck a chord with a much wider community of left-wing elements who were leaning towards a similar position.[25] The ILP held the first meeting of the 'International Socialist States of Europe' in May 1946. It was a small affair attended largely by London Bureau veterans, producing at least one resolution and raising a series of questions to be addressed for the next meeting. For the ILP, Edwards chaired, accompanied by Ridley and McNair. Jacques Robin of the SFIO attended – presumably in place of Pivert, who had fallen ill – as did Gironella (POUM), Germans Heinz Heydorn and Willi Dittmer of the *Sozialdemokratische Partei Deutschlands* (SPD) and Student Socialist Movement respectively, Witte of the Greek Archeio-Marxists, and the former member of the Dutch *Revolutionair Socialistische Partij* Jef Last. French socialists Claude Bourdet and Simon Wichené attended as well, representing the *Conseil national de la Résistance* and the *Union Internationale contre le Racisme* respectively.[26] Once again, the ILP was at the forefront of the organisational effort in July of that year, when at the ILP Summer School it was decided to expand the ILP internal newsletter 'Between Ourselves' to France, benefiting from Pivert's support and editorial assistance, which would last until 1950.[27] This helps in understanding why London was again selected as location for the gathering of socialists who, in February 1947, appointed Edwards as chairman of the International Committee for the United Socialist States of Europe, the first embryonic institution of the MUSSE/MSEUE. The event attracted some prominent figures from France, such as Resistance leader and fervent European federalist Henri Frenay and radical pacifist Robert Jospin. In addition, a handful of anticolonial militants took the stage: South-African-born author Peter Abrahams spoke on behalf of the Pan-African Federation whereas Greek journalist Henry Polydefkis weighed in as representative of the International Union against Racism. A common theme running through the speeches that were delivered throughout the two days of the conference was the necessity to focus on major problems rather than quibble over allegedly minor details. As German socialist Heinz-Joachim Heydorn put it with characteristic brazenness in recalling interwar debates, 'the dispute as to whom the Ruhr mines should belong was idiotic. The issue would not arise if the coal industries of Europe formed a single organism. There was only one real economic problem in Europe and that was how to mobilise its economic resources for the whole continent.'[28]

It is worth stressing that these meetings occurred at a time when the British Labour Party was pressuring the SFIO not to attend ILP-connected events due to the strained relations with its once-affiliated party and the desire to create a new Socialist International, which the emergence of a competing pro-European group could thwart.[29] Yet, while Labour's hostility arguably affected the attitude of SFIO heavyweights such as Guy Mollet or André Philip, who initially preferred to keep their distance from the MUSSE, it had no impact on figures like Pivert, whose relationship with the ILP and record of revolutionary transnational activism was already well established.[30] Even though the MUSSE/MSEUE did not emphasise any kinship – ideological, personal or otherwise – to the London Bureau, the movement could nonetheless build on interwar connections, and could not have come about without them.

Europe as a Third Force?

The idea that a united Europe could establish itself as a Third Force in world affairs – a distinct, autonomous federal bloc capable of successfully mediating between and peacefully coexisting with the two superpowers, the United States and the Soviet Union – was by no means monopolised by the heirs of the London Bureau, not even within the

British public debate. If anything, the period between 1935 and 1945 had been marked by a resurgent interest in various integrationist projects wherein future European supranational authorities would be tasked with far-reaching economic powers. The lure for supranational planning that somewhat peaked between 1940 and 1944 originated from the conviction – fairly common within the more internationally minded British elite – that national planning alone, however necessary, would not provide a sufficient guarantee against what E. H. Carr famously called 'the two scourges' of the 1930s: mass unemployment and war.[31] However, many commentators, civil servants and politicians had no qualms about shelving these plans as soon as it became clear that the newly elected Labour government intended to prioritise domestic reform and struggled financially to retain control over the empire, two factors that undermined its chances of taking the mantle of leadership over continental matters. On the other hand, the MUSSE/MSEUE did not jettison that vision, at least until the fading influence of the ILP over the movement, the launching of the Marshall Plan and a change of mind about the EM brought about a significant softening of its thoroughgoingly anti-capitalist stance. The survival of a Third Force discourse, in spite of its impracticability, can be explained with the desire to escape the binary logic of the looming Cold War, which would force self-styled revolutionary – but steadfastly anti-Stalinist – socialists to pick a side between Washington and Moscow, a choice they found unpalatable.[32]

The concept of a European 'Third Front' featured prominently in the London meeting of February 1947, during which it was presented as 'a powerful instrument for ensuring friendship with and in between the peoples of the U.S.A. and the U.S.S.R.' as well as for establishing a 'planned economy . . . carried out through the organic structure of a real social and economic democracy, based on workers' control and not by any authoritarian medium of either monopoly capitalism or totalitarian state bureaucracy'.[33] Given these premises, it is unsurprising that Ridley and his followers had no appetite for the competing vision of European unity that former Prime Minister Winston Churchill had laid out in Zurich (September 1946), which they dismissed as hopelessly reactionary, and that they blamed first and foremost the Truman Administration for provoking tensions over Germany.[34]

However, by June 1947 – when the MUSSE Inaugural Congress was held in Montrouge, near Paris – some major forces at work were undercutting the appeal of these ideas. Internally, it was becoming increasingly evident that, whatever its ambitions, the ILP lacked the financial resources to operate as MUSSE's powerhouse. In preparation for the February meeting, Pivert and McNair had managed to overcome the rationing in France by having publications and conference materials for the group's French audience produced in London. Nevertheless, these modest costs – coupled with the ILP's campaign to advertise the event, on top of its regular expenses – were enough to exhaust the party's funds and run a deficit: a clear indication of the ILP being hamstrung by its dismal economic condition.[35] The party's crisis was further heightened by the passing in July 1946 of James Maxton, perhaps the last high-profile ILP member in the House of Commons, by its base's staunch refusal to seek re-affiliation with Labour and by the subsequent defection of its three remaining MPs.[36]

The floundering of the ILP goes some way to explaining why the next conference took place in France, and also why the SFIO could now step in as organiser without fear of alienating the British Labour Party. Henceforth, the trajectory of the MUSSE/MSEUE would become more and more entangled with that of the SFIO, and the image projected by the movement would reflect, from time to time, its contiguity with the Parisian cultural and intellectual scene.[37] Still, the growing leverage of French mainstream socialists was perhaps less consequential on the evolution of the MUSSE/MSEUE, at least in the short run, than US Secretary of State George Marshall's speech at Harvard and the launching of the Plan named after him in June 1947. Within many Western European left-wing, non-communist parties, the promise of substantial economic aid led to a reassessment of the contribution Washington could make not only to the economic reconstruction of Europe but also to its political unification, even though there was no consensus about how much interference American dollars would translate into.[38] Moreover, the Plan's inspiring – and carefully crafted – message assuaged fears about America's supposed willingness to impose old-fashioned laissez-faire capitalism abroad.[39] Both in France and Germany, a number of prominent socialists were struck by the boldness of the US initiative and negatively impressed by the Soviet refusal to engage in negotiations.[40] In Britain, left-wing critics who had lambasted the Labour government's pro-American foreign policy were taken aback and some of them – as MP Richard Crossman, until then an eloquent advocate of a Third Force Europe – reversed course.[41]

The position papers for the Montrouge conference, wherein two central tenets of Ridley's vision – radical anti-capitalism and Third Force rhetoric – were markedly scaled down, indicate that a change of mind was already underway. The MUSSE fell back on the much more practical concerns evoked at the opening meeting of 1946, namely the rational planning of European economic assets like coal, transportation and the banking sector. To be sure, some vestiges of the older orientation, implicit in muted criticism of both the United States and the Soviet Union and a promise of humanitarian socialist planning, had survived but the language would be used to refer to something more akin to non-alignment. The MUSSE's newly proposed programme now prudently asserted that the primordial practical task would 'be to . . . [draw] up a plan of production based on the needs of the people [of Europe] which will previously have been ascertained'.[42]

Montrouge would attract some 164 delegates from 14 different countries to the MUSSE's two-day conference, on 21–22 June 1947. Bob Edwards chaired with John McNair as treasurer and secretary. Ridley attended, as did Jacques Robin and Gironella. Heinz-Joachim Heydorn, Willi Dittmer, Jef Last and Witte had all been founding members. The Greek Pafsanias Catsotas was a new face, as was Zygmunt Zaremba, head of the exiled Polish Socialist Party, and several Americans. The conference proceedings indicate that some participants clearly viewed Marshall's speech as a breakthrough. A few, including Robin – who would soon take up the role of MUSSE Co-Secretary – and Brockway, were outspoken about the danger that the Plan might turn into an instrument for an economic colonisation of Europe by American big business; yet they also contended that the risk would be far greater had the Soviet Union and Western European socialists turned down the offer and opted out. In general, participants stressed that Europe's autonomy rested upon its ability to mediate between the two blocs – the metaphor of bridge-building was used – and acknowledged, in one of the resolutions passed, that 'the offer made by General Marshall of aid to Europe corresponds to a vital need but it will only constitute a factor of peace if it is unaccompanied by any form, avowed or unavowed, of political or economic domination'.[43] When, on 2 July 1947, Soviet Foreign Minister Molotov walked out of the Paris conference on the Marshall Plan, thereby rejecting the US proposal, the MUSSE's newsletter decried 'the grave responsibility incurred by the USSR, in, on the one hand, provoking the dividing of Europe in two, and, on the other, prolonging the misery of the Eastern European peoples'.[44] It also concluded that European and American interests were 'exactly complementary', though not without some mild conditions: public negotiations managed exclusively via an international organisation, a European-staffed logistic chain and no military equipment.[45] While MUSSE still resisted the prospect of unreservedly siding with the Western bloc, it no longer aimed to stand halfway between the superpowers.

It took more than another year for the movement to break with the last defining element of the Ridley–Edwards original blueprint, namely the idea that revolutionary socialists were to maintain a strong degree of ideological purity and refuse to band together with non-socialist elements in the edification of a socialist Europe. Although figures like Alexandre

Marc, then General Secretary of the *Union Européenne des Fédéralistes* (UEF), and the already mentioned Henri Frenay, both present at Montrouge, pressed the MUSSE to adopt a more ecumenical attitude, the majority of delegates stood firm.[46] This self-imposed isolation, further strengthened by Churchill's ascendancy over the burgeoning United Europe Movement and by the Labour Party's aloofness, arguably meant that conservative, centre-right federalists were overrepresented within the organising committee of the 1948 Hague Congress.[47] Around that time, the MUSSE 'still prioritised socialism over Europe' insofar as alliances were concerned.[48] Nevertheless, the success of the Hague Congress as well as the fact that one of the Congress's final resolutions recommended a supranational approach to economic integration prompted many MUSSE members to have second thoughts.[49]

The meeting of the MUSSE's International Committee in November 1948 marked a watershed in that respect, for it yielded a new programme, released in December, that substantially revised many of the tenets and strategic guidelines laid out in the previous two years.[50] The MUSSE denounced ongoing efforts by 'Communists and reactionary forces' to suppress democratic rule while praising the role of 'the socialists, Christian Democrats, and non-Communist trade unions' in buttressing parliamentary institutions, especially in France.[51] However, the document stated that national achievements – including the British Labour Party's sweeping social reforms – would 'be of no avail unless they are united in an all-embracing political, economic and social plan at the European level', encompassing minimum wages, collective bargaining, increased levels of production, centralised planning, economic modernisation in industry – facilitated by Marshall funds – the socialisation of the Ruhr's key industries and an 'unshakeable solidarity with all those who are oppressed or threatened in their liberties, in Berlin or Eastern Europe, in Spain or in Greece'.[52] According to this new orientation, the MUSSE – which also stood for a directly and democratically elected 'European Assembly' – would 'support all initiatives, governmental, parliamentary or of any other kind, that constitute a genuine advance' towards those goals.[53] One month later, the MUSSE changed its name to MSEUE and began reaching out to non-socialist politicians, including French Christian Democrats such as Léo Hamon, who would later serve as delegate.[54] In December, it even applied to join the once despised EM.[55] The MSEUE's embrace of a watered-down centre-left federalism, stripped of any reference to the international class struggle and bent on finding a middle ground with other Europeanist organisations, would substantially broaden the movement's appeal among moderate socialists, but left the ILP old guard disenchanted and embittered.[56] By 1950, Edwards –

reflecting on the establishment of the Strasbourg Consultative Assembly, the launching of the Schuman Plan, and the foundation of the European Payments Union – was ready to concede that 'Western European unity in some form or another' was 'inevitable', even though he insisted that 'only a Europe rebuilt on socialist conceptions' would 'guarantee the peace of the world'.[57]

Towards consensus?

The figure who best embodied MSEUE's new course was the French former Minister of the Economy, Finance, and Industry André Philip, who was appointed Chairman in September 1949.[58] A Christian socialist from the SFIO and distinguished member of the French Resistance, Philip was also an academic who had cut his teeth in politics during the Popular Front era. His consistent advocacy of far-reaching economic planning and unflinching *dirigisme*, which triggered his decision to resign from government in 1947, caused him to lose influence at domestic level, up to the point of not being re-elected to the *Assemblée Nationale* in 1951. Yet these setbacks allowed him to focus on the cause of European unity: already a member of the EM and of the parliamentary assembly of the Council of Europe, Philip could raise the profile of the MSEUE through his contacts, experience and aura of respectability.[59] Besides, his brand of federalism displayed the kind of nuance the MSEUE was craving: a true believer in supranational solutions, he nevertheless acknowledged the advantages of a sector-by-sector pooling of resources, as his 1948 proposal for an authority managing the Ruhr's coal and steel demonstrates.[60]

Philip's chairmanship inaugurated a new phase in the activities of the MSEUE: abandoning the rather vague and declamatory statements of the past, its members – divided into small commissions – started hammering out detailed, evidence-based reports that were discussed during congresses. In 1949–50 alone, these addressed topics such as planning in basic industries, Britain's economic ties with the Commonwealth, the integration of agriculture, the German question and the legal challenges posed by the creation of European political authority, and they benefited from the input of the organisation's experts, including German economist Karl Kühne, the Director of the French *Service National des Statistiques* Francis-Louis Closon, and the agronomist and later Food and Agriculture Organisation (FAO) President Michel Cépède.[61] By and large, except for its unrelenting criticism of the political and economic consequences of nationalism – which did not spare the British Labour Party[62] – this body of literature fitted the mould of post-war Western

European social democracy: well-disposed towards parliamentary rule, anti-communist, mildly technocratic in its qualified endorsement of piecemeal social engineering, supportive of worker representation, a more equitable distribution of wealth, higher living standards, full employment and of the expansion of production.[63] Occasionally, Philip too would deploy less idealistic arguments in favour of European integration that echoed the welfarism of the mainstream centre-left discourse.[64] The same outlook would inform the MSEUE's flagship publication from 1953 onwards, a monthly named *Gauche Européenne*, whose first subtitle, 'Fédération et Démocratie Sociale', was a far cry from the ILP's ringing rhetoric deployed in the previous decade.[65] An array of pamphlets released from 1950 also made the language of MSEUE increasingly indistinguishable from that of the resurgent Socialist International, frequently emphasising the tangible benefits of economic unity and rational management of resources over national autarchy and capitalist anarchy.[66]

Yet, when the MSEUE sought to dig deeper into its own identity and articulate a more coherent ideology, a number of problems began to emerge, stemming from the same theoretical difficulties socialism was grappling with in the post-war years.[67] Freeing the organisation from the intellectual baggage associated with the London Bureau was one thing; building consensus around a set of principles that a variety of strands of socialist thought, some of which dated back to the 1920s–30s, could espouse was quite another. Although the very limited archival evidence available makes it impossible to gauge how a wide cohort of militants reacted to MSEUE's decision to venture into the doctrinal field, a few scattered sources can give a glimpse of the unresolved tensions and issues behind the picture of cohesion the MSEUE attempted to project externally.[68]

The MSEUE's Fifth Congress held in Frankfurt in February 1952 was centred on the analysis and identification of a specifically European form of socialism. As usual, several preliminary reports were drafted, one of which by Philip himself.[69] In deliberately sketchy fashion, he first illustrated Marx's failure to predict the evolution of capitalist societies then engaged with the many 'deviations' that contemporary socialist parties were bound to challenge, including what he termed 'economic Malthusianism', that is, employers and employees joining forces to uphold national monopolies and restrict production.[70] In the final section, Philip outlined a possible European 'technical revolution' based on a combination of supranational planning and workers' self-government, hinging upon the strengthening of the alliance with 'American progressive capitalism' on the one hand, and the forging of a 'Federal Socialist Party of Europe' within the recently re-founded Socialist International on the other.[71]

The resolution eventually voted at Frankfurt skipped over many points of Philip's thesis, which he would flesh out elsewhere.[72] Nevertheless, his text caught the attention of the Belgian sociologist and long-time socialist militant Léo Moulin, who sent him an eight-page letter to take issue with his assessment of the state of socialism, which the more pessimistic Moulin depicted as a crippled movement 'forced to survive ... within Europe, a Europe that is bloodless, enfeebled, decaying, partitioned – because of the failure of socialism – and chopped between the two Leviathans, the American and the Soviet'.[73] Despite the friendly tone of the message, Moulin warned that, without a proper 'doctrinal revolution' driven by 'a Christian and realist humanism', Philip's technical revolution would amount to a 'seizure of power by the techno-bureaucratic caste', fostering a dystopian system run by managers that would be antithetical to true socialism.[74]

In this context, the content of Moulin's remarks matters less than the way he hinted at the common milieu he and Philip had shared before the Second World War. Both men were personally and intellectually close to the Belgian theorist and politician Hendrik de Man – whom Moulin praised in the letter – an author who had long argued in favour of a voluntaristic renewal of democratic socialism and whom Moulin and Philip still admired, despite de Man's tarnished reputation and self-exile from Belgium due to his collaboration with the Nazi occupying forces.[75] Arguably, both men had been attracted by de Man's anti-materialism and emphasis on the religious underpinnings of socialism, which also impressed many young francophone Catholics: the Protestant Philip and the agnostic but spiritually inclined Moulin had been contributors to the non-conformist journal *Esprit*, which helped circulate de Man's ideas.[76] Moreover, as young socialists frustrated with reformism, they had been won over by de Man's radical approach to economic planning, better known as 'planism': Philip, having disseminated de Man's critique of Marxism in the late 1920s, became a leading proponent of a French Labour Plan akin to the one de Man had crafted for Belgium and sought to mobilise the SFIO around it in 1934–35, while Moulin entered de Man's inner circle in Brussels.[77] Their heterodox background had put them in touch with the French group *Révolution constructive*, active in the 1930s, which issued one brochure written by Moulin and one prefaced by Philip, and with Dutchman Hendrik Brugmans – another unreconstructed 'planist', European federalist, and first rector of the College of Europe who, by 1952, had gained prominence within both the MSEUE and the EM.[78]

The fact that Moulin sent his letter to de Man as well and that he lauded, within it, another distinguished Europeanist and former member of the interwar 'planist' network – the Belgian former Prime Minister Paul-Henri Spaak who, by that time, had started gravitating towards the MSEUE – suggests that Moulin might have hoped to take advantage of the MSEUE Congress to rekindle a much wider conversation about the foundations of socialism, and perhaps resume the intellectual battle de Man had fought two decades earlier.[79] Although Moulin's initiative eventually bore no fruit, his text gives insight into the interwar roots of the rich and complex political culture MSEUE members and sympathisers had inherited.

Conclusion

While stressing the benefits of a trans-war approach to the study of the creation of the French welfare state after 1945, historian Philip Nord observed that 'there are dangers in such a perspective as well, for it might well create an interpretive bias in favour of continuity'.[80] By the same token, any attempt to interpret the foundation of the MUSSE/MSEUE as a straightforward continuation of the interwar London Bureau is bound to obscure important differences in the way the two organisations understood internationalism and how they seized opportunities offered by the international environment to advance their agendas. Moreover, overstating the role of interwar legacies can easily lead to overlook how the MUSSE/MSEUE adjusted itself to the post-war context.[81] This adaptation involved, among other changes, a shift away from revolutionary phraseology, a less straightforward commitment to a rapid process of decolonisation, and a greater willingness to engage with other political traditions supporting European unity from a non-socialist standpoint, most notably Christian Democracy. The project of a socialist Europe was therefore supplanted by that of a more loosely defined 'social' Europe.[82]

Having said that, highlighting the existence of *fils rouges* and threads of discussion dating back to previous decades can significantly deepen our knowledge of the complex and multifaceted ways certain blueprints for European unity became appealing to parties and movements that had once been indifferent to them, if not outright hostile. It is no accident that a number of recent, ground-breaking studies have stressed the importance of pre-war debates in informing post-war attitudes by socialist parties and trade unions towards European integration: Patrick Pasture has underscored the impact of the First World War and the Great Depression in turning 'Europe' into a meaningful concept and a valuable space for collective action in the eyes of many members of the international labour movement; Christian Bailey has linked Willy Brandt's

Ostpolitik to a tradition of German social democratic thinking about Central and Eastern Europe that emerged during the Locarno era; Brian Shaev has shown how interwar economic conceptions supporting trade liberalisation at regional level provided legitimacy to those socialists who endorsed the creation of a European economic community along the lines of that eventually created in 1957 by the Treaty of Rome – and so on.[83] The more historians investigate the rich, diverse and nuanced sources of socialist Europeanism, the more any rigid, neat distinction between the interwar and the post-war period will come under scrutiny. As this chapter has tried to demonstrate, the study of networks can strengthen this ongoing trend and allow for a more thorough investigation of both European integration *and* European socialism.

Notes

1. See for example Luc-André Brunet, *Forging Europe: Industrial Organisation in France, 1940–1952* (London: Palgrave Macmillan, 2017); Conan Fischer, *A Vision of Europe: Franco-German Relations during the Great Depression, 1929–1932* (Oxford, New York: Oxford University Press, 2017); Stephen Gross, 'Introduction: European Integration across the Twentieth Century', *Contemporary European History* 26, no. 2 (2017): 205–7; Kiran Klaus Patel and Wolfram Kaiser, 'Continuity and Change in European Cooperation during the Twentieth Century', *Contemporary European History* 27, no. 2 (2018).

2. The best published account (up to 1950) remains Wilfried Loth, 'The *Mouvement Socialiste pour les Etats-Unis d'Europe* (MSEUE)' in *Documents on the History of European Integration*, ed. Walter Lipgens and Wilfried Loth, vol. IV (Berlin: De Gruyter, 1991).

3. On these groupings, see Walter Lipgens, *Anfänge der europäischen Einigungspolitik 1945–1950* (Stuttgart: Klet, 1977) and Sergio Pistone, ed., *I movimenti per l'unità europea dal 1945 al 1954* (Milan: Jaca Book, 1992).

4. Talbot Imlay, *The Practice of Socialist Internationalism: European Socialists and International Politics, 1914–1960* (Oxford and New York: Oxford University Press, 2018), 252.

5. For instance, Harold Mock has recently linked Willy Brandt's involvement in the youth branch of the London Bureau to his alleged post-nationalism as German Chancellor: see Harold Mock, 'A Post-National Europe: Brandt's Vision for the European Community between the Superpowers', in *Willy Brandt and International Relations: Europe, the USA, and Latin America*, ed. Bernd Rother and Klaus Larres (London: Bloomsbury, 2018).

6. For a more extensive discussion of the London Bureau, see Willy Buschak, *Das Londoner Büro: Europäische Linkssozialisten in der Zwischenkriegszeit* (Amsterdam: Stichting Internationaal Instituut voor Sociale Geschiedenis, 1985); Michel Dreyfus, 'Bureau de Paris et bureau de Londres: le socialisme de gauche en Europe entre les deux guerres', *Mouvement social* 112 (1980); Michel Dreyfus, 'Socialistes de gauche et trotskystes en Europe 1933–1938', in *Pensiero e azione politica di Lev Trockij*, ed. Francesca Gori, vol. II (Florence: Olschki, 1982); Willy Buschak, 'The London Bureau', in *The Cambridge History of Socialism*, ed. Marcel Van der Linden, vol. II (Cambridge and New York: Cambridge University Press, 2022).

7. According to a leading authority on Trotskyism, 'vastly different concepts' about the New International and the fact that these groups 'disagreed profoundly on a number of programmatic issues' made unity of action practically impossible. Robert J. Alexander, *International Trotskyism, 1929–1985: A Documented Analysis of the Movement* (Durham, NC and London: Duke University Press, 1991), 260.

8. For a recent overview of the tensions between national and transnational forms of anti-fascism, see Kasper Braskén, Nigel Copsey and David J. Featherstone, eds., *Anti-Fascism in a Global Perspective: Transnational Networks, Exile Communities, and Radical Internationalism* (London and New York: Routledge, 2021).

9. As leading figures of the group believed, the 'case for an internationalist and socialist struggle against colonialism was underpinned, and reinforced, by its interpretation as one of the logical outcomes of capitalist oppression. All in all, their anti-colonialism was not closed in on itself, but seen as part of the battle for socialism that must be conducted globally', Quentin Gasteuil, 'A Comparative and Transnational Approach to Socialist Anti-Colonialism: The Fenner Brockway–Marceau Pivert Connection, 1930s–1950s', in *Workers of the Empire, Unite: Radical and Popular Challenges to British Imperialism, 1910s–1960s*, ed. Yann Béliard and Neville Kirk (Liverpool: Liverpool University Press, 2021), 136.

10. See for example the Bureau's 1936 programme of action: *A Lead to World Socialism: on Spain, War, Fascism, Imperialism—Report of Revolutionary Socialist Congress, Brussels, October 31st–November 2nd 1936* (London: POUM for the International Bureau for International Socialist Unity, 1936), 30–32.

11. For a brief but well-documented account of the early years of the ILP-led London Bureau, see Gidon Cohen, *The Failure of a Dream: The Independent Labour Party from Disaffiliation to World War II* (London: Tauris, 2017).

12. The best statement of the ILP's position towards Spain is arguably Fenner Brockway, *The Truth about Barcelona* (n.d.; Independent Labour Party, 1937).

13. On the impact of the London Bureau on the formation of the POUM and on the Spanish Civil War in general, see Victor Alba and Stephen Schwarz, *Spanish Marxism Versus Soviet Communism: A History of the P.O.U.M.* (New Brunswick and Oxford: Transaction Books, 1988) especially 87–110; Michel Dreyfus, 'L'Internationale Ouvrière Socialiste, le Bureau de Londres et la Guerre d'Espagne', in *Internationalism in the Labour Movement 1830–1940*, ed. Frits L. van Holthoon and Marcel van der Linden (Leiden: Brill, 1988), 355–68; Alan Sennet, *Revolutionary Marxism in 1930–1937* (Leiden: Brill, 2014), 200–202. On the ILP contingent, see also Christopher Hall, *'In Spain with Orwell': George Orwell and the Independent Labour Party Volunteers in the Spanish Civil War, 1936–1939* (Perth: Tippermuir Book, 2013) which contains a list of names and useful biographical information.

14. A list was published in *A New Hope for World Socialism (The Resolutions Adopted at the Revolutionary Socialist Congress, Paris, Feb. 19th–25th, 1938, together with the introductory speeches)* (London: International Bureau for Revolutionary Socialist Unity, 1938), 2.

15. On Padmore's anticolonial activism, see in particular Leslie James, *George Padmore and Decolonization from Below: Pan-Africanism, the Cold War, and the End of Empire* (London and New York: Palgrave Macmillan, 2015). C. L. R. James's involvement with the ILP has been thoroughly investigated in several biographies, including the recent one by John L. Williams, *C.L.R. James: A Life beyond the Boundaries* (London: Constable, 2022).

16. On the eve of the Second World War, the ILP was 'a small, insignificant social democratic party whose freedom of thought meant it was deeply divided on most issues', Keith Laybourn, *The Independent Labour Party, 1914–1939: The Political and Cultural History of a Socialist Party* (Abingdon and New York: Routledge, 2020), 149. On the ILP's factionalism, see also Ian Bullock, *Under Siege: The Independent*

Labour Party in Interwar Britain (Edmonton: Athabasca University Press, 2017), 297–314.

17. On Gironella, see Jaume Fabre and Josep Maria Huertas, 'Enric Adroher *Gironella*, vuitanta anys de lluita', *Revista de Girona* 126 (1988), 12–22; on Pivert, see Jacques Kergoat, *Marceau Pivert: 'socialiste de gauche'* (Paris: Les Editions de l'Atelier/Les Editions Ouvrières, 1994), 132–5. In his notebooks, Victor Serge reported that Gironella and Pivert co-authored a political manifesto in 1944: Victor Serge, *Notebooks: 1936–1947*, ed. Claudio Albertani and Claude Rioux (New York: New York Review Books, 2019), 433.

18. On Ridley, see Robert Morrell, *The Gentle Revolutionary: The Life and Works of Frank Ridley, Socialist and Secularist* (London: Freethought History Research Group, 2003); Theo Williams, 'George Padmore and the Soviet Model of the British Commonwealth', *Modern Intellectual History* 16, no. 2 (2019). On Edwards, see Matthew Broad, 'Ignoring Europe? Reassessing the British Labour Party's Policy towards European Integration, 1951–60', *Journal of European Integration History* 24, no 1 (2018); Christopher Andrew, *The Defence of the Realm: The Authorized History of MI5* (London: Allen Lane, 2009), 710–12.

19. F. A. Ridley and Bob Edwards, *The United Socialist States of Europe* (London: National Labour Press Ltd, 1944), 3, 7.

20. Ridley and Edwards, *The United Socialist States of Europe*, 33, 40.

21. Ridley and Edwards, *The United Socialist States of Europe*, 8, 9, 53.

22. Ridley and Edwards, *The United Socialist States of Europe*, 68–75. Ridley would subsequently credit Trotsky's 1926 article *Europe and America* as their main source of inspiration. See for example F. A. Ridley, *Unite or Perish! U.S.S.E., United Socialist States of Europe* (London: ILP, 1947).

23. Ridley and Edwards, *The United Socialist States of Europe*, 101.

24. See for example Fenner Brockway, *The Way Out* (London: ILP, 1942); Walter Padley, *The Economic Problem of the Peace* (London: Gollancz, 1944), especially 89–113. An echo of these arguments can be found in George Orwell's 1947 plea for the Socialist United States of Europe; see George Orwell, 'Toward European Unity', *Partisan Review* 14, no. 4 (1947), 346–51. See also R. N. Berki, 'Marxism and European Unity', in *European Unity in Context: The Interwar Period*, ed. Peter M. R. Stirk (London: Pinter, 1989), 26–41.

25. Michael Newman, 'British Socialists and the Question of European Unity, 1939–45', *European Studies Review* 10 (1980), 80.

26. 'Minutes of the first meeting of the International Socialist States of Europe', London School of Economics, Independent Labour Party Archive, London/LSE/ILP/3/76.

27. 'Minutes of ILP NAC meeting 4–5 August 1946', London/LSE/ILP/3/34. On Pivert's early commitment to socialist Europeanism, see Talbot Imlay, 'Marceau Pivert and the Travails of an International Socialist', in *The Transnational Activist: Transformations and Comparisons from the Anglo-World since the Nineteenth Century*, ed. Stefan Berger and Sean Scalmer (New York and London: Palgrave Macmillan, 2018).

28. See *Report of an International Conference held in London, February 22–23, 1947 in Support of a Campaign for the United Socialist States of Europe* (London: ILP, 1947), 14.

29. On the process leading to the creation of the Socialist International, see at least Ettore Costa, *The Labour Party, Denis Healey and the International Socialist Movement: Rebuilding the Socialist International during the Cold War, 1945–1951* (Cham: Palgrave Macmillan, 2020).

30. On Labour's refusal to attend the February 1947 meeting, see the letter from Windle to McNair, 19 February 1947, Labour History Archive and Study Centre, Manchester, Labour Party Archive, ID/Healey/10/1. On Labour's pressures on the SFIO, see Healey to Mollet, 30 January 1947, ID/Healey/7 and the Pivert-McNair correspondence, January–February 1947, Archives Nationales, Paris, Papers of Marceau Pivert, 559AP/29.

31. See E. H. Carr, 'The Two Scourges', *Times*, 5 December 1940. Carr's wartime fascination with supranational planning is laid bare in his book *Conditions of Peace* (London: Macmillan, 1942). On supranational planning in the British debate, see Peter Wilson, 'The New Europe Debate in Wartime Britain', in *Visions of European Unity*, ed. Philomena Murray and Paul Rich (Boulder, CO: Westview Press, 1996); Mark Gilbert, 'The Sovereign Remedy of European Unity: The Progressive Left and Supranational Government 1935–1945', *International Politics* 46 (2009); Tommaso Milani, 'From Laissez-Faire to Supranational Planning: The Economic Debate within Federal Union (1938–1945)', *European Review of History/Revue européenne d'histoire* 23, no. 4 (2016).

32. Within the British context, this equally applies to left-wing members of the Labour Party who disparaged piecemeal reformism and felt uncomfortable with the Atlanticist orientation of Ernest Bevin's foreign policy. Their views were condensed in the pamphlet *Keep Left* (1947): see Jonathan Schneer, 'Hopes Deferred or Shattered: The British Labour Left and the Third Force Movement, 1945–49', *Journal of Modern History* 56, no. 2 (1984); R. M. Douglas, *The Labour Party, Nationalism and Internationalism, 1939–1951* (London and New York: Routledge, 2004). It is indeed revealing that a few members of Keep Left—R. H. S. Crossman, Michael Foot, Geoffrey Bing and Leslie Hale—agreed to attend the conference held by the MUSSE in Montrouge in June 1947, despite the presence of a strong ILP contingent. See *Rapport de la deuxième conférence internationale pour les États Unis Socialistes d'Europe. Paris, 21 et 22 Juin, 1947* (London: The International Committee of Study and Action for the United Socialist States of Europe, 1947), 8.

33. 'Annual Report of the National Administrative Council of the Independent Labour Party to be submitted at the 55th Annual Conference, The Town Hall, Ayr, April 5th to April 7th, 1947', ILP/5/1947/3.

34. See the already cited *Unite or Perish!* by Ridley where the Truman Doctrine is discussed in some detail.

35. 'National Administrative Council of the ILP—Income and Expenditures Account for the Year ended 29th February 1948', ILP/3/36.

36. See John McNair, *James Maxton: The Beloved Rebel* (London: George Allen & Unwin, 1955), 315–31; William Knox, *James Maxton* (Manchester: Manchester University Press, 1987), 144–5.

37. For an overview, see Hugh McDonnell, *Europeanising Spaces in Paris, c. 1947–1962* (Liverpool: Liverpool University Press, 2016), 104–36.

38. See Richard T. Griffiths, ed., *Socialist Parties and the Question of Europe in the 1950's* (Leiden: Brill, 1992); Othmar Nikola Haberl and Lutz Niethammer, *Der Marshall-Plan und die europäische Linke* (Frankfurt am Main: Europäische Verlagsanstalt, 1986); Jan de Graaf, *Socialism Across the Iron Curtain: Socialist Parties in East and West and the Reconstruction of Europe after 1945* (Cambridge and New York: Cambridge University Press, 2019), especially 243–81.

39. On the 'New Deal synthesis' underlying the Plan, see Michael J. Hogan, *The Marshall Plan: America, Britain, and the Reconstruction of Western Europe, 1947–1952* (Cambridge: Cambridge University Press 1987), 22–3. For a more critical view, see Geoff Eley, *Forging Democracy: The History of the Left in Europe, 1850–2000* (New York and Oxford: Oxford University Press, 2002), 299–304.

40. See for example Gérard Bossuat, *La France, l'aide américaine et la construction européenne*, vol. I (Paris: Comité pour l'histoire économique et financière de la France, 1997), 141–75; Gerard Bailey, *Between Yesterday and Tomorrow: German Visions of Europe, 1926–1950* (New York and Oxford: Berghahn, 2013), 115–44.

41. See Rhiannon Vickers, *The Labour Party and the World: Vol. I—The Evolution of Labour's Foreign Policy, 1900–1951* (Manchester: Manchester University Press, 2004), 168–72.

42. Printed in *Rapport de la deuxième conférence internationale pour les États-Unis Socialistes d'Europe. Paris, 21 et 22 juin, 1947*, 135.

43. *Rapport de la deuxième conférence internationale*, especially 29, 43, 67. For the conference papers, see also International Institute of Social History, Amsterdam, Mouvement Socialiste pour les États-Unis d'Europe Collection.

44. 'Between Ourselves, July 1947', ILP/5/1947/4.

45. 'Between Ourselves, July 1947', ILP/5/1947/4.

46. See for example 'Compte Rendu de la Réunion du Comité d'Études et d'Action pour les États-Unis Socialistes d'Europe', 25–26 October 1947, Historical Archives of the European Union (HAEU, Fiesole), Mouvement européen (ME) Fiesole/EUI/ME-368 and the strong stance taken by the Belgian Raymond Rifflet, 'Vers l'Union occidentale?', *Les Cahiers socialistes: revue indépendante de critique sociale* 20, no. 5 (1948). On the UEF's more flexible line, see Bertrand Vayssière, *Vers une Europe fédérale? Les espoirs et les actions fédéralistes au sortir de la Seconde Guerre mondiale* (Brussels: Peter Lang, 2007), 155–74. On Frenay's attitude towards the MUSSE, see Robert Belot, *Henri Frenay, de la Résistance à l'Europe* (Paris: Seuil, 2003), especially 525–6.

47. See Bertrand Vayssière, 'Le Congrès de La Haye et les fédéralistes ou la quête d'improbables États Généraux de l'Europe', in *Le Congrès de l'Europe à La Haye (1948–2008)*, ed. Jean-Michel Guieu and Christophe Le Dréau (Brussels: Peter Lang, 2009), 79–91. The MUSSE did not take an active role in the Hague Congress and sent only a few observers.

48. Anne-Isabelle Richard, 'The Limits of Solidarity: Europeanism, Anti-colonialism and Socialism at the Congress of the Peoples of Europe, Asia and Africa in Puteaux, 1948', *European Review of History/Revue européenne d'histoire* 21, no. 4 (2014), 527.

49. See the debate taking place at the Puteaux Congress: 'Assemblée Générale du Comité d'étude et d'action pour les États-Unis Socialistes d'Europe—Puteaux, 22 Juin 1948', Fiesole/EUI/ME-87.

50. According to Loth, this was largely a consequence of the SFIO's ascendancy over the MUSSE: see Wilfried Loth, *Sozialismus und Internationalismus: d. franz. Sozialisten u.d. Nachkriegsordnung Europas 1940–1950* (Stuttgart: Deutsche Verlags-Anstalt, 1977), 99–101, 211–14.

51. 'Programme d'action socialiste européenne', *Les Cahiers socialistes: revue indépendante de critique sociale* 22, no. 5 (1948), 18.

52. 'Programme d'action socialiste européenne', 18–19.

53. 'Programme d'action socialiste européenne', 19–20.

54. See the much more diverse list of participants to the Paris Congress of November 1949, Fiesole/EUI/CIF-33. On the change of name, see also Olivier Philip, *Le problème de l'union européenne* (Paris: Éditions de la Baconnière, 1950), 191–3; Henri Brugmans, *L'idée européenne 1920–1970* (Bruges: De Tempel, 1970), 127–8.

55. Letter from Gironella to Rebattet, 2 December 1948, Fiesole/EUI/ME-494.

56. See the dense correspondence, and especially the letter written by Edwards and McNair dated 12 October 1950, between the British section and Gironella in HAEU, Papers of Fernand Dehousse, Fiesole/EUI/FD-80. See also the undated letter from Brockway to Gironella in HAEU, Movimiento federalista europeo (MFE), Fiesole/EUI/MFE-48.

57. *Third European Congress of the Socialist Movement for the United States of Europe* (London: The British Centre of the Socialist Movement for the United States of Europe, 1950), 2. For a critique of the Strasbourg Consultative Assembly from a socialist-federalist perspective, see Enric Gironella, *Le "Serment" de Strasbourg (les raisons d'un échec)* (Paris: MSEUE, 1950).

58. Philip took over from the Luxembourger Michel Rasquin, who had resigned in August out of discomfort with American financial support for the EM and the position of strength British Tories were enjoying within it. See the 'Communiqué de presse' in *Bulletin du Mouvement Socialiste pour les États-Unis d'Europe* 6 (1949), 12–13; 'Lettre du Comité Exécutif International du M.S.E.U.E. à Michel Rasquin', 2 September 1949, and other related documents in Fiesole/EUI/ME-369.

59. On Philip, see Loïc Philip, *André Philip* (Paris: Beauchesne, 1988), especially 9–138; Christian Chevandier and Gilles Morin, eds., *André Philip, socialiste, patriote, chrétien: colloque 'Redécouvrir André Philip' organisé à l'Assemblée nationale les 13 et 14 mars 2003* (Paris: Comité pour l'histoire économique et financière de la France, 2005); Mathieu Fulla, *Les socialistes français et l'économie (1944–1981)* (Paris: Presses de Sciences Po, 2016), especially 70–77.

60. See for example André Philip, 'L'unification économique de l'Europe', *Cahiers du monde nouveau* 5, no. 3 (1949), 32–38; André Philip, *L'unité européenne: l'heure de la décision* (Paris: Editions du M.S.E.U.E., 1950), especially 16–18.

61. See the documentation for the Third and Fourth Congresses – held in Paris in November 1949 and in Strasbourg in November 1950 respectively – in Fiesole/EUI/ME-366 and Fiesole/EUI/ME-365.

62. A full-blown attack came from Philip himself: see André Philip, *Le Socialisme et l'unité européenne: réponse à l'exécutif du Labour Party* (Paris: Editions du M.S.E.U.E, 1950).

63. On the post-war culture of social democracy, see Donald Sassoon, *One Hundred Years of Socialism: The West European Left in the Twentieth Century* (London and New York: I.B. Tauris, 1996), 117–85; Tony Judt, *Postwar: A History of Europe since 1945* (New York: Penguin, 2005), 360–89.

64. See for example André Philip, *L'Europe unie et sa place dans l'économie internationale* (Paris: Presses universitaires de France, 1953), especially 125–66.

65. See for example the opening editorial, 'Notre but . . . la Gauche Européenne', *Gauche Européenne* 1 (March 1953), 1–2.

66. See for example *Mouvement Socialiste pour les États-Unis d'Europe* (Brussels: MSEUE, 1950); Raymond Rifflet, *Europe et socialisme: un bilan politique* (Brussels: MSEUE, 1951); *La Communauté Européenne de Défense (C.E.D) vue par les jeunes du Mouvement Socialiste pour les États-Unis d'Europe* (Bagnolet: MSEUE, 1953); *Le projet de Constitution Européenne: le socialisme et l'Europe* (Brussels: MSEUE, 1953); *La construction de l'Europe vue par les Jeunes du Mouvement Socialiste pour les États-Unis d'Europe* (Brussels: MSEUE, 1953); Raymond Rifflet, *Du fédéralisme utopique au fédéralisme scientifique* (Brussels: MSEUE, 1956).

67. See Dietrich Orlow, *Common Destiny: A Comparative History of the Dutch, French, and German Social Democratic Parties, 1945–1969* (New York and Oxford: Berghahn, 2009), 65–101; Martin Conway, *Western Europe's Democratic Age, 1945–1968* (Princeton: Princeton University Press, 2020), 191–6.

68. It is worth stressing that the MSEUE central archives in Paris were largely destroyed in the 1960s.

69. See André Philip, 'Pour l'étude des principes d'un socialisme européen', Fiesole/EUI/ME-364. Other reports were penned by Herman Louis Brill, Otto Bach, Sébastien Constant, Gérard Jacquet, Hendrik Brugmans and the already cited Gironella and Edwards. Some—including Philip's—were published in *Bulletin du Mouvement Socialiste pour les États-Unis d'Europe* 2 (1951).

70. Philip, 'Pour l'étude des principes d'un socialisme européen'.

71. Philip, 'Pour l'étude des principes d'un socialisme européen'.

72. See for example André Philip, 'Pour l'étude des principes d'un socialisme européen', *Christianisme social* 3–4 (1952), 154–60; André Philip, 'La crise doctrinale du socialisme en Europe', *La revue socialiste* 56 (1952), 346–59. See the official MSEUE 'Résolution sur les principes d'un socialisme européen' in Fiesole/EUI/ME-364.

73. See the letter dated 26 February1952, in Archives Nationales (Paris), Papers of André Philip, 625AP/4.

74. Letter dated 26 February1952, in Archives Nationales (Paris), Papers of André Philip, 625AP/4. Moulin's argument drew heavily on his book, *Socialism of the West: An Attempt to Lay the Foundations of a New Socialist Humanism* (London: Gollancz, 1948).

75. Evidence from de Man's private papers shows that he continued to correspond with Philip and—more frequently and on more substantive issues—with Moulin after 1945. See AMSAB-Instituut voor Sociale Geschiedenis (Ghent), De Man-Lecocq Archive/611–615 and 526–530. On de Man's socialism, see Peter Dodge, 'Voluntaristic Socialism: An Examination of the Implications of Hendrik de Man's Ideology', *International Review of Social History* 3, no. 3 (1958), 385–417. For Philip's and Moulin's appraisals of de Man, see for example André Philip, *Les Socialistes* (Paris: Seuil, 1967), 68–72; Léo Moulin, 'Henri de Man en 1985', *Bulletin de l'Association pour l'étude de l'œuvre d'Henri de Man* 14 (1987), 81–4.

76. See Michel Winock, *Histoire politique de la revue Esprit, 1930–1950* (Paris: Seuil, 1975), 95–7; Léo Moulin, *Libre parcours: itinéraire spirituel d'un agnostique* (Brussels: Racines, 1995), 78–81.

77. See Tommaso Milani, *Hendrik de Man and Social Democracy: The Idea of Planning in Western Europe, 1914–1940* (New York and London: Palgrave Macmillan, 2020), 90–94, 163, 128.

78. See Stéphane Clouet, *De la rénovation à l'utopie socialistes: Révolution constructive, un groupe d'intellectuels socialistes des années 1930* (Nancy: Presses Universitaires de Nancy, 1991) with Moulin's preface (11–14); Henri Brugmans, *À travers le siècle* (Brussels: Presses Interuniversitaires Européennes, 1994); Caroline Vermeulen, *Le Collège d'Europe à l'ère des pionniers (1950–1960)* (Brussels: Peter Lang, 2000), 131–2.

79. See the letter in AMSA-IGS, De Man Archive/539. On Moulin's relationship with Spaak, see his 1988 interview with Alain Dantoing whose transcript can be accessed at the state archives in Brussels (CegeSoma) (AA2268/505) and his letters to Spaak at HAEU (Papers of Paul-Henri Spaak, PHS-502). For Spaak's attitude towards MSEUE in spring 1952, see Paul-Henri Spaak and Jeanne Hersch, 'Les socialistes européens à Francfort', *Monde Nouveau-Paru* 57 (1952), 11–16. Moulin also praised the Belgian monthly *Cahiers socialistes* edited by Rifflet, which frequently published MSEUE contributions while trying to revive a socialist humanism informed by de Man's thought. See Eva Schandevyl, 'Intellectuels belges en quête d'un nouveau socialisme: l'aventure des *Cahiers socialistes* (1944–1953)', *European Review of History/Revue européenne d'histoire* 13, no. 1 (2006); Bertrand Vayssière, *Européiste et*

eurocrate: la vie fédéraliste de Raymond Rifflet (Toulouse: Presses universitaires du Midi, 2018), especially 71–84, 106–8.

80. Philip Nord, *France's New Deal: From the Thirties to the Postwar Era* (Princeton: Princeton University Press, 2010), 13.

81. See for example the speech by Mollet at the Fourth MSEUE Congress, celebrating this flexibility [Fiesole/EUI/MFE-32].

82. See Aurélie Dianara Andry, *Social Europe, the Road not Taken: The Left and European Integration in the Long 1970s* (Oxford and New York: Oxford University Press, 2022).

83. See Patrick Pasture, 'The Interwar Origins of International Labour's European Commitment (1919–1934)', *Contemporary European History* 10, no. 2 (2001); Christian Bailey, 'Socialist Visions of European Unity in Germany: Ostpolitik since the 1920s?', *Contemporary European History* 26, no. 2 (2017); Brian Shaev, 'Liberalising Regional Trade: Socialists and European Economic Integration', *Contemporary European History* 27, no. 2 (2018).

Bibliography

A New Hope for World Socialism (The Resolutions Adopted at the Revolutionary Socialist Congress, Paris, Feb. 19th–25th, 1938, together with the introductory speeches). London: International Bureau for Revolutionary Socialist Unity, 1938.

Alba, Victor and Stephen Schwarz. *Spanish Marxism Versus Soviet Communism: A History of the P.O.U.M*. New Brunswick and Oxford: Transaction Books, 1988.

Alexander, Robert J. *International Trotskyism, 1929–1985: A Documented Analysis of the Movement*. Durham, NC and London: Duke University Press, 1991.

Andrew, Christopher. *The Defence of the Realm: The Authorized History of MI5*. London: Allen Lane, 2009.

Bailey, Christian. 'Socialist Visions of European Unity in Germany: Ostpolitik since the 1920s?' *Contemporary European History* 26, no. 2 (2017): 243–60.

Bailey, Gerard. *Between Yesterday and Tomorrow: German Visions of Europe, 1926–1950*. New York and Oxford: Berghahn, 2013.

Belot, Robert. *Henri Frenay, de la Résistance à l'Europe*. Paris: Seuil, 2003.

Berki, R.N. 'Marxism and European Unity'. In *European Unity in Context: The Interwar Period*, edited by Peter M. R. Stirk, 41–64. London: Pinter, 1989.

Bossuat, Gérard. *La France, l'aide américaine et la construction européenne*, vol. I. Paris: Comité pour l'histoire économique et financière de la France, 1997.

Braskén, Kasper, Nigel Copsey and David J. Featherstone, eds. *Anti-Fascism in a Global Perspective: Transnational Networks, Exile Communities, and Radical Internationalism*. London and New York: Routledge, 2021.

Broad, Matthew. 'Ignoring Europe? Reassessing the British Labour Party's Policy towards European Integration, 1951–60', *Journal of European Integration History* 24, no 1 (2018): 95–114.

Brockway, Fenner. *The Truth about Barcelona*. Independent Labour Party, 1937.

Brockway, Fenner. *The Way Out*. London: ILP, 1942.

Brugmans, Henri. *À travers le siècle*. Brussels: Presses Interuniversitaires Européennes, 1994.

Brugmans, Henri. *L'idée européenne 1920–1970*. Bruges: De Tempel, 1970.

Brunet, Luc-André. *Forging Europe: Industrial Organisation in France, 1940–1952*. London: Palgrave Macmillan, 2017.
Bullock, Ian. *Under Siege: The Independent Labour Party in Interwar Britain*. Edmonton: Athabasca University Press, 2017.
Buschak, Willy. *Das Londoner Büro: Europäische Linkssozialisten in der Zwischenkriegszeit*. Amsterdam: Stichting Internationaal Instituut voor Sociale Geschiedenis 1985.
Buschak, Willy. 'The London Bureau'. In *The Cambridge History of Socialism*, vol. II, edited by Marcel Van der Linden, 542–60. Cambridge and New York: Cambridge University Press, 2022.
Carr, E. H. *Conditions of Peace*. London: Macmillan, 1942.
Chevandier, Christian and Gilles Morin eds. *André Philip, socialiste, patriote, chrétien: colloque 'Redécouvrir André Philip' organisé à l'Assemblée nationale les 13 et 14 mars 2003*. Paris: Comité pour l'histoire économique et financière de la France, 2005.
Clouet, Stéphane. *De la rénovation à l'utopie socialistes: Révolution constructive, un groupe d'intellectuels socialistes des années 1930*. Nancy: Presses Universitaires de Nancy, 1991.
Cohen, Gidon. *The Failure of a Dream: The Independent Labour Party from Disaffiliation to World War II*. London: Tauris, 2017.
Conway, Martin. *Western Europe's Democratic Age, 1945–1968*. Princeton: Princeton University Press, 2020.
Costa, Ettore. *The Labour Party, Denis Healey and the International Socialist Movement: Rebuilding the Socialist International during the Cold War, 1945–1951*. Cham: Palgrave Macmillan, 2020.
de Graaf, Jan. *Socialism Across the Iron Curtain: Socialist Parties in East and West and the Reconstruction of Europe after 1945*. Cambridge and New York: Cambridge University Press, 2019.
Dianara Andry, Aurélie. *Social Europe, the Road not Taken: The Left and European Integration in the Long 1970s*. Oxford and New York: Oxford University Press, 2022.
Dodge, Peter. 'Voluntaristic Socialism: An Examination of the Implications of Hendrik de Man's Ideology', *International Review of Social History* 3, no. 3 (1958): 385–417.
Douglas, R.M. *The Labour Party, Nationalism and Internationalism, 1939–1951*. London and New York: Routledge, 2004.
Dreyfus, Michel. 'Bureau de Paris et bureau de Londres: le socialisme de gauche en Europe entre les deux guerres', *Mouvement social* 112 (1980): 25–55.
Dreyfus, Michel. 'Socialistes de gauche et trotskystes en Europe 1933–1938'. In *Pensiero e azione politica di Lev Trockij*, edited by Francesca Gori, vol. II, 529–60. Florence: Olschki, 1982.

Dreyfus, Michel. 'L'Internationale Ouvrière Socialiste, le Bureau de Londres et la Guerre d'Espagne'. In *Internationalism in the Labour Movement 1830–1940*, edited by Frits L. van Holthoon and Marcel van der Linden, 355–68. Leiden: Brill, 1988.
Eley, Geoff. *Forging Democracy: The History of the Left in Europe, 1850–2000*. New York and Oxford: Oxford University Press, 2002.
Fabre, Jaume and Josep Maria Huertas. 'Enric Adroher *Gironella*, vuitanta anys de lluita', *Revista de Girona* 126 (1988): 12–22.
Fischer, Conan. *A Vision of Europe: Franco-German Relations during the Great Depression, 1929–1932*. Oxford and New York: Oxford University Press, 2017.
Fulla, Mathieu. *Les socialistes français et l'économie (1944–1981)*. Paris: Presses de Sciences Po, 2016.
Gasteuil, Quentin. 'A Comparative and Transnational Approach to Socialist Anti-Colonialism: The Fenner Brockway–Marceau Pivert Connection, 1930s–1950s'. In *Workers of the Empire, Unite: Radical and Popular Challenges to British Imperialism, 1910s–1960s*, edited by Yann Béliard and Neville Kirk, 133–64. Liverpool: Liverpool University Press, 2021.
Gilbert, Mark. 'The Sovereign Remedy of European Unity: The Progressive Left and Supranational Government 1935–1945', *International Politics* 46 (2009): 28–47.
Gironella, Enric. *Le "Serment" de Strasbourg (les raisons d'un échec)*. Paris: MSEUE, 1950.
Griffiths, Richard T. ed., *Socialist Parties and the Question of Europe in the 1950's*. Leiden: Brill, 1992.
Gross, Stephen. 'Introduction: European Integration across the Twentieth Century', *Contemporary European History* 26, no. 2 (2017): 205–7.
Haberl, Othmar Nikola and Lutz Niethammer. *Der Marshall-Plan und die europäische Linke*. Frankfurt am Main: Europäische Verlagsanstalt, 1986.
Hall, Christopher. *'In Spain with Orwell': George Orwell and the Independent Labour Party Volunteers in the Spanish Civil War, 1936–1939*. Perth: Tippermuir Books, 2013.
Hogan, Michael J. *The Marshall Plan: America, Britain, and the Reconstruction of Western Europe, 1947–1952*. Cambridge: Cambridge University Press, 1987.
Imlay, Talbot. 'Marceau Pivert and the Travails of an International Socialist'. In *The Transnational Activist: Transformations and Comparisons from the Anglo-World since the Nineteenth Century*, edited by Stefan Berger and Sean Scalmer, 141–64. New York and London: Palgrave Macmillan, 2018.

Imlay, Talbot. *The Practice of Socialist Internationalism: European Socialists and International Politics, 1914–1960*. Oxford and New York: Oxford University Press, 2018.

James, Leslie. *George Padmore and Decolonization from Below: Pan-Africanism, the Cold War, and the End of Empire*. London and New York: Palgrave Macmillan, 2015.

Judt, Tony. *Postwar: A History of Europe since 1945*. New York: Penguin, 2005.

Kergoat, Jacques. *Marceau Pivert: 'socialiste de gauche'*. Paris: Les Éditions de l'Atelier/Les Éditions Ouvrières, 1994.

Knox, William. *James Maxton*. Manchester: Manchester University Press, 1987.

Laybourn, Keith. *The Independent Labour Party, 1914–1939: The Political and Cultural History of a Socialist Party*. Abingdon and New York: Routledge, 2020.

Lipgens, Walter. *Anfänge der europäischen Einigungspolitik 1945–1950*. Stuttgart: Klet, 1977.

Loth, Wilfried. *Sozialismus und Internationalismus: d. franz. Sozialisten u.d. Nachkriegsordnung Europas 1940–1950*. Stuttgart: Deutsche Verlags-Anstalt, 1977.

Loth, Wilfried. 'The *Mouvement Socialiste pour les Etats-Unis d'Europe* (MSEUE)'. In *Documents on the History of European Integration*, edited by Walter Lipgens and Wilfried Loth, vol. IV, 277–318. Berlin: De Gruyter, 1991.

McDonnell, Hugh. *Europeanising Spaces in Paris, c. 1947–1962*. Liverpool: Liverpool University Press, 2016.

McNair, John. *James Maxton: The Beloved Rebel*. London: George Allen & Unwin, 1955.

Milani, Tommaso. 'From Laissez-Faire to Supranational Planning: The Economic Debate within Federal Union (1938–1945)', *European Review of History/Revue européenne d'histoire* 23, no. 4 (2016): 664–85.

Milani, Tommaso. *Hendrik de Man and Social Democracy: The Idea of Planning in Western Europe, 1914–1940*. New York and London: Palgrave Macmillan, 2020.

Mock, Harold. 'A Post-National Europe: Brandt's Vision for the European Community between the Superpowers'. In *Willy Brandt and International Relations: Europe, the USA, and Latin America*, edited by Bernd Rother and Klaus Larres, 87–107. London: Bloomsbury, 2018.

Morrell, Robert. *The Gentle Revolutionary: The Life and Works of Frank Ridley, Socialist and Secularist*. London: Freethought History Research Group, 2003.

Moulin, Léo. *Socialism of the West: An Attempt to Lay the Foundations of a New Socialist Humanism*. London: Gollancz, 1948.
Moulin, Léo. 'Henri de Man en 1985', *Bulletin de l'Association pour l'étude de l'œuvre d'Henri de Man* 14 (1987): 81–4.
Moulin, Léo. *Libre parcours: itinéraire spirituel d'un agnostique*. Brussels: Racines, 1995.
Newman, Michael. 'British Socialists and the Question of European Unity, 1939–45', *European Studies Review* 10 (1980): 75–100.
Nord, Philip. *France's New Deal: From the Thirties to the Postwar Era*. Princeton: Princeton University Press, 2010.
Orlow, Dietrich. *Common Destiny: A Comparative History of the Dutch, French, and German Social Democratic Parties, 1945–1969*. New York and Oxford: Berghahn, 2009.
Orwell, George. 'Toward European Unity', *Partisan Review* 14, no. 4 (1947): 346–51.
Padley, Walter. *The Economic Problem of the Peace*. London: Gollancz, 1944.
Pasture, Patrick. 'The Interwar Origins of International Labour's European Commitment (1919–1934)'. *Contemporary European History* 10, no. 2 (2001): 221–37.
Patel, Kiran Klaus and Wolfram Kaiser. 'Continuity and Change in European Cooperation during the Twentieth Century', *Contemporary European History* 27, no. 2 (2018): 165–82.
Philip, André. 'L'unification économique de l'Europe', *Cahiers du monde nouveau* 5, no. 3 (1949): 32–38.
Philip, André. *Le Socialisme et l'unité européenne: réponse à l'exécutif du Labour Party*. Paris: Editions du M.S.E.U.E, 1950.
Philip, André. *L'unité européenne: l'heure de la décision*. Paris: Editions du M.S.E.U.E., 1950.
Philip, André. 'La crise doctrinale du socialisme en Europe', *La revue socialiste* 56 (1952): 346–59.
Philip, André. 'Pour l'étude des principes d'un socialisme européen', *Christianisme social* 3–4 (1952): 154–60.
Philip, André. *L'Europe unie et sa place dans l'économie internationale*. Paris: Presses universitaires de France, 1953.
Philip, André. *Les Socialistes*. Paris: Seuil, 1967.
Philip, Loïc. *André Philip*. Paris: Beauchesne, 1988.
Philip, Olivier. *Le problème de l'union européenne*. Paris: Éditions de la Baconnière, 1950.
Pistone, Sergio, ed. *I movimenti per l'unità europea dal 1945 al 1954*. Milan: Jaca Book, 1992.

Richard, Anne-Isabelle. 'The Limits of Solidarity: Europeanism, Anti-colonialism and Socialism at the Congress of the Peoples of Europe, Asia and Africa in Puteaux, 1948', *European Review of History/Revue européenne d'histoire* 21, no. 4 (2014): 519–37.
Ridley, F. A., *Unite or Perish! U.S.S.E., United Socialist States of Europe.* London: ILP, 1947.
Ridley, F. A. and Bob Edwards, *The United Socialist States of Europe.* London: National Labour Press Ltd, 1944.
Rifflet, Raymond. *Du fédéralisme utopique au fédéralisme scientifique.* Brussels: MSEUE, 1956.
Rifflet, Raymond. *Europe et socialisme: un bilan politique.* Brussels: MSEUE, 1951.
Rifflet, Raymond. 'Vers l'Union occidentale?', *Les Cahiers socialistes: revue indépendante de critique sociale* 20, no. 5 (1948) : 1–9.
Sassoon, Donald. *One Hundred Years of Socialism: The West European Left in the Twentieth Century.* London and New York: I.B. Tauris, 1996.
Schandevyl, Eva. 'Intellectuels belges en quête d'un nouveau socialisme: l'aventure des *Cahiers socialistes* (1944–1953)', *European Review of History/Revue européenne d'histoire* 13, no. 1 (2006): 67–82.
Schneer, Jonathan. 'Hopes Deferred or Shattered: The British Labour Left and the Third Force Movement, 1945–49', *Journal of Modern History* 56, no. 2 (1984): 197–226.
Sennet, Alan. *Revolutionary Marxism in 1930–1937.* Leiden: Brill, 2014.
Serge, Victor, *Notebooks: 1936–1947*, edited by Claudio Albertani and Claude Rioux. New York: New York Review Books, 2019.
Shaev, Brian. 'Liberalising Regional Trade: Socialists and European Economic Integration', *Contemporary European History* 27, no. 2 (2018): 258–79.
Spaak, Paul-Henri and Jeanne Hersch, 'Les socialistes européens à Francfort', *Monde Nouveau-Paru* 57 (1952): 11–16.
Vayssière, Bertrand. *Vers une Europe fédérale? Les espoirs et les actions fédéralistes au sortir de la Seconde Guerre mondiale.* Brussels: Peter Lang, 2007.
Vayssière, Bertrand. 'Le Congrès de La Haye et les fédéralistes ou la quête d'improbables États Généraux de l'Europe'. In *Le Congrès de l'Europe à La Haye (1948–2008)*, edited by Jean-Michel Guieu and Christophe Le Dréau, 79–91. Brussels: Peter Lang, 2009.
Vayssière, Bertrand. *Européiste et eurocrate: la vie fédéraliste de Raymond Rifflet.* Toulouse: Presses universitaires du Midi, 2018.
Vermeulen, Caroline. *Le Collège d'Europe à l'ère des pionniers (1950–1960).* Brussels: Peter Lang, 2000.

Vickers, Rhiannon. *The Labour Party and the World: Vol. I – The Evolution of Labour's Foreign Policy, 1900–1951*. Manchester: Manchester University Press, 2004.

Williams, John L. *C.L.R. James: A Life beyond the Boundaries*. London: Constable, 2022.

Williams, Theo. 'George Padmore and the Soviet Model of the British Commonwealth', *Modern Intellectual History* 16, no. 2 (2019): 531–59.

Wilson, Peter. 'The New Europe Debate in Wartime Britain'. In *Visions of European Unity*, edited by Philomena Murray and Paul Rich, 21–38. Boulder, CO: Westview Press, 1996.

Winock, Michel. *Histoire politique de la revue Esprit, 1930–1950*. Paris: Seuil, 1975.

Part II

PATHS NOT TAKEN? EUROPEAN SOCIALISTS AND THE POLITICS OF WORLDMAKING AT THE END OF EMPIRE

Chapter 3

Europe re-imagined? Claude Bourdet, *France-Observateur* and British critics of the Algerian war

Mélanie Torrent

When politician and journalist Claude Bourdet died in 1996 aged 86, his life was celebrated in several obituaries in Britain. He was primarily remembered as a leading figure of the French Resistance, who had led the Movement for National Liberation in the Alpes Maritimes in 1941 and joined the *Conseil national de la Résistance*, before being arrested by the Gestapo in March 1944 and deported to Germany. Central to the emergence of the French new left, he was also the political editor of *Combat* (1942–44, and 1947–50), and the co-founder of *L'Observateur* in 1950 (later *L'Observateur d'aujourd'hui*, 1953–54, and *France-Observateur*, 1954–64).[1] But Bourdet was also remembered for his anticolonial role. Writing in *The Independent*, British historian of France Douglas Johnson remembered meeting him twice: in 1948 at the *Ecole normale supérieure* in Paris when Bourdet spoke against the war in Indochina and hoped that Britain's Labour government 'would become the leader of a united Europe'; and in 1957, when Bourdet, whose writings against the use of torture in Algeria had made the British headlines, denounced French 'misdeeds in Algeria' at Birmingham University, where Johnson had become a history lecturer. If Johnson was later described as 'a kind of ambassador for Charles de Gaulle to the British',[2] a position far removed from Bourdet's, the Birmingham visit was recalled by Johnson as 'a great success'.[3] The lasting impression from Johnson's obituary is that Bourdet stimulated British mobilisation for an alternative world order during the war in Algeria

(1954–62), and by extension, conceptions of the place of Europeans and Western Europe in a decolonising world.

By investigating the web of British contacts of Bourdet and *France-Observateur*,[4] this chapter considers how mobilisation for peace in Algeria in the United Kingdom in 1954–62 intersected with conceptions of Europe and of the European project which was being institutionalised. French policy in North Africa featured prominently in the British press during two important phases of European construction. First, under the premiership of French socialist leader Guy Mollet, the Treaty of Rome of 1957, which France signed with Belgium, Germany, Italy, Luxemburg and the Netherlands, coincided with the intensification of the war in Algeria, a few months after the arrest of Ahmed Ben Bella and his fellow leaders of the *Front de libération nationale* (FLN), and amidst the fallout of the failed Suez expedition. Secondly, in the summer of 1961, Britain's first application to the European Economic Community (EEC) under the Conservative government of Harold Macmillan coincided with the Bizerta crisis in Tunisia, the continued failure of French governments to negotiate a settlement in Algeria and the rise of the *Organisation armée secrète* (OAS), the paramilitary group intent on maintaining 'French Algeria' at all costs. The (neo)colonial intentions behind the EEC, serving the interests of European states and businesses, have generated a growing field of study.[5] As Megan Brown's *The Seventh Member State* has recently shown, the Treaty of Rome was fully part of France's war diplomacy: 'other European states *agreed* that Algeria was a constitutive part of France',[6] while the Six treated citizens of Algeria (and European overseas territories) differently from citizens of the metropoles. Even when opponents of the war in Britain do not seem to have discussed in any great depth, if at all, such legal issues, they did consider the European project in the light of the events happening on both sides of the Mediterranean.

Simultaneously, the war in Algeria, at the nexus of decolonisation and globalisation, had a distinct influence on the emergence of a French 'New Radical Left',[7] and on 'new political cultures'[8] across Western Europe. If, as Daniel Gorman suggests, '[t]ransnational personal relationships were a defining feature of post-war internationalism in Britain',[9] the web of relations formed in support of peace in Algeria (and, in many cases, independence) reveals fluctuations and ambiguities in defining both Europeanism and internationalism in the British non-Communist left, in the wake of the Congress of the Peoples Against Imperialism.[10] More specifically, the correspondence and work of people like Bourdet show that transnational relations influenced ideas of Franco-British comparisons and cooperation outside the governmental spheres: through intermediaries, trusted contacts and 'go-to' people; and through translation and cultural interpretation, deciphering British events to a French audience, and vice versa. The particular interest of Bourdet resides in the breadth of his network, partly due to his excellent command of written and spoken English. Like Bourdet, French Marxist Marceau Pivert, until his death in 1958, had a strong network in the British left.[11] But even if Pivert had lived beyond 1958, he did not have Bourdet's visibility in Britain, within and outside the Labour left. Like Bourdet, who liaised with American and British Quakers, the socialist André Philip, who broke with the SFIO (*Section française de l'internationale ouvrière*) in 1957 over Algeria, corresponded with church groups in the United Kingdom and met Labour MPs. But his anticolonial contacts seem to have been fewer. The same is true of Edouard Depreux, even when he too visited London and exchanged views with the Labour leadership.

Bourdet's business with his British contacts during the war of Algerian independence was conducted in person, in writing and on the telephone – as with Labour MPs Fenner Brockway (1950–64) and Michael Foot (1945–55, 1960–92), who also edited *Tribune* and had a column in the *Daily Herald*.[12] The resulting paper trails shed light on the dynamics of political and cultural translation across two diminishing empires and, importantly for this volume, on the place of the British left in the movement for peace and independence in Algeria, as it developed in Britain. After assessing the place of Bourdet and *France-Observateur* in Britain before 1955, this chapter shows how existing editorial contacts were used to denounce the war in Algeria on both sides of the Channel. It then argues that widening cooperation also nuanced Europe's importance, while socialist connections, if they failed to translate into viable alternative political institutions for Europe, enabled individual and collective rights-based action.

France-Observateur in British and Labour circles: democratic principles and socialist solidarities

In the wake of the uprising in Algeria in November 1954, censorship was established under state-of-emergency legislation on 3 April 1955, and extended in the decree of 17 March 1956. Bourdet's most prominent appearance in the British media can probably be dated to the end of that month, after his arrest in Paris on charges of attempting to demoralise the French army. Featuring on the front page of *The Herald Express* on 31 March, the event was discussed the following day in *The Observer* and reported on the BBC. Bourdet, wrote the British journalist Nora Beloff, 'was charged by a military tribunal for saying in his paper the same things about the horror and futility of the Algerian war as the Socialist leaders themselves had said during the recent election campaign'.[13] *The Times* noted that the arrest of someone 'with an exceptionally fine war record, met with the open disapproval of many people, including those who are by no means in agreement with M. Bourdet's political views'.[14] For *Tribune*, the weekly paper of the left of the Labour Party, Bourdet's arrest was a 'threat to French democracy and Socialism': 'If we value our own liberty', the editorial added, 'we cannot stay silent while the right to print is crushed across the Channel'.[15] As *France-Observateur* argued, reprinting extracts from *Tribune* and *The Economist*, Bourdet's arrest was damaging France's reputation across the British political spectrum.[16]

By 1956, Bourdet was a well-known commentator for the British media, and his contacts in the anticolonial Union of Democratic Control (UDC) believed their relations to have been monitored.[17] Even before *France-Observateur* was first seized in September 1955, Bourdet had featured in *The Guardian* in January 1955, as one of the French intellectuals, alongside François Mauriac, denouncing police brutality and torture in Algeria.[18] A translated version of his article, 'Your Gestapo in Algeria' of 13 January 1955, was circulated by the Movement for Colonial Freedom (MCF), ahead of the publication of a short article – 'Torture by France' – in *Tribune* two weeks after the *Guardian* piece.[19] In the immediate postwar years, Bourdet was a regular guest on the BBC Third Programme, launched in September 1946 and described by art critic and wartime BBC producer Edward Sackville-West as 'the greatest educative and civilising force England has known since the secularisation of the theatre in the sixteenth century'.[20] Beside discussing French foreign policy and international affairs, Bourdet took a direct interest in British politics, in his endeavours to promote world government. In February 1949, he spoke at a meeting of 'The crusade for world government' with the Liberal peer William Beveridge, and was involved in organising the non-Communist Peace congress in London in April 1949. In contact with the Labour MP Henry Usborne, for whom an international legislature charged with defining and enforcing international law was the only path to permanent world peace, Bourdet also spoke at a World Government meeting in Usborne's Birmingham constituency in February 1950, where attendees sought to put 'peace before party'.[21] On issues of peace and world government, Bourdet was also in contact with Ritchie Calder and Brockway, who also liaised with Prime Minister Jawaharlal Nehru in India, and with peace militant Harold Field in the United States.[22]

Key in these endeavours, for Bourdet, was the British Labour Party, whose landslide victory in 1945 made it a central force in European socialist circles, as shown by the negotiations for the revival of the Socialist

International after the war.[23] Even by 1950, when Labour's foreign policy under Ernest Bevin had become firmly Atlanticist, Labour was seen as the best possible government to have in London. Speaking in support of Usborne ahead of the February 1950 general election, Bourdet stated: 'If Labour loses, the Right wing in France will have tremendous impetus. This does not mean more Conservatives but more Fascist organisations in power. On the other hand the Left wing will go Communists [sic]'.[24] On polling day, *The Daily Herald* published Bourdet's 'Your vote and peace':[25] 'the course Britain takes today', he argued, 'will have immediate consequences on the peace of the world', predicting that a Conservative victory would bolster political extremes in Germany and France. This faith in Labour's importance persisted well into the 1950s, even after the electoral defeat of 1951, and particularly after the formation of the Keep Left movement and Aneurin Bevan's resignation over the Korean war. Bevan's support for a third way encouraged Bourdet – and 'all the real socialists in France, whether they belong or not to the Socialist Party', he told Labour MP Ian Mikardo in May 1951 – in his own support for an alternative vision of Europe. With Bevan heralding 'a new orientation of socialism all over the world',[26] *France-Observateur* translated 'Keep Left' for its readers in October 1951. Bourdet regretted what he saw as a Labour tendency to focus primarily on *British* affairs, wishing the 'Bevan bomb' had 'exploded sooner!'[27] But as he later explained, the Bevanites did demonstrate that despite the existence of Stalin's police regime, there was no need to fear Soviet aggression and that Western socialism was mistaken in supporting Atlanticist policies and the over-armament that went with it. 'For a long time, when foreigners asked what our political orientation was,' Bourdet continued, 'many of us would reply: "Something akin to a French bevanism"'.[28]

Bevan was kept informed of what *France-Observateur* published, rectifying the narrative on Labour when required – as in 1953, when he objected to a story that he would become Foreign Secretary if Labour won the election.[29] Shared opposition to the European Defence Community (EDC) led to further collaboration in 1954. After discussions with Labour MP Richard Crossman, Bourdet was hopeful that Labour 'could make French socialists understand a little more clearly' that the EDC could 'gradually sever' Franco-British links and was thus damaging.[30] He also liaised – as did French socialist Lucien Weitz, *Tribune*'s main correspondent in France – with Norman Mackenzie of the *New Statesman and Nation*, Jo Richardson, Mikardo's secretary, and several MPs in the Labour left, including Jennie Lee and Konni Zilliacus.[31] There again, the press stimulated cross-Channel relations. At Foot's request, Bourdet gave *Tribune* a detailed French perspective on the dangers of German rearmament – 'Why Frenchmen are afraid of EDC' – which Foot called 'absolutely first-class'.[32] Simultaneously, Bourdet benefited from the insights of friends such as the Labour MP William Warbey, for whom Pierre Mendès France, as the man who had taken France out of Indochina, had the necessary clout to influence ideas and events in Britain – and, as rather seemed to be happening, to scupper anti-rearmament forces entirely.[33] Writing in *France-Observateur* after the Labour Congress of September 1954, Bourdet concluded that Mendès France's favourable attitude to German rearmament had bolstered the Labour right.[34] Overall, Bevan remained a sort of guiding light for a European third way. As Bourdet put it in March 1955, 'Bevan is not only British':[35] it was his pressure on the Labour leadership which guaranteed parliamentary scrutiny of Conservative policies and held them in check. Bevan's French contacts and their audience therefore saw him as a definite influence on decision-making in international affairs. Extracts from Bevan's major speeches on international policy featured in *France-Observateur*, with a real exegesis sometimes provided. This was the case for his speech against the nuclear bomb in March 1955 – 'a capital document' and 'a historical speech'.[36] A long article by Andrew Roth,[37] the left-wing American journalist who had become a prominent figure on London's media scene, explained to French readers that only Bevan could unite the more 'intellectual' and the more 'sentimental' left-wing of the party. After Labour's new defeat in 1955, Bourdet announced that Bevan was 'not guilty', as Roth stressed that on international affairs, British voters had not been given a choice, given Labour's Atlanticist policies under Clement Attlee.[38] After Bevan lost to Hugh Gaitskell for the post of party treasurer, *France-Observateur* and *Tribune* held joint copyright of Bevan's article 'La signification de mon combat', published in October 1955.[39]

Connections also stemmed from the anticolonial networks that had emerged in the interwar years. K. M. Pannikar, India's Ambassador to China, wrote for *France-Observateur*, while French socialists like Marceau Pivert and Jean Rous kept themselves closely informed of developments in Britain. In 1953, Bourdet's letter to *The Observer*, after the French Embassy questioned critical reporting on North Africa, was never published because Rous's own protest had arrived first.[40] But his letters were published on other occasions, as when he argued to *The Guardian* in December 1953 (optimistically perhaps) that for many in France, 'the real way to deal with Communists in Western Europe is to solve social and colonial problems and not to throw people into gaol, which has never solved anything'.[41] When North Africa gained prominence in British news, Bourdet became one of the key providers of information, notably for the MCF, as shown by correspondence with its chairman, Brockway, and its secretary, Douglas Rogers, in November 1954.[42] Articles in *France-Observateur* (including René Capitant on Indochina and Gilles Martinet on Algeria) were promptly offered as useful sources of information, although Bourdet also indicated a wider range of publications to his British contacts.

Speaking out against the war in Algeria: Bourdet's editorial contacts, between transnational action and national reflection

When questioned by the police in 1956, Bourdet praised the political analysis of the *New Statesman and Nation* as a model,[43] and in a later letter to Rous, the ability of the *Daily Herald* and *News Chronicle* to connect informed writers and the wider public.[44] But in 1956, it was undoubtedly *Tribune* that was used in *France-Observateur* to argue that French policy in Algeria was damaging to the reputation of France, of French socialism and, by extension, of Europe and European socialism in the rest of the world. In June 1956, *France-Observateur* published sections of *Tribune*'s article 'Will Mollet never learn?', which argued that Mollet's policy would result in 'another Indochina' and considered Bourdet's 'criticisms [to be] no stronger than those frequently made in this country of the British government's policy in Cyprus'.[45] Simultaneously, *Tribune* was focusing on repression in European colonies, notably in Kenya and Cyprus, with the MCF organising a large rally in Trafalgar Square in May.[46] Editorial circulations show a real attempt to form a joined-up front against violations. A photograph of the Cyprus rally featured alongside a long article by Weitz on Algeria in mid-May, and Bevan gave *Tribune* and *France-Observateur* joint copyright of an article on military bases in Singapore, Cyprus, Aden and Gibraltar as part of a wider Western strategy, which argued that denying political and social rights to the people living in these territories was a direct threat to international peace.[47]

Editorial cooperation intensified in the autumn of 1956 over Egypt and Algeria. On 13 September, *France-Observateur* published a double page entitled 'English socialism against the adventure', with articles by Bevan and Crossman, and a piece by Roth. The following day, *Tribune* published Weitz's 'When Socialists become small town jingoes', linking the Suez expedition and the Algerian war.[48] 'Mollet attacks free speech', *Tribune* titled on 5 October, charging in its international section: 'Mollet tries to gag French socialists'. A week later, these statements were relayed to French readers, and the end of *Tribune*'s article calling for socialist resistance 'all over the world', translated in full. *France-Observateur* also noted that Bevan was now Labour's treasurer, with Foot openly talking of a Bevanite strategy. *France-Observateur* concluded that Weitz's contributions to *Tribune* – and Alexander Werth's contributions to *Reynold News* – were 'an important link between the French left and the English left. Trying to suppress it is either cynical or stupid'.[49] The following day, *Tribune* quoted Bourdet in *France-Observateur*: 'I hope for a Socialist recovery – but I no longer believe that it can be done except by the elimination of Mollet and his blind supporters'.[50] With the arrest of the FLN leaders on 22 October, *France-Observateur* noted criticism by *The Economist* and *The Times*, but *Tribune* remained its prime contact.[51] On 2 and 9 November, Bourdet was published in *Tribune*. 'The Mollet machine,' he argued, in terms he knew the left and right of Labour would appreciate, 'based on bureaucrats who have no other political idea than anti-Communism, and supported by a large majority of card-carriers can effectively stifle the voice of the real militants'.[52] 'Whether Mollet realises it or not,' Bourdet continued, 'the generals and some of the Ministers are plotting to use general war against the Arabs as a means of establishing a dictatorship in France.' This meant that 'the best hopes' of preventing undemocratic trends abroad and at home was for British Labour to realise that it benefited from 'a huge wave of sympathy and admiration inside the French Left' and 'make things gradually uneasy for Mollet'.[53] In a further piece in *France-Observateur*, Roth claimed that Mollet's policy in Suez and Algeria had united Labour against him.[54] As Claude Estier put it, Labour delegates to the Socialist International, Hugh Gaitskell, Morgan Phillips and Sam Watson, were far from being 'extremists' and all three had supported German rearmament. But all three considered that Mollet was being helped by the French right to conduct un-socialist policies.[55]

The decision of the SFIO leadership in December 1956 to suspend Weitz, following his article of 14 September in *Tribune*, only encouraged the paper's critical stance. Foot, Weitz noted in *France-Observateur*, had called the Suez expedition 'a crime against the world' – which Weitz translated as 'crime against humanity', thereby undoubtedly adding to the discontent of SFIO leaders.[56] Given the use of censorship in several British territories, including Kenya, Weitz's picture of British press freedom was overly positive. But personal correspondence nonetheless confirms that left-wing publications in Britain were seen as useful channels, for British anticolonialists to provide an international perspective to their readers, and for French militants to denounce French and SFIO policy in Algeria to a wider audience, intensifying international pressure. On 4 January 1957, Basil Davidson published in *Tribune* what

France-Observateur described the following week, as it gave Davidson its front page, as 'the most scathing attack ever launched by a socialist publication against Guy Mollet'. For *Tribune* to publish this, the French editorial team added, 'a large majority of Labour militants [must] share the opinion of Basil Davidson'.[57] The article was very much Davidson's, but the material had in fact been partly provided by Bourdet at Davidson's request in mid-October.[58] Perhaps in recognition of this, Davidson wrote to Bourdet on the day of publication, pleased at such a 'broadside' against Mollet.[59] Because it was identified as one of the major motives behind the Suez expedition, French policy in Algeria was given greater scrutiny in British anticolonial circles. The UDC asked Bourdet for a pamphlet, because after Suez 'we feel it is very important for the public of this country to understand the type of policy with which the British government is aligning itself'.[60] While Bourdet had no time to write it himself, he sent the MCF and the UDC a wide range of documentation,[61] from Pierre Henri Simon's *Contre la torture* to newspaper clippings, journals and a letter from the dean of the law faculty in Algiers, Jacques Peyrega, after the death in custody of his former student Ali Boumendjel.[62] Bourdet clarified the context of these publications, the politics and influence of the authors in France (*Témoignage Chrétien*, for instance, had a circulation of 80,000–90,000, was politically liberal but 'strictly Catholic' in all other matters and had been able, unlike *France-Observateur*, to publish long extracts of a Catholic pamphlet against torture in Algeria without censorship).[63]

Contacts stimulated plans for a fairer international order. Davidson, who spent time in Paris, was also interested in socialist plans for a neutral belt in Europe,[64] and put Bourdet in touch with Labour MP Barbara Castle (although there is no evidence that she produced an article for *France-Observateur*).[65] Bourdet was not always the main point of contact. He put Michael Scott of the Africa Bureau in touch with Robert Barrat in May 1957, ahead of Scott's visit to Paris.[66] But it was Robert Barrat who forwarded Brockway's plans for peace in Israel, based on the recognition of the armistice border of 1948 as the condition to all negotiations,[67] and Brockway himself gained many of his insights into French politics from Pivert. But when the group of young socialists around Raphael Samuel formed the *Universities and Left Review* (ULR) after the Soviet repression in Central Europe in 1956, which depleted the British Communist Party, and the imperialist venture of Suez, Bourdet appealed to those wanting 'to recruit students and dons to the Labour Party', while 'stimulat[ing] socialist thought at the University'. *Esprit* was mentioned, but as Stuart Hall later recalled of his time in the first new left, Bourdet 'personified the attempt, after the war, to open a "third way" in European politics'.[68]

The circulation of press articles across the Channel was facilitated by personal visits and public events, advertised beyond left-wing circles. When Bourdet spoke at the ULR Club at the Royal Hotel in Woburn Place in central London in April 1957, *The Guardian* drew attention to it.[69] In its publicity material, ULR noted that Bourdet would speak in English and 'give many details on the repression in Algeria, on the character of the anti-colonial movement in France and on the effect of the war on the French left-wing parties – details not otherwise available in England'.[70] Other ULR speakers in April–June, at meetings which gathered 150–600 people,[71] included the British academics E. P. Thompson (who had left the British Communist Party in 1956) and Eric Hobsbawm (who had not), as well as Doris Lessing and Basil Davidson.[72] While there is no estimation of numbers for the meeting with Bourdet, the secretary of the Harrow West Constituency Labour Party still remembered the 'privilege' of attending it a year later,[73] and Samuel wrote of a 'splendid meeting', telling Bourdet 'it was an indication of the rebirth of internationalism in Britain that people found your meeting so helpful and so moving'.[74] By then, Bourdet was already in touch with the Cambridge University Labour Club, but the ULR conference triggered the interest of the director of extra-mural studies at the University of Glasgow, and of the Oxford Majlis, who invited Bourdet in conjunction with the Oxford Socialist Club.[75] Samuel also started planning ULR lectures in seven university towns, to coincide with Bourdet's attendance of the International Society for Socialist Studies meeting organised by G. D. H. Cole after the summer. There was particular interest from Nottingham, with Pat Jordan liaising with the ULR; Birmingham, with the cooperation of the Birmingham and District Council for African Affairs and the support of Labour MP Tony Benn; Hull, with the involvement of the university's Labour Society and local Labour Party; and Liverpool, with the input of Stan Rushton, who like Jordan had left the Communist Party in 1956.[76] The Liverpool meeting, held on 22 November 1957, was advertised on the front page of the local paper, with Bourdet sharing the platform with UDC's Mervyn Jones.[77]

In the short term, Bourdet's conference at Woburn Place was seized by the MCF to collect signatures for a protest letter to Guy Mollet.[78] On 2 May, *France-Observateur* published a facsimile of *Tribune*'s anti-Mollet front page, while the same issue of *Tribune* gave harrowing extracts from *Des rappelés témoignent*, in which young Frenchmen recalled for military service wrote of the abuses they had witnessed or perpetrated.[79] Labour's *Daily Herald* also published some of the French soldiers' letters and criticised the fact that *France-Observateur* had been seized for printing them.[80] Foot denounced censorship as part of 'The Mollet touch' on 4 May,[81] and on 9 May *France-Observateur* published his 'What is Mollet afraid of?'

For Foot, introduced to French readers as a British MP and editor of *Tribune*, *France-Observateur* was being attacked for publishing the truth. His conclusion was brutal: even if Mollet could temporarily hinder Algerian nationalism and enforce party discipline, he would 'never manage to kill socialist faith in freedom, and particularly in the freedom of the press without which all other freedoms would be derisory'.[82] The next day, Bourdet dominated *Tribune*'s front page, with the title: 'I attack Mollet's methods – then he throws me in jail!' 'Our best defence', *Tribune*'s readers were told, 'is the wave of protests coming from abroad, especially from Britain'.[83]

The views of Foot, Davidson and others in the left-wing press were not, however, dominant in Labour. Bevan's support for the SFIO minority on Algeria created a near diplomatic incident at the Toulouse Congress in June 1957,[84] but overall, the Labour leadership remained cautious. When Bourdet was arrested again in April 1957, Foot's hope 'to see Sir William Haley [*The Times*'s editor] and the Labour Party joining to protest against this menacing attack on freedom'[85] remained unfulfilled. The formation of ULR was a promising development, particularly given the involvement of the Jamaican-born Stuart Hall, whom Bourdet and Weitz had previously met in Paris, and ULR's interest in 'more theoretical material on the economic background to the current struggle, and more material on the sociology of the French colonists', with Samuel specifically requesting issues of *Présence africaine*.[86] And yet Bourdet was struck by the absence of major political figures – there was no Bevan, no Foot. He was also aware that Bevan's interest in Algeria was limited. The Labour Party Conference in Brighton on 30 September–3 October 1957 partly confirmed this. Bourdet was a guest speaker at the *Tribune* and the MCF and ULR meetings on 1 and 2 October, the first time he had attended the party conference since 1954. His friend Mikardo had given him advance notice, stressing that the 'Labour movement here is in desperate need of a bit of information and education about what's happening in France and what's happening in Algeria'.[87] As Bourdet told his audience, and wrote subsequently in *Tribune*, the violations at the heart of France's Algeria policy and the resulting damage to domestic institutions, were 'not only *our* business, but also *yours*. . . . each country's policy affects the other'. But active pressure, he stressed,

> must be a constant pressure, and not only a few short editorials. It must come from the rank and file as well as from the Executive. The British reluctance to be seen meddling in other people's affairs should be discarded here. After all, this is an international problem – and what is Socialism if it is not international Socialism?[88]

Bevan himself had been discussing the contradictions between international socialism and the European project, which he saw as 'an escapist conception in which the play of market forces will take the place of political responsibility'.[89] Bourdet was therefore hoping for a conversation with him during the Congress, even more so after Bevan stunned his audience by opposing a motion on unilateral nuclear disarmament, arguing that without proper plans in place, it would create a diplomatic shambles and increase international instability. Why, Bourdet asked Bevan over lunch, had he allowed nuclear issues, however important they were, to dominate, when they were likely to lead to passionate – rather than constructive – debates?[90] Bourdet does not recount what answer he got from Bevan, who never answered (either?) a list of questions which Bourdet forwarded in early October via Foot, hoping to print an interview in *France-Observateur*.[91] Bourdet's request to Barbara Castle to intercede, specifying that Bevan could ignore some questions and answer concisely, also failed to deliver.[92]

If time constraints played a part in Bevan's silence, he had also begun to give exclusivity to *L'Express* – with a major interview published in February 1957 – after pressure from the editors.[93] Until then, K. S. Karol, *L'Express*'s London correspondent who helped arrange Bevan's personal trips to France – avoiding the French SFIO members Bevan disliked – had acted as a contact for both French papers.[94] He too spoke at a ULR meeting at the Left Book Centre in Soho on 1 May 1957, on 'France in crisis', attended by Mohamed Kellou of the small FLN London bureau and a member of the Muslim Committee for Algeria formed in 1956.[95] Ahead of the Labour conference, Bourdet had written to Foot to make the case for *France-Observateur*. Even though *L'Express* was also critical of Mollet's policies, Bourdet explained, only *France-Observateur* was 'consistently anti-capitalist' and, more importantly, supported ending, rather than merely reforming, the empire.[96] Bourdet's arguments, and reminder that they had been the first to publish Keep Left literature in translation, failed. But Bourdet's reservations about Bevan were voiced in *France-Observateur* even *before* his interview questions were left unanswered. In their Labour Conference report, 'Is Bevan still a Bevanite?', Bourdet and Roth criticised Bevan's abandonment of unilateral disarmament as political opportunism. In *Tribune*, Bourdet saw Bevan 'much more like a statesman than a polemist' and noted that his audience 'responded well to his restraint and gravity'. But in *France-Observateur*, Bourdet and Roth concluded that his stand was tactically wrong, because grassroots voters were unlikely to follow him, and because he had no intellectually matured theoretical or practical plan to offer instead.[97] There is no evidence that this upset Bevan, but Bourdet was aware of the potential impact of questioning Bevan's faithfulness. Writing to Castle the next day, he stressed that he wanted

> to force Nye to bring out with your help (or to support) some really worked-out proposals for a positive foreign policy. On the Middle East and Germany for instance, the Executive's proposals are rather vague and sheepish (although the intentions are good) like what used to come out of the SFIO before it became national-socialist.[98]

The decision of the Labour executive not to send any observer to the first Congress of Bourdet's *Union de la gauche socialiste* (UGS) in December 1957 was an additional disappointment. As he wrote to his friend Mikardo, he read UGS delegates private letters of support from British MPs 'to prevent disgust' against Labour – a strong term, clearly heartfelt.

Intersecting circles of friends: a decreasing place for Europe?

In its issue of 10 October 1957, *France-Observateur* included a roundtable of foreign correspondents: 'Les Français acceptent-ils la guerre d'Algérie?' The panel consisted of Luthar Ruehl of *Die Spiegel*, R. Kornecki of Warsaw's *Tribuna Ludu*, Kamalesh Banerji of *Amrita Bazaar Patrika*, George Williamson of *The Wall Street Journal* and, representing the British press, Nora Beloff of *The Observer*. While Beloff was an obvious choice as the Paris-based correspondent of a nuanced paper, the round table also reflected the internationalisation of the war, the increasingly effective diplomacy of the FLN and mounting critical reporting in the foreign press. By the spring of 1958, the Anglo-American good offices mission after the French bombing of Sakiet made the headlines, while the high-profile trial of the young FLN militant Djamila Bouhired led to public and private appeals from Britons. A turning point for Bourdet seems to have been the publication of an article in *The Economist* on 19 April 1958, which *France-Observateur* reproduced in part the following week. The article was important, French readers were told, because the conservative *Economist*, which 'reflected the views of most of the City, the Foreign Office and the Conservative Party, and influenced these circles and this party', 'now joined and perhaps outdid' the Labour press, the *Manchester Guardian* and *The Observer* 'in its condemnation of France's aberration'.[99] Written after the French National Assembly had rejected Tunisia's Habib Bourguiba offer to mediate, the *Economist* article concluded (and *France-Observateur* reprinted):

As time passes, the chances increase of either a right-wing *coup* or a 'popular front' which would admit the Communists to a share of the power. The Americans have sown money and gathered abuse, without securing any progress towards a solution. What France needs is not gentle persuasion and dollar anaesthetics. It needs the dream to be broken.[100]

, Less than a month later, the coup launched in Algiers by the supporters of a 'French Algeria' raised fears of a military dictatorship in France and Algeria, including with the return to power of General Charles de Gaulle. The details of the coup, and reactions to it in Britain have been studied elsewhere.[101] What is of interest here is how the circulation of articles across the left-wing press in France and Britain shows the tensions between international solidarities, common concerns in managing the end of the European colonial empires, and the strategic, pragmatic need to take national specificities into account. On 29 May, *France-Observateur* published long extracts from *The Daily Herald*'s reports of 17–27 May, which emphasised the dangers posed by the return of de Gaulle and the fears that he might support the military rebels in Algiers.[102] In early July, *Tribune* printed an article by Claude Roy, which the authorities had censored in *France-Observateur* and which argued that only a popular front could repeal the threat of fascism in France, concluding: 'our choice does not lie between the guillotine of Algiers and the gallows of Budapest'.[103] The issue featured an interview with the FLN leader Krim Belkacem, first given to *L'Express*, and an article on die-hard officers in Algeria. *Tribune* remained a key ally, but *France-Observateur* showed that criticism came from across the political spectrum, with a series of translated pieces about de Gaulle's visits to Algeria from *The Guardian*, *The Times* and *The Spectator*.[104] The selection process tended to stress misgivings, consciously or not. *The Times*'s article, for instance, was less critical than suggested, with the paper waiting to see the results of the tour.[105] But there was certainly a wider press interest in the events taking shape in France, notably de Gaulle's speech on 4 September to introduce the new constitution of the Fifth Republic, on which France and its empire would vote on 28 September, and the anti-Gaullist marches that accompanied it. Bourdet would also have been aware of other limits: E.P. Thompson, for instance, assured him that his article for the *New Reasoner* was well received but acknowledged its small circulation.[106] In *France-Observateur*, other outlets were highlighted: *The Observer*, which noted that de Gaulle's enthusiastic audience on 4 September was carefully selected; BBC and *Daily Telegraph* correspondents, who faced police brutality in Paris; and the thoroughness of Italian – rather than British – reporting was appreciated.[107]

Simultaneously, some editing became more influenced by national priorities during the May crisis. The passages edited out of Bevan's *Tribune* article ('De Gaulle') for *France-Observateur* are a case in point. The first two major omissions concerned de Gaulle's 'pompous arrogance so egocentric and so blind, that it is hard to believe that the French people will turn to him even in their present extremity'; and more significantly perhaps, Bevan's direct reference to the threat of 'civil war'.[108] The second set of omissions concerned the similarities and complexities of colonies of settlement. 'In what way and at what pace can the colonial powers adjust themselves to the demands of subject peoples for liberty and national independence?', Bevan asked in *Tribune*, stressing constraints posed by 'emotional overtones', 'racial animosities' and 'property interests' in all settler colonies – Algeria, Kenya, Northern Rhodesia and Nyasaland. Several reasons could explain the omissions. First, space: the focus was the immediate crisis, not a wider discussion of colonial policy and its intricacies. On de Gaulle, despite his misgivings, Bourdet gave his international audience a more nuanced picture than what Bevan had offered. De Gaulle, he wrote in *Africa South*, 'is more realistic than the Socialist politicians, and . . . understands that the hour of independence of the North African peoples has sounded'.[109] At the 'Cry Europe' meeting organised by the ULR Club on 14 July 1958 at St Pancras Town Hall, Bourdet argued that de Gaulle was not a fascist but 'a man of the seventeenth century, an autocrat who has just taught himself democracy, as a person might teach himself mathematics when he is old'.[110] Also absent from *France-Observateur*'s version of Bevan's article was the important disclaimer that '[t]here is no justification for smug self-righteousness on the part of the British people as they hear the news from France. Cyprus, Malta, Kenya all point in the same direction, and pose the same problem.' Consequently, French readers were not aware that Bevan claimed no superiority, nor were they encouraged to think about the broader picture of violence and repression across the European empires. This might have been to maintain attention on the unparalleled dangers posed to French democracy. But it also showed that events in Britain's colonial territories – Cyprus, Malaysia, Malta and Oman – and South Africa only featured occasionally in *France-Observateur*. This does not mean that Bourdet was not involved. He corresponded with leading figures against apartheid, including Michael Scott and the South African unionist Solly Sachs, exiled in Britain since 1953 and who had met Bourdet in Paris, with Audrey Jupp of the UDC a common acquaintance. Bourdet had in fact hoped that on apartheid, Sachs could produce an article 'stressing the analogies and differences (of course, as far as you are acquainted with it) with the situation in North Africa, with some photos and about 3,000 words length'.[111] As mentioned above, Bourdet contributed to *Africa South*, the journal edited by the South African Ronald Segal, also in exile in Britain since 1953, and produced a detailed assessment of the impact of the Algerian war on both global and French politics.[112]

Socialist solidarities should also be considered in the light of other networks, with which they intersected. On Algeria, Bourdet corresponded with the Society of Friends. In 1955, he was contacted by Eric Baker, the general secretary of the National Peace Council in London, which had the support of the Quakers and several churches,[113] and by Earlham College in late 1956, to talk about Algeria to US students enrolled on a Study in France programme.[114] But on refugee relief, the contacts of British Friends were primarily the Moroccan and Tunisian Embassies in London, and various delegations at the United Nations through the American Friends Service Council Conference for Diplomats. In December 1957, Charles Read and George Whiteman of Friends House met Mohamed Kellou, the FLN's representative in London, to discuss ways of assisting the Red Crescent's work in Tunisia.[115] Thanks to US Quaker Howard Reed, contacts were made with Cecil Hourani, Bourguiba's personal assistant, while the British Quaker Horace Alexander facilitated access to Tayeb Slim, the Tunisian ambassador in London.[116] A friend of the late Mahatma Gandhi, Alexander had been involved in negotiations for India's independence after 1945 and was in India as an observer at the time of partition, taking a particular interest in the plight of refugees.[117] British Quakers were also in close contact with Oxfam, particularly after the creation of the UK Committee for Algerian Refugees in 1959.[118]

Much of the important information on Algeria came to British Friends from their American counterparts. But here again, the importance of Bourdet surfaces, as a direct contact for American Friends, who then passed on, commented and interpreted his thoughts back to Friends House in London. Proof of the importance Bourdet gave Quaker networks, one of the longest letters found in his correspondence in English was addressed to the American Friends Service Committee in the spring of 1957.[119] In 1954, Bourdet had spoken to various Quaker groups on the war in Indochina and now wrote them 'a very grave letter and one which, I hope will shock you, and shock you into action'. The war in Algeria, he argued as he sent the same French documentation he forwarded the MCF and ULR, was 'much worse' than Indochina:

> It is worse because the amount of horror is greater; it is worse because the morale of the French people is being very rapidly corrupted; how deeply you will, I am afraid, witness before many years go by; it is also

worse because although the problem <u>ought to be</u> easier to solve, the outlooks for a peaceful settlement are in fact, worse.

Bourdet emphasised 'the general use of tortures and mass murder by the French Army' as the worst aspect of a war waged 'with the feeling that the nationalists must be eradicated and the clock of history turned back' – a war in which Algerian nationalists were still being called 'rebels' or 'terrorists'. American inaction, for Bourdet, was due to the absence of any real Communist threat in North Africa, but the threat would become real if the war led Soviet Russia to become involved. An American reaction, therefore, and a Quaker reaction against the corruption of young soldiers 'taken in a kind of moral trap and begin[ning] to accept what used to disgust them', was crucial. No hope would come from the SFIO. 'More than anything else', Bourdet wrote, 'they fear being called "unpatriotic" as your soft-Liberals feared being called unamerican'.

In Paris, Bourdet was in regular contact with Wolf Mendl, the Quaker International Affairs Representative (QIAR), discussing the plight of refugees in May 1959[120] and international affairs more generally.[121] Overall, Mendl found it easier to liaise with foreign diplomats and men like Bourdet than with the French Foreign Office, and valued the information he was able to obtain.[122] Mendl was not Bourdet's only contact. Josephine Noble, who managed the British Quaker small relief programme for North Africa from 1960, also knew Bourdet from her time working at the Friends International Centre in Paris after 1945. In 1957, she had participated in the silent anti-war demonstration he organised in Paris, attended a large information meeting in Ivry,[123] and the general assembly of the Fellowship of Reconciliation, held at the home of pacifists André and Magda Trocmé near Versailles. Bourdet was not systematically asked to speak on Algeria. When Noble invited him to address a weekly meeting of young diplomats and civil servants in Paris, she asked him to avoid the topic, after it had 'provoked rather regrettable reactions' at a recent meeting on 'Black Africa'.[124] But Mendl does appear to have been a central intermediary with British Friends, as an interpreter of both the French and the French new left. After his conversation with Bourdet in March 1960, he wrote a long letter to British Friends about his 'concern to lay this, the only "major war" in the world, upon the conscience of Friends'. Mendl did not 'necessarily shar[e] Claude's political approach', found him 'a little bit too dogmatic', with 'a Frenchman's capacity to tie up everything very neatly into a logical package, without loose ends and imponderables trailing around'; but he also thought him 'an honest, fearless man and a natural fighter'. It was therefore 'quite certain', in Mendl's view, 'that he is extremely well informed and that when his immediate propaganda zeal is not involved, his judgment is very good'. His conclusion was that on Algeria, he had 'an excellent grasp of the problem'. British Friends learnt from Mendl that Bourdet had told Castle that the FLN had already made a number of 'very substantial concessions' and that any negotiation plans that entailed more concessions was bound to fail.[125] After lunching with Bourdet in November 1960, Mendl further told Alun Davies and Jo Noble in Britain that it was dangerous for the West to underplay the importance of the FLN, with negotiations the only road to peace.[126] Another critical observer for Mendl was Robert Barrat, who shared these concerns. 'Both these conversations', he wrote to British Friends, 'were with men of the left who are extremely critical of de Gaulle. We must therefore take their judgment with some reserve, yet it would be foolish to overlook them.'[127] The later stages of the war shifted dynamics somewhat, with British Quakers investigating community development projects in North Africa from March 1961, rather than simply relief work.[128] By the time independence was celebrated in July 1962, Quaker plans in Algeria focused on cooperation with the Norwegian Friends, through the European Yearly Meetings. By September 1962, the presence of a QIAR for Paris was considered less important, because of direct contacts among European Quakers in North Africa, and given the availability of the American Centre Director, Louise H. Wood, to represent Friends at UNESCO.[129]

In parallel, anticolonial work focused on contacts and insights from outside Europe. Davidson needed Bourdet to enlighten him on French politics, but had had his own access to Ahmed Ben Bella for an interview in 1955.[130] In the autumn of 1957, Bourdet asked Mikardo for an article on Algeria for *France-Observateur*: 'not a technical paper but the sort of crude expostulation which a British Socialist would thunder out at the meeting of a World People Assembly if there was such a thing'.[131] The resulting article, published in late November, was entitled 'The Algerian war seen from Africa', following Mikardo's visit to Ghana and Nigeria.[132] For Mikardo, whose concerns also included South Africa, British East and Central Africa, Algeria was the litmus test for the application of universal suffrage, and a source of 'doubts, reservations, suspicions, in the minds of Africans' about any free and equal partnership with Europe. 'French repression in Algeria', Mikardo concluded, 'is not only morally indefensible and politically stupid in itself: it also causes criminal damage to all interracial cooperation'. His expostulation was rooted not so much in Labour discussions but in his conversations with Africans in Africa. He was inevitably the *European* mouthpiece for such views, but the intention was clearly to convince Europeans of all political shades to mark the shifts in Africa and acknowledge African agency. In *Africa South*, comments on Algeria still came predominantly from British or European or white contributors – Colin Legum, Tony Benn, Catherine Hoskins, Robert Barrat and Bourdet himself – but they emphasised their experience of pan-African conferences, in Accra in 1958 and Tunis in 1960.[133] European rights activists extended relations and developed new contacts outside their own national spheres.[134] Post-Bandung and post-Accra, they were also increasingly only one component of the global liberation networks of African militants, and altogether bypassed at times.[135]

The travails of an alternative European socialist movement: political conceptions and practical limits

From late 1958, Bourdet's relations with the Labour Party suffered from a series of strategic and political differences. First was Labour's refusal to send observers to the congresses of Bourdet's UGS and, after 1960, the newly formed *Parti socialiste unifié* (PSU).[136] Labour criticised the SFIO but made no serious move to have it suspended from the Socialist International, or to sponsor the other French (and European) socialist parties that were not already members. This was partly due to the fundamental difference highlighted by André Philip in *France-Observateur* between Catholic countries, notably France and Italy, where 'the party has become a Church with its dogmas, rites and, above all its fellowship of brothers'; and Protestant countries, which preferred 'an action-group party', bringing together 'the most different philosophical and religious opinions'.[137] Secondly, Labour's defeat in the general election of 1959 was a practical blow to the hopes of renewing socialism in Europe. A survey by Stuart Hall and Andrew Roth, 'Can Labourism renew itself?', was published in *France-Observateur*, which also reprinted one of Bevan's articles from *News of the World*. Bevan's suggestion that defeat was due to the relative economic satisfaction of the under-30s and to general political timidity gave limited hope for the future.[138] Third, the obituary written by Bourdet in *France-Observateur* after Bevan died in July 1960 caused a major rift with Foot. Bourdet suggested that Bevan's interest in international affairs came from domestic concerns and that Bevan 'did not consider himself in the least to be the leader of a world political trend'. His impact on the French new left was not minimised but Bourdet also wrote of an individualistic man who disliked contradiction, theory and method, and who had given Labour no 'complete political doctrine'.[139] What Bevan had nonetheless achieved, was to give enough Labour members the 'courage' to reflect on socialist principles, particularly the young people and the academics around the *New Left Review* (*NLR*), which merged *Universities and Left Review* and *New Reasoner* in 1960.

Bourdet was a sponsor of the *NLR* and knew the editorial team well, particularly Ralph Samuel, Stuart Hall and E.P. Thompson. He spoke at its launch in London in late 1959[140] and publicised it in both *France-Observateur* and *Tribune des peuples*. Writing to Bourdet in November 1961, Samuel spoke of plans to 'internationalise the journal', beginning with 'a full historical and theoretical and detailed discussion of the evolution of Asia, Africa and Latin America', and taking *France-Observateur*, which had changed formats, as a model to give more space to international questions. Samuel also spoke of the change as 'a "European" turn (though not less strongly against the half Europe of the EEC), so that we want to give much more space to articles and material from the continent'.[141] Or as he put it to *ULR*'s contributor Michael Barrat Brown, the objective was that 'Africa and Asia stopped being seen as "colonial" subjects, and America only as the heartland of NATO'.[142] This was not, however, entirely new and several *NLR* members had more radical objectives. For Peter Worsley, reviewing Davidson's *Old Africa Rediscovered* in the first issue of *NLR* in early 1960, 'we can no longer do with a "world" history focussed only on a few European countries. . . . We cannot be satisfied that an intimate knowledge of French or German culture provides an adequate corrective to the notion of the superiority of Western Europe'.[143] History such as Davidson's, he argued, should be part of the British school curriculum, particularly after Suez and the racist violence at Notting Hill. For Perry Anderson, a truly international perspective had methodological implications: as 'any account of a colonial area is one account of the metropolitan country', societies and economies could not be treated interchangeably, and a comparative perspective was essential.[144] There was therefore a conscious attempt to 'translate' national circumstances to a broader audience in the *NLR*, but also in publications like *Africa South*, with Bourdet writing explicitly for 'the British reader' and 'anglo-saxon minds'.[145] This was not a specific call for a transnational or world movement, but an endeavour to analyse a national (French) situation to a national (British) public. By including a self-critical reflection on (anti-)colonialism, these editorial adaptations formed part of the incomplete but significant 'epistemic reversal' described by Christoph Kalter as characteristic of a New Radical Left.[146]

At the turn of the 1960s, Bourdet remained a frequent speaker in Britain, on a wide range of topics rooted in his quest for peace and opposition to colonialism. He was an active supporter of the Campaign for Nuclear Disarmament (CND), formed in 1958, and spoke at a CND conference in Manchester in May 1960, alongside the Soviet writer Ilya Ehrenburg, the German theologian Heinz Kloppenburg and the Labour MPs Will Griffiths and Konni Zilliacus. He also joined a CND meeting in

London in June, with Canon L. John Collins, J. B. Priestley and, again, Ehrenburg.[147] He continued to address students clubs and was involved in getting support for young Frenchmen who had refused to serve in Algeria and gone to Britain.[148] He was on the platform of the 'Stop the War' meeting organised by Tony Benn in central London on 24 June 1960. He spoke to the British media on regular occasions, although he did not always find the questions well informed.[149] He was on the radio in January and May 1961,[150] on ITV in December 1961, spoke on the situation in France in London in February 1962,[151] and participated in the BBC's special programme on de Gaulle in June 1962, which also debated the General's place in the resistance and his immediate post-war career.[152]

Back in 1958, Thompson had suggested to Bourdet that

> if we are to educate public opinion in the direction of policies which break decisively with the whole NATO concept, it is of the utmost importance that we should discuss this question not as Englishmen but as Europeans. Are these opportunities for working towards a European 'Bandung'? . . . Can we link the cause of peace with a new vision of a socialist community of nations in Europe?[153]

By early 1961, plans were in place for a conference to be held in English and French in London on the main theme of NATO and neutralism, 'the occasion – the first for some years – for an exchange of information and views about the reconstruction of the socialist movement in Europe'.[154] People, rather than parties, would be invited from France, Germany, Italy, Switzerland and Yugoslavia; Spanish democrats in exile would also be represented. With Mervyn Jones's contribution, invitations were officially issued by Stuart Hall and E.P. Thompson of *NLR*, Richard Clements of *Tribune*, Nigel Harris of the National Association of Labour Student Organisations, John Horner of the Fire Brigades Union, Bert (H. W.) Wynn of the National Union of Mineworkers, and Professors Ritchie Calder (International Relations, Edinburgh) and Kenneth Muir (Literature, Liverpool). The suggested agenda had four themes: the rebuilding of European socialism; the Cold War and the division of Europe; Socialist perspectives for Europe; and practical proposals for future cooperation. Delegates would have their expenses in London covered, and Bourdet was enlisted by Samuel to help stimulate interest.[155] Bourdet had earlier liaised with Zilliacus and the Italian Socialist Party of Pietro Nenni on a European workshop with the British and German left, and with Jo Richardson, then secretary of the East-West Round Table Conference in early 1960.[156] He encouraged the Belgian Marxist Ernest Mandel to attend, to reinforce the intellectual, theoretical and technical endeavours of the *NLR*,[157] and advertised it with the PSU and the non-Communist left in

France.[158] A few days before it was due to open, the conference was cancelled as several people pulled out, including Marten Lange and Gerhard Gleißberg from *Die Andere Zeitung* in Hamburg, due to parliamentary and electoral events. As Samuel conceded, it 'seemed wiser not to hold a conference with inadequate representation'.[159]

The failure of the conference may account for Bourdet's uncharacteristically positive view of Britain's application to the EEC in late July, which he described as 'perhaps the last chance to avoid sclerosis', despite his strong reservations and his prescient belief that de Gaulle was 'the number one obstacle' to British membership.[160] Britain and Scandinavia had 'a role of progress and mediation' to play, and Scandinavia featured regularly in his correspondence with Zilliacus, who was fluent in Swedish and liaised with the socialist parties there, in a bid to protect the European Free Trade Association (EFTA) ('minus Portugal!',[161] as Zilliacus specified) and Commonwealth connections.[162] But Bourdet did not think that the European Free Trade Association, formed in January 1960, could realistically become a neutral force, even if Yugoslavia ever joined.[163] British membership of the EEC, by contrast, could help counter Franco-German militarism and German economic domination.[164] His view may also have rested on the comparatively positive assessment he made of British attitudes to end-of-empire affairs. Labour's record on colonial policy, Bourdet told Mikardo in 1957, was 'not so bad',[165] and he was also impressed by the Devlin Report of July 1959, which admitted the existence of a 'police state' in Nyasaland after mass arrests and deaths had made the headlines in March, and which demonstrated that repressing nationalism led to cyclical violence. Every *France-Observateur* reader who knew English, Bourdet concluded, should read the report.[166] Bourdet, Jones told him in early 1960, was 'too optimistic in [his] picture of the Labour Party'.[167] But by the summer of 1961, Bourdet's assessment also came from broader international developments, including the departure of South Africa from an expanding Commonwealth of newly independent countries, with Roth penning an article in *France-Observateur* in March.[168] South Africa's 'expulsion', Stuart Hall and Perry Anderson argued, reflected 'the reciprocal communication of new mental and political attitudes back on Britain through the mediation of African and Asian states'.[169] But this, for them, was an additional reason to oppose EEC membership, as the combination of EFTA and Commonwealth circles 'could precipitate precisely the kind of transition of feeling and attitudes in this country upon which a genuine inter-nationalism, viable for the Seventies and Eighties, could be based'.[170] This meant using *British* specificities and staying out of the EEC, at the very least to 'make economic sense of our Commonwealth and EFTA ties' or, more radically, to forge 'a close alliance with, not merely

Europe's neutrals and the Commonwealth, but the emergent powers too'.[171] What Bourdet continued to share with his anti-EEC acquaintances in Britain was a fundamental ideological opposition to the principle of the common market, and he was invited to the New Left Summer School at Ruskin College in Oxford on socialism in Europe in 1961.[172]

As Bourdet's relations with his co-editor Martinet soured at *France-Observateur* in early 1963, Thompson wrote to his friend: 'not only has FO under your directorship been of the greatest inspiration at critical moments to us, but you personally have done more than any other individual to assist a similar tendency into being over here, to give us confidence and assistance at important junctures.'[173] Thompson himself, for whom internationalism should be 'embedded with the national English context',[174] was finding relations within the new left increasingly tense. He thought Hall too involved in CND, and as for the *NLR*, found its general approach 'over-academic, disengaged and perhaps too much influenced by academic sociology'.[175] But the movement for nuclear disarmament was a concern dear to Bourdet, who helped found the French movement against nuclear armament (*Mouvement contre l'armement atomique*) the same month, a 'CND-type organization'.[176] His resignation from *France-Observateur* was lamented by CND members,[177] even though he continued to exchange information with conscientious objector Tony Smythe of the War Resisters' International. As Benn campaigned for re-election in his Bristol constituency in 1963, he too asked Bourdet for a few sentences on 'the things that you would like to see Britain do at the United Nations and in international affairs' so that he could 'use these, as quotations or texts' in his own speeches.[178] Benn also asked others – friends 'in India, Kenya, New Zealand, Yugoslavia, France, the USA, the Soviet Union, Italy and Algeria' – but it shows Bourdet's importance nonetheless. On North Africa, Bourdet remained an important source of contacts and information, particularly on the kidnapping of Mehdi Ben Barka, the leader of the left-wing National Union of Popular Forces in Morocco, in 1965.[179] In fact, Bourdet's role was so central that Brockway admitted to him that 'it would be good if we had another voice' (provided they had Bourdet's 'status' and command of English).[180] Bourdet's earlier connections with anticolonial and Quaker circles also meant that by the mid-1960s he was an equally important source of information, commentary and action on Vietnam. Mendl sought Bourdet's advice on North Vietnam in June 1965 and acted as a transmission belt for British Friends with France, with *Le Monde* deemed a better source of information on Vietnam than the British media.[181] In their correspondence of October 1966, Bourdet and Brockway discussed both the trial in the Ben Barka affair and peace efforts in Vietnam, with Bourdet suggesting speakers and contacts to Brockway's British Council for Peace in Vietnam, including the mathematician Laurent Schwartz, engaged against torture in Algeria, for decolonisation and international peace, and now chair of the *Comité de soutien au peuple vietnamien*.

Conclusion

Thanks to Bourdet's Labour contacts and the cooperation of sympathetic editors, particularly Foot at *Tribune*, *France-Observateur* showed that the war in Algeria mattered across the Channel, and that violations should be ended, if the reputation of socialism was to be salvaged. But interests worked both ways. As Stuart Hall put it, Bourdet was a means of 'translation to a wider stage' of the concerns of *New Left Review*.[182] Bourdet's particular appeal, and influence, came from a notoriety that preceded the Algerian war and from two qualities: a broad humanism that chimed with Labour circles but went beyond them; and an internationalist outlook that brought into his address book individuals in Asia, Africa and America – mirroring and complementing Labour's own contacts outside Europe. If a movement is understood as 'working within society to spread information', 'to raise awareness and organise the population as widely as possible',[183] Bourdet undoubtedly played a key role in helping the left of the Labour Party explain (and at times realise) why events in Algeria should matter to Britons, and to British socialists specifically. Political activism rested on a transnational base, which in turn stimulated contacts across the British left. In 1957–58 for instance, Bourdet's selected documentation against torture, for a negotiated peace and independence, was exchanged several times by the UDC, the MCF and the ULR, as they prepared their own publications.[184] Bourdet also connected generations, in ways that older or younger French anticolonial figures could not, even though Bevan's death did deprive *France-Observateur* of a useful commentator and symbol of European socialism that was never quite replaced. But there was no undisputed intention to translate transnational channels into a transnational Franco-British or European movement. In *France-Observateur*, comparisons remained few. Algeria was on occasion used as a reference point, for instance by Roth when discussing Nyasaland in March 1959, or as a means to attract the readers' attention, as in 'The Commonwealth's Algeria', an article on Kenya, the Rhodesias and South Africa, which made no particular mention of Algeria beyond its title.[185] In *Tribune*, or even *NLR*, Algeria was a unique case, matched only by the denunciation of Portuguese colonial rule, led notably by Davidson, while discussions about the wider French empire – including the war in Cameroon – were marginal. What readers thought of the articles exchanged across the Channel is difficult to assess. Discussions were inter-national rather than transnational as such and resulted in no immediate ground-breaking policy change. But the activities studied above did challenge 'Western' European interpretations of events and trends, at the nexus of party and non-party circles, and contested the restrictive geography of the European Six. Ultimately, the core characteristics of Bourdet's British circle of friends gave it its force and its limits: nationally grounded and European, decentring but not quite decentred. But it was, at the very least, significant for the reflection it pursued on the tensions placed by location, place and space on socialist aspirations *and* practice.

Notes

1. Claude Bourdet in Olivier Wieviorka, *'Nous entrerons dans la carrière': de la résistance à l'exercice du pouvoir* (Paris: Seuil, 1994).
2. Paul Barker, 'Obituary of Douglas Johnson', *The Independent*, 30 April 2005.
3. Douglas Johnson, 'Obituary of Claude Bourdet', *The Independent*, 23 March 1996, 20.
4. Its circulation averaged 100,000; Michel Winock, *Le XXe siècle idéologique et politique* (Paris: Perrin, 2013), 440.
5. Véronique Dimier, *The Invention of a European Development Aid Bureaucracy: Recycling Empire* (Basingstoke: Palgrave, 2014); Peo Hansen and Stefan Jonsson, *Eurafrica: The Untold Story of European Integration and Colonialism* (London: Bloomsbury, 2014); Laura Kottos, *Europe between Imperial Decline and Quest for Integration: Pro-European Groups and the French, Belgian and British Empires (1947–1957)* (Brussels: Peter Lang, 2016); Muriam Haleh Davis and Thomas Serres, eds. *North Africa and the Making of Europe: Governance, institutions and culture* (London: Bloomsbury, 2018).
6. Megan Brown, *The Seventh Member State: Algeria, France and the European Community* (Harvard: Harvard University Press, 2022), 105, 140.
7. Christoph Kalter, *The Discovery of the Third World. Decolonization and the Rise of the New Left in France, c. 1950–1976* (Cambridge: Cambridge University Press, 2016).
8. Andrea Brazzoduro, 'Algeria, Antifascism, and Third Worldism: An Anticolonial Genealogy of the Western European New Left (Algeria, France, Italy, 1957–1975)', *Journal of Imperial and Commonwealth History* 48, no. 5 (2020): 960; also Daniel A. Gordon, 'A "Mediterranean New Left"? Comparing and Contrasting the French PSU and the Italian PSIUP', *Contemporary European History* 19, no. 4 (2010).
9. Daniel Gorman, *Uniting the Nations* (Cambridge: Cambridge University Press, 2022), 185.
10. Isabelle Richard, 'The Limits of Solidarity: Europeanism, Anti-colonialism and Socialism at the Congress of the Peoples of Europe, Asia and Africa in Puteaux, 1948', *European Review of History: Revue européenne d'histoire* 21, no. 4 (2014).
11. Quentin Gasteuil, 'A Comparative and Transnational Approach to Socialist Anti-colonialism: The Fenner Brockway-Marceau Pivert connection, 1930s–1950s', in

Workers of the Empire, Unite: Radical and Popular Challenges to British Imperialism, 1910–1960s, ed. Yann Béliard and Neville Kirk (Liverpool: Liverpool University Press, 2021).

12. In Bourdet to G. H. D. Cole, 20 October 1956; Bourdet to Foot, 24 September 1957, Bibliothèque nationale de France, Papers of Claude Bourdet, NAF 28091/46.

13. Nora Beloff, 'Peace pressure grows in France', *The Observer*, 1 April 1956, 1.

14. 'Paris editor detained. Algeria policy resented. Ministry alleges demoralisation', *The Times*, 2 April 1956, 6.

15. 'Tribune Says': 'Stop this war – and free the man who says so', *Tribune*, 6 April 1956, 1.

16. 'Grande-Bretagne: L'arrestation de Claude Bourdet', *France-Observateur*, 5 April 1956.

17. *Nor Lose the Common Touch. The Memoirs of Audrey Jupp*, 1990 (unpublished), p. 366, Hull History Centre, Papers of Audrey Jupp, GB 50 U DJT/5.

18. 'Charges of police brutality in Algeria', *The Guardian*, 15 January 1955, 5. On the use of torture in Algeria, and on the impact of the war on the metropole, there is a rich literature, including Raphaëlle Branche, *La torture et l'armée pendant la guerre d'Algérie* (Paris, Gallimard, 2016 [2001]); Jean-Pierre Rioux and Jean-François Sirinelli eds, *La guerre d'Algérie et les intellectuels français* (Paris: Éditions Complexe, 1991); Thomas Augais, Mireille Hilsum and Chantal Michel, eds. *Écrire et publier la Guerre d'Algérie. De l'urgence aux résurgences* (Paris: Kimé, 2011).

19. 'Torture by France', *Tribune*, 4 February 1955, 4. Douglas Rogers to Bourdet, 17 January 1955, NAF 28091/45. The *New Statesman and Nation* mentioned torture the following month, but less prominently; 'What follows Mr France?', 12 February 1955, 200; no mention was made of Bourdet or *France-Observateur*, contrary to Rogers's hope.

20. In David Hendy, *The BBC: A People's History* (London: Imprint Books, 2022).

21. *Birmingham Gazette*, 15 February 1950, 5.

22. Bourdet to Field, 15 May 1950, NAF 28091/41.

23. See Guillaume Devin, 'L'internationalisme des socialistes', in *La gauche en Europe depuis 1945. Invariants et mutations du socialisme européen*, ed. Marc Lazar (Paris: Presses universitaires de France, 1996).

24. 'Einstein backs world government', *Birmingham Post*, 21 February 1950, 6.

25. 'Your vote and peace', *The Daily Herald*, 23 February 1950, 3.

26. Bourdet to Mikardo, 3 May 1951, NAF 28091/42.

27. Bourdet to J. Cook, Cardiff Labour Party, 25 June 1951; Bourdet to Mikardo, 3 May 1951, NAF 28091/42.

28. Claude Bourdet, 'Bevan', *France-Observateur*, 14 July 1960, 9.

29. Correspondence between Bourdet and Bevan, 15 and 21 October 1953, NAF 28091/42.

30. Bourdet to Thomas Balogh, 24 September 1953, NAF 28091/43.

31. Labour expelled Zilliacus in 1949 for voting against NATO; he was re-admitted in 1952, regaining a Labour seat in 1955.

32. Foot to Bourdet, 6 April 1954, NAF 28091/44.

33. Warbey to Bourdet, 24 August 1954, NAF 28091/44.

34. Claude Bourdet, 'Ne pas aller à Londres', *France-Observateur*, 9 September 1954, 6; 'Scarborough: M. Mendès-France a facilité l'échec de Bevanistes',

France-Observateur, 30 September 1954, 9. Alexander Werth also believed that 'Mendes's gutless, kowtowing interview for US News' had done much damage, although he equally blamed Labour for not supporting Bevan against German rearmament; Werth to Bourdet, 2 October 1954, NAF 28091/44.

35. Claude Bourdet, 'Bevan n'est pas que britannique', *France-Observateur*, 24 March 1955, 8–9.

36. 'Un document capital: Bevan contre la bombe', 10 March 1955; the issue also included two cartoons from the *Daily Mirror*.

37. Roth was *France-Observateur*'s permanent London correspondent by the autumn of 1950 (Bourdet to Ross, 29 November 1950, NAF 28091/40; H. de Galard to Roth, 2 November 1950, Bishopsgate Institute, Roth Papers, ROTH 2/17). It also followed Bourdet's correspondence with the editors of several left-wing and pro-peace publications in the United States (*The Nation*) and Britain (*New Statesman and Nation, Peace News*). Roth was also in contact with Jean Rous of *Franc Tireur* in 1950, on North Africa, Indochina and international affairs, ROTH 2/16.

38. Claude Bourdet, 'Bevan pas coupable', *France-Observateur*, 2 June 1955, 1; Andrew Roth, 'Les Anglais ont voté "constructif"', *France-Observateur*, 2 June 1955, 9.

39. Aneurin Bevan, 'La signification de mon combat', *France-Observateur*, 13 October 1955, 7.

40. Charles Davy to Bourdet, 12 December 1953, NAF 28091/44. Jean Rous, Letter to the editor, 'France and North Africa', *The Observer*, 6 December 1953.

41. Claude Bourdet, Letter to the editors, *The Guardian*, 5 December 1953, 4.

42. Brockway to Bourdet, 10 November 1954; Bourdet to Brockway, 19 November 1954, NAF 28091/44.

43. Report of police questioning, 13 April 1956, NAF 28091/167.

44. Bourdet to Rous, 23 October 1957, NAF 28091/46.

45. Tribune reporter, 'Will Mollet never learn?', *Tribune*, 22 June 1956.

46. 'Cyprus in Trafalgar Square'; Lucien Weitz, 'That French war', *Tribune*, 18 May 1956, 3. See also Fenner Brockway, 'Kenya: they try to extort "confessions"', *Tribune*, 9 March 1956, 1; 'Kenya: here are the facts', *Tribune*, 15 June 1956, 1 and 6–7.

47. Aneurin Bevan, 'La stratégie occidentale est-elle édifiée sur des sables mouvants?', *France-Observateur*, 31 May 1956, 8. This was partly taken from Aneurin Bevan, 'Bases: the plan that failed', *Tribune*, 25 May 1956, 12.

48. Lucien Weitz, 'When Socialists become small town jingoes', *Tribune*, 14 September 1956, p. 10. Weitz's article was the most prominent on the page, with quotes in bold.

49. '"Tribune" commente l'ostracisme des dirigeants de la SFIO', *France-Observateur*, 11 October 1956, 2.

50. Special correspondent, 'French socialists hit back at Mollet's gag policy', *Tribune*, 12 October 1956, p. 3.

51. Andrew Roth, 'Londres: "Les conséquences seront graves"', *France-Observateur*, 1 November 1956, 16 (US condemnation of French action was also noted).

52. Claude Bourdet, 'Labour can unseat Mollet', *Tribune*, 9 November 1956, 3.

53. Bourdet, 'Labour can unseat Mollet'.

54. London correspondent, 'Les travaillistes contre Mollet', *France-Observateur*, 15 November 1956, 2.

55. Claude Estier, 'L'Internationale socialiste aide les minoritaires de la SFIO', *France-Observateur*, 6 December 1956.

56. Lucien Weitz, 'Mon exclusion de la SFIO', *France-Observateur*, 27 December 1956, 5. Michael Foot, 'A crime against the world', *Tribune*, 2 November 1956, 1 (which also featured Weitz's 'France plunges into lunatic policy over North Africa', 5).

57. '"Tribune": Guy Mollet est-il notre camarade?', *France-Observateur*, 10 January 1957, 1, 5.

58. Davidson to Bourdet, 17 October 1956, NAF 28091/46.

59. Davidson to Bourdet, 4 January 1957, NAF 28091/46.

60. Jupp to Bourdet, 6 February 1957, NAF 28091/46.

61. It is difficult to establish how frequently this occurred; correspondence with the MCF and the UDC suggests that several parcels were dispatched in the spring of 1957.

62. See Malika Rahal, *Ali Boumendjel. Une affaire française, une histoire algérienne* (Paris: Belles Lettres, 2010).

63. Jupp to Bourdet, P. Rushton to Bourdet, 2 May 1957, Bourdet to P. Rushton, 20 May 1957, NAF 28091/46.

64. Davidson to Bourdet, 4 January 1957; Bourdet to Davidson, 16 April 1957, NAF 28091/46. Interest was strong as the right of the party, including Gaitskell and his Shadow Defence Secretary Denis Healey, was investigating options preserving Britain's full commitment to NATO. See for instance Gerald Hughes, '"We are not seeking strength for its own sake": The British Labour Party, West Germany and the Cold War, 1951–64', *Cold War History* 3, no. 1 (2002).

65. Bourdet to Castle, 30 May 1957, NAF 28091/46.

66. Bourdet to Scott, 22 May 1957, NAF 28091/46.

67. Barrat to Bourdet (and others), 22 January 1957, NAF 28091/46.

68. Stuart Hall, 'Life and times of the first new left', *New Left Review*, 61, January–February 2010, 178.

69. *The Guardian*, 24 April 1957, 10.

70. Bishopsgate Institute, Papers of Ralph Samuel, RS 1/002.

71. ULR Club to members and subscribers, April 1957, RS 1/002.

72. On E.P. Thompson, and the changing British left after 1956, see Cal Winslow, ed., *E.P. Thompson and the Making of the New Left. Essays and Polemics* (New York: New York University Press, 2014); Evan Smith and Matthew Worley, eds. *Against the Grain: The British Far Left from 1956* (Manchester: Manchester University Press, 2014).

73. Alan Williams to Bourdet, undated, NAF 28091/46.

74. Samuel to Bourdet, undated, NAF 28091/46.

75. Colin Bell to Bourdet, 1 April 1957, W. Lloyd to Bourdet, 30 April 1957, NAF 28091/46; A. Banerjee to Samuel, 30 June 1957, RS 1/004.

76. Also: P. Rushton to Samuel, 8 July 1957; Otley to Samuel, July and December 1957, RS 1/007; Benn to Samuel, 19 August 1957; Jordan to Samuel, 25 August 1957, RS 1/005.

77. *Liverpool Echo*, 19 November 1957, 1; Kenneth Kaunda, Basil Davidson and Doris Lessing were also considered as possible speakers, alongside Bourdet, Sedgwick to Samuel, Sedgwick Papers, 1/1. The Birmingham meeting seems to have taken place during Bourdet's same visit, Knight to Samuel, 16 November 1957, RS 1/007.

78. Rushton to Bourdet, 1 May 1957, NAF 28091/46.

79. Britain was not spared criticism. The paper featured a photograph of Gladwyn Jebb, the British ambassador in Paris, and a quote from his speech on 14 July 1956:

"We are on your side in Algeria. We understand your pride in your civilizing mission . . . we ardently desire the success of your efforts in Algeria." *Tribune*, 2 May 1956.

80. 'A French soldier writes of butchery in the Algerian fighting / Police ban tales of torture', *Daily Herald*, 7 May 1957, 7.

81. Michael Foot, 'The Mollet touch', *Daily Herald*, 3 and 9 May 1957.

82. Michael Foot, 'De quoi Mollet a-t-il peur?', *France-Observateur*, 9 May 1957, 3 (also listed in the table of contents on the front page).

83. Claude Bourdet, 'I attack Mollet's methods – then he throws me in jail', *Tribune*, 10 May 1957, 1, 4.

84. Claude Estier, 'Après le Congrès de Toulouse: Guy Mollet sur la défensive', *France-Observateur*, 4 July 1957, 5.

85. Foot, 'The Mollet touch', 4.

86. Samuel to Bourdet, undated; Bourdet to Samuel, 5 June 1957, NAF 28091/46.

87. Mikardo to Bourdet, 12 July 1957, NAF 28091/46.

88. Claude Bourdet, 'My appeal won't be in vain!', *Tribune*, 4 October 1957, 7.

89. Aneurin Bevan, 'Back to free markets – and the jungle', *Tribune*, 30 August 1957, 5.

90. Bourdet, 'Bevan'.

91. Bourdet to Foot, 8 October 1957, NAF 28091/46. The list of questions did not feature with the archived letter.

92. Bourdet to Castle, 11 October 1957, NAF 28091/46.

93. 'Deux heures d'entretien avec "Nye" Bevan – Dans la tête d'un vrai socialiste', *L'Express*, 22 February 1957.

94. K. S. Karol, interviewed by Pierre Beuchot, Grands entretiens patrimoniaux de l'INA/Itinéraires, https://entretiens.ina.fr/itineraires/Karol/k-s-karol/print.

95. ULR Club, RS 1/009.

96. Bourdet to Foot, 24 September 1957, NAF 28091/46.

97. Claude Bourdet, 'Bevan reste-t-il toujours bévaniste?', *France-Observateur*, 10 October 1957,

98. Bourdet to Castle, 11 October 1957, NAF 28091/46.

99. 'Les Anglo-Saxons ont assez de la guerre d'Algérie', *France-Observateur*, 24 April 1958, 12.

100. 'France's misdirected fury', *The Economist*, 19 April 1958, 187.

101. See Geoffrey Barei, 'The Algerian War of Independence and the Coming to Power of General Charles de Gaulle: British Reactions', *The Maghreb Review* 37, no. 3–4 (2012); Mélanie Torrent, *Algerian Independence and the British Left: Resistance and Solidarities in a Decolonising World* (London: Bloomsbury, forthcoming).

102. 'Le "Daily Herald" contre les factieux', *France-Observateur*, 29 May 1958, 2.

103. Claude Roy, 'Banned – by order of de Gaulle', *Tribune*, 4 July 1958, 1.

104. 'Le gaullisme inquiète les Anglais', *France-Observateur*, 21 August 1958, 9.

105. 'The General's tour', *The Times*, 19 August 1958, 9.

106. Thompson to Bourdet, 3 July 1958, NAF 28091.

107. 'Pour suivre l'actualité française, faudra-t-il désormais lire la presse étrangère?', *France-Observateur*, 11 September 1958, 5.

108. Aneurin Bevan, 'De Gaulle', *Tribune*, 29 May 1958.

109. Claude Bourdet, 'Algeria and France', *Africa South* 2, no. 3, April–June 1958, 70.

110. In 'London Letter', *The Manchester Guardian*, 15 July 1958, 6.

111. Bourdet to Sachs, 11 April 1957, NAF 28091/46.

112. Bourdet, 'Algeria and France'.

113. Baker to Bourdet, 11 November 1955, NAF 28091/45.

114. Mary Lane Charles to Bourdet, 25 October 1956, NAF 28091/45.

115. Charles Read to Paul Johnson, 5 February 1958, Archives of Friends Service Council, FSC/NAF/2/7.

116. Read to Johnson, 5 February 1958, FSC/NAF/2/7. Read to George Whiteman, 14 February 1958, FSC/NAF/2/7.

117. Geoffrey Carnall and J. Duncan Wood, 'Alexander, Horace Grundy', *Oxford Dictionary of National Biography*, 2004, https://doi.org/10.1093/ref:odnb/38403.

118. Jo Noble, 'Report to Friends Service Council', 5 January 1961, FSC/NAF/2/3.

119. Bourdet to AFSC, undated but c. March 1957, NAF 28091/46.

120. Mendl to various correspondents including Whiteman, 28 May 1959, FSC/NAF/1/10.

121. Mendl to Bourdet, 14 December 1961, NAF 28091/53.

122. FSC Europe Committee minutes, 21 February 1962.

123. Noble, Occasional report, Centre Quaker International, 12 August 1957, FSC/NAF/2/4. She also noted Robert Barrat's activity and Quaker concerns about the impact of the war on young conscripts; Noble, 'Report from the Mill of Peace', July 1957, FSC/NAF/2/4.

124. Noble to Bourdet, 15 March 1957, NAF 28091/46.

125. Mendl to Whiteman and Frank Hunt, 23 March 1960, NAF/1/10.

126. Mendl to Davies, Noble and others, 'Some conversations on the Algerian problem', 22 November 1960, FSC/NAF/1/10.

127. Mendl to Davies, Noble and others, 'Some conversations on the Algerian problem'.

128. Noble, 'Notes on development of Quaker relief in Morocco' for Advisory Group on North Africa Relief, 9 March 1961, FSC/NAF/2/3.

129. 6 September 1962, FSC GP Committee Minutes.

130. Basil Davidson, 'I meet the man the French would like to catch', *Daily Herald*, 8 February 1956, 4.

131. Bourdet to Mikardo, c. October 1957, NAF 28091/46.

132. Ian Mikardo, 'La guerre d'Algérie vue d'Afrique', *France-Observateur*, 28 November 1957.

133. Colin Legum, 'Ghana: the morning after (III) The Accra conference', *Africa South* 3, no. 1, July–September 1958; Catherine Hoskins, 'Tunis Diary', and Tony Benn, 'The Algerian War', *Africa South* 4, no. 4, July–September 1960.

134. Victor Barros, 'The French anticolonial solidarity movement and the liberation of Guinea-Bissau and Cape Verde', *The International History Review* 42, no. 6 (2020).

135. Ismay Milford, *African Activists in a Decolonising World: The Making of an Anticolonial Culture, 1952–1966* (Cambridge: Cambridge University Press, 2023); John

Munro, *The Anticolonial Front: The African American Freedom Struggle and Global Decolonization, 1945–1960* (Cambridge: Cambridge University Press, 2017).

136. On the PSU, see Marc Heurgon, *Histoire du PSU. 1. La fondation et la guerre d'Algérie* (Paris: La Découverte, 1994); Noëlline Castagnez, Laurent Jalabert, Jean-François Sirinelli et al., eds. *Le parti socialiste unifié* (Rennes: Presses universitaires de Rennes, 2013); Bernard Ravenel, *Quand la gauche se réinventait. Le PSU, histoire d'un parti visionnaire, 1960–1989* (Paris: La Découverte, 2016).

137. André Philip, 'Un socialisme pour aujourd'hui', *France-Observateur*, 18 December 1958, 7–8.

138. 'L'opinion de Bevan', *France-Observateur*, 15 October 1959.

139. Claude Bourdet, 'Bevan', *France-Observateur*, 14 July 1960, 9; Foot to Bourdet, 20 July 1960, NAF 28091/51.

140. Janet Hase to Bourdet, 5 November 1959, NAF 28091/49.

141. Samuel to Bourdet, 10 November 1961, NAF 28091/53.

142. Samuel to Barrat Brown, 25 October 1961, RS 1/018.

143. Peter Worsley, 'Africa rediscovered', *New Left Review*, January–February 1960, 59.

144. Perry Anderson, 'Portugal and the end of ultra-colonialism 3', *New Left Review*, Winter 1962, 113.

145. Claude Bourdet, 'The last quarter of an hour', *New Left Review*, January–April 1962, 21. See also Lelio Basso, 'The centre left in Italy', *New Left Review*, Winter 1962, 71; Eric Heffer, 'Conversations in Italy', *New Left Review*, November–December 1960, 57.

146. Kalter, *Discovery*, 96, 432.

147. *The Guardian*, 5–6 May 1960; *The Observer*, 26 June 1960.

148. Bourdet to Briottet, 22 November 1960, NAF 28091/51.

149. Although he seemed disappointed in the BBC's 'The Listener' in January 1961; Bourdet to Bernard Ellis, 20 January 1961, NAF 28091/51.

150. Bourdet to Bernard Ellis, 20 January 1961, NAF 28091/51.

151. *Daily Herald*, 26 February 1962.

152. Philip Donnellan to Bourdet, 12 June 1962, NAF 28091/53.

153. Thompson to Bourdet, 28 February 1958, NAF 28091/47.

154. Samuel to Bourdet, 20 January 1961, RS 1/016.

155. Samuel to Bourdet, 20 January 1961, RS 1/016.

156. Bourdet to Zilliacus, 11 February 1959; Richardson to Bourdet, 3 January 1960, NAF 28091/49.

157. Bourdet to Mandel, 28 February 1961, NAF 28091/52.

158. Bourdet to Samuel, 4 March 1961, RS 1/016.

159. Draft letter from organisers, RS 1/016.

160. Claude Bourdet, 'Une, deux, trois Europes', *France-Observateur*, 3 August 1961.

161. Zilliacus to Bourdet, 9 June 1962, NAF 28091/53.

162. See for instance Zilliacus to Bourdet, 28 December 1961, 22 February 1962, NAF 28091/53.

163. He shared this hope, voiced by Michael Barrat Brown in *NLR*, but did not think it would happen; Michael Barrat Brown, 'Neutralism and the Common Market', *New Left Review*, November–December 1961, 27.

164. Claude Bourdet, 'Une, deux, trois Europes'.

165. Bourdet to Mikardo, October 1957, NAF 28091/46. Mikardo, in his article for *France-Observateur* in late 1957, argued that Ghana and Nigeria had their own constitutional problems and faced foreign-owned companies, but that little blood was shed during their struggle for independence.

166. Claude Bourdet, 'Le rapport Devlin honore l'Angleterre', *France-Observateur*, 30 July 1959, 9–10; Andrew Roth, 'Epreuve de force au Nyasaland', *France-Observateur*, 12 March 1959.

167. Jones to Bourdet, 5 January 1960, NAF 28091/49.

168. Andrew Roth, 'Commonwealth: l'apartheid au coeur des débats', *France-Observateur*, 9 March 1961, 8.

169. Stuart Hall and Perry Anderson, 'The politics of the Common Market', *New Left Review*, July/August 1961, 13.

170. Hall and Anderson, 'The politics of the Common Market', 14.

171. Hall and Anderson, 'The politics of the Common Market', 14.

172. John Thurwell to Bourdet, NAF 28091/52.

173. Thompson to Bourdet, 28 February 1963, NAF 28091/54.

174. Stefan Berger and Christian Wicke, 'A very rooted cosmopolitan: E.P. Thompson's Englishness and his transnational activism', in *The Transnational Activist: Transformations and Comparisons from the Anglo-World since the Nineteenth Century*, ed. Stefan Berger and Sean Scalmer (Basingstoke: Palgrave Macmillan, 2018), 258.

175. Thompson to Bourdet, 28 February 1963, NAF 28091/54.

176. Bourdet to Dan Elwyn Jones, 28 January 1963, NAF 28091/54.

177. Evelyn Antal to Bourdet, 27 August 1963, NAF 28091/54.

178. Benn to Bourdet, 5 August 1963, NAF 28091/54.

179. *Birmingham Daily Post*, 10 May 1966, 33.

180. Brockway to Bourdet, 28 October 1966, NAF 28091/55.

181. Mendl to Bourdet, 11 June 1965, NAF 28091/55.

182. Hall, 'Life and Times', 182.

183. Olivier Wieviorka, 'France' in *Resistance in Western Europe*, ed. B. Moore (Oxford/New York: Berg, 2000), 130.

184. Bourdet to Samuel, 5 June 1957, NAF 28091/46, and Bastable to Samuel, 11 February 1958, RS 1/009.

185. Emile R. Braudi, 'L'Algérie du Commonwealth', *France-Observateur*, 3 May 1962, 11–12.

Bibliography

Augais, Thomas, Mireille Hilsum and Chantal Michel, eds. *Écrire et publier la Guerre d'Algérie. De l'urgence aux résurgences*. Paris: Kimé, 2011.

Barei, Geoffrey. 'The Algerian War of Independence and the Coming to Power of General Charles de Gaulle: British Reactions', *The Maghreb Review* 37, no. 3–4 (2012): 259–83.

Barros, Victor. 'The French Anticolonial Solidarity Movement and the Liberation of Guinea-Bissau and Cape Verde', *The International History Review* 42, no. 6 (2020): 1297–318.

Berger, Stefan, and Christian Wicke. 'A Very Rooted Cosmopolitan: E.P. Thompson's Englishness and his Transnational Activism'. In *The Transnational Activist: Transformations and Comparisons from the Anglo-World since the Nineteenth Century*, edited by Stefan Berger and Sean Scalmer, 257–81. Basingstoke: Palgrave Macmillan, 2018.

Branche, Raphaëlle. *La torture et l'armée pendant la guerre d'Algérie*. Paris, Gallimard, 2016 (2001).

Brazzoduro, Andrea. 'Algeria, Antifascism, and Third Worldism: An Anticolonial Genealogy of the Western European New Left (Algeria, France, Italy, 1957–1975)', *Journal of Imperial and Commonwealth History* 48, no. 5 (2020): 958–78.

Brown, Megan. *The Seventh Member State: Algeria, France and the European Community*. Harvard: Harvard University Press, 2022.

Castagnez, Noëlline, Laurent Jalabert, Jean-François Sirinelli, et al., eds. *Le parti socialiste unifié*. Rennes: Presses universitaires de Rennes, 2013.

Davis, Muriam Haleh, and Thomas Serres, eds. *North Africa and the Making of Europe: Governance, Institutions and Culture*. London: Bloomsbury, 2018.

Devin, Guillaume, 'L'internationalisme des socialistes'. In *La gauche en Europe depuis 1945. Invariants et mutations du socialisme européen*, edited by Marc Lazar, 413–31. Paris: Presses universitaires de France, 1996.

Dimier, Véronique. *The Invention of a European Development Aid Bureaucracy: Recycling Empire*. Basingstoke: Palgrave, 2014.

Gasteuil, Quentin. 'A Comparative and Transnational Approach to Socialist Anti-colonialism: The Fenner Brockway-Marceau Pivert Connection, 1930s–1950s'. In *Workers of the Empire, Unite: Radical and Popular Challenges to British Imperialism, 1910–1960s* edited by Yann Béliard and Neville Kirk, 133–64. Liverpool: Liverpool University Press, 2021.

Gordon, Daniel A. 'A "Mediterranean New Left"? Comparing and Contrasting the French PSU and the Italian PSIUP', *Contemporary European History* 19, no. 4 (2010): 309–30.

Gorman, Daniel. *Uniting the Nations*. Cambridge: Cambridge University Press, 2022.

Hansen, Peo, and Stefan Jonsson. *Eurafrica: The Untold Story of European Integration and Colonialism*. London: Bloomsbury, 2014.

Hendy, David. *The BBC: A People's History*. London: Imprint Books, 2022.

Heurgon, Marc. *Histoire du PSU. 1. La fondation et la guerre d'Algérie*. Paris: La Découverte, 1994.

Hughes, Gerald. '"We are not seeking strength for its own sake": The British Labour Party, West Germany and the Cold War, 1951–64', *Cold War History* 3, no. 1 (2002): 64–94.

Kalter, Christoph. *The Discovery of the Third World. Decolonization and the Rise of the New Left in France, c. 1950–1976*. Cambridge: Cambridge University Press, 2016.

Kottos, Laura. *Europe between Imperial Decline and Quest for Integration: Pro-European Groups and the French, Belgian and British Empires (1947–1957)*. Brussels: Peter Lang, 2016.

Milford, Ismay. *African Activists in a Decolonising World: The Making of an Anticolonial Culture, 1952–1966*. Cambridge: Cambridge University Press, 2023.

Munro, John. *The Anticolonial Front: The African American Freedom Struggle and Global Decolonization, 1945–1960*. Cambridge: Cambridge University Press, 2017.

Rahal, Malika. *Ali Boumendjel. Une affaire française, une histoire algérienne*. Paris: Belles Lettres, 2010.

Ravenel, Bernard. *Quand la gauche se réinventait. Le PSU, histoire d'un parti visionnaire, 1960–1989*. Paris: La Découverte, 2016.

Richard, Isabelle. 'The Limits of Solidarity: Europeanism, Anti-colonialism and Socialism at the Congress of the Peoples of Europe, Asia and Africa in Puteaux, 1948', *European Review of History: Revue européenne d'histoire* 21, no. 4 (2014): 519–37.

Rioux, Jean-Pierre, and Jean-François Sirinelli, eds. *La guerre d'Algérie et les intellectuels français*. Paris: Éditions Complexe, 1991.

Smith, Evan, and Matthew Worley, eds. *Against the Grain: The British Far Left from 1956*. Manchester: Manchester University Press, 2014.

Torrent, Mélanie. *Algerian Independence and the British Left: Resistance and Solidarities in a Decolonising World*. London: Bloomsbury, forthcoming.

Wieviorka, Olivier. *'Nous entrerons dans la carrière': de la résistance à l'exercice du pouvoir*. Paris: Seuil, 1994.

Wieviorka, Olivier. 'France'. In *Resistance in Western Europe*, edited by B. Moore, 125–56. Oxford/New York: Berg, 2000.
Winock, Michel. *Le XXe siècle idéologique et politique*. Paris: Perrin, 2013.
Winslow, Cal, ed. *E.P. Thompson and the Making of the New Left. Essays and Polemics*. New York, New York University Press, 2014.

Chapter 4

Social activism in the age of decolonisation: Basil Davidson and the liberation struggles in Lusophone Africa, c. 1954-75[1]

Pedro Aires Oliveira

It is now a well-established fact that in the early 1970s the gains made by the independence movements of Portuguese Africa were as dependent on the sympathies they were able to earn among sectors of international public opinion as from real military achievements.[2] The historiography of the colonial wars in Lusophone Africa, for instance, has long highlighted the crippling divisions among the nationalists in Angola that allowed the Portuguese to gain the upper hand there until the collapse of the colonial regime in April 1974 (the military balance was more even in Mozambique and in many aspects favourable to the forces of the *Partido Africano da Independência da Guiné e Cabo Verde* [PAIGC] in Guinea-Bissau).[3]

Coinciding with the American stalemate in Vietnam, the strength of *tiersmondisme* among left-leaning movements around the world, the quasi-universal repudiation of apartheid and the supremacy of the anti-colonial bloc in the General Assembly of the United Nations (UN), the liberation movements of Guinea-Bissau, Angola and Mozambique were able to attract greater attention to their causes after years of relative neglect by the mainstream media in the West. Television reports and documentaries depicting the popular mobilisation and 'social work' carried out in the so-called 'liberated areas' reached significant audiences. Among the horrors portrayed featured the use of napalm, and the practice of war crimes and other rogue initiatives undertaken by the

Portuguese military (such as during the failed invasion of Guinea-Conakry in 1970, or the Wiriyamu massacre of 1972). These events made the headlines on several occasions and were condemned by multiple UN bodies and other entities. In addition, civil society groups protested against controversial development projects like the Cahora Bassa dam in Mozambique or the presence of American oil companies in Angola. In the early months of 1974, the 'Republic of Guinea-Bissau', proclaimed by the PAIGC in the 'liberated area' of Madina do Boé (24 September 1973), had already been recognised by nearly eighty states at the UN – a major blow to the Portuguese claim of being able to sustain the integrity of their pluri-continental empire against armed nationalist movements.[4]

The aim of this chapter is to draw attention to the ways in which the Portuguese 'colonial issue' and the independence struggles in Lusophone Africa became a feature of the anti-imperialist networks operating within the British left from the late 1950s to the mid-1970s. In order to do this, the chapter follows the trajectory of a pivotal figure in those circles: Basil Davidson (1914–2010). Davidson was a pioneer British historian of Africa, a freelance writer and reporter for numerous publications in the United Kingdom and elsewhere, as well as a member of several anticolonial and pro-Third World NGOs and committees, and a well-connected individual within the Labour Party (at least among its leftist sections) and other socialist circles in post-war Britain. Of particular interest here is his role as a cultural intermediary between those socialist circles and the Lusophone African leaders, most of them from a Portuguese and Francophone background (and often struggling to make themselves understood in English), as well as Portuguese émigrés who had settled in the United Kingdom.

The chapter also considers how the antagonisms of the Cold War and its rigid ideological polarisations set the parameters of the socialists' engagement with the African independence struggles – for instance, how far solidarity with the 'underdog' could be limited by the *realpolitik* of the Cold War when Labour was in office. The chapter will thus contribute to ongoing discussions about the engagement of left-wing individuals and groups with anti-imperialist struggles after the Second World War and in the 'long 1960s', either on a national or a transnational level, an increasingly prominent historiographical concern.[5] To what extent, for instance, might the unravelling of Britain's decolonisation since the 1940s have made a difference in the engagement of civil society and party structures with Lusophone African liberation struggles? And how did the situation in Britain compare with other European states, which also faced the dilemma of wanting to maintain cordial relations with a NATO ally, and at the same time wished to distance themselves from Lisbon's die-hard imperialism and build friendly relations with emerging Third World nations?

Finally, the chapter will try to provide an assessment of the sort of impact which activists and experts like Davidson may have had in the foreign policy process in Britain in the period under consideration, particularly in those years in which Labour was in office.[6]

The making of an Africanist

Basil Davidson's engagement with African issues in the early 1950s was, to some extent, an unintended consequence of the Cold War. A self-educated journalist with a gift for foreign languages, Davidson became the Paris correspondent of the *Economist* in 1938, at the age of 24, and then the diplomatic correspondent of the London based *Star*, with 'a crafty ear to the gossip of all the chancelleries in Europe'.[7] When the war broke out, he was recruited by MI6 and sent to Hungary where he pretended to run a news service in Budapest, but was in fact acting as a liaison agent with anti-Axis elements. He later moved to Belgrade, was captured by Italian forces, and returned to Britain as part of an exchange of prisoners. From 1942, and for the remainder of the war, he worked for the Special Operations Executive (SOE), acting as chief of its Cairo section, and then as liaison officer with Tito's partisans in Yugoslavia until 1944, as well as with the Italian anti-Fascist forces in Liguria and Genoa in 1945 – experiences he evokes in two of his books, *Partisan Picture* (1946) and *Special Operations Europe* (1980).

Known for attracting young idealist socialists and communist sympathisers, SOE and its missions in Axis-occupied Europe were a formative experience for Davidson, who for ever became enamoured with the egalitarian spirit of the Partisans' war, and the sort of progressive democratic prospects that seemed to be opening up with the overthrow of fascism and the remains of the social *ancien régime* in several parts of Europe. With the dissolution of the organisation in 1946, Davidson, who ended the war as Lieutenant-Colonel with a Military Cross (and the American Bronze Star),[8] apparently severed his ties with British intelligence as well. He resumed his journalistic career with an appointment as the Paris correspondent (1945–47) of *The Times*, and then as its foreign leader writer. Somewhat ironically in the light of future developments, he was banned from travelling to parts of Eastern Europe and the Balkans on account of his previous connections with the Secret Intelligence Service.[9]

In the heightened Cold War tensions of the late 1940s, Davidson began to attract suspicions for his political views and friendships. Some of his close friends and intellectual companions (among them, the academics John Desmond Bernal[10] and Thomas Hodgkin[11]) were indeed members of the Communist Party, and many were under surveillance by the security services. His critical opinion on the western intervention in the Greek civil war probably cost him his job at *The Times*. He was able to find a part-time job in the left of centre *New Statesman and Nation*, then edited by Kingsley Martin, a journalist with a pacifist background and an 'erratic' posture towards the Soviet Union (he was mentioned in the famous list of 'fellow travellers' which George Orwell handed to the Information Research Department in 1949).[12] Martin seems to have also been an important influence in another job that Davidson took up in those years, the position of secretary-general of the Union of Democratic Control (UDC), a pressure group set up in 1914 to scrutinise the military's influence in politics and, after the Second World War, to press for the cause of world disarmament (again, a suspicious activity when the United States had a clear lead over the Soviet Union in terms of nuclear capacity). Some of its mentors now wanted it to devote greater attention to colonial issues as well, an area in which Labour's pragmatic foreign and imperial policy had not pleased many in the party.[13]

Davidson's engagement with UDC went well beyond a simple 'managerial' capacity. He was a prolific writer of pamphlets on current affairs (a genre in which he was particularly talented), addressing topics such as the Greek civil war, German rearmament or the political situation in Spain. His views were, in many instances, on the left of the Labour Party's 'official' positions, to the point of raising concerns among the security apparatus of Cold War Britain, who viewed the UDC as a 'front organisation'.[14] MI5 set up a surveillance operation on Davidson (and his family) which would go on for several years.[15]

Barred from travelling to Eastern Europe, Davidson redirected his interests to a part of the world still very much neglected by the media in Britain. Through an invitation by a group of South African trade unionists (the Garment Workers' Union, mostly comprised of women, but directed by Solly Sachs, a member of the South African Labour Party and former communist militant), he travelled to the country where the apartheid regime had recently been established. From this trip he collected material for his first book on African affairs, *Report on Southern Africa* (1952), a critical overview of the segregationist policies of the apartheid state and the social and political conditions in the then-British-controlled territories of Basutoland (Lesotho), Southern Rhodesia (Zimbabwe), and Northern Rhodesia (Zambia).[16] The contents of the book, and some of the reporting which preceded it in the pages of the *New Statesman and Nation*, deepened the suspicions that had provided the pretext for MI5's surveillance operation. There was now ample concern among colonial governments in British Africa, as well as in South Africa, about the repercussions of Davidson's writings. He was soon declared a 'prohibited immigrant' by Daniel Malan's government, while other British Crown colonies, like Kenya, sounded out the Colonial Office about the possibility of following the South African example.[17] These official misapprehensions, most likely hissed to the directorship of the *New Statesman and Nation*, in addition to his difficult relation with Kingsley Martin's partner, Dorothy Woodman, led to Davidson's removal from the permanent staff of the journal in 1953.[18]

In the following ten years, he was employed by the *Daily Herald* (1954–57) and then by the *Daily Mirror* (1959–61). His reporting of the Hungarian uprising in 1956 eventually helped to dissipate his reputation of communist sympathiser since his coverage of the crushing of the nationalist revolt led by Imre Nagy was extremely critical of Moscow's intervention.[19] But the core of his international reporting was now mainly located in West, Central and Eastern Africa, partly on account of the *Mirror*'s publishing interests in Nigeria, but most likely because Davidson was sensing a sea-change in the political situation of the continent.[20]

For the purposes of this chapter, it makes sense to highlight one of his trips to Africa in this period, one which took him to the Belgian Congo and Angola in 1954. The funding partly came from an American organisation (the Foundation for World Government, based in Charlottesville, Virginia) and *Harper's*, the US monthly magazine (which half a century before had commissioned Henry Nevinson's famous reportage on the 'new African slaveries'). This allowed Davidson to pen a series of articles, later developed into his book *African Awakening* (1955), largely devoted to the operation of the 'contract system' in Angola and the archipelago of São Tomé and Príncipe.[21]

Davidson's comparisons of the two colonial contexts were highly unfavourable to the Portuguese. Whereas the Belgian colony struck him with its febrile pace of industrial development, and the rise of a new African proletariat in fast-growing towns, Angola was a colonial backwater run by the Portuguese with extremely archaic methods. His main conclusion could be summarised as follows: the labour system that prevailed in the Portuguese colonies was more human than in Nevinson's time, but its functioning remained practically unchanged. In other words, Africans continued to be forcibly enlisted to work on plantations, in mines, railways and public works; their working conditions, despite some improvements in food, accommodation and medical care, remained almost as harsh as at the beginning of the century; and the Portuguese authorities, from the Ministry of Colonies in Lisbon to the modest chief of post in the interior of Angola, not only continued to provide coverage to and reap dividends from this degrading process, but they did not appear to have any remorse about it.

Davidson also contrasted the modest but, in some ways, meaningful civil and political liberties in parts of French West Africa and Northern Rhodesia, with the total denial of opportunities for political participation in the Portuguese colonies. Portuguese colonialism brought together the worst defects of other European empires, without having a single of its 'qualities'. Its administration was corrupt and repressive, economic, social, and educational innovations practically non-existent, and Africans continued to be treated like beasts of burden, without any civic and political rights.

The publication of *African Awakening*, widely reviewed in the United Kingdom and elsewhere, immediately established his reputation as an African expert not aligned with pro-empire views. The book was translated into French (*L'éveil de l'Afrique*) and published by *Présence Africaine* in 1957. It was read avidly by many African intellectuals, including those who collaborated with the journal and frequented Africanist circles in Paris, among them Mário Pinto de Andrade, one of the founders of the *Movimento Popular de Libertação de Angola* (MPLA).[22]

Davidson's denunciation of the 'contract system' in Angola galvanised the critics of Portuguese colonialism, who soon got in touch and found in him an invaluable facilitator of contacts among Labour Party and other anti-imperialist circles in the United Kingdom. His London flat became, in his own words, a 'port of call' for many leading figures of the liberation movements that were emerging, as clandestine movements, in the Portuguese territories.[23] Since the 1950s, he had established close friendships with Pinto de Andrade and the future leader of the MPLA, Agostinho Neto, with Marcelino dos Santos and Eduardo Mondlane, both Mozambicans and the latter the leader of FRELIMO (*Frente de Libertação de Moçambique*) until his assassination in 1969, and with the Guinean Amílcar Cabral, founder and leader of the PAIGC (and also a victim of a deadly conspiracy in 1973).

An important document anthology of the early years of the MPLA, published by one of its key figures, Lúcio Lara, provides evidence of the sort of comradely services that Davidson was able to offer the nationalists, from the translation of texts to the writing of articles that drew attention to the hardening of political repression in Angola. In 1959, the *New Statesman and Nation* published one of his most celebrated articles, 'The Time of the Leaflet', a three-column piece that described the growing signs of unrest among the colonial authorities and their heavy-handed attitude towards members of the African intelligentsia in Angola. The article also underlined the persistence of forced labour in the Portuguese territories, two years after Portugal signed the 1930 International Labour Organisation (ILO) convention which banned all forms of compulsory labour. Again, Davidson singled out the Portuguese as an especially unreconstructed imperial power: 'Britain, France, Belgium may all move towards a reconciliation with the ideas of African quality. But not the Portugal of Salazar: not the boyo with the gun.'[24]

The following year, Davidson received Cabral in his own apartment and assisted him in the translation of *The Facts About Portugal's African Colonies*, to which he also contributed a preface.[25] In the 'year of Africa' at the UN, with the accession of thirteen new independent countries emerging from British, French and Belgian decolonisation, the pamphlet was a powerful rebuttal of Portugal's claims of being a slower, but no less accomplished, 'civilizing power' in Africa. When Lisbon was still refusing to provide the UN General-Secretary with data on the social and educational progress in its overseas territories, Cabral's pamphlet, published by UDC, underlined the appalling shortcomings of Portugal's colonial rule in those fields.

By now Davidson was already a familiar figure among the Portuguese diplomatic and security apparatus. *African Awakening* had enjoyed excellent critical acclaim in various countries, only to be followed by two volumes on African history that also became best-sellers. Davidson's articles were reprinted around the world, including in India, a country with whom Portugal had an ongoing territorial dispute over the fate of its colonial enclaves of Goa, Damão and Diu. He also took the initiative of sending his field notes from his Angolan trip to the ILO headquarters, drawing the attention of the Geneva secretariat to the 'archaic' Portuguese labour conditions in the colony.[26] Excerpts of his *Harper's* reportage were circulating at the ILO headquarters in the bulletin of the Anti-Slavery Society, an additional reason for embarrassment being an unflattering reference in Davidson's text to the Portuguese candidate for the Non-Metropolitan Territories Commission.[27] At some point, Salazar's government considered sponsoring an anonymous pamphlet to discredit Davidson's allegations,[28] but at the end of the day decided to follow a more 'constructive' path and commissioned a pamphlet with a pro-Portuguese apologia from an old Salazar admirer, F. C. C. Egerton (*Angola without Prejudice*, 1955), and subsequently a book (*Angola in Perspective*, 1957). Davidson did not let pass the opportunity to 'cross swords' with Egerton, who had managed to secure a prestigious publishing house to print his apology (Routledge and Kegan Paul), and wrote a demolishing review for *West Africa*, to which he was a regular contributor.[29]

It was now evident that the repressive nature of the *Estado Novo*, as well as its retrograde colonial policies, were increasingly seen as 'historical anomalies' among progressive and liberal circles in the United Kingdom – a perception reflected in some of the comments elicited by Queen Elizabeth II's rather grandiose state visit to Portugal in March 1957, including a provocative article by Kingsley Martin, 'Fascism in the Name of Jesus', and a letter to the *New Statesman and Nation* editor signed by Basil Davidson – both of which were to have some circulation as a pamphlet printed by the Indian authorities.[30]

Campaigns and platforms

The unveiling of the harshest realities of the colonial situation in Portuguese Africa would be accelerated by the outbreak of the war in Angola in the early months of 1961, the 'annus horribilis' of the Lisbon dictatorship. The coverage of the events by the British press was significant, with the national papers devoting ample space to the explosion of vigilante violence against the African population of Luanda's shanty towns (*musseques*), in February, and subsequently to the *União das Populações de Angola* (UPA) March uprising in the coffee districts of the north-east of the colony, and the quite ferocious counterattack by Portuguese settler militias and armed forces.[31] The interest of British audiences for the under-reported situation in Portugal and its colonies had already been aroused by other events, such as the hijacking of the *Santa Maria* liner by a Luso-Spanish anti-fascist commando (January–February 1961). The prospect of a possible 'insurrectional detour' of the ship to Luanda had attracted a significant number of international journalists to the colony's capital, including several British ones. Some were able to report the early stages of the anticolonial upheavals. The colonial authorities tried to control the news flux from the territory by inviting reporters from more trustworthy newspapers, such as *The Times* or *The Daily Telegraph*, to travel 'embedded' with Portuguese troops, but the results did not always meet their objectives.[32]

Already banned from travelling to Angola, Davidson was nevertheless a regular contributor to *New Statesman and Nation* and other newspapers, taking advantage of his wealth of contacts inside the colony and among the African émigrés and anti-Salazarist oppositionists in the United Kingdom. Again under the auspices of UDC, he published a pamphlet (*Angola, 1961. The Factual Record*) which presented a detailed chronology of the insurgency in Angola and the Portuguese military and vigilante response.[33] Davidson also made an interesting connection between the campaign led by the Congo Reform Association between 1904 and 1913, in which the founder of the UDC, Edmund Morel, had played a key role, and the humanitarian outrage towards Portuguese actions in Angola. Writing in the summer of 1961, when Cold War solidarities meant the United States and other NATO members were already cooling down their initial criticism of Portuguese policies in the UN's Security Council, Davidson was well aware of the need to present the sufferings of the Angolans as a cause of concern for the enlightened and 'non-partisan' opinion in the West.

Indeed, the plight of Portuguese oppositionists and Angolan nationalists was by then a relevant cause for British human rights activists. Peter Benenson, a Catholic lawyer, was in the process of launching Amnesty International, soon to evolve into one of the major humanitarian activist groups in the second half of the twentieth century. The event which apparently caused the 'epiphany' that encouraged him to start his humanitarian crusade was a discreet news item in a London newspaper related to an arbitrary arrest of two students in Coimbra (for raising a toast to freedom).[34] But the Lusophone figure who came under the spotlight in his 'Forgotten Prisoners' article in *The Observer* of 28 May 1961, the launchpad for the 'Appeal for Amnesty' campaign, was Agostinho Neto, the physician held under captivity by the Portuguese, and leader of the MPLA.[35]

Davidson's role as 'broker' between African nationalists and the Labour Party should also be underlined since events in Angola in 1961 were the pretext for several heated debates in Westminster between ministers in Macmillan's government and opposition MPs.[36] A card-carrying member of the party since the late 1940s, he had at one point been sounded to run for winnable parliamentary seats but ended up deciding to focus on civic activism and his intellectual pursuits.[37] He nevertheless cultivated contacts among the more radical and 'non-aligned' sections of the party, many of whom he would meet not only at UDC meetings but also in the Movement for Colonial Freedom, a pressure group he helped to set up in 1954 and which can be counted, in the words of one author, 'among the most important post-war British political pressure groups'.[38] At the UDC he kept up a close dialogue with the Fabian Colonial Bureau (FCB), a small think-tank established in 1940 to advise Labour MPs and leaders on colonial issues. But his preference for 'socialist' solutions as the final outcome of the process of imperial dissolution was not exactly welcomed by the gradualist FCB and the 'centrist' elements of the Labour Party.[39] Together with Thomas Hodgkin, he organised several important meetings on Africa which brought together politicians, academics and African nationalists. In 1953, Davidson was also the author of a damning critique of the colonial sections of Labour's policy document, *Challenge to Britain*, written, as remarked historian Stephen Howe, from 'the newly influential perspective of an intimate relationship between economic exploitation, political and racial injustice in the colonies, and the prospects for socialism in Britain'.[40] Not without some reason, Hugh Gaitskell, Labour's centrist leader between 1955 and 1963, is supposed to have used his influence to get Davidson sacked from the Labour Party-oriented *Daily Herald* a few years later.[41] Seen as too much of a radical by these sectors of the Party, Davidson was nevertheless able to work with other elements who still had a degree of influence in Westminster, as well as among the 'rank and file' members and other sectors of British opinion. In 1960, along with several MPs (including Tony Benn and Fenner Brockway), and with the representative of the MPLA in London, and secretary of the Goan League, João Cabral, he helped to organise the visit of a delegation of several Lusophone African nationalists. One of its highlights was the staging of a press conference in the House of Commons, following an invitation by James Callaghan, then head of Labour's National Executive Committee and its spokesman for colonial affairs. The event took place on 6 December 1960, shortly after a major defeat for Portugal in a vote at the UN's Fourth Committee in New York. In their address to the House of Commons conference, Mário Pinto de Andrade, Américo Boavida, Viriato da Cruz (MPLA), Matthew Mayole and C. Nahala (Mozambique Makonde Union), Alfredo Bangura (PAIGC),[42] and João Cabral (Goan League), asked for the recognition of their people's right to self-determination, an amnesty for political prisoners, the restoration of basic civil rights and liberties, as well as the withdrawal of the political police and Portuguese armed forces from their territories.[43] They were nevertheless advised by the Labour MPs to refrain from using the expression 'armed struggle', as this was perceived as a term which could alienate most of the British public. Tony Benn tried to ascertain the Foreign Office's willingness to meet unofficially with some of the nationalists who 'in ten years' time' might be holding office in their countries, but his suggestion was not met with success.[44]

Davidson's contacts were not limited to the universe of African nationalists. Since the late 1950s he had also been cultivating friendships among the small, but growing community of Portuguese expatriates and political émigrés in the United Kingdom. Many of them were students, artists, young professionals or political dissidents trying to survive with odd jobs. A few could be counted as militants of the Portuguese Communist Party, which had recently adopted an unambiguous stance towards self-determination in the African colonies. Some of these elements were behind the launching of the Council of Freedom in Portugal and Colonies in 1960, under the chairmanship of Sir Leslie Plummer, a Labour MP with a long record of involvement in colonial issues and matters of racial discrimination, and someone attentive to the human rights situation in Francoist Spain. Other notable members included several Labour MPs, university professors, clergymen and human rights lawyers. In the MPLA communiqué announcing the setting up of the new body, Davidson was singled out as 'the author of the book *L'Eveil de l'Afrique* – Editions Présence Africaine, Paris, which denounced the existence of forced labour in Angola'.[45] While a few years before Davidson had expressed some misgivings about the 'shyness' of the Portuguese opposition vis-à-vis the emancipation of the colonies, he was now more at ease with the younger generation of activists who were trying to organise some protest initiatives in the United Kingdom and other European countries. In 1962, he gave his patronage to the British Committee for Portuguese Amnesty, part of a larger West European Conference for Amnesty for Portuguese Prisoners and Exiles, with branches in France and Italy. Other eminent personalities included Doris Lessing, J. D. Bernal, Julian Huxley, Henry Moore and the Labour MPs Tom Driberg and Judith Hart. Davidson was particularly helpful to António Figueiredo, a Portuguese emigré who had benefitted from asylum protection in the United Kingdom since 1959 (acting as General Humberto Delgado's representative in Britain), securing him temporary jobs in places like the Anti-Slavery Society, contributions to *Anti-Apartheid News*, *Tribune* and *The Guardian,* as well as an introduction to Victor Gollancz, who in 1961 published Figueiredo's book, *Portugal and Its Empire: the Truth*, a volume that for many years was to be a reference book on twentieth-century Portugal, from the standpoint of the anti-Salazarist opposition.[46] Figueiredo was one of the Portuguese exiles who was able to gain the confidence of the Lusophone African nationalists that occasionally visited the United Kingdom and acted as one of the 'bridge builders' between these two groups, together with some other expatriates and exiles who had made acquaintances with the latter during their student days in post-war Lisbon.

Marching with the guerrillas

In the late 1960s, along with Southern Rhodesia, and to some extent South Africa, the Portuguese African territories remained one of the 'unfinished businesses' of European decolonisation. Armed struggle in Angola had been followed by equivalent insurgencies in Guinea-Bissau (1963) and Mozambique (1964). But while some observers had predicted that the colonialist regime in Lisbon would not concede easily to independence claims, the resilience of Portugal's 'ultra-colonialism' took many by surprise (including the *New Left Review*, which introduced the concept in 1962).⁴⁷ The 'Euro-Atlanticist' priorities of the western alliance had gradually reasserted themselves after some brief flirtation in the early months of Kennedy's administration with the cause of African liberation. Under Lyndon B. Johnson, Portugal was able to gain some respite and even if NATO's backing for its colonial wars could not be taken for granted,⁴⁸ the country's acceptance as part of the American sphere of influence, including its most important military alliance, was the source of many trump cards. Until 1974 Portugal enjoyed impressive growth rates, benefiting from its inclusion in the European Free Trade Area and other trade agreements, a significant flow of foreign investment and a measure of political solidarity from its western partners in the UN and other international bodies. Lusophone African leaders also met some difficulties in travelling to many western countries and were unable to be received by governmental representatives or other official bodies. This was particularly the case of the United Kingdom, even during Harold Wilson's first stint in Downing Street (1964–70). Commercial reasons, NATO commitments and the 'old alliance' links, as well as the fear of a Portuguese collusion with the white minority in Salisbury, were behind Labour's appeasement of Salazar in the 1960s.⁴⁹

In the British media, the wars in Portuguese Africa were gradually relegated to the inside pages of most newspapers, partly for the lack of major 'breakthroughs' from the guerrillas, partly due to the eruption of crises and conflicts on an altogether greater scale and with a greater salience in the international news, such as the Vietnam War, the Six-Day War (1967) and its aftermath in the Middle East, the secession of Biafra, not to mention Rhodesia's Unilateral Declaration of Independence.

The situation correspondingly demanded a 'public relations' offensive from the Lusophone African nationalists at this stage, and Davidson was uniquely well placed to assist those with whom he had built a close rapport: the PAIGC in Guinea-Bissau, the MPLA in Angola and FRELIMO in Mozambique. They were the 'modernist' (and Marxist) movements that claimed to wage a people's war based on the political mobilisation of the peasant masses, having as their final goal a complete overthrow of the structures of inequality erected by the colonial power, to be followed by the establishment of socialist regimes – though not necessarily modelled on the 'real existing socialism' of the Soviet bloc or Maoist China.⁵⁰ Given that such 'subtleties' were not easily understood by the less politicised sectors of western audiences, Davidson's role as the 'interpreter' of their message was particularly valued. He needed to make the essentially 'non-aligned' outlook of the Lusophone independence movements better known to the wider world and thereby give a strong rebuttal to the Portuguese claim that Cabral, Neto and Mondlane were hostages to Soviet global designs or champions of 'anti-white' and 'anti-western' ideologies.

Between 1968 and 1971, he made two long incursions to the 'liberated areas' of Guinea-Bissau and Angola, travelling 'embedded' with the guerrillas, as well as a brief visit to Mozambique, to attend the second congress of FRELIMO (July 1968), in one of the 'liberated areas' of Niassa province.

The kind of voyage undertaken by Davidson to the Guinean *maquis* controlled by the PAIGC had become a regular feature of the guerrilla war in the Portuguese colony. Cabral was adamant that he had to seize every opportunity to make his cause known in western countries and give assurances as to the PAIGC's determination to pursue a realistic nation-building project (along socialist lines but avoiding a dogmatic emulation of 'foreign' models), as well as an autonomous foreign policy.[51] The timing of Davidson's travel was probably related to the awareness that Portugal's armed forces were trying to regain the initiative, with a more efficient use of air power and the appointment of a more 'forward-looking' commander, General António de Spínola, who did not hesitate to carry out armed incursions into the neighbouring states (Senegal and Guinea-Conakry) that provided sanctuaries to the PAIGC's guerrillas. Some of Davidson's observations were conveyed in a series of reports in European newspapers (*New Statesman*, *Le Monde diplomatique*), but they achieved greater notoriety through his book *The Liberation of Guinea*, published in 1969. Along with filmmakers, photographers, politicians and fellow journalists, Davidson was one of several western enthusiasts who helped to popularise the 'David versus Goliath' struggle that was raging in the little-known Portuguese colony, praising the cunning and bravery of the PAIGC's fighters, as well as the clear-sightedness and sense of moderation that distinguished Cabral.[52] But his account was also somewhat appealing to more radical audiences, with its emphasis on grassroots mobilisation, egalitarian practices, and social and educational improvements in the 'liberated areas', as well as direct comparisons to Mao's 'Long March' in the 1930s, the Viet Minh in Indochina, and 'surgical' quotes from Fanon, Marx and V. N. Giap.

In the late 1960s, Davidson had already established his reputation as one of the United Kingdom's foremost 'Africanists'. Indeed, he had a leading role in creating a new study field, helping to correct decades, if not centuries, of crude stereotypes about the continent, its peoples and its cultures.[53] Without an academic position, he made his living as a published author and although attracting some unsympathetic remarks for his lack of 'critical detachment' (the 'fellow travelling' accusations having in the meantime subsided), he enjoyed significant critical acclaim. His book on Guinea was his third with Penguin's 'African Library' series, launched in 1962 by the South African exile, and anti-apartheid activist, Ronald Segal. It soon became a mass-market paperback, in a collection which included other well-known radical authors (academics, activists, as well as politicians) and was easily recognisable by its striking cover.[54]

The timing of his small odyssey among the Angolan guerrillas was no less relevant; indeed it can be said that it was even a more pressing endeavour. The MPLA's position was in many ways more complicated than the one of its fellow 'progressive' organisations in Guinea and Mozambique. It had a recent history of internal dissension and faced the competition of two other movements, UPA and UNITA (*União Nacional para a Independência Total de Angola*), with whom it maintained a belligerent relationship. Apart from scattered groups fighting in the Cabinda enclave and the Dembos region (north-east of Luanda), its military operations were quite reduced. Agostinho Neto lacked the skills to direct an effective guerrilla campaign and was mostly an 'exile politician', subject to growing internal criticism.[55] In the early 1970s, his leadership would face two important challenges which culminated in two splits – the *Revolta de Leste* (Eastern Revolt), led by the charismatic commander Daniel Chipenda, and the *Revolta Activa* (Active Revolt), led by Mário Pinto de Andrade, one the most respected intellectuals of the movement.[56] Davidson however remained loyal to Neto and his close circle of associates and his reports can to some extent be read as an attempt to bolster Neto's faltering authority (this is particularly evident in the photographs published in some newspapers,[57] and later in the book which resulted from his wanderings with the MPLA, which portraited Neto ostensibly holding an AK-47 assault rifle).

In the Eye of the Storm: Angola's People was originally published in 1972 by Longman, only appearing in Penguin's African Library collection in 1975, the year of Angola's independence. It was a more scholarly volume than the previous one, with its first two chapters (out of four) devoted to the historical trajectory of Angola, from pre-colonial times to the eve of the 1961 uprising. In the third chapter, Davidson discussed at length the unravelling of the revolt and tried to throw some light on the factional divisions among the Angolan nationalists. The concluding chapter offered a more theoretical discussion about the possibilities of a meaningful decolonisation in Angola, that is, one which would avoid the pitfalls of other independence transitions which had become hostage to 'neo-colonialist' machinations. Again, Davidson was keen to stress the 'revolutionary potential' of the sort of 'people's war' which the MPLA was waging thanks to the mobilisation of the peasants, the setting up of 'democratic' or egalitarian structures, and the political education of the rural communities by a 'vanguard party'. Evidence that Davidson was eager to keep up with debates among the anti-imperialist left is easy to spot in the last sections, where extensive references to the works of neo-Marxist dependency theorists like André Gunder Frank and Samir Amin are made.[58]

Indeed, in the early 1970s a revival of Marxist currents of thought was discernible among the sort of intellectual circles which Davidson frequented. He was close to several figures of the New Left in Britain, many of them former communists who had left the Party after their disillusion with the crushing of the Hungarian rising. Among them were Ralph Miliband and John Saville, editors of *The Socialist Register*, to which Davidson was a regular contributor in the 1960s and 1970s. In the United Kingdom, with the near completion of the 'transfer of power' phase of decolonisation, anti-imperial activists were now more aware of the modalities of subtle or not-so-subtle postcolonial influence facilitated by aid schemes, foreign investments and other economic arrangements. Davidson plunged into some of these debates which also involved the Portuguese territories, where the economic boom experienced in the early 1970s ('the Angolan miracle') gave way to apprehensions about a 'flag independence' masterminded by neo-colonial interests, with the imperial centre handing the levers of power to a 'comprador' African elite and some pragmatic white settlers.[59]

Making Portugal look toxic

The temporising attitude towards Portuguese colonialism adopted by the Wilson administrations, and afterwards by Edward Heath's Conservative government (1970–74), encouraged a small group of British activists, headed by Anthony Gifford, a human rights lawyer, Labour peer in the House of Lords and a speaker in Movement for Colonial Freedom (MCF) events, who launched a solidarity committee devoted to the liberation struggles in Portuguese Africa in 1967 – the Committee for Freedom in Mozambique, Angola and Guinea (CFMAG). The suggestion had been conveyed to him by Polly Gaster, a young activist who had worked for the Mozambican Institute in Dar es Salaam, FRELIMO's educational think-tank and *cadres* training centre (and, coincidentally, a friend of Thomas Hodgkin, Davidson's close associate since the 1950s).[60] According to FRELIMO's president, Eduardo Mondlane, the time was ripe for FRELIMO to have a more direct channel to present its views to the British public, dispensing with the mediation of the Portuguese exiles established in London.

As the major populariser of the liberation struggles in Lusophone Africa in the United Kingdom, Davidson was approached by Gifford to become one of its initial sponsors. A few years later he became more engaged and, along with his wife Marion, worked as a full member in the committee, carrying out several tasks in its busiest years (1971–75), including the writing of pro-PAIGC brochures.[61] His links to CFMAG would also allow him to interact more closely with some of the solidarity committees that had emerged in the late 1960s in several European countries, particularly in France, the Netherlands and Scandinavia, usually bringing together the younger and more radical elements of the established Social Democratic parties as well as militants from the various currents that made up the European far left.[62]

CFMAG's initial efforts had been associated with opposition to the construction of the massive Cahora Bassa dam in Mozambique, and the indirect participation of British firms and banks in various aspects of the project – a topic about which Davidson wrote a short essay for *Présence Africaine*.[63] Apart from acting as the formal representative of the socialist-oriented liberation movements in the United Kingdom, CFMAG organised the visits made by their leaders to the British Isles and promoted the visits of journalists and other individuals to the 'liberated areas' in the Portuguese African territories. Additionally, the group dealt with the production and distribution of informative material and propaganda (including a newsletter entitled *O Guerrilheiro* and pamphlets with the translation of speeches by the leaders of the liberation movements) and made links with parties, churches and other elements of British civil society, as well as with the Portuguese exile community.[64]

While being run with the characteristic professionalism of British NGOs, CFMAG also benefited from the enthusiasm and sense of improvisation and imagination of its activists. In addition to the production of the usual pamphlets, press releases, postcards and flyers, the Committee held meetings and seminars at universities that helped to create some excitement in a public willing to join protest events against 'imperialism' and 'racism', and was also keen to produce educational kits for secondary schools.[65]

In terms of major public events, one highlight was the visit paid by Amílcar Cabral to the United Kingdom in October 1971. It was a carefully planned event, occurring at the height of Cabral's prestige, in which various solidarity and civic bodies were involved. CFMAG organised a speaking tour that took him to Central Hall in London and the Free Trade Hall in Manchester, both attended by hundreds of people. Cabral gave several press interviews, and brochures with his translated speeches were circulated by CFMAG.[66] The intervention of the Labour MP Joan Lester in the London event was in many ways revealing. When mentioning Labour's endorsement of anticolonial struggles in Portuguese Africa, she was booed by the audience – a clear sign of the disenchantment that many left-wingers felt towards what they perceived as Labour's compromising stance on a series of issues, from nuclear disarmament to the Vietnam War.[67]

CFMAG also played a pivotal role in a second episode that brought Portugal's resistance to decolonisation to the forefront of public debates in Britain and elsewhere: the protests staged against the official visit of Marcelo Caetano, Salazar's successor, to London, on the pretext of the celebration of the sixth centenary of the Anglo-Portuguese alliance (1373–1973).[68] When the celebrations were announced, the visit was immediately seized on by CFMAG and other groups as an opportunity to raise awareness of one of the most protracted conflicts in Africa, and of the lack of freedom and democracy in one of Britain's partners in NATO and, until recently, the European Free Trade Association (EFTA). A broad anti-fascist and anticolonial coalition was then assembled – the End the Alliance Campaign, which promoted workshops, symbolic protests and mass meetings prior to and during Caetano's visit. Although Davidson was not, according to CFMAG's chairman, 'much at ease in the language of campaigning',[69] he did take part in several events, such as the conference held at the University of Manchester to 'explore and discuss the anachronism of Portuguese colonialism in the context of modern imperialism', with speakers including academics and journalists, such as Fred Halliday, Bob Sutcliffe and Paul Foot, the South African exile Joe Slovo, as well as Marcelino dos Santos and Aquino de Bragança, two of the FRELIMO leaders with responsibilities for external relations.[70] At the beginning of the year, he had also kept an active presence in the media, writing on Amílcar Cabral's assassination, a crime perpetrated by internal dissenters, but which Davidson believed to have involved the participation of the Portuguese secret police and Guinea's colonial government.[71] It was, it should be remembered, the second assassination which targeted a major figure of the Lusophone liberation movements, the first being Eduardo Mondlane, the leader of FRELIMO, killed on 3 February 1969 when opening a parcel-bomb sent to his office in Dar es Salaam (the circumstances have since remained wrapped in mystery, but strong suspicions of Portuguese involvement were also raised in the press).[72]

Portugal was indeed becoming a 'toxic' ally and the revelation of a horrific massacre by Portuguese commandos against unarmed civilians in the province of Tete, central Mozambique, on the front page of the London *Times* (10 July 1973), only made things worse for Caetano and his hosts. As press coverage of Wiryamu and the circumstances of Caetano's visit have fully been described elsewhere,[73] we shall not dwell on them here. Suffice it to say that although Wilson's support for the anti-Caetano campaign was seen as 'lukewarm' by the CFMAG leadership, it seems undoubtable that the public outcry against the Portuguese Prime Minister's visit, and the wide international repercussions of the Wiriyamu scandal (the subject of an inquiry commission set up by the UN in August 1973), encouraged the Labour Party to reconsider its stance vis-à-vis Portugal on the eve of the 1974 general election. Its foreign policy programme, presented in May 1973, had already repudiated 'the Portuguese assertion that its overseas provinces were part of mainland Portugal', and made a pledge to follow a more restrictive investment policy in Portugal, to pursue the cancellation of the commercial agreement celebrated between Lisbon and the EEC in 1972, to press for Portugal's temporary suspension from NATO and take steps to prevent future British arms sales to Portugal, among other 'drastic' measures.[74]

Following the February 1974 election, which saw Wilson return to Downing Street with a narrow margin of four seats, the composition of the new Cabinet showed a significant number of former anticolonial and human rights activists, some of them with junior ministerial posts at the Foreign and Commonwealth Office, like Joan Lester, Judith Hart and David Ennals. Wilson's second government took office in mid-March, just a few weeks before the military coup that put an end to the oldest colonial empire in Africa and the longest surviving dictatorship in Western Europe. Its influence on this outcome was negligible if it can be said to have existed at all. But in the subsequent months, several events showed that some of these choices did have a meaningful impact on the course of the relationship between the United Kingdom and the new Lusophone African states. Indeed, some of the personal links forged in the context of the public campaigns and solidarity committees helped the Wilson administration to start its relationship with FRELIMO's government on the right footing (to the point of receiving an invitation to attend the independence ceremonies in Maputo on 25 June 1975, contrary to other NATO members), to initiate an aid programme which aimed to earn the confidence of the new regime in Maputo (an important step to isolate the minority regime in Rhodesia), as well as to explore channels to prevent the MPLA government in Luanda, headed by his long time friend Dr Agostinho Neto, from becoming even more dependent on the USSR and its closest allies.[75]

Concluding remarks

As we have seen in parts of this chapter, attitudes among British socialists towards the specific case of the independence struggles in Portuguese Africa were inevitably conditioned by Labour's commitments as a party of government and the constraints which resulted from the defence and foreign policy arrangements of the Cold War. The sympathies which some of its more openly anti-imperialist militants, MPs or voters expressed towards the aspirations of Lusophone African nationalists were not replicated at a more official level when Labour held office. Symbolic manifestations of solidarity were sometimes expressed (such as the House of Commons' 1960 press conference with several Lusophone African nationalists) when the Party was in opposition. A fairly similar pattern occurred in West Germany when Willy Brandt's Social Democratic Party (SPD) entered the 'grand coalition' with the Christian Democratic Union (CDU) in 1966 and then became the senior partner of the ruling coalition with the Free Democratic Party (FDP) from 1969 to the end of the 1970s. The Social Democrats' desire to ingratiate themselves with progressive forces in West Germany, Europe and the Third World, and earn support for their foreign policy initiatives in the UN and other fora, was in many ways checked by their fear of alienating Portugal, a partner in NATO and a country which had provided defence facilities to the Bundeswehr since 1960, as well as a few investment opportunities in an industrialising peripheral economy.[76] A marked contrast in Western Europe is provided by neutral Sweden, where a strong 'thirdworldist' stance among the Social Democrats imposed a withdrawal of Swedish firms from the Cahora Bassa dam project and assured a significant flow of aid to the Lusophone liberation movements.[77]

At most, the prevalent realpolitik attitudes in London and Bonn were mitigated by the activism of grassroots militants and less 'officially aligned' figures among Party ranks. Davidson was a good example of these 'fellow travellers' of the independence parties and the anti-imperialist *movida* who not only found ways to harness support for their causes, but also worked to open channels of dialogue. His repertoire of connections was in many ways impressive, ranging from the more centrist personalities of the Labour Party to some of its 'maverick' elements (among which people like Tony Benn or Fenner Brockway), as well as including a broad range of individuals from the 'progressive' circles of Britain's intellectual life in the second half of the twentieth century. On several occasions, he was able to reach out to influential MPs and Cabinet ministers in order to convey the views or support the interests of the liberation movements to whom he was closely associated. But Davidson's personal trajectory also highlights the sort of closed doors which someone with his views had to face. From the late 1940s and 1950s, the label 'fellow traveller' was a term of opprobrium that had quite a negative impact on his professional career as a journalist, at times even threatening his job security. He also faced a number of travel restrictions in British territories across Africa in the 1950s and was apparently vetoed for a job opportunity at UNESCO, when his reputation as a foremost historian of Africa was already well established.[78] Throughout the 1960s and early 1970s, Davidson's views on decolonisation ceased to be perceived as completely at odds with the British 'official mind' or with 'middle-of-the road' published opinion. Britain had dismantled most of its African empire, decolonisation by then received near unanimous support at the UN, and the condemnation of South Africa's apartheid and Portugal's 'ultra-colonialism' was now shared by large sections of society in most western countries. The expectations towards the future development of the newly independent states in Africa were still fairly optimistic at the time, even if disillusionment and scepticism were beginning to gain ground by the end of the 1960s in Britain and other western countries. But Davidson's quasi-millenarist enthusiasm with the 'revolutionary prospects' in Lusophone Africa, and his close identification with the Marxist 'vanguard parties' in power in Bissau, Luanda and Maputo (not to mention his support for Siad Barre's regime in Somalia),[79] helped to rekindle ancient suspicions and reservations in official circles.[80] The high hopes which he and the *tiermondiste* sectors of the British left placed in the political developments in Southern Africa shortly after the collapse of the Portuguese colonial regime in 1974 came up against the hawkish attitudes prevailing in Whitehall in the aftermath of the Soviet and Cuban intervention in Angola and the Ogaden war between Ethiopia and Somalia.[81] As such, his counsel and expertise continued to be disregarded by the Foreign and Commonwealth Office under the Labour governments of the second half of the 1970s.

Notes

1. Research for this chapter was carried out in the framework of IHC – NOVA FCSH / IN2PAST. The IHC is funded by FCT – Fundação para a Ciência e a Tecnologia, I.P., under the projects UIDB/04209/2020, UIDP/04209/2020, and LA/P/0132/2020.

2. For a nuanced account of the war in Guinea (the thornier war theatre for the Portuguese), see Mustafah Dhada, *Warriors at Work: How Guinea Was Really Set Free* (Niwot, CO: University Press of Colorado, 1993). On the importance of the diplomatic dimension of the liberation struggle, see Norrie MacQueen, *The Decolonization of*

Portuguese Africa: Metropolitan Revolution and the Dissolution of Empire (London: Longman, 1997).

3. For the Angolan context, see Stephen L. Weigert, *Angola: A Modern Military History 1961–2002* (Basingstoke: Palgrave, 2011). For the other theatres, see MacQueen, *Decolonization*; John P. Cann, *Counterinsurgency in Africa: The Portuguese Way of War 1961–1974* (Westport CT: Greenwood Press, 1997).

4. Norrie MacQueen, 'Belated Decolonization and UN Politics against the Backdrop of the Cold War: Portugal, Britain and Guinea-Bissau's Proclamation of Independence, 1973–1974', *Journal of Cold War Studies* 8, no. 4 (2006); Pedro Aires Oliveira, *Os Despojos da Aliança. A Grã-Bretanha e a Questão Colonial Portuguesa 1945–1975* (Lisbon: Tinta da China, 2007).

5. There is a fast-expanding literature on this topic, which is difficult to summarise. In the context of this chapter, important references are Stephen Howe, *Anticolonialism in British Politics: The Left and the End of Empire 1918–1964* (Oxford: Oxford University Press, 1993); Robert Gildea, James Mark and Niek Pas, 'European Radicals and the "Third World". Imagined Solidarities and Radical Networks, 1958–1973', *Cultural and Social History* 8, no. 4 (2011); Kostis Kornetis, '"Cuban Europe"? Greek and Iberian *thirdmondisme* in the "Long 1960s"', *Journal of Contemporary History* 50, no. 3 (2015); Christoph Kalter, *The Discovery of the Third World: Decolonization and the Rise of the New Left in France* (Cambridge: Cambridge University Press, 2016); Nils Schliehe, 'West German Solidarity Movements and the Struggle for the Decolonization of Lusophone Africa', *Revista Crítica de Ciências Sociais*, 118 (2019); Victor Barros, 'The French Anticolonial Solidarity Movement and the Liberation of Guinea and Cape Verde', *International History Review* 42, no. 6 (2020), as well as Zeina Maasri, Cathy Burgin and Francesca Burke, eds. *Transnational Solidarity: Anticolonialism in the Global Sixties* (Manchester: Manchester University Press, 2022).

6. A useful survey of the Labour Party and foreign policy in the second half of the twentieth century is provided by Stephen Howe, 'Labour and International Affairs', in Pat Thane, Nick Tiratsoo, Duncan Tanner, eds. *Labour's First Century* (Cambridge: Cambridge University Press, 2000).

7. Basil Davidson, *Special Operations Europe: Scenes from the Anti-Nazi War* (London: Gollancz, 1980), 51. For an overview of his life and literary achievements, see the obituary by Victoria Brittain, 'Basil Davidson', *The Guardian*, 9 July 2010, as well as the special issue devoted to him by *Race & Class* in 1994, particularly the contributions by Barry Munslow, 'Basil Davidson and Africa: A Biographical Essay', *Race & Class* 36, no. 2 (1994), and Stephen Howe, 'The Interpreter: Basil Davidson as Public Intellectual', *Race & Class* 36, no. 2 (1994).

8. Munslow, 'Basil Davidson and Africa', 3.

9. According to Brittain, Davidson was mentioned as a British intelligence agent in the László Rajk process in Budapest in 1949.

10. J.D. Bernal's son, historian Martin Bernal, alludes to this friendship while noting that his parents had some reservations towards Davidson, most likely on account of his 'Titoist' sympathies. Martin Bernal, 'Basil Davidson: A Personal Appreciation', *Race & Class* 36, no. 2 (1994), 101.

11. See Hodgkin's evocation of their friendship in Thomas Hodgkin, 'Where the Paths Began', in *African Studies since 1945: A Tribute to Basil Davidson*, ed. Christopher Fyfe (London: Longman, 1976), and the biography by Michael Wolfers, *Thomas Hodgkin: Wandering Scholar* (Monmouth: Merlin Press, 2007). Thomas Hodgkin's MI5 files at the UK's National Archives (KV series [Security Service]) cover a period from 1949 to 1958.

12. See Peter Davison, ed., *Orwell and Politics* (Harmondsworth: Penguin Books, 2001), 501–9.

13. See Howe, *Anticolonialism*, 190–95, for an overview of UDC's commitment to anti-imperialism after the Second World War, and Munslow, 'Basil Davidson and Africa', 8–9.

14. The National Archives (TNA), KV-2-3691-1, 84. See also Union of Democratic Control (UDC), propaganda directed to trade Unions 1952–1954, TNA, FCO 141/4972.

15. There are eleven files on the KV series (Security Service) on Davidson, covering a period from 1952 to 1958.

16. Basil Davidson, *Report on Southern Africa* (London: Jonathan Cape, 1952).

17. Basil Davidson, *The Search for Africa* (London: James Currey, 1994), 99.

18. Brittain, 'Basil Davidson'.

19. Basil Davidson, *What Really Happened in Hungary: A Personal Record* (London: UDC, 1957).

20. Munslow, 'Basil Davidson and Africa'; Brittain, 'Basil Davidson'.

21. Some pieces of reportage were also published in *New Statesman and Nation*, *Reporter* (a US bi-weekly current affairs magazine) and in *West Africa*, a British monthly magazine.

22. See Michel Laban, *Mário Pinto de Andrade. Uma Entrevista* (Lisbon: Ed. João Sá da Costa, 1997) and Lúcio Lara, *Documentos e Comentários para a História do MPLA. Até Fev. 1961* (Lisbon: Dom Quixote, 1999).

23. Davidson, *The Search for Africa*, 180.

24. Basil Davidson, 'The Time of the Leaflet', *New Statesman and Nation*, 21 November 1959.

25. Abel Djassi (alias of Amílcar Cabral), *The Fact About Portugal's Colonies* (London: UDC, 1960).

26. Basil Davidson, Report for the ILO – UN Special Committee of Forced Labour – Forced Labour in Angola, 3 June 1954, ILO Archive, Series FLC, number 1-3-4 Jacket 1. ILO\ - \UN\ Special \Committee\ on \Forced Labour\ - \Correspondence\ with Basil Davidson, London.

27. Dispatch from J. Luís Archer (Bern embassy) to Ministry of Foreign Affairs (Portugal), 25 November 1954, Arquivo Histórico-Diplomático (AHD), Lisbon, PAA – 124.

28. Dispatch from P. Teotónio Pereira to Ministry of Foreign Affairs (Portugal), 16 September 1955 forwarding a letter from a London solicitor advising against such a course of action, AHD, PAA – 324.

29. Basil Davidson, 'Angola in Perspective' (book review), *West Africa*, 6 April 1957.

30. Both were reprinted as an 8-page pamphlet by the North-American bureau of the Information Service of India, *Fascism in the Name of Jesus* (Washington DC, 1957).

31. A detailed account of the British newspaper coverage is provided by Tânia Alves, *1961 – Sob o Viés da Imprensa. Os jornais portugueses, britânicos e franceses na conjuntura da eclosão da guerra no império português* (Unpubl. PhD dissertation, University of Lisbon, 2018).

32. Aires Oliveira, *Os Despojos*, chapter 5.

33. Basil Davidson, *Angola, 1961. The Factual Record* (London: UDC, 1961).

34. Tom Buchanan, '"The Truth Will Set You Free": The Making of Amnesty International', *Journal of Contemporary History* 37, no. 4 (2002).

35. Peter Benenson, *Persecution 1961* (Harmondsworth: Penguin, 1961).

36. Aires Oliveira, *Os Despojos*, chapter 5.
37. Munslow, 'Basil Davidson and Africa', 4.
38. Howe, *Anticolonialism*, 231.
39. Howe, *Anticolonialism*, 193–94.
40. Howe, *Anticolonialism*, 220–21.
41. Richard Gott, 'Basil Davidson: a fine writer and fighter', 7 May 2011. https://www.redpepper.org.uk/basil-davidson-a-fine-writer-and-fighter/ [accessed 7 January 2021].
42. Alfredo Bangura was the pseudonym of Aristides Pereira, who became the first head of state of Cape Verde (1975–1991).
43. Press statement, 6 December 1960, Fundação Mário Soares (Lisboa), Casa Comum/Amílcar Cabral Archive, folder 07058.017.032, http://casacomum.org/cc/visualizador?pasta=07058.017.032 [accessed 1 March 2021].
44. Meeting of Portuguese Nationalist Leaders, H.F.T. Smith, 7 December 1960, TNA, FO 371/147256.
45. Lúcio Lara ed., *Um Amplo Movimento . . . : Itinerário do MPLA através de documentos de Lúcio Lara: 1961–1962* (Luanda: Edição do Autor, 2006), 53–4.
46. A. de Figueiredo, 'The Times of Utopia', *New African*, November 2004, 60–61.
47. Perry Anderson, 'Portugal and the End of Ultracolonialism (Part. 1)', *New Left Review* 15, no. 1 (1962), 83–102, whose first line read: 'It is now clear that the Portuguese empire is coming to an end.'
48. At least in an overt fashion. But some NATO equipment seems to have been regularly diverted to the African theatres, and British, French and West German matériel (including fighter jets, light aircraft and helicopters) gave the Portuguese armed forces an important edge throughout most of the conflict.
49. Aires Oliveira, *Os Despojos*, chapter 6.
50. Patrick Chabal et al., *A History of Postcolonial Lusophone Africa* (London: Hurst & Co., 2002), chapters 1 and 2.
51. See Patrick Chabal, *Amilcar Cabral: Revolutionary Leadership and People's War* (London: Hurst & Co., 2002 [original edn 1983]).
52. António Tomás, *O Fazedor de Utopias. Uma biografia de Amílcar Cabral* (Lisbon: Tinta da China, 2008), chapter 8.
53. Brief assessments of his contributions to the post-war African historiography can be found in Stephen Ellis, 'Writing Histories of Contemporary Africa', *Journal of African History* 43 (2003), and Jason Parker and Richard Rathbone, *African History: A Very Short Introduction* (Oxford: Oxford University Press, 2007).
54. Basil Davidson, *The Liberation of Guinea: Aspects of an African Revolution* (Harmondsworth: Penguin Books, 1969). For the Penguin African Library, see the post by Josh McPhee ('111: Penguin African Library: Part 1) in https://justseeds.org/jbbtc-111-penguin-african-library-pt-1/ [accessed 12 March 2021] and Alistair McCleery, 'Minding Their Own Business: Penguin in Southern Africa', *Journal of Southern African Studies* 44, no. 3 (2018).
55. See Dalila Cabrita Mateus and Álvaro Pereira, *Purga em Angola. O 27 de Maio de 1977* (Lisbon: Texto, 2009), chapter 2; Lara Pawson, *In the Name of the People: Angola's Forgotten Massacre* (London: I.B. Tauris, 2014).
56. These internal dissensions are presented in great detail in Jean-Michel Mabeko-Tali, *Guerrilhas e Lutas Sociais. O MPLA Perante si Próprio 1960–1977* (Lisbon: Mercado das Letras, 2018 [original edn 2001]).

57. Basil Davidson, 'Advance in Angola: Guerrillas head for the Atlantic', *Sunday Times*, 16 August 1970.

58. See the chapters 'The neo-colonial variant' and 'The road ahead' in Basil Davidson, *In the Eye of the Storm: Angola's People* (Harmondsworth: Penguin Books, 1975 [original ed. 1972]).

59. See Basil Davidson, 'South Africa and Portugal', *Issue: A Journal of Opinion* 4, no. 2 (1974), and Basil Davidson *Can Africa Survive? Arguments Against Growth without Development* (Heineman: London, 1974).

60. Anthony Gifford, 'Basil Davidson and the African Liberation Struggle', *Race & Class* 36, no. 2 (1994).

61. See Basil Davidson, *Growing from Grassroots: The State of Guinea-Bissau* (CFMAG: London, 1973).

62. See Victor Barros, 'Connected Struggles: Networks of Anticolonial Solidarity and the Liberation Movements of the Portuguese Colonies in Africa', in *Transnational Solidarity*, ed. Maasri et al. 131–52. Minutes on some of the 'pan-European' conferences of these solidarity committees in the early 1970s are held in the collection of the Committee for the Freedom in Mozambique, Angola and Guinea (CFMAG) at the Bishopgate Institute, London.

63. Basil Davidson, 'Cahora Bàssa', *Présence Africaine* 82 (1972), 39–51.

64. Pedro Aires Oliveira, 'Generous Albion? Portuguese Anti-Salazarists in the United Kingdom, c. 1960–1974', *Portuguese Studies* 27, no. 2 (2011).

65. Samples of these materials, as well as some correspondence and other documentation, can be found in the CFMAG collection.

66. See the brochure 'Speech at a Mass Meeting in Central Hall, London, on 26th October 1971', CFMAG collection.

67. Telegram from Portuguese embassy in London to MFA (Lisbon), 27 October 1971, AHD, Collection of Telegrams London-Lisbon.

68. See Norrie MacQueen and Pedro Aires Oliveira, '"Grocer meets Butcher": Marcello Caetano's London Visit of 1973 and the Last Days of Portugal's Estado Novo', *Cold War History* 10, no. 1 (2010).

69. Gifford, 'Basil Davidson', 87.

70. Report from the Metropolitan Police/Special Branch, 22 May 1973, Arquivo Nacional Torre do Tombo (Lisbon), PIDE/DGS Archive. SC. CI (2). UI 7690.

71. Basil Davidson, 'The men who killed black Africa's top guerrilla', *Sunday Times*, 8 April 1973.

72. See José Manuel Duarte de Jesus, *Eduardo Mondlane. Um homem a abater* (Coimbra: Almedina, 2010) and George Roberts, 'The Assassination of Eduardo Mondlane: FRELIMO, Tanzania, and the Politics of Exile in Dar es Salaam', *Cold War History* 17, no. 1 (2017).

73. See MacQueen and Aires Oliveira, '"Grocer Meets Butcher"', and Mustafah Dhada, *The Portuguese Massacre of Wiryamu in Colonial Mozambique, 1964–2013* (New York: Bloomsbury Academic, 2016).

74. Aerogram 81 from Portuguese embassy in London to MFA, 25 May 1973, AHD, PEA/26 (1974).

75. Pedro Aires Oliveira, 'The UK and the Independence of Portuguese Africa 1974–1976: Stakes, Perceptions and Policy Options', *Revue Française de Civilisation Britanique* 18, no. 2 (2013).

76. See Schliehe, *West German Solidarity*, and Rui Lopes, *West Germany and the Portuguese Dictatorship 1968–1974* (Basingstoke: Palgrave Macmillan, 2014).

77. See Tor Sellström, *Sweden and National Liberation in Southern Africa*, 2 vols. (Uppsala: Nordiska Afrikainstitutet, 1999).

78. Brittain, 'Basil Davidson'.

79. Howe, 'The Interpreter', 25. Davidson's post-1974 unqualified support for Neto and the MPLA is critically mentioned in Pawson, *In the Name of the People*, namely in the context of the Nito Alves 'failed coup' of 27 May 1977 and the fierce retaliations commanded by the Angolan President.

80. An FCO profile about Davidson dated August 1979 described him as 'sometimes hostile to HMG, but not exclusively extreme. He remains a Marxist and strongly "anti-colonialist", and he is still associated, though not very actively, with certain front organisations.' TNA, FCO 106/82.

81. Concerning the UK's stance in relation to Angola and Mozambique after 1974 see Oliveira, 'The UK and the Independence', and Geraint Hughes, 'Soldiers of Misfortune: the Angolan Civil War, The British Mercenary Intervention, and UK Policy towards Southern Africa, 1975–6', *The International History Review* 36, no. 3 (2014).

Bibliography

Alves, Tânia. *1961 – Sob o Viés da Imprensa. Os jornais portugueses, britânicos e franceses na conjuntura da eclosão da guerra no império português*. Unpubl. PhD dissertation, University of Lisbon, 2018.
Barros, Victor. 'The French Anticolonial Solidarity Movement and the Liberation of Guinea and Cape Verde'. *International History Review* 42, no. 6 (2020): 1297–318.
Barros, Victor, 'Connected Struggles: Networks of Anticolonial Solidarity and the Liberation Movements of the Portuguese Colonies in Africa'. In *Transnational Solidarity: Anticolonialism in the Global Sixties*, edited by Zeina Maasri, Cathy Burgin and Francesca Burke, 131–53. Manchester: Manchester University Press, 2022.
Benenson, Peter. *Persecution 1961*. Harmondsworth: Penguin, 1961.
Bernal, Martin. 'Basil Davidson: A Personal Appreciation', *Race & Class* 36, no. 2 (1994).
Buchanan, Tom. '"The Truth Will Set You Free": The Making of Amnesty International', *Journal of Contemporary History* 37, no. 4 (2002): 375–97.
Cann, John P. *Counterinsurgency in Africa: The Portuguese Way of War 1961–1974*. Westport CT: Greenwood Press, 1997.
Chabal, Patrick et al. *A History of Postcolonial Lusophone Africa*. London: Hurst & Co., 2002.
Chabal, Patrick. *Amilcar Cabral: Revolutionary Leadership and People's War*. London: Hurst & Co., 2002 (1983).
Davidson, Basil. *Report on Southern Africa*. London: Jonathan Cape, 1952.
Davidson, Basil. *What Really Happened in Hungary: A Personal Record*. London: UDC, 1957.
Davidson, Basil. *Angola, 1961. The Factual Record*. London: UDC, 1961.
Davidson, Basil. *The Liberation of Guinea: Aspects of an African Revolution*. Harmondsworth: Penguin Books, 1969.
Davidson, Basil. 'Cahora Bassa', *Présence Africaine* 82 (1972): 39–51.
Davidson, Basil. *Growing from Grassroots: The State of Guinea-Bissau*. CFMAG: London, 1973.
Davidson, Basil. *Can Africa Survive? Arguments Against Growth without Development*. Heineman: London, 1974.
Davidson, Basil. 'South Africa and Portugal', *Issue: A Journal of Opinion* 4, no. 2 (1974): 9–20.
Davidson, Basil. *In the Eye of the Storm: Angola's People*. Harmondsworth: Penguin Books, 1975 (original edn 1972).
Davidson, Basil. *Special Operations Europe: Scenes from the Anti-Nazi War*. London: Gollancz, 1980.

Davidson, Basil. *The Search for Africa*. London: James Currey, 1994.
Davison, Peter, ed. *Orwell and Politics*. Harmondsworth: Penguin Books, 2001.
Dhada, Mustafah. *Warriors at Work: How Guinea Was Really Set Free*. Niwot, CO: University Press of Colorado, 1993.
Dhada, Mustafah. *The Portuguese Massacre of Wiryamu in Colonial Mozambique, 1964–2013*. New York: Bloomsbury Academic, 2016.
Djassi, Abel (alias of Amílcar Cabral). *The Fact About Portugal's Colonies*. London: UDC, 1960.
Duarte de Jesus, José Manuel. *Eduardo Mondlane. Um homem a abater*. Coimbra: Almedina, 2010.
Ellis, Stephen, 'Writing Histories of Contemporary Africa', *Journal of African History* 43 (2003): 1–26.
Fyfe, Christopher, ed. *African Studies since 1945: A Tribute to Basil Davidson*. London: Longman, 1976.
Gifford, Anthony. 'Basil Davidson and the African Liberation Struggle', *Race & Class* 36, no. 2 (1994): 85–8.
Gildea, Robert, James Mark and Niek Pas. 'European Radicals and the "Third World". Imagined Solidarities and Radical Networks, 1958–1973', *Cultural and Social History* 8, no. 4 (2011): 449–71.
Hodgkin, Thomas. 'Where the Paths Began'. In *African Studies since 1945: A Tribute to Basil Davidson*, edited by Christopher Fyfe. London: Longman, 1976.
Howe, Stephen. *Anticolonialism in British Politics: The Left and the End of Empire 1918–1964*. Oxford: Oxford University Press, 1993.
Howe, Stephen. 'The Interpreter: Basil Davidson as Public Intellectual', *Race & Class* 36, no. 2 (1994): 19–43.
Howe, Stephen. 'Labour and International Affairs'. In *Labour's First Century*, edited by Pat Thane, Nick Tiratsoo, Duncan Tanner, 119–50. Cambridge: Cambridge University Press, 2000.
Hughes, Geraint. 'Soldiers of Misfortune: The Angolan Civil War, The British Mercenary Intervention, and UK Policy towards Southern Africa, 1975–6', *The International History Review* 36, no. 3 (2014): 493–512.
Kalter, Christoph. *The Discovery of the Third World: Decolonization and the Rise of the New Left in France*. Cambridge: Cambridge University Press, 2016.
Kornetis, Kostis. '"Cuban Europe"? Greek and Iberian *thirdmondisme* in the "Long 1960s"', *Journal of Contemporary History* 50, no. 3 (2015): 1–30.
Laban, Michel. *Mário Pinto de Andrade. Uma Entrevista*. Lisbon: João Sá da Costa, 1997.

Lara, Lúcio. *Documentos e Comentários para a História do MPLA. Até Fev. 1961*. Lisbon: Dom Quixote, 1999.

Lara, Lúcio, ed. *Um Amplo Movimento . . . : Itinerário do MPLA através de documentos de Lúcio Lara: 1961–1962*. Luanda: Edição do Autor, 2006.

Lopes, Rui. *West Germany and the Portuguese Dictatorship 1968–1974*. Basingstoke: Palgrave Macmillan, 2014.

Mabeko-Tali, Jean-Michel. *Guerrilhas e Lutas Sociais. O MPLA Perante si Próprio 1960–1977*. Lisbon: Mercado das Letras, 2018 (2001).

MacQueen, Norrie. *The Decolonization of Portuguese Africa: Metropolitan Revolution and the Dissolution of Empire*. London: Longman, 1997.

MacQueen, Norrie. 'Belated Decolonization and UN Politics against the Backdrop of the Cold War: Portugal, Britain and Guinea-Bissau's Proclamation of Independence, 1973–1974', *Journal of Cold War Studies* 8, no. 4 (2006): 29–56.

MacQueen, Norrie and Pedro Aires Oliveira. '"Grocer meets Butcher": Marcello Caetano's London visit of 1973 and the last days of Portugal's Estado Novo', *Cold War History* 10, no. 1 (2010): 29–50.

Maasri, Zeina, Cathy Burgin and Francesca Burke, eds. *Transnational Solidarity: Anticolonialism in the Global Sixties*. Manchester: Manchester University Press, 2022.

Mateus, Dalila Cabrita and Álvaro Pereira. *Purga em Angola. O 27 de Maio de 1977*. Lisbon: Texto, 2009.

McCleery, Alistair. 'Minding Their Own Business: Penguin in Southern Africa', *Journal of Southern African Studies* 44, no. 3 (2018): 509–17.

Munslow, Barry. 'Basil Davidson and Africa: A Biographical Essay', *Race & Class* 36, no. 2 (1994): 1–17.

Oliveira, Pedro Aires. 'Generous Albion? Portuguese Anti-Salazarists in the United Kingdom, c. 1960–1974', *Portuguese Studies* 27, no. 2 (2011): 175–207.

Oliveira, Pedro Aires. *Os Despojos da Aliança. A Grã-Bretanha e a Questão Colonial Portuguesa 1945–1975*. Lisbon: Tinta da China, 2007.

Oliveira, Pedro Aires. 'The UK and the Independence of Portuguese Africa 1974–1976: Stakes, Perceptions and Policy Options', *Revue Française de Civilisation Britannique* 18, no. 2 (2013): 105–28.

Parker, Jason and Richard Rathbone. *African History: A Very Short Introduction*. Oxford: Oxford University Press, 2007.

Pawson, Lara. *In the Name of the People: Angola's Forgotten Massacre*. London: I.B. Tauris, 2014.

Roberts, George. 'The Assassination of Eduardo Mondlane: FRELIMO, Tanzania, and the Politics of Exile in Dar es Salaam', *Cold War History* 17, no. 1 (2017): 1–19.

Schliehe, Nils. 'West German Solidarity Movements and the Struggle for the Decolonization of Lusophone Africa', *Revista Crítica de Ciências Sociais* 118 (2019): 173–94.

Sellström, Tor. *Sweden and National Liberation in Southern Africa*. Uppsala: Nordiska Afrikainstitutet, 1999.

Tomás, António. *O Fazedor de Utopias. Uma biografia de Amílcar Cabral*. Lisbon: Tinta da China, 2008.

Weigert, Stephen L. *Angola: A Modern Military History 1961–2002*. Basingstoke: Palgrave, 2011.

Wolfers, Michael. *Thomas Hodgkin: Wandering Scholar*. Monmouth: Merlin Press, 2007.

Chapter 5

Olof Palme, Sweden and the Vietnam War: An outspoken socialist among European socialists

Lubna Z. Qureshi

To the dismay of US President Lyndon B. Johnson, no Western European nation contributed troops to the American military intervention in Southeast Asia. For the most part, Western Europeans did not consider South Vietnam worth the investment.[1] The reunification of distant Vietnam under Communist rule would not threaten the security of their own continent. This did not mean that Western European leaders collectively spoke out against the war. In fact, a few conservatives even defended it, including West German chancellor Ludwig Erhard, who was in office from 1963 to 1966, and British Prime Minister Alec Douglas-Home, who briefly held power from 1963 to 1964.[2] Even the arrival of Labourite Harold Wilson at 10 Downing Street in October 1964 brought about no substantial alteration in British policy on Vietnam. Once Operation Rolling Thunder, Johnson's bombing campaign against North Vietnam, got underway, Wilson stood in the House of Commons to make 'absolutely plain our support of the American stand against the Communist infiltration of South Vietnam'.[3] Pressure from within his own Labour party forced Wilson to express mild regret after the 1966 bombing of major metropolitan areas in North Vietnam, but apart from that, Wilson remained publicly supportive of Lyndon Johnson. It was the firm policy of the British government to please Washington.[4] Even in a private meeting with Swedish leader of the Social Democratic Party (1969–1986) and Prime Minister Olof Palme in 1970, Wilson defended the Vietnam policy of the new American president, Richard M. Nixon.[5]

Olof Palme of Sweden was not the first leader in Western Europe to boldly and passionately criticise the American war in Vietnam. Eight years before Palme assumed his office in 1969, French President Charles de Gaulle had warned his American counterpart, John F. Kennedy, against the pursuit of a neo-colonial role in Vietnam. He warned the younger man with profound foresight:

> You will find that intervention in this area will be an endless entanglement. Once a nation has been aroused, no foreign power, however young, can impose its will upon it. You will discover this for yourselves ... You Americans wanted to take our place in Indo-China. Now you want to take over where we let off and revive a war which we brought to an end. I predict that you will sink step by step into a bottomless military and political quagmire, however much you spend in men and money.[6]

In 1966, as the war raged under Johnson, Kennedy's successor, the French president publicly condemned the Vietnam War as a 'murderous' violation of the Vietnamese people's right to self-determination.[7] De Gaulle was a man who was hard to place politically, and his opposition to the war was primarily strategic and tactical, rather than moral. De Gaulle decried the 'exorbitant privilege' enjoyed by the United States, when the dollar functioned as the reserve currency for the franc and when the value of the dollar, in turn, depended on the American supply of gold. Even before the formal abandonment of the gold standard in 1971, Washington relied on deficit spending, regardless of the supply of that precious metal. Deficit spending led to the inflation of the dollar, and consequently, the franc.[8] Most importantly, de Gaulle challenged the Vietnam War as part of the Cold War system that divided the world on bipolar terms. De Gaulle aspired toward a multipolar system that would enhance the status of France, allowing it a dominant role in Europe, and believed that Paris deserved as much of a say in world affairs as Washington and Moscow. De Gaulle's ambitions for an expansive French role in the Third World of the 1960s also influenced his thinking and strategy over the Vietnam War.[9] Simultaneously, de Gaulle assumed that the Vietnam War would weaken the United States, rendering it less able to counter the Soviet Union in Europe, which in turn, would have a deleterious effect on France. The war in Southeast Asia could have potentially resulted in the withdrawal of US forces from West Germany, obliging the French to make up the difference in ground forces. De Gaulle dreaded the prospect of an enlarged French troop presence in West Germany, for he wished to concentrate French expenditure on France's independent programme for nuclear weapons.[10] Once de Gaulle realised that the Johnson administration would not withdraw any US forces from Western Europe, he had less to say about Vietnam.[11] In 1968, his government started to discourage, and in some cases even prevent, antiwar demonstrations in Paris.[12]

Neutral Sweden also opposed the US intervention in Vietnam, but with far greater moral intensity. Paradoxically, this opposition was sustained *both* by Swedish collaboration with other Western European countries *and* by Swedish neutrality.

Growing Swedish outrage

Long before the Vietnam War consumed the world's attention, Olof Palme questioned its morality. The US dollar may have also backed the Swedish krona, but his concerns transcended monetary considerations. When Palme, as minister without portfolio, addressed the issue in 1965, he saw the popular Vietnamese struggle as part of a broader colonial fight for liberation in Asia and Africa: 'We must learn to live with it and perhaps also for it.'[13] Yet, once he became Prime Minister, Palme conducted a delicate balancing act. While he actively opposed the US intervention in Vietnam, he strove to maintain a relationship with Washington. When he visited the United States in June 1970, his criticism of the war was measured and cautious. 'You say that the people of Vietnam should have had the opportunity for self-determination,' an interviewer noted on *The Today Show*, a programme on the NBC television network. 'Do you think they would have that opportunity if the North Vietnamese and the Vietcong took over'?[14] Palme began in a hesitant fashion: 'It's very difficult to say. We can't speak of democracy in the same way as we do in our countries'.[15] The Prime Minister, however, did go on to explicitly state: 'Only that I think the NLF [National Liberation Front], to a large extent, has represented the national aspirations of the Vietnamese people'.[16]

Palme employed his rhetoric, polite though it was, as an expression of official Swedish neutrality. He opposed the Vietnam War for its violation of Vietnamese self-determination. Superpower aggression against one small country threatened all the others. Addressing his American audience during his June 1970 visit, Palme said: 'The superpowers are in a position to destroy themselves, but in so doing they will destroy the others. But the small nations cannot escape being affected by their actions. This is why the small nations would like to have a word in the councils'.[17] On that same trip, Palme also said: 'When we express opinions on different questions they are based on our own independent judgment. This is fully compatible with a foreign policy based on strict neutrality as far as national security is concerned'.[18]

Toward the end of 1972, Hanoi was subjected to terror from the air. Starting on Friday 6 October, the United States attacked the North Vietnamese capital with a particular ferocity that did not end until Monday 9 October. Ambassador Jean-Christophe Öberg survived a relatively close call on that first day. 'During Friday's raids an American missile was fired, which is said to be the type known as the "Shrike",[19] toward the city centre and claimed twenty-six dead and injured,' Öberg reported. 'The missile fell less than 300 meters from the embassy and hit a residential block'.[20]

Shortly before noon on 12 October, the French diplomatic mission in Hanoi did not prove as fortunate as the Swedish embassy. Even though the French mission was located in a diplomatic area, far from any industrial targets or North Vietnamese government buildings, its residence was all but destroyed in yet another US bombing raid over the North Vietnamese capital. Pierre Susini, the delegate-general, was trapped in the rubble. The Swedish ambassador immediately visited the affected site, even trying to dig Susini out with a shovel. A Vietnamese soldier stopped Öberg, warning him that the bombing could resume. Öberg recounted that, even though he had neglected to bring his helmet:

> I remained on the spot until Pierre Susini was dug out and carried away by ambulance. He still was conscious. The day before, he had borrowed a record from me, Mozart's 'Piano Concerto No. 23 in A major.' The theme of Elvira Madigan [a 1967 film by Swedish director Bo Widerberg]. The album cover lay scorched among the ruins. It was unreal, like a dream.[21]

Determined to help in some way, Öberg informed Stockholm via radio of the catastrophe: 'The French radio connection was broken off. We were suddenly the only link with Western Europe'.[22] Quickly getting word, Swedish Foreign Minister Krister Wickman addressed the atrocity before the UN General Assembly in New York that very day.[23] As soon as he could, Öberg made available the Swedish embassy's own radio system to other members of the French delegation. They reached the French embassy in Stockholm.[24] Courtesy of the Swedish embassy in Hanoi, Susini's deputy could then communicate with his superiors in Paris.[25] The Swedish ambassador closely monitored the condition of the comatose Susini, who bore third-degree burns on more than half his body, among other injuries. Against the recommendation of his Vietnamese doctors, who insisted that Susini was in no condition to travel, the delegate-general was flown back to France several days later for additional medical care.[26] Susini would die on 19 October in a Lyon hospital.[27]

Initially, US Secretary of Defence Melvin Laird and Secretary of State William Rogers attempted to blame North Vietnamese anti-aircraft missiles for the bombing of the French delegation's residence. Öberg had been very intimate friends with Susini, frequently meeting to play tennis together. He had also known Susini's partner, Aleya, who had been killed instantly.[28] Wiring Stockholm as Susini lay dying, the Swedish ambassador bitterly scoffed at Laird's explanation:

> One could maybe begin by asking Defence Secretary Laird how come the Vietnamese civil defense immediately after the direct hit found three additional, undetonated American bombs in the delegation's immediate vicinity right after the direct hit. One can further ask the American Defense Secretary how he can explain that an additional building in the delegation's neighborhood was totally destroyed by two American bombs, of which one could be identified.[29]

Shortly afterward, a French commission of inquiry determined that the bombs did, in fact, come from the United States.[30] It was only then that the Americans owned up to their mistake.[31] The Swedish ambassador's humanitarianism was duly acknowledged, with French Foreign Minister Maurice Schumann personally thanking the Swedish government for Öberg's aid after the bombing.[32]

In spite of the unofficial agreement reached by National Security Advisor Henry Kissinger and North Vietnamese diplomat Le Duc Tho in Paris in December of 1972, Nixon ordered the bombing of the North Vietnamese cities of Hanoi and Haiphong shortly before Christmas. Officially known as Linebacker[33] II, since the original Linebacker campaign had taken place earlier that year, the so-called Christmas Bombings lasted from 18 to 27 December. Linebacker II was mainly a signal to the government in Saigon that the US president would maintain his commitment to the regime after the withdrawal of American troops.[34] Some 40,000 tons of bombs fell on Hanoi and 15,000 on Haiphong, leaving more than 1,600 people dead.[35]

Particularly offensive to the Swedes, and to Palme himself, was that the fact that Bach Mai hospital in Hanoi had also been hit. The destruction of the hospital was a blow not only for North Vietnam but for the Swedes as well, given the fact that Sweden had contributed a great deal of aid to it.[36] Whether deliberate or not, hospitals were frequently hit in the bombing raids over North Vietnam in 1972. Bach Mai had, in fact, already been damaged in a bombing raid that June as well.[37]

Outraged, Palme sent a telegram in French to North Vietnamese Prime Minister Pham Van Dong: 'In this moment of new difficult tests for your people I express our sympathy with the victims of the bombings and confirm our solidarity with the demand for a speedy settlement that secures the Vietnamese people's right to determine their own future'.[38] Yet, Palme felt compelled to do more than reassure the North Vietnamese; he had to confront the Americans. Palme, therefore, decided to take a stand. He sought the advice of his Social Democratic counterparts in Austria and West Germany, Bruno Kreisky and Willy Brandt, respectively.[39]

Palme, Kreisky and Brandt

The three leaders shared strong cultural connections. Palme was a native of Stockholm, but had grown up speaking German with his mother, a progeny of the ethnic German nobility of Latvia.[40] Both chancellors had close ties to Sweden. Kreisky, an Austrian of Jewish descent and an active socialist, had spent the Second World War in Stockholm. He had obtained a Swedish visa through the efforts of Torsten Nilsson, who was active in the International Socialist Youth, and who would later serve as Palme's first foreign minister.[41] The German Brandt, also a socialist opponent of the Nazis, had found refuge in Sweden as well as Norway.[42] The Social Democratic movement in Sweden would shape the political development of the two refugees, whose friendship began there. They also made the acquaintance of the economist Gunnar Myrdal and his wife, the sociologist Alva Myrdal. The Myrdals were leading intellectual lights in the Social Democratic movement.[43] As Kreisky observed: 'In Scandinavia, we not only felt at home . . . the political ideals that we held coincided with the aims of our Scandinavian friends'.[44] Brandt later recalled that in 'Swedish Social Democracy, even more conspicuously than in its Norwegian counterpart, I saw an undogmatic, free, popular, and confident movement'.[45] Soon after the war, Kreisky returned to Stockholm as the diplomatic representative for Austria. His job was to establish an embassy, but he lacked the money to fulfil it. The Swedish Foreign Ministry covered his expenses with a greatly appreciated loan.[46] When Kreisky and Brandt got to know Palme in the 1960s, they were already well disposed toward Sweden.[47]

Palme and Brandt both reached the pinnacle of power in October of 1969, and Kreisky would do so the following year. When it came to the Vietnam War, Kreisky and Brandt agreed with Palme. 'Surprising as it may sound,' Kreisky reflected later, 'Olof Palme proved himself to be truly pro-American when by campaigning for an end to the Vietnam conflict he tried to spare the American people a military defeat. Those who thought they had to pursue a policy of strength achieved precisely the opposite'.[48] Notwithstanding Kreisky's personal opposition to war, his archive, held in Vienna, contains no record of any public statement against the Christmas Bombings.[49] Like Sweden, Austria was a neutral country. In contrast to the Swedish policy of non-alignment, which was officially declared but still informal, Austria's version was officially ratified by the Austrian State Treaty of 1955 and enshrined in the national constitution.[50] As early as 1959, Kreisky had concluded that Austrian neutrality relied on 'an international equilibrium . . . It follows, then, that Austrian foreign policy must always aim to help maintain the balance of power by contributing in all ways possible toward lessening international tensions'.[51] Certainly, Palme's rhetoric increased international tensions, which the Austrian chancellor sought to avoid. Formal constraints prevented Kreisky from speaking out. Moreover, the Socialist International had given Kreisky the job of attending to the intractable Israeli–Palestine conflict, while Vietnam was officially made Palme's domain. After the Vietnam War, and once he relinquished office, Kreisky would conclude with remarkable prescience: 'Never has such an irresponsible and pointless war been fought more than that one, and we do not know if it will be the last'.[52]

Brandt, for his part, had his own reasons to disapprove of the war. Not only did the West German chancellor suspect that the conflict in Southeast Asia would eventually result in an American military evacuation from Europe, which was a terrifying prospect for him, he also objected to the war on moral grounds. At the same time, Brandt refrained from criticising the Nixon administration directly.[53] West Germany, unlike Austria, belonged to the North Atlantic Treaty Organization (NATO). The United States was a guarantor for West Berlin. In addition, Brandt needed Washington's support for his *Ostpolitik*, or his policy of rapprochement with East Germany and the rest of Eastern Europe.[54] According to the minutes of his telephone conversation with Brandt, Palme 'said that the bombings now involved systematic destruction of a country', sincerely expressing in private the same sentiments that he would very soon be expressing in public.[55] The West German chancellor mentioned that he had been in touch with General Secretary Leonid Brezhnev of the Soviet Union, whose reaction to the Christmas Bombings was 'entirely undramatic'.[56] Understanding Brezhnev's muted response, the Swedish Prime Minister observed 'that Russians clearly were "patient" and that they also were economically dependent on the U.S.A'.[57] Palme also suspected that Brezhnev believed the American war in Vietnam would somehow exculpate any future Soviet intervention in a Eastern European country.[58]

As for West Germany, the Swedish Prime Minister proposed that Brandt and French President Georges Pompidou 'propose mediation or at least make a public statement'.[59] Brandt claimed that his government had already issued a quiet démarche to the Nixon administration, and added that he was thinking about making a public statement. The Swedish Prime Minister promptly reported to Hanoi what the West German chancellor had said.[60]

The Christmas Bombing speech: Palme's outspokenness, Nixon's fury

Palme also consulted with his mentor and predecessor, former Prime Minister Tage Erlander, and with the Myrdals. Another advisor, Anders Ferm, wrote a draft of a speech, which the Prime Minister revised in his own words at his own kitchen table at home on the night of 22 December.[61] As evidence of the Prime Minister's literary contribution, a draft of the speech in Palme's own handwriting is available at the Labour Movement Archive in Sweden.[62] 'It was not an instant reaction,' Palme later recounted. 'It was building up inside of me since the bombing resumed. We had many discussions on it over a period of five days or so. And then, that evening, I knew what I had to say about it.'[63] The Prime Minister knew what he had to say, even without the counsel of his own Foreign Ministry.[64] 'He didn't ask anybody for permission', remembered Kai Falkman of the Swedish Foreign Ministry, nor did he 'gather the government, and said: "Do you think that . . . ?" Then, there would be compromises and he didn't want that. But he was so strong'.[65]

On 23 December, Palme recorded a speech that was first broadcast on Swedish radio, and then textually transmitted to the international media. He also gave an encore on film for Swedish television. In this speech, Palme dispensed with his customary tact. He had no fear of offending Washington.[66] 'We should call things by their proper names,' Palme began, speaking from the heart. 'What is going on in Vietnam today is a form of torture.' North Vietnam was no threat to the United States, so Nixon's action had no justification at all: 'People are being punished, a nation is being punished in order to humiliate it, to force it to submit to force'.[67] He compared the Christmas Bombings to the Jewish Holocaust of the Second World War, the German and Italian bombing of the doomed Spanish town of Guernica in 1937, the 1940 mass execution of Polish officers by the Soviet Union, and the 1960 massacre of black demonstrators in Sharpeville, South Africa. Thus, Palme closed his speech with a roll call of atrocities: 'Guernica, Oradour, Babi Yar, Katyn, Lidice, Sharpeville, and Treblinka. Now a new name will be added to the list: Hanoi, Christmas 1972'.[68]

The text of the speech arrived at the Washington embassy via telex on Saturday 23 December. As the officer on duty, First Secretary Jan Eliasson found his holiday weekend disturbed: 'It wasn't a regular working day. I remember I came to the embassy, and it was not open'.[69] Once inside, Eliasson examined the telex, and concluded: 'This is dynamite'.[70] Swedish Ambasssador Hubert de Besche planned to visit friends in Virginia, but Eliasson realised the situation was urgent. 'And I called him and said, "Ambassador, I have the sense that you should not leave town",' Eliasson recounted, adding: 'You will have a reaction during the day from someone, I'm sure'.[71] De Besche, therefore, awaited the inevitable summons from the State Department.

Although the reaction from the Nixon administration would come that same day, telegrams from the Swedish embassy in Hanoi gave the Prime Minister no reason to take back what he had said. Chargé d'affaires Eskil Lundberg reported that the bombing raids on 19 and 22 December that had struck Bach Mai hospital had killed one surgeon, fifteen nurses, one pharmacist and six medical students. Three buildings in the medical complex, including the central laboratory, were damaged.[72] With the rest of the local diplomatic corps, Lundberg soon inspected the damage for himself, which turned out to be even worse than expected: 'One can conclude that the material damage with regard to the buildings is now total'.[73] Visiting the hospital himself two weeks later, Ambassador Öberg concurred with the assessment of his chargé d'affaires. He reported that 'the destruction there was total, repeat total. Of the buildings that remain none should be used further'.[74] The ambassador noted that the casualty toll was even higher now, with thirty people dead, including five doctors.[75] The US president, who could never handle criticism with good grace, was very angry.[76]

True, many Western countries officially criticised the aerial assault on Hanoi and Haiphong. For instance, Mitchell Sharp, Canada's secretary of state for external affairs and deputy prime minister under the Liberal Pierre Trudeau, stated: 'We've made clear our opposition to bombing and to any escalation of the war'.[77] The chancellor of West Germany privately described the Christmas Bombings as 'disgusting and unfathomable', but for all the encouragement that he had given Palme, Brandt did not officially speak out.[78] According to Bernd Greiner, the prominent German historian and Americanist:

> Brandt never made a public statement – nor did he press the American government behind the scenes, i.e. diplomatically, to speed up the

efforts for a cease-fire or peace treaty in Vietnam. He did not even voice any disapproval in private talks with members of the Nixon administration. Whatever misgivings he had, he kept them to himself.[79]

Indeed, I have not found a record of any démarche from Bonn among American records. A spokesman for Brandt merely lamented the lack of a peace agreement in Vietnam, indicating the wish that the peace talks would 'soon achieve results'.[80] Brandt did discreetly defend Palme once Swedish–American relations had descended to a new low. Conversing with Kissinger at a Washington dinner, Brandt 'explained how very much the Swede was a product of his student years in the USA: Palme's reaction was like that of the younger Americans'.[81] In 1948, Palme had earned a bachelor's degree at Kenyon College in Ohio.[82] Later, Brandt attributed his own diplomatic tact to moral guilt:

> I thought it was certainly not for us Germans to put ourselves forward as lecturers in international politics and certainly not as moral judges; nor did I feel it advisable to interfere with the American Government in an area it said was vital. Consequently, I swallowed my grave doubts and held my tongue when it might have been better to make my opposition explicit on the one hand, and on the other make open display of my suppressed sympathies.[83]

The anti-Nazi Brandt had conducted himself impeccably during the Second World War. If any German had the right to make moral judgements, it was Willy Brandt. Yet, even the Socialist Brandt felt obligated to continue Bonn's non-military aid programme for South Vietnam, a holdover from the Erhard administration.[84]

Not that Palme blamed Brandt for his cautious approach, as veteran Swedish diplomat Rolf Ekéus noted:

> Willy Brandt became so important for Sweden, and for Palme, to the end of his life . . . I think Brandt made clear to Palme that: 'We, West Germany, cannot be, so to say, not be loyal to the United States . . . we have the Soviet Union. We have East Germany. We have these crazy guys.' So one can understand . . . it was just like a rational fear . . . I even participated in conversations with Brandt-Palme . . . one had to be careful. Palme was very, very smart. He understood it absolutely. Absolutely.[85]

Sweden's Nordic neighbours, Finland and Denmark, also had their say about the 1972 Christmas Bombings. 'It is especially difficult to understand on what arguments the vast bombardments of the North Vietnam territory have been based', commented Finnish Foreign Minister Ahti

Karjalainen, a political centrist.[86] Similarly to Austria, an international treaty had established the post-war neutrality of Finland.[87] Also similarly to Austria, Finland preferred a tone of restraint.[88] Danish Prime Minister Anker Jørgensen, a left-wing Social Democrat, was naturally more outspoken. That October, Jørgensen had publicly stated, 'USA out of Indochina!'[89] In response to the Christmas Bombings, Jørgensen said that prospects for ending the war and for a post-war reconstruction of Vietnam 'suffered a tragic setback . . . the parties and particularly the United States assume a heavy responsibility'.[90] Going further, Jørgensen said that Denmark would '"reconsider" its relationship with NATO'. Denmark retained its NATO membership, of course, and not even Jørgensen conveyed the same passion as Palme did. By then, the Labour party of Harold Wilson had lost power to the Conservatives, with the new Prime Minister, Edward Heath, being supportive of the Christmas Bombings. Speaking to *The New York Times* the following January, Heath stated: 'I can't forget that people were saying the bombing of Hanoi and Haiphong would start World War III – and it didn't'.[91]

The most grateful response to Palme's speech probably came via telegram from Prime Minister Pham Van Dong of North Vietnam. 'Thank you very sincerely for your concern during the new escalation of the extremely barbaric war of the United States, and at the same time for your warm support for the Vietnamese people's just fight'.[92] Using Ambassador Öberg as an intermediary shortly afterward, Dong not only re-expressed his gratitude to Palme, but extended another invitation to visit Hanoi. 'He added that no head of government enjoyed such confidence and popularity here as the Swedish prime minister', Öberg recounted. The North Vietnamese leader also rewarded Palme with a gift, a painting made by a local defence unit.[93]

For all his compliments for Palme, Dong was not quite so complimentary about French President Georges Pompidou, a political conservative who cared more about cultivating a close relationship with the United States than had his predecessor, de Gaulle. 'The prime minister offered scathing criticism of Pompidou's collaborative silence on the Vietnam question', Öberg wrote. 'France was more anxious to protect its colonial remnants in South Vietnam than to play an honourable role in Vietnam'.[94] The late President de Gaulle had removed his country's air defences and Mediterranean fleet from the NATO command structure, and had forbidden the placement of US tactical nuclear weapons in France.[95] By 1966, he had decided to remove French forces entirely from the NATO command structure, and expel any foreign military presence from France the following year.[96] Nevertheless, France had never left NATO and it was membership of NATO, as well as Pompidou's friendlier attitude toward the United States, that held France back from criticising the Christmas Bombing. After all, both Nixon and Kissinger hoped to create a new 'special relationship' with France, for which they regarded Pompidou as the vital linchpin.[97]

West German chancellor Willy Brant had been equally silent, but Dong bore him no ill-will. 'He said he understood the federal chancellor's difficulties in speaking publicly in plain language', the Swedish ambassador informed Palme. 'Pham Van Dong knows that you were in contact with Brandt during the climax of the bombing right before Christmas'.[98] The North Vietnamese Prime Minister was therefore aware that Brandt had advised Palme on his Christmas Bombing speech.

Most Western European leaders publicly opposed the continuation of the Vietnam War. The Prime Minister of Sweden felt freer to speak his mind than the rest. His comments stood apart in the comparison he drew between the Christmas Bombings and Nazi atrocities.[99] In the Second World War, Nixon had served as a naval lieutenant in the Pacific and even though the former logistics officer had faced little danger, and only from the Japanese, the American President now found the comparison with the Nazis impossible to stomach.[100] Kissinger reported that Palme's reference to the Third Reich was 'an aching wisdom tooth' for the President.[101] Although my evidence is circumstantial, I would suggest that the Swedish Prime Minister's words inflicted an even sharper toothache in the mouth of the national security advisor. Nixon had spent much of the Second World War in the South Pacific, but Kissinger, a member of a German-Jewish family, had suffered from direct contact with the Nazi menace. In 1938, he fled with his immediate family to the United States. At least thirteen relatives who had remained behind perished in the Holocaust.[102] During the Second World War, the young refugee then returned to his native land as an intelligence officer in the US Army.[103] 'Consciousness that societies can take a very evil turn,' Kissinger said later. 'This separates me from many Americans, who have never seen it, can't imagine it.'[104] Kissinger could have applied that statement to the Swedes. As Kissinger probably saw it, Palme knew nothing of evil – only he did. The overly sensitive Nixon and Kissinger should have realised that the best way to avoid comparisons to Nazis would have been to refrain from committing atrocities themselves. 'But Kissinger resented all the criticism directed at him', no matter what the reason, observed the historian Robert Dallek.[105]

It is important to remember that Kreisky himself had lost even more relatives to the Holocaust than Kissinger had, over twenty members of his extended family.[106] Despite his own painful personal history, Kreisky never criticised the Swedish Prime Minister's speech. In a collective letter to Palme and Kreisky written three months before the Christmas

Bombings, Brandt had pondered that 'after Auschwitz and Hiroshima, after Nuremberg and Song My [My Lai], we have just realized the barbarity into which the human being can fall, what strong forces oppose and fight attempts to organize peace and a humane community'.[107] Palme concurred with Brandt, and Kreisky raised no objection.[108]

On the very day that Palme delivered his speech, US Undersecretary of State for Political Affairs U. Alexis Johnson requested the appearance of Ambassador de Besche at the State Department in Washington at noon. Functioning as Acting Secretary of State, since everybody else was on vacation, Johnson made a statement to the Swedish ambassador that was authorised from the highest level:

> I am acting on direct personal instructions of the president. Let me say first, that personally I cannot recall any case of two states with diplomatic and friendly relations, where the chief of government of one state made such outrageous statements with regard to the government of the other state. I cannot recall any statement by the Swedish government about Nazi Germany same as what is now said in regard to the US. The president feels that given the Swedish government's relations with Nazi Germany, and what he feels was the cooperation, that statement comes with singular ill grace.[109]

Obviously, Palme had borne no responsibility for Sweden's provision of iron ore to Nazi Germany, or the permitted use of its territory for the transport of German troops to occupied Norway. Nixon, on the other hand, did bear direct responsibility for his own policy in Southeast Asia. Therefore, the US President's comment about Nazi Germany was the one that came with singular ill grace. Concluding his version of a history lesson, Under-Secretary Johnson went on:

> The US government, therefore, cannot come to any other conclusion than that the Swedish government attaches very little importance or value to its relations with the US, or the attitude of the US government towards Sweden. In consequence hereof, the charge d'affaires John Guthrie, who is now in the US, will not be returning to Sweden. It is further the view of the US government that it would not be useful for the successor to Ambassador De Besche, who has already got agreement, to come to the US at this time.[110]

So, Yngve Möller, de Besche's newly appointed replacement, would not be received in Washington, and John Guthrie, who had come home just for Christmas, would remain in the United States.[111] Furthermore, US Ambassador Jerome Holland had left Stockholm in August, and Washington would not replace him anytime soon.[112] De Besche was understandably incensed: 'I terminated the conversation by concluding that in the U.S.A., one found Palme's statement "outrageous" – in Sweden, one found the American bombing "outrageous"'.[113] Stockholm and Washington would not re-establish full diplomatic relations at the ambassadorial level for more than a year.

Conclusion: the significance of Swedish neutrality

In spite of these tensions, it would be a mistake to label the Palme government as anti-American. It was far more pro-American than publicly understood at the time. Historically distrustful of the Soviet Union, Sweden engaged in military collaboration with the United States within Europe.[114] Many critics of US foreign policy must have been sorely disappointed by this fact. In spite of this collaboration, Stockholm avoided collaboration with NATO. Sweden sought to preserve its independence by avoiding the US-dominated military organisation. By collaborating with the United States alone, was Sweden still not deferring to American authority? What difference did it make?

As an explanation, Ekéus referred to the concept of the Nordic Balance, with neutral Sweden effectively functioning as a buffer zone between the two blocs.[115]

More recently, Ekéus noted, Kissinger himself had recommended another buffer zone. In 2014, more than two decades after the dissolution of the Soviet Union, the former US Secretary of State endorsed the non-alignment of Ukraine: 'Far too often the Ukrainian issue is posed as a showdown: whether Ukraine joins the East or the West. But if Ukraine is to survive and thrive, it must not be either side's outpost against the other – it should function as a bridge between them'.[116]

Therefore, the former Secretary of State advised Ukraine against seeking official membership in NATO: 'internationally, they should pursue a posture comparable to that of Finland. The nation leaves no doubt about its fierce independence and cooperates with the West in most fields but carefully avoids institutional hostility toward Russia'.[117] In response to the Russian invasion of Ukraine in 2022, Kissinger would change his mind. Ekéus may have been critical of the retired American diplomat, but he also believed that Kissinger's initial thesis was relevant to the rest of Northern Europe:

> We should not build a sharp line between NATO and Russia up there, which would totally change the security structure in Europe. And that was, of course, American policy during that time, and our policy also.

We should not increase the tension. That meant also that Sweden couldn't be a base, shouldn't be a base, for attacks on the Soviet Union, now Russia ... So I think that is a policy which is a contribution to stability and peace in Northern Europe ... It would be real, serious undermining of European security if we, maybe with the Finns, start to build up a major front, a new front towards Russia.[118]

During the Cold War, official Swedish neutrality not only provided Northern Europe with a secure buffer zone, it allowed Stockholm greater independence of action in other international matters. Neutral Sweden was not a polite fiction, but something that existed in reality. In the phrasing of international relations scholar Ann-Marie Ekengren, Stockholm exercised a form of 'flexible neutrality'.[119] Regardless of Sweden's friendship with the United States, the Scandinavian country did not feel obligated to consult with the members of the North Atlantic Alliance before acting. From time to time, the Swedes could even challenge the Western superpower itself, as they did over the war in Vietnam.

Palme's commitment to socialism, the socialism that he shared with his colleagues Kreisky and Brandt, inspired the construction of his foreign policy. The key principles of that foreign policy were the rule of international law, the development of the Third World, self-determination of smaller countries, and Swedish sovereignty.[120] But it was the commitment to Swedish neutrality and their shared socialist beliefs that made that foreign policy possible.

Palme's wartime exchanges with the West German chancellor, conducted entirely in Swedish, proved particularly fruitful.[121] In 1976, one year after the war in Vietnam had ended, Palme would become vice president of the Socialist International, sharing the post with Kreisky and several others. The former Prime Minister, who would eventually return to his post, would then begin to work even more closely with the former chancellor, now chairman of the organisation. But the Palme–Brandt partnership had truly begun during the Vietnam War.[122]

Notes

1. Fredrik Logevall, 'The American Effort to Draw European States into the War', in *La Guerre du Vietnam et l'Europe*, ed. Christopher Goscha and Maurice Vaïsse (Brussels: Bruylant, 2003), 4, fn2.

2. Logevall, 'The American Effort', 8; Hubert Zimmerman, 'The Quiet German: The Vietnam War and the Federal Republic of Germany', in *La Guerre du Vietnam et l'Europe*, ed. Goscha and Vaïsse, 53.

3. John W. Young, 'British governments and the Vietnam War', in *La Guerre du Vietnam et l'Europe*, ed. Goscha and Vaïsse, 122.

4. Saki Dockrill (2003) 'The Anglo-US Linkage between Vietnam and the Pound: 1964 and 1968', in *La Guerre du Vietnam et l'Europe*, ed. Goscha and Vaïsse, 72; and Young, 'British governments', 122, 124. See also Rhiannon Vickers, 'Harold Wilson, the British Labour Party, and the War in Vietnam', *Journal of Cold War Studies* 10, no. 2 (2008). On British opinion of the war, see Sylvia A. Ellis, 'Promoting Solidarity at Home and Abroad: The Goals and Tactics of the Anti-Vietnam War Movement in Britain', *European Review of History: Revue européenne d'histoire* 21, no. 4 (2014).

5. Transcript of Harold Wilson's conversation with Olof Palme, 7 April 1970, The National Archives (London), PREM 13/3552 (courtesy of David Prentice).

6. Charles de Gaulle, *Memoirs of Hope: Renewal and Endeavor*, translated by Terence Kilmartin (New York: Simon and Schuster, 1971), 256.

7. Frédéric Bozo, *French Foreign Policy since 1945: An Introduction*, translated by Jonathan Hensher (New York: Berghahn Books, 2016), 72.

8. Hubert Zimmerman, 'Who Paid for America's War? Vietnam and the International Monetary System, 1960–1975', in *America, the Vietnam War, and the World: Comparative and International Perspectives*, ed. Andreas W. Daum, Lloyd C. Gardner and Wilfried Mausbach (Cambridge/New York: Cambridge University Press, 2003), 151–3, 156, 160–61. Electronic mail correspondence with Omar Choudhry, M.A., Economics, University of California, Berkeley, 18 January 2021; and with Professor Lori Maguire, University of Reims, 20 January 2021.

9. See for instance Joaquín Fermandois, 'The Hero on the Latin American Scene', in *Globalizing de Gaulle: International Perspectives on French Foreign Policies, 1958–1969*, ed. Christian Nuenlist, Anna Locher and Garret Martin (Lanham, MD: Lexington Books, 2010).

10. Mark Kramer, 'Introduction: De Gaulle and Gaullism in France's Cold War Foreign Policy', in *Globalizing de Gaulle*, ed. Nuenlist, Locher and Martin, 2, 15. Yuko Torikata, 'The U.S. Escalation in Vietnam and de Gaulle's Secret Search for Peace, 1964–1966', in *Globalizing de Gaulle*, ed. Nuenlist, Locher and Martin, 156–8.

11. Torikata, 'The U.S. Escalation in Vietnam', 171.

12. Bethany S. Keenan, '"The US Embassy Has Been Particularly Sensitive about This": Diplomacy, Antiwar Protests, and the French Ministry of Foreign Affairs during 1968', *French Historical Studies* 41, no. 2 (2018).

13. Prime Minister Palme's speech at the Congress of the Brotherhood in Gävle on 30 July 1965 (*Statsrådet Palmes anförande vid Broderskapsrörelsens kongress i Gävle den 30 juli 1965*), Swedish Labour Movement's Archives and Library, Olof Palme Archive (hereafter OPA), *Talserien*, vol. 676/2/4/0: 005. Electronic mail correspondence with Professor Erik Lindberg, Uppsala University, 27 June 2021; and with Professor Lars Magnusson, Uppsala University, 28 June 2021.

14. 'The Today Show: Television Interview', National Broadcasting Company, 9 June 1970, Swedish Information Service, OPA, *Talserien*, vol. 2.4.0: 021.

15. 'The Today Show: Television Interview'.

16. 'The Today Show: Television Interview'.

17. 'Address by Olof Palme at Kenyon College, Ohio, June 6, 1970', OPA, *Talserien*, vol. 2.4.0: 021.

18. 'Address by the Swedish Prime Minister, Mr. Olof Palme, to the National Press Club, Friday, June 5, 1970', OPA, *Talserien*, vol. 2.40: 021.

19. The Shrike was an anti-radiation air-to-ground missile that deliberately detected and then targeted anti-aircraft radar. Vice Admiral James Stockdale of the US Navy

later described the Shrike as 'an anti-radar honing missile', James Stockdale and Sybil Stockdale, *In Love and War: The Story of a Family's Ordeal and Sacrifice During the Vietnam Years* (New York: Harper and Row, 1984), 90.

20. Telegram 502 from Ambassador Jean-Christophe Öberg to Cabinet Stockholm, 'Amerikanska Bombningar mot DRV för Pol och Press', 9 October 1972, Riksarkivet (Arninge, Sweden; hereafter RA), HP 38:29, UD HP-Dossierer, Vietnamkriget, Mål:H. Hanoi politik, juli-december 1972.

21. Kaj Falkman, *Ekot från Vietnam: En diplomats minnen från kriget och återbesök fyrtio år senare* (Stockholm: Carlssons, 2014), 148. A. Lewis, 'Abroad at Home', *The New York Times*, 14 October 1972.

22. Falkman, *Ekot från Vietnam*, 148.

23. Falkman, *Ekot från Vietnam*, 148.

24. Falkman, *Ekot från Vietnam*, 148.

25. Falkman, *Ekot från Vietnam*, 92. Telegram 50 from Ambassador Jean-Christophe Öberg in Hanoi to Cabinet Stockholm, 11 October 1972, RA, HP 38:29, HP-Dossierer, Vietnamkriget, Mål: H. Hanoi politik, juli-december 1972.

26. 'A Career Diplomat', *The New York Times*, 21 October 1972, 3. Telegram 513 from Ambassador Jean-Christophe Öberg in Hanoi to Cabinet Stockholm, 11 October 1972. Telegram 516 from Öberg to Cabinet Stockholm, 12 October 1972. Telegram 527 from Öberg in Hanoi to Cabinet Stockholm, 17 October 1972; RA, HP 38:29, HP-Dossierer, Vietnamkriget, Mål: H. Hanoi politik, juli-december 1972.

27. 'A Career Diplomat'. Falkman, *Ekot från Vietnam*, 148.

28. Falkman, *Ekot från Vietnam*, 147–9.

29. Telegram 514 from Ambassador Jean-Christophe Öberg to Cabinet Stockholm, 'Amerikanska Bombningar Hanoi Onsday 11 Okt.', 12 October 1972, RA, HP 38:29, HP-Dossierer, Vietnamkriget, Mål: H. Hanoi politik, juli-december 1972.

30. Telegram 530 from Ambassador Jean-Christophe Öberg to Cabinet Stockholm, 17 October 1972, RA, HP 38:29, HP-Dossierer, Vietnamkriget, Mål: H. Hanoi politik, juli-december 1972.

31. Falkman, *Ekot från Vietnam*, 149.

32. Telegram 447 from Hamilton at the Swedish Embassy in Paris to Cabinet Stockholm, 13 October 1972, RA, HP 38:29, HP-Dossierer, Vietnamkriget, Mål: H. Hanoi politik, juli-december 1972.

33. A linebacker, incidentally, is a playing position in American football, Nixon's favourite spectator sport.

34. Marilyn Young, *The Vietnam Wars: 1945–1990* (New York: HarperPerennial, 1991), 278.

35. James William Gibson, *The Perfect War: Technowar in Vietnam* (Boston and New York: The Atlantic Monthly Press, 1986), 417.

36. Telegram 621 from Lundberg of the Swedish Embassy in Hanoi to Cabinet Stockholm, 'Re Fortsätta Bombningarna Hanoi-Området', 22 December 1972, RA, HP 38:30, HP-Dossierer, Vietnamkriget, Mål: H. Hanoi politik, 1972–1975.

37. 'Declaration of the DRVN Ministry of Public Health on the deliberate attacks ordered by the Nixon administration against hospitals and other sanitary institutions in North Viet Nam', 7 July 1972, forwarded by Ambassador Öberg in Hanoi to the Swedish Foreign Ministry, 'Bombningar av hälsovårdsetablissemang i DRV', 21 July 1972, RA, HP 38:29, HP-Dossierer, Vietnamkriget, Mål: H. Hanoi politik, juli-december 1972.

38. Telegram från statsminister Olof Palme till DRV:s regeringschef Pham Van Dong' 20 December 1972; press communiqué, Pressbyrån, Foreign Affairs Department, RA, HP 38:58, HP-Dossierer, Vietnamkriget, 1972–1974.

39. Memorandum by Sverker Åstrom of the Swedish Foreign Ministry, 21 December 1972, Foreign Affairs Department, RA, HP 38:58, HP-Dossierer, Vietnamkriget, 1972–1974.

40. Christian Salm, *Transnational Socialist Networks in the 1970s: European Community Development Aid and Southern Enlargement* (Basingstoke: Palgrave Macmillan, 2016), 37–8.

41. Bruno Kreisky, *The Struggle for a Democratic Austria: Bruno Kreisky on Peace and Social Justice* [edited by Matthew Paul Berg, in collaboration with Jill Lewis and Oliver Rathkolb, and translated by Helen Atkins and Matthew Paul Berg] (New York/Oxford: Berghahn Books, 2000), 168.

42. Hélène Miard-Delacroix, *Willy Brandt: The Life of a Statesman*, translated by Isabelle Chaize (London: I.B. Tauris, 2016), 31; Salm, *Transnational Socialist Networks*, 38.

43. Kreisky, *The Struggle for a Democratic Austria*, 69, 190–91, 200–201, 209–13; Willy Brandt, *My Life in Politics* (London: Hamish Hamilton, 1992), 118; Miard-Delacroix, *Willy Brandt*, 35; Salm, *Transnational Socialist Networks*, 38.

44. Kreisky, *The Struggle for a Democratic Austria*, 295.

45. Brandt, *My Life in Politics*, 117.

46. Kreisky, *The Struggle for a Democratic Austria*, 229.

47. Salm, *Transnational Socialist Networks*, 38.

48. Kreisky, *The Struggle for a Democratic Austria*, 218.

49. Electronic mail correspondence with Maria Steiner, *Bruno Kreisky Archiv*, Vienna, 27 January 2021.

50. Bruno Kreisky, 'Austria Draws the Balance', *Foreign Affairs* 37, no. 2 (1959), 273–4; Kreisky, *The Struggle for a Democratic Austria*, 273, n. 20–21. Ove Bring, *Neutralitetens uppgång och fall: eller de gemensamma säkerhetens historia* (Stockholm: Atlantis, 2008), 261; Ulf Bjereld, *Kritiker eller medlare? Sveriges utrikespolitiska roller 1945–1990* (Stockholm: Nerenius & Santérus Förlag, 1992), 166.

51. Kreisky, 'Austria Draws the Balance', 277. B. Vivekanandan, *Global Visions of Olof Palme, Bruno Kreisky, and Willy Brandt: International Peace and Security, Co-operation, and Development* (Cham: Palgrave Macmillan, 2016), 163.

52. Kreisky, *The Struggle for a Democratic Austria*, 327. Vivekanandan, *Global Visions of Olof Palme, Bruno Kreisky, and Willy Brandt*, 237. Statement by Professor Oliver Rathkolb of the University of Vienna in electronic mail from Professor Guenter J. Bischof, University of New Orleans, 13 February 2024.

53. Miard-Delacroix, *Willy Brandt*, 106–7.

54. Electronic mail correspondence with Professor Bernd Greiner, *Universität Hamburg*, 28 January 2021.

55. Memorandum by Sverker Åstrom, Swedish Foreign Ministry, 21 December 1972.

56. Memorandum by Sverker Åstrom, Swedish Foreign Ministry, 21 December 1972. 'Former West German Social Democratic Party Leader Tells Swedes What He Thinks about Kissinger Speech and Kissinger Protest', telegram from the US Embassy in Stockholm to US Secretary of State William P. Rogers, 26 April 1973 (Courtesy of John Powers, US National Archives and Records Administration, Electronic Telegrams, 1973).

57. Memorandum by Sverker Åstrom, 21 December 1972.
58. Memorandum by Sverker Åstrom, 21 December 1972.
59. Memorandum by Sverker Åstrom, 21 December 1972.
60. Memorandum by Sverker Åstrom, 21 December 1972.
61. Henrik Berggren, *Underbara dagar framför oss: en biografi över Olof Palme* (Stockholm: Norstedts, 2010), 463; Alvin Schuster, 'Swedish Chilliness Toward U.S. is Limited to Vietnam', *The New York Times*, 8 January 1973, 8.
62. Palme's draft of Christmas Bombing speech, OPA, vol. 2.4.0: 044, *Tal 1972*.
63. Schuster, 'Swedish Chilliness'.
64. Schuster, 'Swedish Chilliness'.
65. Kai Falkman, Interview with author, Stockholm, Sweden, 6 July 2016.
66. Palme phoned in his speech to the Swedish news agency *Tidningarnas Telegrambyrå*. Berggren, *Underbara dagar*, 463. Göran Hägg, *Retorik i Tiden: 23 historiska recept för framgång* (Stockholm: Norstedts, 2011), 189–91. Electronic mail correspondence with Jan Stellan Andersson, Archivist Emeritus, ARAB, 7 November 2019.
67. Gunilla Banks, ed., *Olof Palme Speaking: Articles and speeches* (Stockholm: Premiss förlag, 2006), 141–2.
68. Banks, ed., *Olof Palme Speaking*, 141–2.
69. Jan Eliasson, Interview with author, Stockholm, Sweden, 7 June 2017.
70. Eliasson, Interview with author, Stockholm, Sweden, 7 June 2017.
71. Eliasson, Interview with author, Stockholm, Sweden, 7 June 2017.
72. Telegram 626 from Lundberg of the Swedish Embassy in Hanoi to Cabinet Stockholm, 'Re Bombningar Bach Mai-Sjukhuset', 24 December 1972, RA, HP 38:30, UD HP-Dossierer, Vietnamkriget, Mål: H. Hanoi politik, 1972–1975.
73. Telegram 629 from Lundberg of the Swedish Embassy in Hanoi to Cabinet Stockholm, 'Re Bombningarna Bach Mai-Sjukhuset', 27 December 1972, RA, HP 38:30, UD HP-Dossierer, Vietnamkriget, Mål: H. Hanoi politik, 1972–1975.
74. Telegram from Ambassador Jean-Christophe Öberg in Hanoi to Cabinet Stockholm, 10 January 1973, RA, HP 38:30, UD HP-Dossierer, Vietnamkriget, Mål: H. Hanoi politik, 1972–1975.
75. Telegram from Ambassador Jean-Christophe Öberg, 10 January 1973.
76. See Lubna Z. Qureshi, *Nixon, Kissinger, and Allende: U.S. Involvement in the 1973 Coup in Chile* (Lanham, MD: Lexington Books, 2009). Stanley I. Kutler, *The Wars of Watergate: The Last Crisis of Richard Nixon* (New York: W.W. Norton & Company, 1992); and Stanley I. Kutler, *Abuse of Power: The New Nixon Tapes* (New York: Touchstone, 1998). For an audio sampling of the true Nixon personality, I would recommend nixontapes.org.
77. Telegram 1651 from Ambassador Hubert de Besche in Washington to Cabinet Stockholm, 'För pol och press', 21 December 1972, RA, HP 38:15, UD HP-Dossierer, Vietnamkriget, Mål: C. USA politik, augusti-december 1972, 1972–1973. See John Boyko, *The Devil's Trick: How Canada Fought the Vietnam War* (Toronto: Alfred A. Knopf Canada, 2021) and Jessica Squires, *Building Sanctuary: The Movement to Support Vietnam War Resisters in Canada, 1965–73* (Vancouver: UBC Press, 2013).
78. Robert Burns, '. . . As Others See Us', *The New York Times*, 8 January 1973, 38; Paul Hofmann, 'War Raids Incite Anti-U.S. Feelings in Italy', *The New York Times*, 3 January 1973, 8.

79. Electronic mail correspondence with Bernd Greiner, *Universität Hamburg*, and Bernd Rother, Bundeskanzler Willy Brandt Stiftung, 16 and 17 December 2020.

80. Burns, '... As Others See Us'; Hofmann, 'War Raids'.

81. Brandt, *My Life in Politics*, 364.

82. Berggren, *Underbara dagar*, 119, 123–4, 129–33. Kjell Östberg, *I takt med tiden: Olof Palme 1927–1969* (Stockholm: Leopard Förlag, 2012), 61–3.

83. Brandt, *My Life in Politics*, 394.

84. Zimmerman, 'The Quiet German', 53, 58.

85. Rolf Ekéus, Interview with author, Stockholm, Sweden, 19 January 2016.

86. Telegram 1651 from Ambassador Hubert de Besche, 21 December 1972.

87. The 1955 renewal of the 1948 Soviet-Finnish Treaty of Friendship, Cooperation, and Mutual Assistance formalised Finnish neutrality. Juhana Aunesluoma and Johanna Rainio-Niemi, 'Neutrality as Identity? Finland's Quest for Security in the Cold War', *Journal of Cold War Studies* 18, no. 4 (2016), 53–4.

88. Aunesluoma and Rainio-Niemi, 'Neutrality as Identity?', 56.

89. P. Høi, '"Kissinger: Anker Jørgensen er en tørvetriller"', *Berlingske*, 8 March 2015, https://www.berlingske.dk/samfund/kissinger-anker-joergensen-er-en-toervetriller, Courtesy of Ron Ridenour.

90. Telegram 1651 from Ambassador Hubert de Besche, 21 December 1972, 105. Matthew Jones, '"The Blue-Eyed Boys": The Heath Government, Anglo-American Relations, and the Bombing of North Vietnam in 1972', *The International History Review* 44, no. 1 (2022), 104–5, 107.

91. Høi, 'Kissinger'.

92. Telegram from Prime Minister Pham Van Dong of the Democratic Republic of Vietnam to Swedish Prime Minister Olof Palme, 25 December 1972, OPA, Brevsamling, vol. 3.2/82 (courtesy of Joakim Palme).

93. Coded Telegram 26 from Ambassador Jean-Christophe Öberg in Hanoi for Prime Minister Olof Palme, 19 January 1973, RA, HP 38:30, UD HP-Dossierer, Vietnamkriget, Mål: H, Hanoi politik, 1972–1975.

94. Coded Telegram 26 from Ambassador Öberg for Prime Minister Palme, 19 January 1973.

95. Bozo, *French Foreign Policy*, 51.

96. Bozo, *French Foreign Policy*, 70–71.

97. Bozo, *French Foreign Policy*, 85.

98. Coded Telegram 26 from Ambassador Öberg for Prime Minister Palme, 19 January 1973.

99. Hägg, *Retorik i Tiden*, 189, 191.

100. Stephen E. Ambrose, *Nixon: The Education of a Politician 1913–1962* (New York: Simon & Schuster, 1987), 105–16; Schuster, 'Swedish Chilliness'; Richard H. Immerman, 'Confessions of an Eisenhower Revisionist: An Agonizing Reappraisal', *Diplomatic History* 14, no. 3 (1990), 337.

101. Berggren, *Underbara dagar*, 508.

102. Walter Isaacson, *Kissinger: A Biography* (New York: Simon & Schuster, 1992), 21–32.

103. Isaacson, *Kissinger*, 43–56.

104. In *The Trials of Henry Kissinger*, a documentary film directed by Jarecki (New York: First Run Features, 2002).

105. Electronic mail correspondence with Robert Dallek, 7 October 2020.

106. Kreisky, *The Struggle for a Democratic Austria*, 45; Vivekanandan, *Global Visions*, 175. Correspondence with Maria Steiner, *Bruno Kreisky Archiv*.

107. Letter from Willy Brandt to Olof Palme and Bruno Kreisky, 17 September 1972 in Willy Brandt, Bruno Kreisky and Olof Palme, *Brev Och Samtal* (Kristianstad, Sweden: *Tidens Förlag*, 1976), 48.

108. Letter from Olof Palme to Willy Brandt and Bruno Kreisky, 10 May 1973 in Brandt, Kreisky and Palme, *Brev Och Samtal*, 74.

109. In Telegram 235 from the Swedish Embassy in Washington to Cabinet Stockholm, 17 March 1983 (originally written by Ambassador Hubert de Besche, 23 December 1972), RA, HP 38:38, Foreign Affairs Department, *HP-Dossierer, Vietnamkriget, 1972–1974*, and HP 38:58.

110. Telegram 235, from the Swedish Embassy in Washington to Cabinet Stockholm.

111. Berggren, *Underbara dagar*, 464.

112. Schuster, 'Swedish Chilliness'.

113. Telegram 235, from the Swedish Embassy in Washington to Cabinet Stockholm.

114. Rolf Ekéus led a historical investigation of Swedish Cold War policy; see Rolf Ekéus, Mathias Mossberg and Birgitta Arvidsson, eds. *Fred och säkerhet: Svensk säkerhetspolitik, 1969–1989* (Stockholm: Fritzes offentliga publikationer, 2002). See also Ulf Bjereld, Alf W. Johansson and Karl Molin, *Sveriges säkerhet och världens fred: svensk utrikespolitik under kalla kriget* (Stockholm: Santérus Förlag, 2008).

115. Ekéus interview.

116. Henry A. Kissinger, 'To settle the Ukraine crisis, start at the end', *The Washington Post*, 5 March 2014.

117. Kissinger, 'To settle the Ukraine crisis, start at the end'.

118. Ekéus interview. Laura Secor, 'Henry Kissinger is Worried About "Disequilibrium"', *The Wall Street Journal*, 12 August 2022.

119. Ann-Marie Ekengren, 'Den långa vägen mot NATO', a panel at the Swedish Institute of International Affairs, Stockholm, Sweden, 6 November 2023. See also Douglas Brommesson, Ann-Marie Ekengren and Anna Michalski, 'Sweden's Policy of Neutrality: Success Through Flexibility?' in *Successful Public Policy in the Nordic Countries*, ed. Caroline de Porte et al. (Oxford: Oxford University Press, 2022), 284, 301.

120. Ann-Marie Ekengren, *Olof Palme och utrikespolitiken: Europa och Tredje* (Umeå: Boréa, 2005), 46–7.

121. Kreisky also spoke Swedish, but I don't know if he spoke Swedish with Palme. Rolf Ekéus, who listened to Palme's telephone conversations with Brandt, said they spoke Swedish.

122. Ekéus interview; and J.S. Andersson, 'Democracy and Disarmament – Some Notes on Public Opinion, Peace Movements, and the Disarmament Process in the Early 1980s', Conference on Swedish Disarmament Policy, Stockholm University, Stockholm, Sweden, 26 November 2012. Miard-Delecroix, *Willy Brandt: Life of a Statesman*, 170. Electronic mail correspondence with Jan Stellan Andersson, Archivist Emeritus, ARAB, 15 February 2024.

Bibliography

Ambrose, Stephen E. *Nixon: The Education of a Politician 1913–1962*. New York: Simon & Schuster, 1987.

Aunesluoma, Juhana and Johanna Rainio-Niemi. 'Neutrality as Identity? Finland's Quest for Security in the Cold War', *Journal of Cold War Studies* 18, no. 4 (2016): 51–78.

Banks, Gunilla, ed. *Olof Palme Speaking: Articles and speeches*. Stockholm: Premiss förlag, 2006.

Berggren, Henrik. *Underbara dagar framför oss: en biografi över Olof Palme*. Stockholm: Norstedts, 2020.

Bjereld, Ulf. *Kritiker eller medlare?: Sveriges utrikespolitiska roller 1945–1990*. Stockholm: Nerenius & Santérus Förlag, 1992.

Bjereld, Ulf, Alf W. Johansson and Karl Molin. *Sveriges säkerhet och världens fred*. Stockholm: Santérus Förlag, 2008.

Boyko, John. *The Devil's Trick: How Canada Fought the Vietnam War*. Toronto: Alfred A. Knopf Canada, 2021.

Brandt, Willy. *My Life in Politics*. London: Hamish Hamilton, 1992.

Brandt, Willy, Bruno Kreisky and Olof Palme, *Brev Och Samtal*. Kristianstad, Sweden: Tidens Förlag, 1976.

Brommesson, Douglas, Ann-Marie Ekengren and Anna Michalski. 'Sweden's Policy of Neutrality: Success Through Flexibility?' In *Successful Public Policy in the Nordic Countries*, edited by Caroline de Porte et al., 284–305. Oxford: Oxford University Press, 2022.

Bozo, Frédéric. *French Foreign Policy since 1945: An Introduction* (translated by Jonathan Hensher). New York: Berghahn Books, 2016.

Bring, Ove. *Neutralitetens uppgång och fall: Eller De Gemensamma Säkerhetens Historia*. Stockholm: Atlantis, 2008.

de Gaulle, Charles. *Memoirs of Hope: Renewal and Endeavor*, translated by Terence Kilmartin. New York: Simon and Schuster, 1971.

Dockrill, Saki. 'The Anglo-US Linkage between Vietnam and the Pound: 1964 and 1968'. In *La Guerre du Vietnam et l'Europe*, edited by Christopher Goscha and Maurice Vaïsse, 65–78. Brussels, Bruylant, 2003.

Ekengren, Ann-Marie. *Olof Palme och utrikespolitiken*. Umeå, Sweden: Boréa, 2005.

Ekéus, Rolf, Mathias Mossberg and Birgitta Arvidsson, eds. *Fred och säkerhet: Svensk säkerhetspolitik, 1969–1989*. Stockholm: Fritzes offentliga publikationer, 2002.

Ellis, Sylvia A. 'Promoting Solidarity at Home and Abroad: The Goals and Tactics of the Anti-Vietnam War Movement in Britain', *European Review of History: Revue européenne d'histoire* 21, no. 4 (2014): 557–76.

Falkman, Kaj. *Ekot från Vietnam: En diplomats minnen från kriget och återbesök fyrtio år senare*. Stockholm: Carlssons, 2014.

Fermandois, Joaquín. 'The Hero on the Latin American Scene'. In *Globalizing de Gaulle: International Perspectives on French Foreign Policies, 1958–1969*, edited by Christian Nuenlist, Anna Locher and Garret Martin, 271–90. Lanham, MD: Lexington Books, 2010.

Gibson, James William. *The Perfect War: Technowar in Vietnam*. Boston and New York: The Atlantic Monthly Press, 1986.

Hägg, Göran. *Retorik i Tiden: 23 historiska recept för framgång*. Stockholm: Norstedts, 2011.

Immerman, Richard H. 'Confessions of an Eisenhower Revisionist: An Agonizing Reappraisal', *Diplomatic History* 14, no. 3 (1990): 319–42.

Isaacson, Walter. *Kissinger: A Biography*. New York: Simon & Schuster, 1992.

Jones, Matthew. '"The Blue-Eyed Boys": The Heath Government, Anglo-American Relations, and the Bombing of North Vietnam in 1972', *The International History Review* 44, no. 1 (2022): 92–112.

Keenan, Bethany S. '"The US Embassy Has Been Particularly Sensitive about This": Diplomacy, Antiwar Protests, and the French Ministry of Foreign Affairs during 1968', *French Historical Studies* 41, no. 2 (2018): 253–73.

Kramer, Mark. 'Introduction: De Gaulle and Gaullism in France's Cold War Foreign Policy'. In *Globalizing de Gaulle: International Perspectives on French Foreign Policies, 1958–1969*, edited by Christian Nuenlist, Anna Locher and Garret Martin, 1–22. Lanham, MD: Lexington Books, 2010.

Kreisky, Bruno. 'Austria Draws the Balance', *Foreign Affairs* 37, no. 2 (1959): 269–81.

Kreisky, Bruno. *The Struggle for a Democratic Austria: Bruno Kreisky on Peace and Social Justice* (edited by Matthew Paul Berg, in collaboration with Jill Lewis and Oliver Rathkolb, and translated by Helen Atkins and Matthew Paul Berg). New York/Oxford: Berghahn Books, 2000.

Kutler, Stanley I. *The Wars of Watergate: The Last Crisis of Richard Nixon*. New York: W.W. Norton & Company, 1992.

Kutler, Stanley I. *Abuse of Power: The New Nixon Tapes*. New York: Touchstone, 1998.

Logevall, Fredrik. 'The American Effort to Draw European States into the War'. In *La Guerre du Vietnam et l'Europe*, edited by Christopher Goscha and Maurice Vaïsse, 3–16. Brussels: Bruylant, 2003.

Miard-Delacroix, Hélène. *Willy Brandt: The Life of a Statesman* (translated by Isabelle Chaize). London: I.B. Tauris, 2016.

Östberg, Kjell. *I takt med tiden: Olof Palme 1927–1969*. Stockholm: Leopard Förlag, 2012.
Qureshi, Lubna Z. *Nixon, Kissinger, and Allende: U.S. Involvement in the 1973 Coup in Chile*. Lanham, Maryland: Lexington Books, 2009.
Salm, Christian. *Transnational Socialist Networks in the 1970s: European Community Development Aid and Southern Enlargement*. London: Palgrave Macmillan, 2016.
Squires, Jessica. *Building Sanctuary: The Movement to Support Vietnam War Resisters in Canada, 1965–73*. Vancouver: UBC Press, 2013.
Stockdale, James and Sybil Stockdale. *In Love and War: The Story of a Family's Ordeal and Sacrifice During the Vietnam Years*. New York: Harper and Row Publishers, 1984.
Torikata, Yuko. 'The U.S. Escalation in Vietnam and de Gaulle's Secret Search for Peace, 1964–1966'. In *Globalizing de Gaulle: International Perspectives on French Foreign Policies, 1958–1969*, edited by Christian Nuenlist, Anna Locher and Garret Martin, 155–80. Lanham, MD: Lexington Books, 2010.
Vickers, Rhiannon. 'Harold Wilson, the British Labour Party, and the War in Vietnam', *Journal of Cold War Studies* 10, no. 2 (2008): 41–70.
Vivekanandan, B. *Global Visions of Olof Palme, Bruno Kreisky, and Willy Brandt: International Peace and Security, Co-operation, and Development*. Cham, Switzerland: Palgrave Macmillan, 2016.
Young, John W. 'British governments and the Vietnam War'. In *La Guerre du Vietnam et l'Europe*, edited by Christopher Goscha and Maurice Vaïsse, 117–30. Brussels: Bruylant, 2003.
Young, Marilyn. *The Vietnam Wars: 1945–1990*. New York: HarperPerennial, 1991.
Zimmerman, Hubert. 'The Quiet German: The Vietnam War and the Federal Republic of Germany'. In *La Guerre du Vietnam et l'Europe*, edited by Christopher Goscha and Maurice Vaisse, 50–64. Brussels: Bruylant, 2003.
Zimmerman, Hubert. 'Who Paid for America's War? Vietnam and the International Monetary System, 1960–1975'. In *America, the Vietnam War, and the World: Comparative and International Perspectives*, edited by Andreas W. Daum, Lloyd C. Gardner and Wilfried Mausbach, 151–74. Cambridge/New York: Cambridge University Press, 2003.

Part III

REDEFINING EUROPE AND REASSESSING EUROPEANISATION: SOCIALIST READINGS OF INTERNATIONALISM AND LIBERALISM

Chapter 6

European socialists and international solidarity with Palestine: towards a socialist European network of solidarity in the 1970s and 1980s?

Thomas Maineult

The attitude of European socialists towards the Israeli–Palestinian conflict changed during the 1970s. From unconditional support for the state of Israel, it became more sympathetic to the Palestinians and this shift translated into a desire to establish close ties with them. This chapter begins by analysing the relations of European socialist and social democratic parties with the state of Israel, and in particular with the Israeli Labour Party (*Mifléguet Poalei Eretz Israel*, or MAPAÏ). The case of France is then analysed to show that the 1970s marked a turning point in the way socialists considered Palestinians. Finally, the 1980s were marked by dramatic events but they did not, as this chapter shows, call into question the support of European socialists for the Palestinian cause.

European socialists and Israel: a friendly relationship

Most socialist and social democrat parties in Western Europe welcomed the creation of the state of Israel in 1948, as a symbol of a socialist achievement. The enthusiastic partnership with a new socialist state lasted for more than two decades. During the Suez crisis in 1956, European socialists were in tune with Israel. The French case clearly illustrates a deep commitment to the defence of Israel. French Premier Guy Mollet took sides with the Conservative government in the United Kingdom to support Israel against Egypt. Nasser was portrayed as a 'new Hitler' in the French press. The attitude of the SFIO – the French Socialist Party – was just the same eleven years later when a new major outburst of violence occurred in the Middle East.[1]

The Six-Day War of June 1967 is usually interpreted as a turning point in the relations between the French left and Israel. However, the war was just the beginning of a slow, long-term process that lasted throughout the 1970s until the beginning of the 1980s. Indeed, Mollet, who was now leading his party from the opposition benches,[2] strongly affirmed complete solidarity between the SFIO and MAPAÏ a few days before the outbreak of the Six-Day War. Golda Meir, a prominent figure of the Israeli left, was invited to the 56th Congress of the SFIO which took place at the end of June 1967 in Suresnes, a city whose mayor was Robert Pontillon, a well-known figure of French socialism who was for many years in charge of international affairs within the French Socialist Party. Golda Meir delivered a speech in which she strongly accused the Arab states, and Egyptian president Nasser in particular, of aggression and asked her French counterparts to support the right for the state of Israel to live in peace:

> One doesn't have to be a military expert to recognise the real danger that Israel was facing. It's a small country with very few airfields. If we had as many airfields as Egypt, there would be no room on Israeli territory for anything other than these airfields. We know full well that the problem was very simple: whoever destroys their opponent's air force first will have won the war. (Applause) We did what was necessary, we destroyed the enemy's air force and this is how we won the war, but we don't want to be, we refuse to be, dead heroes. (Applause) (Bravos in the audience) And we ask our friends, especially our Socialist friends, our friends who are members of the workers' movement, to recognise our right to live. We cannot accept that the right of self-defence should be reserved to all peoples except one, which is to say ours, just to please our friends. (Applause) [. . .] If Nasser had won, no Israeli would have been able to take time out of your day to speak at this Congress. (Applause) Because what Nasser has decreed is holy war, and in holy war you take no prisoners, in holy war you have to kill all your opponents, and according to Nasser every Israeli is an enemy. We are accused on all sides of being guilty of a lot of imaginary things, that don't exist. I only admit guilt in one sense: that of having won this war. (Applause)[3]

At the end of her long speech, Golda Meir was warmly applauded by the French socialists, and celebrated with the singing of the 'International'.

This situation was quite similar to that in other European countries during the 1967 war. In the United Kingdom, the Labour government led by Harold Wilson clearly supported Israel even though some of its leaders may have had more pro-Arab ties. As June Edmunds puts it:

> despite its public statements of neutrality, virtually the whole Cabinet sided with Israel, with the Prime Minister, Harold Wilson, and other senior members initially wanting Britain and America to intervene on Israel's behalf; a position that stemmed from the government's commitment to Atlanticism. Even the Foreign Secretary George Brown, who had a reputation for being pro-Arab, adopted a pro-Israeli stance behind the scenes. Brown's concern to prevent the Soviet Union from gaining a power base in the Middle East overrode his pro-Arab sympathies.[4]

The spectre of a new genocide against Jews was also a reason for the support of French socialists and social democrats for Israel. Many of them had been Resistance fighters during the Second World War and some were of Jewish origin. Christian Pineau, a prominent member of the SFIO, was an important Resistance fighter and became Minister of Foreign Affairs in France in 1956. Daniel Mayer, a member of France's second most important left-wing party in France, the *Parti socialiste unifié* (PSU), was also a former Resistance fighter, fearing massacres against Jews during the Six-Day War. In the 1950s and 1960s, many activists on the French left, including Mayer, broke with the SFIO over the Algerian War. The French socialists had pursued a colonial policy in Algeria and fought the Algerian national liberation movement. The PSU was created to the left of the SFIO by bringing together activists in favour of Algerian independence and decolonisation movements in general.[5] But Mayer could no longer remain a member of the PSU after 1967, precisely because he disagreed with the pro-Arab stance of this party and returned to the SFIO in 1970.

More broadly, the memory of the Shoah remained very present in the European left in the 1960s. Many activists in France and in the rest of Europe had experienced the concentration camps. This memory was a driving force in the fight against anti-Semitism and in the European socialists' friendship with the state of Israel. In Italy, Pietro Nenni, the leader of the Italian Socialist Party whose daughter had died at Auschwitz, claimed that 'the Israeli population is composed by the survivors of Hitler's "final solution" and has given birth to "a political and social experience that blends the ideals of democracy and socialism"'.[6] Such a consideration underlines the fact that the state of Israel was seen as the archetype of a truly, deeply socialist state.

Even in opposition to their respective governments, European socialists adopted a pro-Israel stance, and it seemed inconceivable to criticise the Israeli government. As a serious contender against Charles de Gaulle for the French presidency, François Mitterrand was closely linked to support for Israel. A small club – the *Convention des Institutions Républicaines* (CIR) – was created around Mitterrand to help him rally pro-Israeli voices to the French Socialist camp in the 1960s. The CIR was very diverse, bringing together activists from many different backgrounds. Claude Estier, a journalist and member of this club, had a keen interest in the Middle East, particularly after a trip to Egypt in 1964–65. Estier, who also edited one of the publications that relayed François Mitterrand's positions, remained a singular figure in this organisation,[7]. On Israel, he was clearly concerned by the fate of the Palestinian people and a strong supporter of the resolution of the conflict between Israel and the Arab states through a general disarmament of the regional powers. Writing a report on the situation for Mitterrand, he pleaded for a demilitarisation of Israel.[8] Mitterrand, however, opposed Estier's idea and rejected any such discussion, saying emphatically: 'if it is just to claim the right for Israel to defend itself, then the means to allow its protection must be guaranteed'.[9]

In West Germany, Foreign Minister and Social-Democrat leader Willy Brandt tried to deal with Israel in an even-handed way. Relations between the Arab states and West Germany were suspended in 1965 and 'formal ties' were then established with Israel.[10] However, when he became German Chancellor and leader of the coalition between the Social Democrats (*Sozialdemokratische Partei Deutschlands*, SPD) and the centrist Free Democratic Party (*Freie Demokratische Partei*, FDP) in 1969, Brandt turned out to be far more open to the Arab states. Willy Brandt's policy was characterised by the re-establishment of diplomatic relations with the Arab countries and a desire to keep an equal distance between the Arabs and the Israelis, which was coined as 'a policy of even-handedness (*Ausgewogenheit*)'.[11]

The 1970s: a turning point for French socialists

Support for the Palestinians was not self-evident in the socialist milieus of the late 1960s. When support occurred, it caused divisions between and within many different political organisations. In France, the CIR gradually asserted itself as a laboratory of ideas conducive to the development of a more pro-Arab, or pro-Palestinian, approach to the conflict, that gained ground in the following years while the Socialist Party was going through a major period of restructuring – a transition period that began with the election of Alain Savary at the head of a new party in 1969 until it ended in 1971, when the Socialist Party was officially launched after the Épinay Congress, which also saw the victory of François Mitterrand to the leadership. Interest in Palestine and the Palestinians grew within the CIR, as evidenced by several articles which appeared in the journal *Dire*, which was founded and edited by Estier to air the ideas of the political club among a wider public. As an experienced journalist, who worked for *France Observateur* and *Le Monde*, Estier delivered his analyses and published the articles of several Israeli militants for the Palestinian cause. They included Uri Avnery, an Israeli journalist and left-wing activist who campaigned for peace between Israelis and Palestinians, who participated in the creation of the party *Haolam Hazeh – Koach Hadash* (This World – New Force) in 1965 and became one of its representatives in the Knesset, and who would later meet Yasser Arafat in 1982. *Dire* also published articles by Simha Flapan, an active member of the Israeli far-left party Mapam (*Mifleget HaPoalim HaMeuhedet*, the party of united workers, formed in 1948) and a contributor to *New Outlook*, a magazine dedicated to dialogue between Israelis and Palestinians, and who became increasingly critical of Zionism in the 1970s. In 1970, Estier published a thorough investigation of the situation in the Middle East, where he had an impressive network of contacts. In the 1960s, he managed to meet both the Egyptian president Gamal Abdel Nasser and one of the spokesmen of the Palestine Liberation Organisation (PLO). A form of embryonic partisan diplomacy was already emerging within the CIR in the 1970s, which prefigured in part what was to become the diplomacy emanating from the Socialist Party from 1971 to 1981.

Claude Estier maintained close links with François Mitterrand and had privileged access to the socialist leader, even though Mitterrand did not always follow Estier in his pro-Arab analyses. Mitterrand personally tried to preserve a certain balance between support for the state of Israel and respect for the rights of the Arab peoples. In the 'Socialist Contract' of the CIR established in 1969, it was clearly stated that 'the socialists recognise the Palestinian national fact in the same way as they have always recognised the Israeli state', and at the beginning of 1970 in the French newspaper *Le Monde*, Mitterrand also indicated that 'just as one cannot deny the existence of the state of Israel, one cannot deny the Palestinian people'.[12] This middle-of-the-road position suited the tactical game he was conducting to win over opposite factions within the PS. This was reflected during the Epinay Congress in June 1971 when Mitterrand succeeded in rallying the supporters of a more left-wing line and those inclined to third worldism, like the *Centre d'études, de recherches et d'éducation socialiste* (CERES) of Jean-Pierre Chevènement, with the supporters of a traditional line, closer to Israel, represented by Pierre Mauroy. Although international issues were not the main focus of the Socialists during this congress, the new leader of the party succeeded in rallying around him supporters of the traditional party line, which was in favour of Israel, and younger activists from different backgrounds, whose sensitivity to Third World issues was much more pronounced. Throughout his time at the head of the party, François Mitterrand would never cease to seek a balance between these different tendencies within the party in order to maintain a form of unity.

From the formal creation of the Socialist Party (PS) after the Epinay Congress, relations with the Palestinians gradually become more institutionalised and the party's orientations evolved due to various changes in the structure and composition of the party. French Socialists who supported the Palestinian cause were given positions within the party. In the international relations secretariat, for example, Lionel Jospin had become an active supporter of the Palestinians, in stark contrast to the previous party leadership. He made several trips to the Middle East to meet Arab and Palestinian leaders. If the reversal of values was not total, the Party was nonetheless subjected to a whole series of new influences over the course of the decade. The policy of the Socialist Party consisted in leaving a great freedom of expression to the different factions which composed the Party while displaying a central, single position in the public debate and in particular in the relation with the other parties of the left. For example, the *Programme Commun de Gouvernement*, a political alliance between the PS, the French Communist Party (PCF) and the Radicals of the Left, established in June 1972, used specific terms to evoke the conflict in the Middle East:

> It [the government] will strive to contribute to the restoration of peace and security in the Middle East, while respecting the right to exist and the sovereignty of all the states of the region, including the state of Israel, as well as the national rights of the Arab people of Palestine. It will base its activity in this sense on the Security Council resolution of 22 November 1967.[13]

Ambiguity remains in this formulation because of the necessity to recognise the right of Israel to exist as a state, whereas the 'Arab people of Palestine' (and not the 'Palestinians' or the 'people of Palestine') only have 'national rights', leaving the question of statehood unanswered. Palestinians could thus form a nation without a state if this logic were followed.

Several factors explain the changing attitude of socialist activists during the 1970s. While the PS had to reconcile different tendencies and promote a fairly balanced line on the Palestinian question, its First Secretary accorded a significant place to more committed voices in favour of the Palestinians and discovered for himself the reality of the conditions in which the Palestinians lived. François Mitterrand's position evolved, primarily because of the contacts that he made throughout the decade, which allowed him to see the situation for himself on the ground, and to meet Palestinians.

These contacts began in 1972 with a visit to Gaza where he met Rachad Chawa, the city's mayor. Mitterrand saw the living conditions of the Palestinian refugees for himself, which had a profound impact on him. He also appreciated the contacts he made in Gaza, in particular Chawa, who was a moderate figure far removed from the nationalist positions of the PLO.[14] This decision to meet with the Palestinians is important to understand the attitude of Mitterrand towards the PLO and Yasser Arafat in the years that followed. Two other trips were a milestone for Mitterrand. First was a trip to Cairo in 1974 where he met Yasser Arafat for the first time. He also met President Muhammad Anwar es-Sadat and several Egyptian officials, including the Minister of Foreign Affairs. His meeting with Yasser Arafat was not planned: it was an informal meeting organised by a newspaper, at the insistence of the Egyptians. The conversation was very short and nothing concrete came out of it.[15] Then came a trip to Hebron in 1976 where Mitterrand met several mayors of Palestinian municipalities. During these trips, he also surrounded himself with specialists or experts of the Palestinian question and the Middle East, both those closer to the Palestinians such as Estier, as well as those closer to Israel like Pontillon.

Another element that explains why pro-Arab voices were increasingly heard within the PS lies in the direction in which the Party was taken by Mitterrand. This spoke to the balance between left-wing and more moderate currents within the party that Mitterrand was encouraging. Mitterrand's strategy was to promote groups that were firmly on the left of the party and more moderate ones. The CERES acquired more and more influence in the debate on the Palestinian question and regularly echoed it in its publications, in particular in *Frontières* and *Repères*, on the left of the Socialist Party. They printed numerous articles in which Israel's policies were strongly criticised, with the CERES itself advocating a negotiated solution to the Israeli–Palestinian conflict and the recognition of a future Palestinian state.

In preparation for the PS Congress in Grenoble in June 1973, and as stated in its journal *Frontière*, which also drew up a table of the differences between the motions within the Party, Jean-Pierre Chevènement's CERES presented a motion clearly stating its desire to see the creation of a Palestinian state within secure and recognised borders.[16] The CERES stated that it was 'committed to the implementation of the Security Council resolution of November 1967, which included, on the part of the state of Israel the renunciation of any annexation, and the recognition of Israel's right to exist as well as a Palestinian state with internationally secure and recognised borders'.[17] But the CERES was still one of the few groups in the party to raise the idea of a Palestinian state. The rest of the Socialist Party-sponsored motions did not even mention the fate of the Palestinians and remained very vague on the international questions. The CERES seems to have been part of a competition within the socialist ranks on how to support the Palestinian cause and it claimed to be resolutely in favour of all peoples struggling for their national liberation. The fact that any mention of the Middle East was absent from the motion presented by its opponents reinforces the idea that Chevènement's CERES was at the forefront of thinking about the plight of the Palestinians. A few months later, when the Yom Kippur War broke out, tensions arose between the Paris Federation of the PS, where the ideas of the CERES were in vogue, and the Party's Executive Bureau. The Paris Federation then published a text in which it 'no longer mention[ed] the need to provide the state of Israel with borders, call[ed] for the restitution of all land to establish a Palestinian state and ma[de] Israel responsible for the affront'.[18] The Executive Bureau considered this position not to be in accordance with the position of the party. Despite these criticisms, the CERES continued throughout the 1970s to include in its proposals for international relations the creation of a Palestinian state. This was the first example of a solidly pro-Palestinian current within the PS, whereas previously this commitment appeared more individual and was only subscribed to by a few individuals.

This transformation within the PS was also beneficial for Estier, a pioneer of the Palestinian cause among socialists. When he became director of *L'Unité*, the weekly magazine of the PS, in 1972, he carried out a considerable amount of work: the aim was not only to give his point of view but to provide a regular account of the evolving situation in the Middle East and to give a forum to the various protagonists in the conflict, both Israeli and Palestinian. For example, in December 1977, the Socialist newspaper interviewed the PLO representative in Paris, Ezzedine Kalak, who reaffirmed the necessity of a recognition of a Palestinian state:

> The international community now recognises the Palestinian problem as the very basis of the Arab-Israeli conflict. So repeating this obvious

truth is nothing new. Today, the struggle of the Palestinian people is going through a decisive stage: that of Palestinian representation. Who represents the national rights of the Palestinians today? The Palestinian people have given their answer: the PLO. As we have seen in previous colonial wars, whether in Algeria or Vietnam, the colonisers have always tried to find weak interlocutors to seek some sort of solution. But these interlocutors never solved any problems. The same thing is happening today: the Israeli leaders think they can solve the Palestinian problem with certain Palestinian individuals in the West Bank or in the Gaza Strip, in collaboration with King Hussein's regime. We regret that President Sadat has gone down this road. I repeat that we want a genuine, real and lasting peace, and this cannot be achieved with individuals who represent only themselves.[19]

An equally important theme of this decade and one which also explains why the PS changed its attitude, was the arrival of new militants within the Party. This was especially true after the *Assises du socialisme*, a debate organised in October 1974 within the party, enabled a number of Christian activists to join the Socialist Party, such as Michel Rocard, a former member of the PSU who became an important figure in the Socialist Party between 1970 and 1980 (before he became Prime Minister from 1988 to 1991, under President Mitterrand).[20] When Rocard and part of the PSU joined the PS, the support for Third World struggles and the Palestinian cause held a central place in their thinking. Rocard maintained close links with the Palestinian representatives in Paris. The ideas of the newcomers, armed with this international background, made their way into the PS, although the PSU had not been deserted by all its pro-Palestinian militants. The group around Rocard expressed itself in the journal *Faire*, established in 1975, which was committed to the defence of the Palestinian cause and relied on several experts such as Xavier Baron, a journalist with the *Agence France Presse* (AFP) in the Middle East. However, the magazine's interest in international relations and the Middle East appeared less present than in other socialist factions, such as the CERES.

What the moment of the *Assises du socialisme* reveals more generally is a whole network of activists that had been rehabilitated by Christianity and that had come to believe in the PS.[21] Although a fraction of the Christian Left, represented by Robert Buron, had already rallied the PS at the Congress of Epinay in 1971, in particular through the K motion calling for mass revolutionary action and union with the Communists,[22] the *Assises du socialisme* of October 1974 saw the arrival of a whole series of Christian groups, often linked to trade unionism, through the *Confédération*

Française Démocratique du Travail (CFDT), *Jeunesse Ouvrière Chrétienne* (JOC) and *Jeunesse Étudiante Chrétienne* (JEC).[23]

Among these groups, one publication stands out: *Témoignage Chrétien*, edited by Pierre-Luc Séguillon. The flagship newspaper of the Christian Left was a bastion of the defence of the Palestinian cause in France. Séguillon, who was a journalist for *Témoignage Chrétien* before becoming its editor, was a member of many Christian groups and committees for Palestine and had a degree in Arabic theology from the University of Saint Joseph in Beirut. He was thus active in these Christian circles composed of those who can be called 'left-wing Christians'.[24] He also met socialist activists committed to the defence of the Palestinians, such as Lionel Jospin and Didier Motchane, and worked with Chevènement at the CERES. Other members of the PS like Maurice Buttin, a lawyer for the family of Moroccan socialist Mehdi Ben Barka[25] in France, were committed to supporting the Palestinians. Buttin was involved in various groups such as the *Groupe de Recherche et d'Action pour le règlement du Problème Palestinien* (GRAPP), and the *Association de Solidarité Franco-Arabe* (ASFA),[26] both of which aimed to support the Palestinian cause. Another central figure in the PS was Alain Chenal, lecturer in public law at the University of Nanterre since 1968, who was responsible for the Mediterranean sector within the PS's National Secretariat for the Third World and subsequently within the PS's National Secretariat for International Relations, working closely with their director Lionel Jospin. Chenal and Jospin were very active in the years 1975–79, attempting to sway the PS to take the side of the Palestinians. They were both in contact with Yasser Arafat, with the approval of Mitterrand.[27]

European socialism and the Israeli–Palestinian conflict in the 1980s: a deeper commitment

Another element explaining such a change in the 1970s within the PS was the general revolution in European social democracy during this decade. The European socialist or social-democratic parties were turning more and more towards Palestine in these years and one can surmise that the PS and its First Secretary were not insensitive to this change of wider and greater magnitude. Indeed, the Israeli–Palestinian conflict affected many European states, especially as regards terrorism. France, and Europe more broadly, were the scene of pro-Palestinian attacks and settling of accounts between Palestinian fighters and the Israeli secret services. Moreover, several leaders of the PLO in Paris, known to several socialist activists, were assassinated there.[28] This prominence of the Israeli–

Palestinian conflict in Europe led the socialist political forces to include the Palestinian dimension in their policy grid. This change in attitude should also be seen in the context of the profound changes in Israeli political life at the turn of the 1970s and 1980s, when the Israeli Labour Party, which had been in power since 1948, was defeated by the conservatives of Likud and Menachem Begin.

Bruno Kreisky in Austria, Olof Palme in Sweden and Willy Brandt in the Federal Republic of Germany all turned their gaze towards the Palestinians during their time in office. During the 1970s, Bruno Kreisky travelled several times to the Middle East. He had close connections with Arab leaders, and especially with Yasser Arafat. Between 1976 and 1983, Olof Palme's close adviser Bernt Carlsson was Secretary General of the Socialist International and developed a strong relationship with Yasser Arafat's envoy to the Socialist International, Issam Sartawi. As discussed by Lubna Qureshi in this volume, Kreisky, Brandt and Palme were important social democratic leaders in Europe in the 1970s, and formed what Oliver Rathkolb calls a 'triumvirate' within the Socialist International and within European institutions such as the EEC, aiming to forge relations with the countries of the South and in particular with the countries of the Middle East. Brandt was head of the Independent Commission on International Development Issues and Kreisky co-chaired the first North–South summit in Cancun in 1980. Thanks to their intensive work, the PLO became an important partner in negotiations to resolve the conflict.[29]

In France, the situation slowly changed after Mitterrand's election as President in May 1981. On the eve of the 1981 presidential election, Mitterrand answered questions from Daniel Mayer, the former socialist leader, activist in favour of Israel, and president of the International Federation of Human Rights (FIDH) in the 1970s and the 1980s. Mayer pressed Mitterrand about the policy that he would implement in the Middle East if he became President of the French Republic. To the following question, 'Do you want France to invite Arafat to Paris, given that the terrorists who are in Europe are in collusion with him?', Mitterrand's response was clear: 'I for my part have never said or written that I would take such an initiative'.[30] Nevertheless, the question of the PLO as a diplomatic actor was more difficult to answer for the French Socialist leader. According to Mitterrand:

> the PLO today is probably the most representative organization of the Palestinian aspirations. It is a part of the problem that every responsible politician must take into consideration, without implying an adherence to the objectives and methods it uses. I am a foe of indiscriminate and terrorist violence. It devalues in a perhaps irreversible

way the scope of the political discourse that it is supposed to convey. As I have already said, the PLO will deny itself the ability that it claims as long as it does not acknowledge the existence of the state of Israel. Some states like Lebanon are trying to use for their own benefit the human and military capital built up by the various branches of the PLO. I will simply say that the PLO has everything to lose in these gambles with powers that are more concerned with their own interests, and on the contrary, it would have everything to gain in a recognition of the state of Israel on the basis I have indicated above.[31]

These two questions were crucial for the socialist leader since they were the ones he would have to answer during a large part of his presidency. It was not until eight years later, in May 1989, that Arafat set foot on French soil for the first time, for an official visit. During his speech at the *Institut du monde arabe*, he stated that the PLO Charter was 'null and void' with regard to the non-recognition of Israel, which in effect paved the way for formal recognition of the State of Israel by the PLO.

The 1980s were marked by increasingly violent conflicts in the Middle East, making it difficult for the French Socialist president to act. During his visit to Israel in March 1982, he decided to set the tone of his policy in a speech delivered in front of the Knesset, in which he explained to Israeli MPs why he thought that it was a necessity to recognise the rights of the Palestinians:

> Why did I want the Arab inhabitants of the West Bank and Gaza to have a homeland? Because no one can be asked to give up their identity. . . . It is up to the Palestinians, I repeat, as it is up to the others, whatever their origin, to decide their own fate. On the condition that they situate their right within the respect of the right of others, in the respect of international law and in dialogue instead of violence. . . . Dialogue presupposes the prior and mutual recognition of the right of others to exist, the prior and mutual renunciation of war, whether direct or indirect. . . . Dialogue presupposes that each party can go to the end of its right, which, for the Palestinians as for others, may in due course mean a state. France will approve any dialogue or approach to dialogue as well as observe with concern any unilateral action which on one side or the other would delay the time for peace.[32]

Mitterrand reiterated his desire that the Palestinians should renounce their ambitions to destroy the state of Israel but took a further step in their direction by clearly using the term 'State' in conjunction with 'Palestinian', which marked another turning point in his Middle Eastern policy. From then on, he no longer spoke of a Palestinian 'national fact' or 'national rights' for the Palestinians but of a state, which implied the redrawing of borders and major geopolitical upheavals. However, his speech did not calm tensions in the Middle East, at a time when the Israelis embarked on a military operation called 'Peace in Galilee' in the summer of 1982 in Lebanon. In September 1982, Christian militias massacred Palestinians in Sabra and Shatila.[33] Following these events, the situation in the Middle East was taken very seriously by the Socialist International. The Socialist International became increasingly concerned about the plight of the Palestinians and the Social Democratic leaders appeared to be more active and committed on this issue than the French Socialists at first. At the request of its President Willy Brandt, and Mario Soares, the President of its group on the Middle East, the Socialist International sent a six-person delegation to Beirut. Socialist International Secretary General Carlsson, who was very close to the Palestinians, was a member of the delegation, as was French Socialist Jacques Huntzinger. Upon his return to France the latter recorded his assessment of the chaotic situation in which Lebanon found itself for the French Socialist magazine *L'Unité*:

> We arrive at one of the PLO's 'headquarters', Fahkrani. Behind the sandbags protecting the entrance of a collapsed building, two kerosene lamps illuminate a display of rockets and bombs. A corridor leads to a small room without doors or windows. Yasser Arafat joins us there and welcomes us. The setting is somewhat sordid, but the leader of the PLO has been 'at home' in this building for years and he is still there for a few days. We have the strange impression of meeting a man who wants above all to remain faithful to a certain image, that of the United Nations, the vice-chairman of the Non-Aligned Movement, the man who talks with heads of state. He wants to make us forget the derisory framework in which we find ourselves. . . . He ends his interview by thanking the Europeans for their solidarity with the population of Beirut and the Palestinian people and insists on the fact that there would have been no agreement on the withdrawal of the Palestinians without the arrival of the French troops.[34]

Here was an interesting example of a member of the French Socialist Party who was given a mission by the Socialist International and who would use this international competence in his later functions.[35] One can see the tension between French intervention and Socialist diplomacy, but we can also understand that this meeting with Arafat was also a way to get him to admit that it was the French troops that had allowed the Palestinian withdrawal from Beirut. The meetings held by Jacques Huntzinger on behalf of the Socialist International and the Socialist Party were in line with French diplomacy, which was keen to preserve its links with the Palestinians. In parallel with these missions, Socialist leaders, including Prime Minister Pierre Mauroy and the Socialist Party's First Secretary Lionel Jospin, conducted intensive negotiations with the Palestinians.

Finally, some European and French socialists were given new prominence in the 1980s in their governments' relations with the Palestinians. In France, this was the case of pro-Palestinian figures such as Claude Cheysson, the Minister of Foreign Affairs in 1981–84, and Roland Dumas, who succeeded him from 1984 to 1986 and from 1988 to 1993. Cheysson, who had been an observer in Palestine in 1948, kept a certain freedom of speech throughout his presence at the Quai d'Orsay, causing some interference with statements by Mitterrand. Dumas, a lawyer committed to the fight against colonialism, was also very close to the Arab world.

The turning point of the 1970s was confirmed in the following decade, with the Palestinian question being increasingly taken into consideration. European socialist leaders accepted the right of the Palestinians to participate in the congress of the Socialist International in Albufeira, Portugal, in April 1983. It was during this congress that Arafat's special envoy, Issam Sartawi, was assassinated by a commando linked to the terrorist Sabri al-Banna, alias Abu Nidal, whose group had seceded from the PLO in 1974. This terrorist attack was aimed at preventing the efforts of Carlsson and the European socialist leaders from finding a peaceful solution to the Middle East conflict. The visit of Arafat's envoy Issam Sartawi to Portugal was also not without difficulties, as the Israeli socialist leader Shimon Peres was strongly opposed to it. The Socialist International was thus caught up in the turmoil of events in the Middle East. Carlsson was forced to resign from his position in the Socialist International and died in 1988 in the Lockerbie bombing.

Some conclusions

European socialists underwent a profound change in their attitude to the Israeli–Palestinian conflict in the 1970s and 1980s. While the attraction for Israel was predominant in the 1960s and early 1970s, consideration for the Palestinians became increasingly strong, specifically in the 1970s and 1980s due to the increasingly worrying situation of Palestinian refugees and the development of the PLO. Support for Israel also declined as a result of its policy towards the Palestinians and the fact that the Israeli Labour Party was defeated by the Israeli Right in the late 1970s. The State of Israel no longer appeared to be an ideal socialist state and its relations with European socialists gradually deteriorated.

Notes

1. François Lafon, *Guy Mollet: itinéraire d'un socialiste controversé (1905–1975)* (Paris: Fayard, 2006); Denis Lefebvre, *Les secrets de l'expédition de Suez: 1956* (Paris: CNRS éditions, 2019); Alain Herberth, *Les socialistes, les juifs & Israël: de la question juive à la question d'Israël* (Paris: L'Harmattan, 2021).

2. Guy Mollet remained the leader of the SFIO until the creation of the new Socialist Party in 1969.

3. Fondation Jean Jaurès, Centre des Archives Socialistes, *Compte-rendu sténographique du 56ème Congrès national de Suresnes*, 29 June to 2 July 1967.

4. June Edmunds, 'The Evolution of British Labour Party Policy on Israel from 1967 to the Intifada', *Twentieth Century British History* 11, no. 1 (2000), 25.

5. Bernard Ravenel, *Quand la gauche se réinventait: le PSU, histoire d'un parti visionnaire, 1960–1989* (Paris: La Découverte, 2016); Jacques Sauvageot, *Le PSU, des idées pour un socialisme au XXIè siècle* (Rennes: Presses universitaires de Rennes, 2012); Marc Heurgon, *Histoire du PSU: La fondation et la guerre d'Algérie (1958–1962)* (Paris: La Découverte, 1994).

6. Claudio Brillanti, 'The Italian Communists and Socialists' Reading of the Six-Day War and its Consequences', in *The European Left and the Jewish Question, 1848–1992, Between Zionism and Antisemitism*, ed. Alessandra Tarquini (London: Palgrave Macmillan, 2021), 246.

7. Laurent Jalabert, 'La Convention des institutions républicaines (1964–1971)', *Vingtième Siècle. Revue d'histoire* 104, no. 4 (2009), 139.

8. 'Origines et conséquences de la crise au Moyen-Orient', 4–5 November 1967, 11, Fondation Jean Jaurès, Centre des Archives Socialistes, Papers of Claude Estier, F FP 5/30.

9. Jean-Pierre Filiu, *Mitterrand et la Palestine* (Paris: Fayard, 2005), 32–3.

10. Carole Fink, '"The Most Difficult Journey of All": Willy Brandt's Trip to Israel in June 1973', *The International History Review* 37, no. 3 (2015), 504.

11. Fink, 'The Most Difficult Journey of All', 504.

12. Filiu, *Mitterrand et la Palestine*, 34.

13. Parti socialiste, Parti communiste français, Mouvement des Radicaux de gauche, *Programme commun de gouvernement* (Paris: Flammarion, 1973).

14. Filiu, *Mitterrand et la Palestine*, 38.

15. Filiu, *Mitterrand et la Palestine*, 44.

16. *Le poing et la rose* 16, juin 1973, 8, http://62.210.214.201/cg-ps/documents/pdf/cong-1973-06-22-1-jnl2.pdf.

17. 'Avant le congrès de Grenoble, Tableau comparé des motions présentées aux militants du parti socialiste', *Frontière* 7, June 1973, 4–13.

18. Laurence Coulon, *L'opinion française, Israël et le conflit israélo-arabe 1947–1987* (Paris: Honoré Champion, 2009), 266.

19. 'Ezzedine Kalak (OLP): "Que l'existence nationale du peuple palestinien soit reconnue!"', *L'Unité*, 2 December 1977, 23.

20. For more on Rocard, see Pierre-Emmanuel Guigo, *Michel Rocard* (Paris: Perrin, 2020).

21. François Kraus, *Les Assises du socialisme ou l'échec d'une tentative de rénovation d'un parti*, Les Notes de la fondation Jean Jaurès, no 31, July 2002, 74.

22. Robert Buron, a Christian Democrat and former minister under the Fourth Republic, joined the PS and embodied a very minor tendency of the centre-left within the party. On Buron and these debates, see Roberto Colozza, 'Robert Buron: parcours d'un chrétien de gauche (1962–1973), *Parlement(s), Revue d'histoire politique* 30, no. 3 (2019).

23. These groups were Christian-led trade unions who played a significant role in the 1968 uprising in France. They called for more liberty in the working class and for 'autogestion'. Many of its members joined the PS in the 1970s after having been members of the PSU.

24. Denis Pelletier and Jean-Louis Schlegel, eds. *À la gauche du Christ: les chrétiens de gauche en France de 1945 à nos jours* (Paris: Seuil, 2012). They did not call themselves left-wing Christians but the term was coined by historians to describe them.

25. Mehdi Ben Barka was a Moroccan socialist who opposed King Hassan II and supported Third World causes. He was kidnapped in Paris 1965 and his body was never found.

26. The GRAPP (Group of Research and Action to solve the Palestinian Problem) was a group of intellectuals around orientalist Maxime Rodinson which gathered journalists and intellectuals on the left who were interested in defending the Palestinian cause. The ASFA (Association for Franco-Arab Solidarity) is a group created by former Gaullist minister Louis Terrenoire aimed at gathering journalists, lawyers and politicians from various political backgrounds around support to the Palestinians. It can be considered as a pro-Arab lobby in French politics.

27. Lionel Jospin, *Lionel raconte Jospin: entretiens avec Pierre Favier et Patrick Rotman* (Paris: Seuil, 2010).

28. Mahmoud Hamchari was assassinated in Paris in 1972 by Mossad in retaliation for the assassination of Israeli athletes by Palestinian terrorists during the Munich Olympic Games in September 1972. Ezzedine Kalak, his successor, was assassinated by the Abu Nidal Organization, a Palestinian terrorist organisation, in Paris in 1978.

29. Oliver Rathkolb, 'Brandt, Kreisky and Palme as Policy Entrepreneurs: Social Democratic Networks in Europe's Policy Towards the Middle East', in *Transnational Networks in Regional Integration, Governing Europe 1945–83*, ed. Wolfram Kaiser, Brigitte Leucht and Michael Gehler (London: Palgrave Macmillan, 2010) 152–75.

30. *Perspectives France-Israël*, n° 95, April–May 1981, Centre d'histoire de Sciences Po (CHSP), Papers of Daniel Mayer, 2 MA 8 (Middle East).

31. *Perspectives France-Israël*, n° 95, April–May 1981.

32. François Mitterrand, Speech at the Knesset, 4 March 1982, https://www.vie-publique.fr/discours/136068-discours-de-m-francois-mitterrand-president-de-la-republique-la-kne.

33. The Sabra and Chatila camps were refugee camps near Beirut in Lebanon. They were inhabited by Palestinian refugees and fighters. In September 1982, the Israeli army let the Lebanese Christian militias enter the camp in order to kill the Palestinian resistance. The militias massacred thousands of Palestinians and the horror of this event remained in the Palestinian as well as in the Western memory as a shock.

34. Jacques Huntzinger, 'Ce que j'ai vu et entendu à Beyrouth', *L'Unité*, n° 479, 10 September 1982, 13–14. At the request of the Lebanese government, a UN force made up of French troops was sent to Lebanon to oversee the evacuation of Yasser Arafat and the Palestinian fedayeen from Beirut, where they were besieged by the Israeli army.

35. He was the French ambassador to Israel from 1999 to 2003.

Bibliography

Brillanti, Claudio. 'The Italian Communists and Socialists' Reading of the Six-Day War and its Consequences'. In *The European Left and the Jewish Question, 1848–1992: Between Zionism and Antisemitism*, edited by Alessandra Tarquini, 243–62. London: Palgrave Macmillan, 2021.

Colozza, Roberto. 'Robert Buron: parcours d'un chrétien de gauche (1962–1973)', *Parlement(s), Revue d'histoire politique* 30, no. 3 (2019): 171–86.

Coulon, Laurence. *L'opinion française, Israël et le conflit israélo-arabe 1947–1987*. Paris: Honoré Champion, 2009.

Edmunds, June. 'The Evolution of British Labour Party Policy on Israel from 1967 to the Intifada', *Twentieth Century British History* 11, no. 1 (2000): 23–41.

Filiu, Jean-Pierre. *Mitterrand et la Palestine*. Paris: Fayard, 2005.

Fink, Carole. '"The Most Difficult Journey of All": Willy Brandt's Trip to Israel in June 1973', *The International History Review* 37, no. 3 (2015): 503–18.

Guigo, Pierre-Emmanuel. *Michel Rocard*. Paris: Perrin, 2020.

Herberth, Alain. *Les socialistes, les juifs & Israël: de la question juive à la question d'Israël*. Paris: L'Harmattan, 2021.

Heurgon, Marc. *Histoire du PSU: La fondation et la guerre d'Algérie (1958–1962)*. Paris: La Découverte, 1994.

Jalabert, Laurent. 'La Convention des institutions républicaines (1964–1971)', *Vingtième Siècle. Revue d'histoire* 104, no. 4 (2009): 123–39.

Jospin, Lionel. *Lionel raconte Jospin: entretiens avec Pierre Favier et Patrick Rotman*. Paris: Seuil, 2010.

Kraus, François. *Les Assises du socialisme ou l'échec d'une tentative de rénovation d'un parti*. Les Notes de la fondation Jean Jaurès, no 31 (July 2002).

Lafon, François. *Guy Mollet: itinéraire d'un socialiste controversé (1905–1975)*. Paris: Fayard, 2006.

Lefebvre, Denis. *Les secrets de l'expédition de Suez: 1956*. Paris: CNRS éditions, 2019.

Pelletier, Denis and Jean-Louis Schlegel, eds. *À la gauche du Christ: les chrétiens de gauche en France de 1945 à nos jours*. Paris: Seuil, 2012.

Rathkolb, Oliver, 'Brandt, Kreisky and Palme as Policy Entrepreneurs: Social Democratic Networks in Europe's Policy Towards the Middle East'. In *Transnational Networks in Regional Integration, Governing Europe 1945–83*, edited by Wolfram Kaiser, Brigitte Leucht and Michael Gehler, 152–75. London: Palgrave Macmillan, 2010.

Ravenel, Bernard. *Quand la gauche se réinventait: le PSU, histoire d'un parti visionnaire, 1960–1989*. Paris: La Découverte, 2016.

Sauvageot, Jacques. *Le PSU, des idées pour un socialisme au XXIè siècle*. Rennes: Presses universitaires de Rennes, 2012.

Chapter 7

Black British Labour leaders and the Europeanisation of antiracism, 1986–93

Pamela Ohene-Nyako

In 1986, the announcement of a Single European market to be implemented by 1992 led to many critiques and to the formation of several local and transnational initiatives for social justice led by people of colour in Europe. These initiatives were responses to the consolidation of the European integration process that enforced patterns of exclusion and further gave rise to the term 'Fortress Europe'.[1] This expression was at first used by American business men and women in the late twentieth century to express the fears that Western Europe was closing itself to foreign trade.[2] However, for antiracist activists and intellectuals at the turn of the late 1980s and early 1990s, the expression progressively designated the conflation at the European level of national legislations aiming to limit immigration, citizenship and asylum.

As a means of contestation, many among these 'activist intellectuals' – as coined by Imaobong Umoren[3] – issued research and documentation to denounce the increased political disenfranchisement of European minorities.[4] Alongside these publications, social scientists analysed the effects of Europeanisation on social movements, and accounted for the ways European integration led to an "NGO-sation" of many organisations.[5] On the side of historical investigation however, only few studies have so far paid attention to the activism and political agitation of racialised minorities in response to Europeanisation at the turn of the 1980s.[6] Daniel Gordon's 2015 article on British and French transnational activism stands as a milestone in showing how increased political integration from the

1970s onwards led to further mutual exchanges among activists of the radical left on both sides of the Channel and minorities in Germany.[7] His study has convincingly shown how these influences remained relatively limited to a few individuals and asymmetrical, in the sense that French and German activists tended to be more receptive to British influences than the reverse, British activists being usually held as 'bolder' and 'more advanced' in challenging racism.[8] However, the author paid little attention to the female activists who played a significant role in shaping antiracist activism across Western Europe. On that note, Tiffany Florvil's recent publications on the Black German movement in the 1980s and 1990s, and the transnational activism of feminist poet and intellectual May Ayim have been valuable contributions on the agency of Black European women and men.[9] Drawing from activists' accounts and archival material, Florvil's work documents how Afro-Germans actively coalesced with other Black and racialised Europeans amid European integration and growing racial violence in a reunifying Germany. In the same scope, my own publications have retraced how Black and racialised women built and relied on pan-European networks to inform themselves about European developments and their impact on minorities.[10]

This chapter thus builds upon this historiography. It provides additional insights on British antiracist socialists in the context of Europeanisation while contributing to the growing historiography on Black internationalism in gendered perspective.[11] More precisely, my aim is to pay attention to mobilisations that took place mostly outside of European institutions but from which British antiracist activists and socialists sought funding and support. To do so, I draw from archival material produced by the protagonists themselves,[12] or the intermediaries they were working with, to analyse more closely two initiatives that emerged in Britain and became pan-European in their scope: the Standing Conference for Racial Equality in Europe (SCORE) and the Black Women and Europe Network (BWEN). The reason of my focusing on these two initiatives is because their chairs, respectively Bernie Grant and Martha Osamor, were Black leaders within the British Labour Party. Also, neither of them has been subjected to historical scrutiny to this day, except in the work of Philomena Essed who, in addition to being an academic, participated in the Dutch women's movement and transnational antiracist initiatives through which she was informed about BWEN.[13] Yet both initiatives are particularly insightful for two reasons. First, they provide historical perspectives on how matters of race, immigration, citizenship, and gender intersected in the case of people of colour when building European transnational networks for social justice. Second, they are also historical examples from which contemporary civil society actors and politicians can draw insights as regards the European Union and pan-European networks organised around matters of racism, migration, asylum and equality.

This chapter thus seeks to introduce SCORE and BWEN, and to illuminate some of the key challenges they faced at the time of their creation between 1990 and 1993. To do so, I address three sets of questions. First, what was at stake for British socialists of colour and why did the announcement of the Single Market become their focus of transnational antiracism? Second, what were their demands pertaining to the Single Market and how did they try to influence its policies? Finally, why did organising as people of colour or as women of colour, the same as networking at a transnational level, become the strategy they sought? The chapter first gives a brief presentation of the context that preceded the emergence of these groups, before presenting and analysing each one of them with regards to the above-mentioned questions.

Fears of 'Fortress Europe'

Britain joined the European Economic Community (EEC) in 1973, the same year that its 1971 Immigration Act came into force. Under these provisions, EEC migrants seeking jobs in the UK could enter the country more easily than Commonwealth citizens of colour (non-Patrials).[14] This situation led to local mobilisations and denunciations by Labour leaders against what was considered a racist piece of legislation that affected not only the entry of racialised immigrants but also the perceptions held on minorities living in the country.[15] But the issue was mostly understood as a domestic matter until the end of the 1970s and resulted in few political incentives to network with other antiracist Europeans of colour or reaching out to EEC institutions.[16] The political context of the 1981 Brixton riots alongside the signing of the British Nationality Act the same year acted as catalysts for a few British antiracist activists and leftist MPs. As recalled by Ann Dummett, a white British female activist involved in organising one of the first informative conferences on the issue in 1983: 'The event had to be organized so as to provide a starting-point for a completely new kind of discussion, bringing together people who had never before had to consider British immigration policy with others who had working experience of it and with people who know about other countries'.[17] Among the participants who hadn't had to consider immigration for themselves until then was Lord Pitt. He was a London-based antiracist activist and Labour MP born in Grenada and who migrated as a British subject in the 1930s. Yet, he had to re-register under the new 1981 Nationality Act, which came into force in January 1983 and which tightened the conditions under which British citizenship could be acquired.[18] The representatives who, on the other hand, were perceived as more knowledgeable about the internal impact of immigration policies than their British counterparts provided insights on the French, German, Dutch and Swedish contexts, alongside case studies taken from Canada, Australia and the United States.

Amid political disenfranchisement and because their country was a relative latecomer in the European Community (EC), British activists and political leaders increasingly felt the need to come to terms with EC politics and disenclave their national experiences. Eventually, the signature and announcement of the Single European Act (SEA) in 1986 (ratified in 1987) provided them with new urgency to inform themselves and come into closer contact with other antiracist politicians and activists in continental Europe. The Act set 1992 as the date for the completion of the European Single Market that would result in the free movement of goods, services, people and capital among the twelve member states.[19] This announcement, its mediatisation, and the fact that it took place in a conservative political context marked by the rise of far-right political parties nourished the anxieties already felt by antiracist organisations and individuals. During the last decade, they had been witnessing a general tightening of legislation pertaining to immigration, citizenship and asylum that increasingly affected them.[20] Concerns were namely raised on the degree, areas and consequences of such policy harmonisation on racialised minorities.

In Britain, fears around the 1986 Act firstly pertained to the status of third-country nationals. Commonwealth citizens living in Britain and registered in 1981 still had the same social and political rights as British citizens, but they were not understood as citizens under the British EC agreement. Thus, questions were raised about the impact of the liberalisation of services and people, and the likelihood that it would negatively impact the economic sectors where (working-class) Black and minority people were mainly concentrated. The latter was of particular concern since Commonwealth citizens could not benefit in turn from freedom of movement in the EC because they were not considered citizens under EC law.[21] On the other hand, British antiracist activists and leftist politicians equally feared for the protection of British citizens of colour who could circulate and potentially benefit from the liberalisation of services and people. These fears were rooted in the numerous experiences made by British tourists of colour in France who had been racially harassed by customs officers.[22] They were also direct responses to the racial violence in Germany and France being featured in the British press, and of reports of the racial profiling of Black people framed as illegal immigrants.[23] The question then was on what basis would any harmonisation of antiracist legislation take place, when no country in Europe had the equivalent of the British Race Relations Act of 1976.[24] On that note, British antiracist and critical leftist political leaders were also worried about the TREVI group, formed in 1976 to coordinate policies on terrorism, radicalism, extremism and international violence (hence its name), and the Schengen group on mobility, established following the signing of the agreement of the same name in 1985. Both were perceived as secret intergovernmental meetings aiming to limit immigration and increase security measures upon racialised people.[25] Antiracist actors feared that decisions taken within those groups would be the basis for European harmonisation on racism and immigration, and lead to further tightening of legislation. Finally, with regards to women of colour, the EC presented some advances, as article 119 of the Treaty of Rome stated equality between women and men in employment. Nonetheless, this provision did not consider the racialised dimension of gender discrimination for women of colour.[26] Furthermore, since the Treaty of Rome did not cover non-citizens, women with third-country citizenship could not benefit from its legislation.

The Standing Conference on Racial Equality in Europe (SCORE)

Antiracists' anxieties depicted above led to several local conferences, studies and the creation of groups in Britain and across Europe.[27] The British Commission for Racial Equality, established by the 1976 Race Relations Act,[28] was among the bodies to take action on the matter. Initially set to eliminate racism and promote equality within Britain, its mission progressively extended to 'identify[ing] possible discriminatory effects contained in the . . . implement[ation] of the Single market'.[29] In June 1990, it convened a conference with the aim of coordinating efforts among groups with very diverse agendas and understandings of the impact of the SEA. The conference gave birth to a working group comprising of representatives of the Commission for Racial Equality, the British Council of Churches, the Trades Union Congress, the Greater London Action for Race Equality, the Confederation of Indian Workers, Labour MP Bernie Grant and the Runnymede Trust, among others. These various bodies and leaders had a history of collaborating with each other on matters pertaining to racism in Britain at least since the late 1970s.[30] In 1990, their discussion centred on whether to create a national information group – in order to remedy the lack of knowledge on the SEA's implications for Britain and for European institutions – or to become a campaigning group lobbying British and European institutions. The Standing Conference on Racial Equality in Europe (SCORE) was the outcome of these debates, and it was launched in Birmingham on 24 November 1990. It aimed to facilitate the exchange of information; to work for the equality of all residents of EC member states; to promote action and legislation at a European level; and to cooperate with other groups in the EC.[31] Throughout its lifespan, it benefited from grants and support by the Commission for Racial Equality, the World Council of Churches, the Churches Committee for Migrants in Europe and the Commission of Churches for Racial Justice.[32]

Labour MP Bernie Grant was elected as SCORE's chair and was influential during its initial stages in pushing for an organisation that would be led by people of colour and focused on racism in Europe. Born and raised in Guyana, Grant was a man of African descent who migrated to London in the early 1960s. There, he became involved in trade union politics and joined the Labour Party in 1973. In 1978, he was elected councillor of the Borough of Haringey, an activity he led in parallel to founding and working full-time for the Black Trade Unionists Solidarity Movement.[33] By 1985, he was the leader of the Haringey Council, a position from which he notoriously denounced the murderous effects of police brutality following the death of Cynthia Jarret and the uprising at the Broadwater Farm Estate.[34] It is in that context that he generated strong activist ties with Nigerian-born activist Martha Osamor, whom I will return to subsequently.[35] In 1987, Grant was the leader of the Black Sections – an internal Black pressure group within the Labour Party – and one of the four Black people to enter the House of Commons alongside Diane Abbott, Keith Vaz and Paul Boateng.[36] All had been known for their previous engagement with antiracism and gender equality in Afro-Asian communities in Britain, and their elections coincided with the re-instatement of the Conservative government headed by Margaret Thatcher as Prime Minister. Amid this political context and mounting racial tensions in the country, the four Black MPs joined forces with Lord Pitt, mentioned above, and founded the Parliamentary Black Caucus inspired by the American Congressional Black Caucus.[37] The difference between the two was their numbers – the British Black Caucus being only composed of five members – and their understanding of racial identification – the British Black Caucus forming along the lines of political blackness, a politically constructed identification along which radical British activists of colour had been organising since the 1960s and 1970s.[38] In this sense, Black referred to all racialised minorities who faced colonial legacies, anti-immigration policies and the effects of structural racism regardless of whether they were of African descent. Such 'politics of solidarity' – as Nydia Swaby refers to[39] – also reverberated in SCORE's racial understanding and coalition building both inside Britain and across Europe.

Before SCORE's creation and its willingness to foster a pan-European perspective on racism and antiracism, Grant had already toured Europe as a Labour MP. For example, he, Keith Vaz and Martha Osamor were part of a UK-delegation of twenty people who participated in a pan-European conference titled 'Immigration and Citizenship in Europe' that was held in Amiens, France, in October 1989, in conjunction with the celebrations of the Bicentenary of the French Revolution.[40] There, they networked with local and European deputies of colour, such as Djida Tazdaït and Nora Zaidi, both members of the European Greens. The aim of the conference was to gather information about measures taken by local politicians of colour to tackle matters of racism, immigration, civil rights and citizenship. Grant's time in Amiens and subsequent travels to Belgium, Portugal and Germany led to his feeling that the centrality of racism was missing in those countries, and that 'the dominant concept was still Assimilation'.[41] He also deplored his party's lack of a clear position on matters of racialised and ethnic minority groups, a situation he considered as 'an important gap in policy provision'.[42] On matters of race, he and other members of the Black Sections already disagreed with mainstream Labour MPs because they felt their conceptions of racism remained liberal and not critical enough with regard to police brutality and structural racism.[43] Thus, SCORE was an additional attempt to put race and racism on the political and European agenda of leftist politicians in a general context that was prone to deny their ongoing relevance to understand postcolonial European contexts.[44] Nevertheless, Grant oversimplified continental antiracist responses in equating them to 'assimilation' when in fact many grassroots activist groups were also race-conscious and challenging the denial of European racism. But he was right in insisting that many continental European politicians and publicly recognised leaders objected to using race as a signifying and political category, the same way they were less prone to push forth the leadership of people of colour as was advocated in British critical activist and leftist contexts.[45] SCORE did both: it focused on European racism and its leadership was held by people of colour.

Despite differences in experiences, identifications, and in apprehending race, SCORE's members admitted they still needed to network with their continental counterparts. In doing so, they extended their political concerns and activities to the European level when the latter became relevant and potentially impactful. Hence, the accelerated process of Europeanisation through the Single European Act led to a Europeanisation of British social justice initiatives, a conclusion which Gordon also comes to.[46] My understanding of 'Europeanisation' builds upon the definition suggested by historians Ulrike von Hirschhausen and Kiran Patel.[47] I use the term to address the transnationalisation of activists' agendas, strategies and collective identities which led to the creation of networks, groups and campaigns with a European scope, even if not all European countries were involved. I thus consider the impact of political Europeanisation on social movements even when they took place outside of European institutions; I therefore depart from a purely institutional perspective on the matter.[48] I also contend that Europeanisation never resulted in the abandonment of national or global concerns, but rather evolved simultaneously with them. In fact, mobilisations at a city-level and national level remained far more significant even when targeting 'Fortress Europe'.[49] As such, SCORE was one of the few British initiatives that responded to European integration by actively seeking transnational outreach across the Channel. But like other cross-national initiatives of its time, it remained British-centred in terms of its power base and in its approach to race and political blackness.[50]

Indeed, in terms of networking, SCORE's strategy was first to secure branches across the United Kingdom (in Wales, the Midlands, the North West, the South West and Scotland) and then to encourage the establishment of SCORE branches in other European states.[51] The latter would then be granted associate membership.[52] In Britain, more than 200 organisations and individuals joined during its first year, among which were the Joint Council for the Welfare of Immigrants, the Council of Churches for Britain and Ireland, the Trades Union Congress and the Commission for Racial Equality, as well as local authorities, academics and people from civil society.[53] At a European level, SCORE was in contact with groups in France, Portugal, Denmark, Germany, Spain, Italy, Greece and the Netherlands.[54] The latter identified along a variety of lines, including as immigrants or under national lines; only a few people who were not of African descent called themselves Black in the political sense. Josephine Ocloo, SCORE's vice-president, played an important role in developing these transnational networks. SCORE's Alternative Summits were also important transnational venues which took place in parallel to EC Council of Ministers meetings (Edinburgh in 1992, and Brussels in 1993).[55] The first one happened in Maastricht and Brussels in 1991 on signature of the treaty, and was 'an attempt by SCORE (UK) to bring together Black and Minority ethnic groups together ... as a first step towards the establishment of a permanent European wide networking system for Black and Minority Ethnic people'.[56] Attendees also participated in a picket in front of the building where European Ministers were having their Summit, and gave press conferences.

Regarding lobbying, Bernie Grant's political position facilitated SCORE's communication with other Members of the European Parliament (MEPs) and other Euro-deputies, as well as with British and German Prime Ministers because he more legitimately had access to them. In 1992, Britain – still led by the Conservatives but now under John Major – presided over the European Community, and therefore SCORE counted on the country's leadership to push for 1) an amendment of the Treaty of Rome that would give the European Commission competence in the field of antiracism and protection of minority people, migrants and asylum seekers; 2) EC antiracist legislation that would bind EC states to implement antiracist legislation nationally; and 3) freedom of movement for third-country nationals established in EC countries.[57] The response of the Home Office was that it would not encourage EC legislation, but rather support and advise each EC member state. It also stated that only nationals would be concerned by EC provisions on freedom of movement.[58] Despite this negative response, SCORE continued to lobby British and European parliamentarians, in the context of the European elections of 1994. To do so, it formulated its 'Black Manifesto for Europe' which, again, demanded an amendment of the Treaty of Rome to outlaw racial discrimination; free movement for all EU residents; the end of racial violence and harassment; the creation of 'an anti-racist and anti-sexist' immigration policy; an independent status for 'Black, Migrant and Minority' women, and the mainstreaming of their issues across Europe. The Manifesto also called for all Black, Migrant and Minority residents to have the right to vote, equal housing, equal education inclusive of their own specificities, equal health and social services, as well as the right to family reunion.[59]

In terms of gender, around 1993, SCORE established a Black Women Sub-Committee, chaired by Anne-Marie Harding and which put Black women's issues on SCORE's general agenda.[60] The sub-committee denounced racist and sexist immigration policies in Europe, and demanded that women who migrated as a result of family reunion have an independent status from their husbands. They also pushed for the mainstreaming of Black women's specific issues.[61] Thus, SCORE opted for a women's section within the main group in order for sexism to be considered in its articulation with class and racial discrimination. The archives consulted don't allow me to investigate the gendered dynamics within SCORE, nor how women's agendas were effectively promoted. But Black women seem to have been in leadership positions as testified by Ocloo's appointment as the organisation's vice-president and Harding as the leader of its women's section. But again, these facts say little about the overall gender dynamics. On the other hand, Britain had one of the most vibrant Black women's movements in 1980s Europe, and many of its participants had experience in shaping gender inclusive agendas and in organising as Black women.[62] Like for others, the passing of the Single European Act raised the anxieties of several Black feminist activists in Britain who feared that more regional integration would lead to further political disenfranchisement for women of colour. The closer the term to 'Europe 92', the more they felt called to organise. As a result, they launched the Black Women and Europe Network (BWEN) in 1993.

The Black Women and Europe Network (BWEN)

When BWEN was in the process of being created, initiatives with a European scope and inclusive of minority women's specific issues existed.[63] As seen above, this was the case of SCORE, but also of the Cross-Cultural Black Women's Studies Institute established in London in 1987 or of the World Council of Churches' subprogram Women under Racism, created in 1980.[64] Some of BWEN's constituents even participated in their activities and collaborated with their members. For example, Bernie Grant and Martha Osamor, who went on to become BWEN's first chair, worked together within the Black Trade Unionists Solidarity Movement and the Black Sections. As mentioned above, they also travelled together in Europe in 1989 to network with other antiracist protagonists. Furthermore, once established, BWEN used SCORE's bi-monthly newsletter *Scoreboard* to advertise its actions and boost its membership.[65] But what characterised BWEN was that it sought to be an independent and minority women-led initiative guided by self-determination which put minority women's issues at the forefront of its actions.

BWEN was the direct result of two meetings held in 1991. The first was a one-day seminar in February convened by a group of Women's Equality officers in London who had emerged from the British Black women's movement. The meeting focused on the impact of the Single European Act 'for black, migrant and refugee women' within the British context.[66] The event gathered about 130 women from the UK and was chaired by Valerie Amos, a woman of Guyanese descent, who was then the Chief Executive of the Equal Opportunities Commission.[67] The panellists were female researchers, equality officers, professionals, social workers, members of women's organisations and European lobbyists of African and Asian descent – such as Wangui Wa Goro, Naseem Khan and Umran Beeler – as well as white women allies such as MEP Pauline Green. Most of these women had been active during the women's movement of the 1970s and 1980s and were now at the forefront of experiencing and gathering knowledge about the Single European Act. The meeting resulted in a set of thirty-one recommendations which included gathering expertise and documentation on European institutions and policies; demanding that all women, no matter their civil status, have access to the same rights as EC citizens; creating national and 'cross-European networks'; and the formation of a 'black, migrant, and refugee Women's lobby in Europe' as a long-term goal.[68]

The second meeting that stimulated the creation of BWEN was convened by the European Green Party nine months later, in November 1991, under the leadership of Euro-deputy Djida Tazdaït. Tazdaït was a French politician of Algerian background who had been the co-founder of the Maghrebi women's group *Zaâma d'banlieue* (women from the suburbs) and an activist against racial discrimination. She had formerly met Grant and Osamor in Amiens in 1989, and had taken part in SCORE's Alternative Summit in Maastricht in 1991.[69] Her activism translated in the aims of the November gathering, which were to articulate the issues facing Black and minority women in Europe, and to create a 'pressure group at European level' as soon as possible.[70] Consequently, the British delegates of the November conference networked with the organisers of the February seminar and took the initiative to create such a network that was to be politically independent.

The steering group named itself 'Black Women and Europe Network' and elected Martha Osamor as its interim president. Osamor was a Nigerian London-based community activist, trade-unionist, and member of the Labour Party. She had co-founded the United Black Women Action Group in Tottenham – Bernie Grant's constituency – in the mid-1970s, and the Group had been a member of the Organisation for Women of African and African/Asian Descent (OWAAD) from 1978 to 1982.[71] In 1977, she worked for the Tottenham Law Centre where she met Bernie Grant. By 1980, she was a member of the local Labour Party and eventually became the national vice-chair of the Black Sections.[72] She, however, remained committed to grassroots activism and co-founded the British Movement for Civil Rights and Justice in 1987 after the murder of Cynthia Jarret which sparked the Broadwater Farm uprising in 1985.[73] In this context, she and Bernie Grant took a radical public stand against police brutality and racial inequality. In 1986, Osamor became Labour Councillor for the Borough of Haringey, a position she kept until 1990 when she was nominated Deputy leader of the Haringey council.[74] She was thus an active Labour leader when she was chosen as BWEN's first chair.

BWEN was officially launched in April 1993 at its constitutional meeting. The latter was financed by European grants and attended by more than sixty women from eleven European countries, some of which were not part of the EEC: twenty-six participants were from the United Kingdom; thirteen from France; eight from Germany; six from Spain; four from the Netherlands; two from Denmark; one each from Ireland, Greece and Norway.[75] This representation speaks of an understanding of Europe in more geographical terms than political. Since most of the women present came from women's groups, female self-determination was to be the basis of the BWEN, as stressed by Tazdaït: 'We mobilise together because we want to avoid marginalization, discrimination and subordination. Most importantly, if we do not mobilise to do this, no one else, no matter how liberal they might be, can achieve this for us'.[76] Black and minority female self-determination was thus understood as being the only effective way for Black and minority women's issues to be central to the fight against racism and 'Fortress Europe'. Given the context, I suggest that this stance emerged out of their experiences of working in or with male-led groups, in addition to a practice of organising autonomously as women. Nevertheless, this posture did not exclude working in partnership with mixed or male-led groups, nor did it mean that larger community issues were not tackled, as testified by the BWEN's initial objectives and collaboration with SCORE with which it was aligned. Its main aims were to voice the special needs of 'black, migrant, refugee, and asylum-seeking women' and to combat all forms of discrimination, including the distinction between non-citizens and citizens.[77] To do so, it envisaged linking women's groups at a national and transnational level to produce information and knowledge on women specifically, and their communities in general; to act as a consulting body vis-à-vis European institutions and as a pressure group both at the European and national levels; and to conduct transnational campaigns. Some of its British and Dutch members thus joined the European Women's Lobby to increase their impact through multi-affiliations.

This agenda testifies to the founders' understanding of themselves as racialised minority women whose struggle for social justice included oppressions linked to race, class and gender (sexuality was left out) and aimed at the liberation of themselves and their communities. Yet, they did not publicly call themselves feminists since they still equated the term with white women's struggle solely based on sex oppression (a conception in itself limited).[78] Thus, in the same way as SCORE, the BWEN was not only responding to political Europeanisation, but also aiming to Europeanise the fight for social justice from an autonomous Black women's standpoint. Their strategy was rooted in the idea that a cross-border coalition was a necessary and relevant strategy in the face of such a regional geopolitical development. Nevertheless, due to the BWEN seeking a transnational scope, debates around membership and the group's identity were raised from its foundation. As was also the case of

SCORE, BWEN's initiators identified as politically Black regardless of whether they were of African descent. Thus, for them, the focus of the network was to be for women commonly seen and oppressed as non-European due to their phenotype and/or cultural attributes; it did not comprise white European immigrants who had immigrated to another European state as contracted workers (such as Portuguese women in France).[79] In this sense, political blackness applied to people 'marked as racially different' through dominant gazes.[80] On the other hand, other participants did not identify as 'Black', either because they were not of African descent (i.e. Turkish women in Germany, the Netherlands and Belgium) or because they did not endorse a racialised identity but rather a national identity (i.e. Cameroonian) or an identity based on their civil status (i.e. immigrant).[81] As a result, alternative names to 'Black Women in Europe' were suggested. In the end, the name 'Black Women and Europe Network: Black, Migrant, Refugee, Asylum Seeking Women in Europe' was chosen.[82]

This choice of name, I argue, reveals that a compromise was sought between participants embracing the notion of political blackness, and others identifying differently, perhaps as migrant, refugee, asylum seeking, and so on. Nevertheless, 'Black Women in Europe' – without its extension – remained the common name used by the network. Whether this was the result of an embrace of political blackness with time by all the members, a lack of contestation, or the departure of those who still didn't identify with the name remains to be further researched. The name also testifies to an attempt to Europeanise a concept and strategy that initially sprung from the British context, at a time where political blackness as a collective identity and politics of solidarity was challenged in the country itself.[83] Thus, it could also be that BWEN's insistence on focusing on political blackness as a collective identity was perceived as British and Anglo-Saxon domination, which could explain why the number of active members at a transnational level dropped from sixty to a dozen the year after.[84] Indeed, as much as BWEN sought to Europeanise its scope, not only did its member organisations remain more active at a national level, but its base and leadership remained mainly British until 1997. In this sense, it shared a similar fate to SCORE, which also remained a British-centred initiative despite its initial ambitions towards continental Europe.

Conclusion

As presented, SCORE and BWEN were responses to political Europeanisation at a time when its policies were understood as direct threats to

British and other European people of colour's freedom of movement within the EU, their socio-economic welfare, and their protection from racism and xenophobia. The networks' chairs were elected Labour leaders and their members had been politically socialised in minority-led antiracist and/or antisexist groups prior to their transnational mobilisations. Building upon their political and activists' practices, they further decided to organise collectively and publicly against 'Fortress Europe' as a consequence of the shared fears and sense of urgency surrounding the announcement of the Single European Act, while embracing the idea that a regional development necessitated a transnational reply. Their main demands were to grant non-citizens the same right to circulate and establish within the Single Market, and to amend the Treaty of Rome so that it included an explicit provision covering racial discrimination. Networking and building coalitions, outside and autonomously from EU institutions, became important, first in order to gather information across borders, then to attempt to put more pressure on European states by increasing their ranks.[85] Consequently, not only were they responding to Europeanisation, but, in turn, also contributing to producing a Europeanisation of social justice on the basis of British understanding of race and political blackness.

SCORE and BWEN were not the only British initiatives with a European scope. Another example is the European Action for Racial Equality and Social Justice (European Action group) formed in London in November 1990 and co-chaired by London-based activist and publisher John La Rose and lawyer Ian Macdonald. The association's membership was racially mixed yet overwhelmingly constituted by men. During its lifespan, between 1991 and 1993, European Action had coordinators in Germany (Nii Addy from the *Initiativ Schwarze Deutsche* (ISD)-Berlin) and in France (Mogniss Abdallah from Rock Against Police – RAP).[86] Another initiative was the European Race Audit launched in 1992 by the Institute of Race Relations (IRR) with the aim of collecting data on racism in Europe and undertaking analysis of its different expressions depending on context.[87] Whether these initiatives were successful in reaching all their aims and effectively impacting governments' decisions on racism still needs to be scrutinised. But antiracist provisions were inserted into the Amsterdam Treaty of 1997.

Notes

1. See Les Black and Anoop Nayak, eds., *Invisible Europeans? Black People in the "New Europe"* (Birmingham: AFFOR, 1993), 1–2.

2. Desmond Dinan, *Europe Recast: A History of European Union* (London: Lynne Rienner Publishers, 2004), 222.

3. Imaobong Denis Umoren, *Race Women Internationalists: Activist-Intellectuals and Global Freedom Struggles* (Oakland: University of California Press, 2018).

4. Eleonore Kofman and Rosemary Sales, 'Towards Fortress Europe?', *Women's Studies International Forum* 15, no. 1 (1992); Frances Webber, 'From Ethnocentrism to Euro-Racism', *Race & Class* 32, no. 3 (1991); Tony Bunyan, 'Towards an Authoritarian European State', *Race & Class* 32, no. 3 (1991); Ann Dummett, 'Racial Equality and "1992"', *Feminist Review* 39, no. 1 (1991); Mirjana Morokvasic, 'Fortress Europe and Migrant Women', *Feminist Review*, no. 39 (1991). Doug Imig, 'Contestation in the Streets: European Protest and the Emerging Euro-Polity', *Comparative Political Studies* 35, no. 8 (2002); Doug Imig and Sidney Tarrow, 'Political Contention in a Europeanising Polity', *West European Politics* 23, no. 4 (2000); Donatella della Porta and Manuela Caiani, *Social Movements and Europeanization* (Oxford: Oxford University Press, 2009).

5. Imig, 'Contestation in the Streets'; Imig and Tarrow, 'Political Contention in a Europeanising Polity'; della Porta and Caiani, *Social Movements and Europeanization*; Ruud Koopmans et al., *Contested Citizenship. Immigration and Cultural Diversity in Europe* (Minneapolis, London: University of Minnesota Press, 2005).

6. Research on racism and antiracist activism in Europe is however expanding. For recent comparative studies in European scope, see namely Rita Chin, *The Crisis of Multiculturalism in Europe: A History* (Princeton: Princeton University Press, 2017); Elizabeth Buettner, *Europe after Empire: Decolonization, Society, and Culture* (Cambridge: Cambridge University Press, 2016); Britta Timm Knudsen et al., eds., *Decolonizing Colonial Heritage: New Agendas, Actors and Practices in and beyond Europe* (London: Routledge, 2021); Gurminder K. Bhambra and John Narayan, eds., *European Cosmopolitanism: Colonial Histories and Postcolonial Societies* (Abingdon/New York: Routledge, 2017); Natasha A. Kelly and Olive Vassell, eds., *Mapping Black Europe: Monuments, Markers, Memories* (Bielefeld: Transcript, 2023).

7. Daniel A. Gordon, 'French and British Anti-Racists Since the 1960s: A "Rendez-Vous Manqué"?', *Journal of Contemporary History* 50, no. 3 (2015).

8. Chin, *The Crisis of Multiculturalism*, 84, 93–94; Gordon, 'French and British Anti-Racists', 24.

9. Tiffany N. Florvil, *Mobilizing Black Germany: Afro-German Women and the Making of Transnational Movement* (Urbana: University of Illinois Press, 2020), and Tiffany N. Florvil, 'May Ayim's Cosmopolitanism from Below in Europe', *History Workshop* (blog), 2 October 2023, https://www.historyworkshop.org.uk/feminism/may-ayims-cosmopolitanism-from-below-in-europe/.

10. Pamela Ohene-Nyako, 'Black Women's Transnational Activism and the World Council of Churches', *Open Cultural Studies* 3, no. 1 (2019), and Pamela Ohene-Nyako, 'Contexts and Spaces of Intersectionality: The Black Feminism and Internationalism of Lydie Dooh-Bunya, 1970–1990', *Journal of Women's History* 35, no. 3 (2023).

11. Among recent publications following this perspective: Florvil, *Mobilizing Black Germany*; Keisha Blain and Tiffany Gill, eds., *To Turn the Whole World Over: Black Women and Internationalism* (Urbana: University of Illinois Press, 2019); Félix F. Germain and Silyane Larcher, eds., *Black French Women and the Struggle for Equality, 1848–2016* (Lincoln: University of Nebraska Press, 2018); Quito Swan, 'Giving Berth: Fiji, Black Women's Internationalism, and the Pacific Women's Conference of 1975', *Journal of Civil and Human Rights* 4, no. 1 (2018); Cheryl Higashida, *Black Internationalist Feminism: Women Writers of the Black Left, 1945–1995* (Urbana: University of Illinois Press, 2013).

12. More specifically correspondence, minutes, pamphlets, circulars and publications.

13. Philomena Essed, 'Gender, Migration and Cross-Ethnic Coalition Building', in *Crossfires. Nationalism, Racism and Gender in Europe*, ed. Helma Lutz, Ann Phoenix and Nira Yuval-Davis (London: Pluto Press, 1995); Philomena Essed, 'Transnationality. The Diaspora of Women of Colour in Europe', in *Diversity. Gender, Color, and Culture*, ed. Philomena Essed (Amherst: University of Massachusetts Press, 1996).

14. Ann Dummet, 'The Law of Citizenship and Nationality', in *Immigrant Voice Supplement*, undated, Pennsylvania State University, University Libraries, Special Collections Library, Rare Books and Manuscripts, Ann Dummett papers (hereafter Dummett Papers) (9466), Box 1, file 1.4. See also Buettner, *Europe after Empire*; Kathleen Paul, *Whitewashing Britain: Race and Citizenship in the Postwar Era* (Ithaca: Cornell University Press, 1997).

15. George Padmore Institute Archives (hereafter GPI), Black Panthers News, file 17, *Freedom News*, editorial, 19 February 1972; Black Panthers Movement, 'Stop the racist immigration bill', March 1971; Chin, *The Crisis of Multiculturalism*, 93.

16. Jenny Bourne, 'IRR: The Story Continues', *Race & Class* 50, no. 2 (2008); Gordon, 'French and British Anti-Racists'; Report on the AGIN conference concerning Reform of British Immigration Law and its Administration, Somerville College, Oxford, 1–3 July 1983, Dummett papers (9466), Box 1, file 1.4

17. Report on the AGIN conference, 2.

18. Report on the AGIN conference, 3–4.

19. Which included France, the Federal Republic of Germany, Italy, Belgium, Luxemburg, the Netherlands, the United Kingdom, Ireland, Denmark, Greece, Portugal and Spain.

20. Buettner, *Europe after Empire*.

21. Minutes of conference launch 24 November 1990, Bishopsgate Institute Archives – Bernie Grant Collection/SCORE.

22. Gordon, 'French and British Anti-Racists', 25.

23. Minutes of conference launch 24 November 1990.

24. Minutes of conference launch 24 November 1990. Expanding on the Race Relations Act of 1965 and 1968, the new legislation in 1976 included indirect discrimination in its definition of the term, and established a new body, the Commission for Racial Equality, which was given responsibility to enforce legislation and advise British governments on issues of race relations.

25. Working group meeting minutes, Bernie Grant Collection/SCORE 6/1. More generally on Trevi and Schengen, see Virginie Guiraudon, 'Schengen: une crise en trompe l'oeil', *Politique étrangère*, no. 4 (2011), 773.

26. Minutes of conference launch 24 November 1990.

27. Proposal to set up a Standing Conference, undated, Bernie Grant Collection/ SCORE 6/1. See also Black and Nayak, *Invisible Europeans?*

28. The body was disbanded in 2007 and replaced by the Equality and Human Rights Commission.

29. 'Commission for racial equality. Submission to the European parliament's committee enquiry into racism and xenophobia', undated but before 1992, Dummett Papers (9466), Box 1, file 1.33.

30. They were namely present at the 1983 conference mentioned previously. Report on the AGIN conference.

31. Constitution, Bernie Grant Collection/SCORE 4/1.

32. Report 1993/1994, 4, Bernie Grant Collection/SCORE file 4/2.

33. For more information, see biographical note accompanying his archival records https://www.bishopsgate.org.uk/collections/bernie-grant.

34. https://www.bishopsgate.org.uk/collections/bernie-grant.

35. Harmit Athwal and Jenny Bourne, 'It Has to Change: An Interview with Martha Osamo', *Race & Class* 50, no. 1 (2016), 91.

36. Athwal and Bourne, 'It Has to Change', 91.

37. Bernie Grant Collection PBC files 1–5.

38. James G. Cantres, *Blackening Britain* (Lanham: Rowman & Littlefield, 2020).

39. Nydia A. Swaby, '"Disparate in Voice, Sympathetic in Direction": Gendered Political Blackness and the Politics of Solidarity', *Feminist Review* 108, no. 1 (2014).

40. Rapport du colloque d'Amiens, Centre des Archives du Féminisme (Angers), Papers of the feminist network Ruptures, 49AF88.

41. Working group meeting minutes, undated but most likely 1990, Bernie Grant Collection/SCORE 6/1.

42. Working group meeting minutes, most likely 1990, Bernie Grant Collection.

43. Athwal and Bourne, 'It Has to Change', 90–91.

44. On Europe's relation to race and racism, see David Theo Goldberg, 'Racial Europeanization', *Ethnic and Racial Studies* 29, no. 2 (2006); Fatima El-Tayeb, *European Others: Queering Ethnicity in Postnational Europe* (Minneapolis: University of Minnesota Press, 2011); Buettner, *Europe after Empire*; Philomena Essed and Kwame Nimako, 'Designs and (Co)Incidents: Cultures of Scholarship and Public Policy on Immigrants/Minorities in the Netherlands', *International Journal of Comparative Sociology* 47, no. 3–4 (2006); Gloria Wekker, *White Innocence. Paradoxes of Colonialism and Race* (Durham and London: Duke University Press, 2016); Alana Lentin, 'Europe and the Silence about Race', *European Journal of Social Theory* 11, no. 4 (2008); Chin, *The Crisis of Multiculturalism*; Rita Chin et al., *After the Nazi Racial State. Difference and Democracy in Germany and Europe* (Ann Arbor: University of Michigan Press, 2009).

45. El-Tayeb, *European Others*; Florvil, *Mobilizing Black Germany*; Gordon, 'French and British Anti-Racists'; Ohene-Nyako, 'Contexts and Spaces of Intersectionality'.

46. Gordon, 'French and British Anti-Racists'. See also Florvil, 'May Ayim's Cosmopolitanism'.

47. Ulrike von Hirschhausen and Kiran K. Patel, 'Europeanization in History: An Introduction' in *Europeanization in the Twentieth Century. Historical Approaches*, ed. Martin Conway and Kiran K. Patel (Basingstoke: Palgrave Macmillan, 2010), 2–3.

48. Johan P. Olsen, 'The Many Faces of Europeanization', *JCMS: Journal of Common Market Studies* 40, no. 5 (2002).

49. Della Porta and Caiani, *Social Movements and Europeanization*; Pierre Monforte, *Europeanizing Contention: The Protest against "Fortress Europe" in France and Germany* (New York: Berghahn Books, 2014).

50. On activists' British-centredness, see Gordon, 'French and British Anti-Racists', 23–5.

51. Briefing. Undated but probably end of 1992, Bernie Grant Collection/SCORE 2/2.

52. Briefing. Undated but probably end of 1992, Bernie Grant Collection/SCORE 2/2.

53. Grant to Clarke, 18 August 1992, Bernie Grant Collection/SCORE 2/2.

54. Report 1993/1994, 9, Bernie Grant Collection/SCORE file 4/2.

55. Report 1993/1994, 5, Bernie Grant Collection/SCORE file 4/2.

56. Invitation to Maastricht Alternative Summit, November 1991, Bernie Grant Collection/SCORE 10/1, 1.

57. Grant to Clarke, 18 August 1992, Bernie Grant Collection/SCORE 2/2.

58. Letter from Peter Lloyd to Bernie Grant, 2 October 1992; Letter from John Major to Bernie Grant, 24 December 1992, Bernie Grant Collection/SCORE 2/2.

59. Report 1993/1994, Black Manifesto for Europe, 4, Bernie Grant Collection/SCORE file 4/2.

60. Report 1993/1994, Black Manifesto for Europe, 4, Bernie Grant Collection/SCORE file 4/2, 4.

61. Report 1993/1994, Black Manifesto for Europe, 4, Bernie Grant Collection/SCORE file 4/2, 4.

62. Julia Sudbury, *'Other Kinds of Dreams': Black Women's Organisations and the Politics of Transformation* (London: Routledge, 2003); Natalie Thomlinson, *Race, Ethnicity and the Women's Movement in England, 1968–1993* (Basingstoke: Palgrave Macmillan, 2016); Swaby, 'Disparate in Voice, Sympathetic in Direction'.

63. Ohene-Nyako, 'Black Women's Transnational Activism'.

64. Ohene-Nyako, 'Black Women's Transnational Activism'; Florvil, *Mobilizing Black Germany*, 166–77.

65. *Scoreboard*, April 1995, Bernie Grant Collection/SCORE file 5/8. The documents consulted do not allow me to determine precisely the number of issues released, nor its readership.

66. *The Effects of 1992 and the Single European Market on Black, Migrant, and Refugee Women. A report of a seminar held in February 1991*, 2, GPI – EAC file 02/02/04/05.

67. Amos, a member of the Labour Party, was appointed to the House of Lords in 1997. She is notably known for being the first Black woman to become a British Minister in 2003 and the director of a higher education institution in 2015 when she became head of SOAS.

68. *The Effects of 1992*, 33–35, GPI – EAC file 02/02/04/05.

69. Déclaration de Maastricht, 7–8 November 1991, Bernie Grant Collection/SCORE 9/8.

70. Minutes of the constitutional conference, 16–17 April 1993, London, Atria Archives, Personal papers of Helen Felter, folder 17.

71. Athwal and Bourne, 'It Has to Change', 87–90.

72. Athwal and Bourne, 'It Has to Change', 91.

73. The Black Cultural Archives – Martha Osamor's personal papers/file 2 and Oral/1/28/1-3, Martha Osamor interviewed by Hayley Reid, March 2009 (with transcript).

74. In 2018, Martha Osamor was granted the title of Baroness.

75. Minutes of the constitutional conference, 16–17 April 1993, Felter Papers/17.

76. Minutes of the constitutional conference, 16–17 April 1993, Felter Papers/17.

77. BWEN constitution, Felter Papers/17.

78. For a more nuanced understanding of the women's movement in Britain, see Thomlinson, *Race, Ethnicity and the Women's Movement in England*.

79. Minutes of the constitutional conference, 16–17 April 1993, Felter Papers/17.

80. Minutes of the constitutional conference, 16–17 April 1993, Felter Papers/17. See also Noémi Michel and Joëlle Scacchi, 'Enoncés dans le présent, Les actes de discours racialisés ravivent une longue histoire d'exclusion et de violence', *Tangram*, no. 33 (2014).

81. Minutes of the constitutional conference, 16–17 April 1993, Felter Papers/17.

82. Minutes of the constitutional conference, 16–17 April 1993, Felter Papers/17.

83. Namely due to the rise of islamophobia leading to limited solidarity with Muslim Asians who then formed identities around their racialised religious oppression, Buettner, *Europe after Empire*.

84. 'Report BWEN Office 13–14 August 1994', France, Felter Papers/17.

85. Briefing. Undated but probably end of 1992, Bernie Grant Collection/SCORE 2/2.

86. GPI – EAC files (01 and 02). See also Gordon, 'French and British Anti-Racists'; Florvil, 'May Ayim's Cosmopolitanism'.

87. Bourne, 'IRR'.

Bibliography

Athwal, Harmit and Jenny Bourne. 'It Has to Change: An Interview with Martha Osamor', *Race & Class* 58, no. 1 (2016): 85–93.

Bhambra, Gurminder K. and John Narayan, eds. *European Cosmopolitanism: Colonial Histories and Postcolonial Societies*. Abingdon and New York: Routledge, 2017.

Black, Les and Anoop Nayak, eds. *Invisible Europeans? Black People in the "New Europe"*. Birmingham: AFFOR, 1993.

Blain, Keisha and Tiffany Gill, eds. *To Turn the Whole World Over: Black Women and Internationalism*. Urbana, Illinois: University of Illinois Press, 2019.

Bourne, Jenny. 'IRR: The Story Continues', *Race & Class* 50, no. 2 (2008): 31–9.

Buettner, Elizabeth. *Europe after Empire: Decolonization, Society, and Culture*. Cambridge: Cambridge University Press, 2016.

Bunyan, Tony. 'Towards an Authoritarian European State', *Race & Class* 32, no. 3 (1991): 19–27.

Cantres, James G. *Blackening Britain*. Lanham: Rowman & Littlefield, 2020.

Chin, Rita. *The Crisis of Multiculturalism in Europe: A History*. Princeton: Princeton University Press, 2017.

Chin, Rita, Heide Fehrenbach, Geoff Eley and Atina Grossmann. *After the Nazi Racial State. Difference and Democracy in Germany and Europe*. Ann Arbor: University of Michigan Press, 2009.

Dinan, Desmond. *Europe Recast: A History of European Union*. London: Lynne Rienner Publishers, 2004.

Dummett, Ann. 'Racial Equality and "1992"', *Feminist Review* 39, no. 1 (1991): 85–90.

El-Tayeb, Fatima. *European Others: Queering Ethnicity in Postnational Europe*. Minneapolis: University of Minnesota Press, 2011.

Essed, Philomena. 'Gender, Migration and Cross-Ethnic Coalition Building'. In *Crossfires. Nationalism, Racism and Gender in Europe*, edited by Helma Lutz, Ann Phoenix and Nira Yuval-Davis, 48–64. London: Pluto Press, 1995.

Essed, Philomena. 'Transnationality. The Diaspora of Women of Colour in Europe'. In *Diversity. Gender, Color, and Culture*, edited by Philomena Essed, 104–18. Amherst: University of Massachusetts Press, 1996.

Essed, Philomena and Kwame Nimako. 'Designs and (Co)Incidents: Cultures of Scholarship and Public Policy on Immigrants/Minorities in the Netherlands', *International Journal of Comparative Sociology* 47, no. 3–4 (2006): 281–312.

Florvil, Tiffany N. *Mobilizing Black Germany. Afro-German Women and the Making of Transnational Movement.* Urbana Chicago Springfield: University of Illinois Press, 2020.

Florvil, Tiffany N. 'May Ayim's Cosmopolitanism from Below in Europe', *History Workshop* (blog), 2 October 2023, https://www.historyworkshop.org.uk/feminism/may-ayims-cosmopolitanism-from-below-in-europe/.

Germain, Félix F. and Silyane Larcher, eds. *Black French Women and the Struggle for Equality, 1848–2016.* Lincoln: University of Nebraska Press, 2018.

Goldberg, David Theo. 'Racial Europeanization', *Ethnic and Racial Studies* 29, no. 2 (2006): 331–64.

Gordon, Daniel A. 'French and British Anti-Racists Since the 1960s: A "Rendez-Vous Manqué"?' *Journal of Contemporary History* 50, no. 3 (2015) : 606–31.

Guiraudon, Virginie. 'Schengen: une crise en trompe l'œil', *Politique étrangère*, no. 4 (2011) : 773–84.

Higashida, Cheryl. *Black Internationalist Feminism: Women Writers of the Black Left, 1945–1995.* Urbana Chicago Springfield: University of Illinois Press, 2013.

Hirschhausen, Ulrike von and Kiran K. Patel. 'Europeanization in History: An Introduction', In *Europeanization in the Twentieth Century. Historical Approaches*, edited by Martin Conway and Kiran K. Patel, 1–18. Basingstoke: Palgrave Macmillan, 2010.

Imig, Doug. 'Contestation in the Streets: European Protest and the Emerging Euro-Polity', *Comparative Political Studies* 35, no. 8 (2002): 914–33.

Imig, Doug and Sidney Tarrow. 'Political Contention in a Europeanising Polity', *West European Politics* 23, no. 4 (2000): 73–93.

Kelly, Natasha A. and Olive Vassell, eds. *Mapping Black Europe: Monuments, Markers, Memories.* Bielefeld: Transcript, 2023.

Knudsen, Britta Timm, John Oldfield, Elizabeth Buettner and Elvan Zabunyan, eds. *Decolonizing Colonial Heritage: New Agendas, Actors and Practices in and beyond Europe.* London: Routledge, 2021.

Kofman, Eleonore and Rosemary Sales. 'Towards Fortress Europe?' *Women's Studies International Forum* 15, no. 1 (1992): 29–39.

Koopmans, Ruud, Paul Statham, Marco Giugni and Florence Passy. *Contested Citizenship: Immigration and Cultural Diversity in Europe.* Minneapolis: University of Minnesota, 2005.

Lentin, Alana. 'Europe and the Silence about Race', *European Journal of Social Theory* 11, no. 4 (2008): 487–503.

Michel, Noémi and Joëlle Scacchi. 'Énoncés dans le présent, les actes de discours racialisés ravivent une longue histoire d'exclusion et de violence', *Tangram*, no. 33 (2014): 38–43.

Monforte, Pierre. *Europeanizing Contention: The Protest against "Fortress Europe" in France and Germany*. New York: Berghahn Books, 2014.

Morokvasic, Mirjana. 'Fortress Europe and Migrant Women', *Feminist Review*, no. 39 (1991): 69–84.

Ohene-Nyako, Pamela. 'Black Women's Transnational Activism and the World Council of Churches', *Open Cultural Studies* 3, no. 1 (2019): 219–31.

Ohene-Nyako, Pamela. 'Contexts and Spaces of Intersectionality: The Black Feminism and Internationalism of Lydie Dooh-Bunya, 1970–1990', *Journal of Women's History* 35, no. 3 (2023): 125–45.

Olsen, Johan P. 'The Many Faces of Europeanization', *JCMS: Journal of Common Market Studies* 40, no. 5 (2002): 921–52.

Paul, Kathleen. *Whitewashing Britain: Race and Citizenship in the Postwar Era*. Ithaca: Cornell University Press, 1997.

Porta, Donatella della and Manuela Caiani. *Social Movements and Europeanization*. Oxford: Oxford University Press, 2009.

Sudbury, Julia. *"Other Kinds of Dreams": Black Women's Organisations and the Politics of Transformation*. London: Routledge, 2003.

Swaby, Nydia A. '"Disparate in Voice, Sympathetic in Direction": Gendered Political Blackness and the Politics of Solidarity", *Feminist Review* 108, no. 1 (2014): 11–25.

Swan, Quito. 'Giving Berth: Fiji, Black Women's Internationalism, and the Pacific Women's Conference of 1975', *Journal of Civil and Human Rights* 4, no. 1 (2018): 37–63.

Thomlinson, Natalie. *Race, Ethnicity and the Women's Movement in England, 1968–1993*. Basingstoke: Palgrave Macmillan, 2016.

Umoren, Imaobong Denis. *Race Women Internationalists: Activist-Intellectuals and Global Freedom Struggles*. Oakland: University of California Press, 2018.

Webber, Frances. 'From Ethnocentrism to Euro-Racism', *Race & Class* 32, no. 3 (1991): 11–17.

Wekker, Gloria. *White Innocence. Paradoxes of Colonialism and Race*. Durham, NC and London: Duke University Press, 2016.

Chapter 8

From dark to light: the fate of two European socialist employment initiatives in an age of austerity

Mathieu Fulla

On 26 March 1985, a working group created by the Confederation of the Socialist Parties of the European Community (CSPEC) in 1983 adopted an ambitious document entitled 'More Jobs for Europe'. This collective research project was coordinated by Willy Claes, a former Belgian Economic Affairs minister and senior member of the Flemish-speaking Christian Socialists who mobilised approximately thirty politicians and experts for the group. The report's authors highlighted the fact that over twelve million European citizens were unemployed, a crisis that they urged the member states of the European Economic Community (EEC) to mitigate by substituting concerted macroeconomic, industrial and employment policies for what they described as the dominant 'neoliberal approach'.[1]

Eight years later, in early December 1993, the rejuvenated Party of European Socialists (PES) – the successor of the CSPEC that was founded shortly after the end of the Cold War and the 1992 Maastricht Treaty – supported a 'European Employment Initiative' (EEI) before the European Council. This proposal had been prepared by a working group of politicians and experts chaired by the former Swedish Minister of Finance, Allan Larsson (1990–91). A newcomer to European socialist circles, Larsson had delivered a provocative but well-received talk a year earlier to the Socialist Group in European Parliament (SGEP) entitled 'Can Europe Afford to Work?'[2]

A casual observer might conclude that European socialists' approach to mass unemployment remained unchanged throughout this period. The Claes and Larsson groups both rejected the claim put forward by West European governments that a lack of financial resources hindered their ability to resolve the employment crisis. Both groups alerted European elites to the threat of desocialisation induced by long-term unemployment, particularly among younger and senior workers. Both also called for a 'New Deal for Europe' founded on active budgetary policies and massive public investment in new technologies and infrastructure, coupled with a radical restructuring of working time.

The two groups' documents pursued remarkably different paths, however. 'More Jobs for Europe' exerted minimal influence beyond the CSPEC. Neither the socialist leaders in office nor the European Commission, headed by Jacques Delors, a French Social Democrat, gave serious consideration to the Claes group's recommendations. The EEI, by contrast, was warmly received by the socialist leadership. Jacques Delors took note of the EEI's recommendations concerning employment policy in the White Paper on growth, competitiveness and employment, which he concurrently presented to the Brussels European Council.[3] The socialist EEI was thus one – but not the only – principal inspiration for the specific employment title that was inserted into the 1997 Amsterdam Treaty.[4]

This chapter discusses the principal factors that contributed to the divergent courses of the two documents. Structural and ideological differences in the experts' approaches in the Larsson and Claes groups naturally played a significant role in shaping their trajectories. Nevertheless, the contents of the two documents do not adequately explain their divergent paths. Understanding the failure of European socialists to influence European policymaking in the 1980s – which they successfully managed to accomplish during the next decade – requires an understanding of three closely interconnected factors: the climate of the socialist 'Europarty' at the time of the Claes and Larsson groups; the ideological background of their experts; and the relationships between the two groups and the Delors Commission.

The literature regarding the history of West European socialism and economic development sheds significant light on the first issue. In his seminal book *One Hundred Years of Socialism*, Donald Sassoon argued that socialists had 'run out of ideas' on economic and social affairs after the Berlin Wall collapsed.[5] More recent studies have helped nuance this assertion. Considering European socialism in light of its supranational organisations rather than of the national parties, as Sassoon had, several political scientists have emphasised the persistence of a 'Euro-Keynesian' approach to economic and social issues that had been initiated in the

1970s and updated in the 1980s. Andreas Aust observed that the CSPEC, as well as the PES, 'has developed into an organization that is increasingly trying to coordinate the European policies of Social Democratic actors in the EU'.[6] Regarding the institutional history of the CSPEC and PES, Gerassimos Moschonas demonstrated convincingly the contribution of the EEC's institutional architecture, and later of the European Union (EU), 'to the consolidation and deepening of the great identity change of social democracy and, at the same time, an obstacle to the *re*-social democratisation of its programmatic options'.[7] This body of work has provided researchers with a detailed perspective on the history of the 'Europarties',[8] underlining the structural weaknesses that prevented them from playing a more significant role in European policymaking. As Knut Heidar bluntly noted, 'Europarties' were – and remain – 'second-order parties'.[9] The genesis of the Claes and Larsson reports remains largely unknown, however. This chapter suggests that a close examination of the networks of experts mobilised by West European socialists at the time – and the institutional and organisational frameworks in which they operated – offers an interesting case study of the channels through which 'Europarties' could influence European policymaking.

Opening the 'black box' of the Claes and Larsson reports required examining a variety of archival sources, including the archives of Delors's presidency of the European Commission,[10] and the unclassified archives of Delors's internal think tank, the Forward Studies Unit (*Cellule de Prospective*), which played a prominent role in the architecture of the 1993 White Paper, held at the Historical Archives of the European Commission in Brussels. This research is also based on the archives of the European Socialist Party (PES) and the Socialist International at the Fondation Jean Jaurès, a French Socialist think tank in Paris, and the archives of SAMAK, 'the cooperation committee between the social democratic parties and trade union confederations in the Nordic countries' whose perspectives on employment policy greatly influenced Allan Larsson, in the Swedish Labour Movement's Archives and Library in Stockholm.[11]

Understanding the failure of 'More Jobs for Europe' and the success of 'Put Europe to Work' requires a systematic comparison of the development of the Claes and Larsson reports. The first section of this chapter highlights the structural weaknesses of the CSPEC, which undermined the legitimacy of the Claes group outside of the 'Europarty', whereas the revival of the PES and the greater involvement of socialist leaders in the Larsson group's activities considerably enhanced the credibility of Larsson's work. The following section examines the sociological and cultural background of the experts involved in drafting the projects. While the Claes group of experts remained faithful to the 'Euro-Keynesian' approach to economic and employment policies that developed in the 1970s, the Larsson group proposed a major change of course that gained traction not only among socialist politicians but also in European institutions. The third section illustrates the crucial role of the working relations between the Larsson group and the Delors cabinet in the group's rise to political legitimacy. The President of the European Commission, although supportive of the CSPEC, had never regarded the organisation as a reliable partner. By contrast, Delors and his aides forged a strong relationship with Allan Larsson, thereby facilitating the circulation of ideas between the PES and the Commission, which was drafting its White Paper. After a decade of ineffectiveness, the PES acquired a voice in European policy-making by marginalising its 'Euro-Keynesian' activists, who continued, however vainly, to call for a break with the Economic and Monetary Union (EMU) established by the Maastricht Treaty.

Attracting the interest of socialist leaders: a challenging proposition

During the 1980s, democratic socialism encountered significant hardships. At the national level, socialist governments, particularly in France and Southern Europe (Greece, Spain and Portugal), failed to lastingly implement alternative economic and social policies. They quickly endorsed austerity measures and prioritised curbing inflation as a means of vying with the US and Japanese economies. Some scholars have concluded, somewhat hastily, that these decisions pushed the socialists in office to 'embrace neoliberalism'.[12] While in no way disregarding the current debate over the role of 'neoliberalism' in the radical transformation of Western capitalism (and social democracy) in the past decade,[13] the prevailing mood among socialist leaders at the time was one of resignation rather than enthusiasm. In 1983, when the French Socialist government officialised its conversion to austerity – a turn it had discreetly initiated from late 1981 onwards[14] – socialist heads of state and government held a series of meetings organised by the French Socialist Party. Confidential records from these meetings highlight the growing doubts of socialist party members about the possibility of building a socialist alternative in economic and social policy. The concerns expressed by the French Prime Minister Pierre Mauroy and his Swedish and Greek counterparts, Olof Palme and Andreas Papandreou, resoundingly echoed the cool, straightforward analysis of Mario Soares, the

Portuguese president. Soares proclaimed (in fluent French, which he learned in exile in Paris under Salazar's dictatorship):

> In southern Europe, we came to power not through expansion (as in the North), but in crisis and because of the crisis. The problem is then how not to disappoint and to retain power. . . . In Portugal, we had a revolution, but it veered in the direction of a popular democratic type of regime. The Socialist Party opposed it. [We] reintroduced market-based elements into a quasi-collectivised economy. As a result, we were unable to either conduct a social policy or satisfy the capitalists. We regained power because the conservatives failed! We are going to defend the mechanisms that we denounce (such as the IMF [International Monetary Fund]). How can this contradiction be reconciled?[15]

At the turn of the 1990s, this mentality prevailed among central socialist leaders and experts in Northern and Southern Europe, most of whom accepted the 1986 Single European Act (SEA) and EMU, which were founded on pro-market principles. In France, the then Prime Minister Pierre Bérégovoy relentlessly professed his faith in a hard currency as the architect of the *politique du franc fort*, which prioritised economic policies that favoured a balanced budget and decreased inflation over full employment.[16] In Sweden, the administration of Olof Palme initiated a major shift in economic policy in 1985. Palme's objective was to curb inflation, but the tools he deployed marked 'the beginning of a set of austerity budgets' that transformed employment 'from a social citizenship entitlement to a market variable'.[17] The Soares and Felipe González administrations in Portugal and Spain endorsed similar policies to avert economic crisis, characterised by the rampant protectionism championed for years by Salazarism and Francoism. The political scientist Cornel Ban described the policies implemented by González and his aides as 'embedded neoliberalism'.[18]

Although most socialist politicians and experts contended that the SEA and the Maastricht Treaty 'removed the option of national Keynesianism',[19] a minority refused to renounce Keynes's ideas. Most of these actors were affiliated with the CSPEC and/or the Socialist International. In conjunction with the meetings of the *Acteurs du changement* (Agents of Change), Joop den Uyl, the CSPEC president and the leader of the Dutch Labour Party (PvdA) from 1966 to 1986, informed his comrades at the Bureau that a working group chaired by Willy Claes intended to address mass unemployment in the EEC. The group's members supported a 'Euro-Keynesian' approach to economic policy that differed significantly from the austerity policies being put in place by

Socialist national governments. The Claes group appeared to be the most active of the CSPEC's working groups during the 1980s. Its first responsibility was to draft the article that addressed economic and social issues for the manifesto presented by the CSPEC for the 1984 European elections. The document endorsed what experts in the Claes group called the '3Rs': 'a selective and planned *recovery*'; the *restructuring* of national economies 'through the modernization of the European framework based on the development of research and the diffusion of technological advancements'; and 'radical *redistribution* of work and wealth'.[20] In other words, economic recovery required a concerted relaunch coupled with the regulation of multinational firms and an improvement in annual working time.[21] Although these principles were updated to reflect an increasingly globalised and Europeanised economic framework, they underscored the clear connection between the intellectual roots of the Claes group's experts and ideas espoused by left-leaning members of the British Labour Party and French Socialist Party in the 1970s.[22] Although there were huge differences in terms of institutional structures, political culture, electoral trends and governmental experience, the economic programmes designed by both parties in the early and late 1970s developed very similar analyses of the capitalist crisis and the solutions to get out of it. On the economic and social levels, the strong similarities between the Alternative Economic Strategy (AES) developed by the left wing of the Labour Party and the *Programme commun de gouvernement* concluded by the French Socialist Party and the French Communist Party in June 1972 were striking.[23] Both documents called to radically reshape capitalism through the reinforcement of the public sector, stronger economic planning in which the trade unions should play a prominent role, and the setting up of self-management within private and public firms.[24] The common cultural background of the experts who wrote these political programmes undoubtedly contributed to this unexpected convergence. Their common readings – notably the US neo-marxists like Paul Baran and Paul Sweezy as well as John Kenneth Galbraith – and their socialist engagement also led them to call for the introduction of harsh regulations to control multinationals at the national and European levels.

The Claes group strove to promote an updated version of this legacy. The '3Rs' failed to gain an audience outside of CSPEC circles, as illustrated during an informal meeting of European socialist elites a few days before the 1984 elections. At the conclusion of the meeting, the leaders issued a statement asserting their faith in a concerted economic relaunch facilitated by EEC member states to overcome mass unemployment. Confidential recordings of the meeting provide a conflicting account, however. Security issues were the central topic of the meeting, whereas economic issues were scarcely addressed. Joop den Uyl expressed frustration at the uncooperativeness of the Danish and British Socialists. Tensions escalated when the topic of Euromissiles was broached. Neil Kinnock, the new Labour Party leader, argued that a Labour administration would facilitate the removal of missiles from the United Kingdom to which Mario Soares abruptly replied: 'We speak foreign languages. If Labour must withdraw the cruise missiles, then I prefer that they lose the election'.[25] These divergences between socialist leaders' priorities on the national level and the Bureau of the CSPEC demonstrate why 'More Jobs for Europe' failed to influence European social policy.

By 1993, the political climate among socialist elites had shifted radically. Socialist Members of the European Parliament (MEPs) and their CSPEC colleagues felt a need to rejuvenate their approach to social Europe, which had reached a stalemate, as the president of the Socialist Group in the European Parliament (SGEP), the French Socialist Jean-Pierre Cot, stated during a meeting between the group and the CSPEC in May 1992.[26] Having previously supported rapid ratification of the Maastricht Treaty, which was unpopular among the citizens of member states (as illustrated by its defeat in the Danish referendum), MEPs called for 'a political response to social injustice, unemployment, and growing regional imbalances' at a European level to address inequalities perpetuated by the single market.[27] In this atmosphere of uncertainty, the speech that Allan Larsson delivered to the SGEP in Stockholm sparked significant interest.[28] Larsson's growing influence in European socialist circles can be attributed to this speech and his work as both a politician and an expert within SAMAK.[29]

In early September 1993, the PES leadership held a two-day conference in Arrabida, Portugal. The persistent issue of unemployment was the central focus of debates. The Spanish Prime Minister Felipe González suggested that the PES establish a high-level working group for the purpose of developing a socialist employment initiative. His proposal was widely welcomed by his comrades.[30] Socialist leaders formally asked the Swedish Social Democratic Party (SAP) to draft a working paper addressing the following objectives: reducing unemployment, creating new jobs, preserving European competitiveness and modernising social protections for workers. The SAP leader, former Prime Minister Ingvar Carlsson, delegated the task to Allan Larsson, his former finance minister.[31] Whereas Larsson benefited from broad PES support, his Belgian counterpart Willy Claes had navigated a considerably weaker and more divided institutional framework a few years earlier.

The triumph of politics over expertise in the (Euro)party

Despite their mutual political affiliation, the Claes and Larsson groups operated within two different organisations. The archives of the CSPEC highlight perpetual internal conflicts throughout the 1980s, not only between the Bureau and the national leaders of the Socialist MEPs, but also within the Bureau. Accordingly, the Claes group's recommendations failed to appeal to a wider audience beyond socialists who already subscribed to these principles. As Edgard Pisani noted in an impassioned speech to the members of the Bureau: 'Where is the obstacle? It is in the presence of the British; not because they are nasty, but because they are different and the Group did not attempt to make the necessary synthesis among the different European socialisms'.[32] Although most members in European socialist circles expressed their concerns less abrasively than Pisani, all of them acknowledged how problematic the Labour Party's approach to European issues was. The situation remained relatively unchanged until 1987; without being the sole cause, Labour's rampant Euroscepticism nurtured persistent divisions within the CSPEC as well as the Socialist Group in the European Parliament, which prevented them from weighing in on European affairs. Regarding the Spanish Socialist Enrique Barón's initial defeat in the presidential election of the European Parliament, Joop den Uyl decried the 'general weakness of social-democracy' – albeit in a more diplomatic tone than Pisani.[33]

Throughout this period, the Claes group was weighed down by an internal political lack of cohesiveness. A few days after the Bureau ratified what its members considered the final draft of 'More Jobs for Europe' in March 1984, the Labour Party sent a telex calling for numerous amendments. Unlike the Common Agricultural Policy (CAP) and the European Monetary System (EMS), which British Labour staunchly opposed, employment policy did not figure prominently in the Party's grievances. Nevertheless, their points of disagreement with the original document were significant enough for the Bureau to convene a special meeting to address the challenges posed by the Labour Party's position. Increasingly irritated by internal CSPEC divisions, the French Socialist Party leader, Lionel Jospin, decided to personally attend the meeting. The participants failed to reach an agreement on the Claes text, however, and chose to exclude the report from the forthcoming CSPEC Congress, while encouraging Claes to further develop ideas as a 'basis for an extraordinary conference, a workshop, a special meeting of the Bureau, or the setting up of a "conference of workers"'.[34] In other words, the members of the

Bureau 'elegantly' stripped the document of political legitimacy. Shortly after the 'disguised funeral' of the Claes report, Jospin fiercely criticised the incompetence of the CSPEC:

> I believe that the first observation we should make, on the eve of the Congress of the Union of EEC Socialist Parties, is that the union of our parties is not up to its task. I wish to say it clearly because this is our sentiment. The European Economic Community is very important for our countries, and I would even say increasingly important . . . But the Union of EEC Socialist Parties is not considered by us as an important political organization. I believe that it is best to be honest with ourselves: in any case, this is how we, in the French Socialist Party, see it.[35]

Lamenting the failure of the Party and the SGEP to influence European policymaking, Jospin contended that until radical structural reforms were initiated by the CSPEC, the documents produced by the organisation would remain confidential. The CSPEC could continue to uphold the status quo or submit to new guidelines:

> A number of meetings, bilateral or between several leaders, have allowed for often-exciting political exchanges, focused on the most important problems. I am thinking, for example, of the meetings of Southern Europe where leaders saw each other during two days and compared their internal political situations, discussed the problems of socialism in Italy, in Greece, in France, in Spain, in Portugal, and had the highest-level political exchanges centred on the main issues. These were meetings that we always found very, very useful and very exciting.[36]

Jospin's intervention sparked a lively debate. Joop den Uyl again denounced the British and Danish socialists for undermining the CSPEC. Nevertheless, few changes in the CSPEC occurred following this meeting. The situation that Jospin described in 1985 remained at an impasse until the birth of the PES in November 1992. Although European socialists relentlessly called for a 'Social Europe', their positions on the topic remained ambiguous throughout the 1980s.[37]

The creation of the more structured PES signified an improvement in relations between elite party members, fostering an 'intimate atmosphere' that was propitious to ambitious initiatives such as the EEI.[38] Like Delors, the PES advocated for 'the shaping of capital-labour relations at a supranational level', one of the goals supported by promoters of a socially oriented European framework.[39] Larsson was especially shrewd in capitalising on the opportunity afforded by the founding of the PES. The preliminary stages of the EEI demonstrated that Larsson took particular care to inform socialist leaders and the Delors cabinet of each development.[40] By contrast, the CSPEC had been unsuccessful in establishing a close working relationship with the Delors cabinet, socialist commissioners, or socialist leaders of European nations. The reconfiguration of the party contributed significantly to the growth of a large coalition among European socialists. Nevertheless, these new developments would not have occurred if the Larsson group had supported the 'Euro-Keynesian' approach promoted by the Claes group in the previous decade.

A farewell to 'Euro-Keynesianism'

The Claes group consisted of approximately thirty experts but only two members of the German Socialist Party, probably due to significant ideological divisions within the organisation,[41] whereas the French Socialist Party, the Belgian Flemish Socialist Party, the Spanish Socialist Party and the British Labour Party were represented by four or five experts. The archives of the working group offer historians insights into the experts' principal intellectual influences. Paradoxically, although the British Labour Party had rejected numerous recommendations of the Claes group, the analytical framework of 'More Jobs for Europe' was chiefly inspired by British economists close to the left wing of the party. These individuals had played a central role in the architecture of the Alternative Economic Strategy, which the Labour leadership reluctantly endorsed during Wilson's term in the early 1970s – and championed more enthusiastically under the leadership of Michael Foot after Labour's 1979 electoral defeat. The academic 'Euro-Keynesian' economist and British MP Stuart Holland acted as an intermediary, connecting the analysis developed by the 'Out of Crisis Project', an informal research group he created in the late 1970s, with the CSPEC and the Socialist International, which began drafting their reflections on economic crisis at the same time.

The volume published by the members of the 'Out of Crisis Project' in 1983 synthesised ten years of research. In his preface, Holland highlighted the foundation of the group's economic approach: 'Several members of the group had criticised Keynesian analysis for its failures to account for changes in the supply structure of capital some time before the new "supply side economics" emerged from the monetarists'.[42] He also noted that most members of the group – among them Delors[43] – were now ministers, MPs, executive party members or advisers to top socialist leaders. Holland also emphasised the persistent faith of group members in planning economic models. Like the left wing of the British Labour Party in the 1970s and early 1980s and later the Claes group, the 'Out of Crisis Project' advocated an economic alternative founded on the '3Rs' – reflate, restructure, redistribute – to counter the trend towards 'beggar-thy-neighbour' deflation. The design of the '3R' strategy suggested recourse to econometric models, particularly the model forged by the Cambridge Economic Policy Group (CEPG).[44] These scholars, who worked closely with the left-wing experts of the British Labour Party, offered support to the architecture of the AES, whose neo-protectionist philosophy was inspired by Nicholas Kaldor's work.[45] Like Holland and Kaldor, some of the scholars themselves (such as Wynne Godley and Francis Cripps) were committed to the left wing of the Labour Party.

The influence of this Labour Party economic faction, which was discernible in the Party manifesto for the 1983 general election, rapidly declined after their overwhelming electoral loss to Margaret Thatcher. Stuart Holland presumably responded to his intellectual marginalisation within the party by moving towards more receptive European socialist circles. He relied on close contacts within the CEPG when he began working for the Socialist International a few months after the publication of the 'Out of Crisis Project'. The Socialist International had indeed decided to propose an economic and social alternative to austerity at the same time as the formation of the Claes group. In April 1983, the Albufeira Congress of the Socialist International recognised the need for a set of policies aimed at recovery and reform of the world economy. To this end, the Bureau established the Socialist International Committee on Economic Policy. Michael Manley, President of the People's National Party in Jamaica, was elected chairman, and Oscar Debunne, International Secretary of the Socialist Party of Belgium, became secretary. The Committee's inaugural meeting began at the Socialist International Bureau meeting in Brussels in November 1983.[46] The Manley group endorsed the political recommendations issued in a series of documents drafted between the mid-1970s and the early 1980s: the declaration for a new international economic order adopted by the UN General Assembly dominated by the G-77 in May 1974; the Charter of Economic Rights and Duties for States adopted in the same arena in December 1974; the report on Common security issued by the Palme Commission in 1983; and above all, both reports issued by the Brandt Commission in 1980 and 1983.[47] Their common goal was to reshape the existing economic international order within which mass poverty and inequalities were increasingly growing. Like the Brandt Commission,[48] the Socialist International strove to find a third way between the neoliberal order defended by the Ronald Reagan administration and the radical 'new international economic order' the G-77 at the United Nations called for in the middle of the 1970s.[49] In 1985, the Socialist International presented an alternative to monetarism and the international economic order embodied by the so-called 'adjustment policies' that the IMF required of Southern countries in exchange for loans.[50] This report, entitled *Global Challenge*, was based on the reflections developed within the Manley group. The document urged the Reagan administration to break with its monetary policy based on overvalued dollar and high interest rates induced by the famous 1979 Volcker Shock. Far from limiting itself to economic and social issues, this document conflated and closely linked the three main preoccupations of the Socialist International since Willy Brandt took its presidency in 1976: common security, North–South dialogue and human rights.[51] The internal debates of the Manley group, however, showed that its members were worried about their ability to weigh in on the policymaking of West European socialist parties in office. As Manley's opening address to the Kingston meeting in Jamaica illustrated, distrust was the dominant feeling – and the Jamaican leader openly emphasised their disappointing record.[52] These concerns were founded. *Global Challenge* failed to arouse any attention among Western European national socialist elites.

Nor did it really spark the interest of the CSPEC. Despite common concerns, the Claes group did not develop any renewed ideas about the transformation of the economic international order. Its members remained clearly focused on the issue of mass unemployment within the EEC. Regarding the global challenges, especially the relationship with Southern countries, they only endorsed the recommendations of the Brandt reports. A few months before the elections to the European Parliament in June 1984, the Claes group published a pamphlet entitled 'European Solution to the Crisis', which was a contribution to the common electoral manifesto adopted at the end of the Conference of the CSPEC in Luxemburg on 8–9 March. Only half a page out of fifteen specifically dealt with the issue of solidarity with Southern countries, whereas the conclusion of the document very succinctly called for a new monetary international system inspired by the recommendations inserted into the second Brandt report in 1983.[53]

An 'epistemic community'[54] subsequently emerged from the collective research of the New Cambridge School, the 'Out of Crisis Project', the Manley group of the Socialist International, and the Claes group. Experts such as Jan Pronk and Stuart Holland circulated easily from one group to another, conveying a set of economic and social ideas based on the '3Rs'. Both played a crucial role in the design of *Global Challenge*. In a similar vein, Oscar Debunne's nephew, Georges Debunne, played a prominent role in the Claes group at the time, composing an article on flexibility and the reduction of working time that was inserted into an updated version of 'More Jobs for Europe'.[55]

These groups all met in Brussels, strengthening the ties between politicians and experts. One of the most active experts in the Claes group, the Belgian economist Ludo Cuyvers, acknowledged his debt to the FERE (*Fédération européenne de recherches économiques*) working group, 'Europe in the World Economy', whose research used

> a neo-Keynesian (Kaldorian) model originally developed by the Cambridge Economic Policy Group (Department of Applied Economics, University of Cambridge, UK), which encompasses the world economy as a closed system and in which real income and spending in the nine world blocs of countries are linked to each other via changes in the international trade flows.[56]

Similarly, 'More Jobs for Europe' explicitly referenced the 1985 Manley report produced by the Socialist International to rationalise the socialist appeal of a concerted relaunch.[57]

Strictly speaking, the working papers produced by the different supranational socialist organisations endorsed the same analytical framework that was formalised by the experts of the 'Out of Crisis Project'. As previously mentioned, this body of work failed to gain an audience outside the narrow circles of 'Euro-Keynesian' politicians and experts. The prevailing economic culture among European socialist leaders and their aides – not to mention the senior civil servants implementing economic policy at national and EEC levels – was simply too dissimilar for a dialogue to be initiated. The pleas for a concerted relaunch and structural reforms to capitalism were brushed aside.[58] Like many other initiatives, 'More Jobs for Europe' was dismissed primarily because its call for flexible employment policy was inserted into a broader proposal to radically reform capitalism.

Nevertheless, 'Euro-Keynesianism' remained influential within the PES when Larsson was appointed as a lead expert. Despite the warm reception that socialist leaders gave Larsson's 'active employment policy', the Nordic approach to the labour market did not immediately become dominant in European socialist circles. In December 1992, the PES had created a working group on economic and social issues co-chaired by the French Socialist Gérard Fuchs (a close colleague of the former Prime Minister Michel Rocard and a vice-president of the PES) and Mario Didò, a senior member of the Italian Socialist Party (PSI) who had just regained his seat as an MEP.[59] The Southern European Socialists were considerably more influential in the group than its Nordic members. According to the list of affiliates, only two of the thirty members belonged to a Nordic social democratic party. In August 1993, the group issued a paper entitled 'Eight Recommendations for Growth and Employment'. The document characterised its analytical framework as a derivative of 'communitarian

Keynesianism', largely inspired by the European Growth Initiative adopted by member states at the Edinburgh European Council meeting in December 1992. The Fuchs–Didò group supported a voluntarist industrial policy, which echoed the 'neo-mercantilist' initiatives developed by the European Commission in the early 1980s.[60] In light of protectionist Japanese and US industries, the report's authors called for a significant increase in the EU budget to support large-scale investment in research and development. This return to neo-mercantilist principles was coupled with a call for the adoption of the principle of *préférence communautaire*, or community preference, in the EU commercial policy, that is, giving priority to member states when a non-EU country failed to provide minimal social protections for its workforce.[61] Moreover, the working group raised the controversial issue of working time reduction, which was strongly opposed by the British Labour Party and the Greek Pan-Hellenic Socialist Movement, PASOK. Symbolically Larsson, who was supposed to attend, never attended a meeting of the group.[62] In September, the Fuchs–Didò document was submitted to the socialist leadership in Arrabida, but it failed to spark their interest; Larsson's ideas prevailed.

Consequently, the Fuchs–Didò group was abruptly sidelined in favour of the Larsson group, whose members promoted an approach to employment policy that the leaders considered more practical within the EMU framework and closer to their own vision of economic policy. From Larsson's perspective, Europe would be well advised to follow the precedent set by Japan, which had succeeded in combining strong economic growth with a decrease in unemployment and inflation in the 1980s. Although Larsson understood that Japanese employment policy was not replicable in a European context, he nevertheless called attention to the European labour market's contrasting inability to create numerous jobs despite economic expansions. Larsson's analysis addressed three challenges: the rigidity of the European labour market, the growing shortage of skilled labour that created a 'mismatch' between supply and demand, and the insufficiency of the EMU for providing jobs and welfare for all Europeans. To resolve these issues, Larsson encouraged European leaders to closely study the Japanese model of youth education and training. He called for an active and developing employment policy, for which Nordic – from his perspective, Swedish – and Japanese models could provide vital inspiration. The Swedish MP underlined the need for increased flexibility – a taboo word among the European socialist milieu – in the labour market, coupled with improvements in the welfare of workers.

Although the Larsson group had the advantage of working within a more efficient organisation, its chairman was keenly aware of the necessity of proposing a social alternative that did not challenge the macroeconomic and monetary framework of the EMU. This strategy enabled 'Put Europe to Work' to gain credibility outside socialist circles, particularly at the head of the European Commission.

The key role of Jacques Delors and his cabinet

Shortly before assuming the leadership of the European Commission, Delors was cordially welcomed at a CSPEC meeting. Addressing the attendees, he underscored the deep divisions between member states on a wide range of topics. During the debate, Delors claimed that the Commission would propose a challenge to 'Reaganism' and the Japanese export industries through the creation of a large European internal market. He stressed that this concept of a common market would be inextricably linked with the promotion of 'an original social model' and that the CSPEC could count on the support of the socialist commissioners. Willy Claes seized this opportunity to mention the activities of his working group and asked Delors whether a close collaboration over socio-economic issues would be possible. The President of the European Commission responded favourably to Claes's call.[63]

Despite his many obligations, which included the implementation of the SEA, Delors honoured his commitment. Presenting the activities of his group at a Bureau meeting in December 1985, Claes informed his colleagues that the head of the European Commission had sent him a working paper suggesting six axes to restore competitiveness in the EEC. Joop den Uyl congratulated Claes on his new-found cooperation with Delors, although their amicable relationship never resulted in a firm partnership.[64] In 1987 and 1989, Christine Verger, a new representative of the Delors cabinet,[65] attended the CSPEC Congresses in Lisbon and Brussels. Her analysis of both was consistent: the resolutions supported by the 'Europarty' were ambiguous and were significantly weakened by internal conflicts between the British Labour Party and other member parties.[66] As a result, Verger dismissed the documents as politically unviable. Her summary of the manifesto designed by the CSPEC for the 1989 election to the European Parliament crystallised the grievances of the Delors cabinet towards the organisation:

> The proposed Manifest developed under the leadership of E. BARON has been the focus of several difficult meetings that have resulted in a 24-page text with 78 points, extremely dense, and in any case scarcely usable for the outside . . . the sum of compromises in nearly every area, some of its passages remain highly controversial, particularly for the Danes and the British.[67]

Relations between the CSPEC and the Commission were similarly a disappointment for European socialists, as noted by the SGEP president, SPD member Rudi Arndt, during a meeting of the Bureau.[68]

This cordial but ineffective partnership between CSPEC and Delors resulted in three interconnected developments. First, the positions adopted by the 'Europarty' were deemed too radical and vague to be inserted into the Commission's own work. As Moschonas stated, many 'socialists and social democrats want a powerful, more left-oriented Europe' through a strong social policy, particularly regarding employment, but 'they do not possess the requisite institutional and political means, perhaps not even the ideas, for refocusing integration'.[69] Moreover, the Delors Commission prioritised the establishment of Economic and Monetary Union over employment policy and the broader conception of a 'Social Europe' throughout its first term.[70] Last, the working papers that Delors sent to the Claes group were again greeted with scepticism by the British Labour Party. Although it conceded the fact that an agreement could be reached concerning five of the six axes to restore European competitiveness as proposed by Delors, its representatives remained firmly opposed to his approach to the European internal market. From their perspective, the SEA would exacerbate regional inequalities, severely limit the macroeconomic flexibility of national governments by preventing them from enacting a voluntarist industrial policy and inviting a general movement towards deregulation. Their statement on the matter was openly disparaging of Delors:

> The internal market is a political mechanism intended to extend the field of action of market forces and weaken the role of government and labour unions. We reject the free-market principle on which it is based, and, at the same time, we believe that the concrete effects of these proposals would be extremely pernicious.[71]

The President of the European Commission nevertheless maintained his ambition that 'the new architecture of Europe pivoted on a triptych: competition-cooperation-solidarity'.[72] Following his celebrated speech to the Trades Union Congress in Bournemouth in 1988, Delors at last succeeded in rallying the Labour Party and British trade unions to his cause.[73] His initiative contributed to the accelerated reshaping of Labour's European policy initiated by Labour leader Neil Kinnock one year earlier, when he launched a general 'Policy Review'. According to Patricia Hewitt, the Review's coordinator, Kinnock aimed at making Labour 'a modern European democratic socialist party'.[74] At the turn of the 1990s, Eurosceptic supporters did not vanish within the Labour Party, but they had been sidelined by the leadership. Kinnock's European turn thus greatly facilitated the participation of British Labour members in supranational initiatives.

Two years later, the Larsson group benefited from improved relations with the British Labour movement by establishing a strong working relationship with Delors based on their shared affinity for the Nordic approach to employment policy, which promoted increased flexibility and security within the workforce. The Delors cabinet thus welcomed the Larsson initiative with enthusiasm. As Chris Boyd wrote in a note to Delors after a trip to Sweden, during which he met with Larsson and Ingvar Carlsson, 'Larsson is taking very seriously his task of writing the paper on employment for the Socialist leaders. All are pleased that he was asked to do it and wish it to complement the Commission's White Paper'.[75] The leader of the Commission was amenable to supporting Larsson's efforts, as his own diagnosis of the structural crisis of the EU and his approach to employment policy were compatible with those promoted by the Swedish MP. Several members of the Delors cabinet were closely involved with the Larsson group. In early November, Jérôme Vignon, the chair of the Forward Studies Unit and one of Delors's closest advisers, addressed a series of comments that were inserted into the final draft of the text.[76] Numerous records of the correspondence between Delors's aides and members of the Larsson group are contained in the archives of the Forward Studies Unit.[77] Conversely, the EEI exerted a tangible influence on the social chapters of the Commission White Paper, although the document was never officially cited. Jacques Delors wished to avoid potential criticism of a supposed partiality in favour of European social democracy.[78] Nevertheless, and although the final version echoed numerous elements of the EEI, the White Paper should not be interpreted as a direct translation of the document. In the interest of adopting a single currency by the late 1990s, the Commission adhered to the macroeconomic criteria established by the Maastricht Treaty and opposed substantive changes to the strict regulation of the budgetary policies of member states, whereas the EEI adopted a more voluntarist approach in its call for a 'New Deal for Europe'.[79]

The contents of the Commission's White Paper nonetheless show that Delors partially fulfilled his expressed goal of using 'his office to implement at least parts of a Social Democratic agenda'.[80] The arguments about employment policy contained in the White Paper affirmed the proximity of Larsson's and Delors's viewpoints: 'Both the White Paper and the Larsson report can be seen as efforts towards a coherent Social democratic strategy against recession and unemployment which would not question the only recently ratified Maastricht Treaty'.[81] Both documents called for a supply-side economic relaunch through private and public investment rather than through consumption, which would induce inflation due to wage increases. Both underscored the necessity of increased flexibility in the labour market of member states. The break with 'Euro-Keynesianism' was thereby officialised.

Conclusion

Contrary to popular belief, European socialist movements did not unanimously convert to austerity policies in the 1980s, nor did Keynesian approaches to economic and social issues vanish during the decade. Nevertheless, as illustrated by the Claes group of the CSPEC and the Manley group of the Socialist International, the proponents of these alternatives remained circumscribed to narrow circles in supranational organisations that lacked the political leverage to influence European policy making, which was then dominated by an 'ordoliberal' approach to economic and social affairs. The defence of free enterprise 'anchored in framework treaties, with a primary focus on ensuring respect for property and contracts, protecting free competition, and honouring monetary prudence' largely prevailed.[82] As several scholars have astutely observed, the SEA and the Maastricht Treaty monopolised the political discourse of the time, rendering alternatives to the set of macroeconomic and monetary constraints it had created obsolete. Socialist leaders at the national level were aware that they had helped shape this dynamic. Like Jacques Delors, however, they were willing to reconceptualise their approach to the European community. One of the key objectives of the Larsson group was to mediate these complexities by proposing a Nordic approach to employment policy that was fully compatible with the Maastricht framework. The skill of its Swedish chairman in navigating the complex maze of European institutions facilitated his appointment as Director General of DG V (the Directorate General for Social Affairs) in 1995.[83] European socialists thus succeeded in regaining a voice in European policy making. The strategies they used to achieve this, however, caused them to embrace a moderate 'Third Way' that could be regarded as a precursor to more radical ideological projects such as Tony Blair's 'Third Way' and Gerhard Schröder's *Neue Mitte* that emerged in the second half of the 1990s.

Notes

1. Working group on economic policy of the CSPEC, 'More Jobs for Europe', 26 March 1985. Archives of the CSPEC, Centre of Socialist Archives at the Fondation Jean Jaurès in Paris (below CAS-FJJ), Archives of the CSPEC, 50 RI UPSCE 1985.

2. Allan Larsson, speech at the meeting of the Socialist Group of the European Parliament, 2–3 July 1992. Alan Larsson, 'En havstang till arbete', 21 April 1992,

Swedish Labour Movement Archives and Library in Stockholm (below SLMAL), Archives of the Arbetarrörelsens nordiska samarbetskommité (SAMAK), 1213/F/1/5. Allan Larsson, 'Put Europe to Work', Report over the European Employment Initiative to the Leaders of the member parties of the PES', 3 December 1993, CAS-FJJ, Archives of the PES, PS 50 RI – PSE 1993.

3. European Commission, *Growth, Competitiveness, Employment: The Challenges and Ways forward into the 21st Century. White Paper* (Luxembourg: Office for Official Publications of the European Communities, 1994).

4. Karl Magnus Johansson, 'Tracing the Employment Title in the Amsterdam Treaty: Uncovering Transnational Coalitions', *Journal of European Public Policy* 6, no. 1 (1999), 85. This employment title pointed out that employment was 'a matter of common concern' and called for member states and the EU to 'work towards developing a co-ordinating strategy for employment'.

5. Donald Sassoon, *One Hundred Years of Socialism: The West European Left in the Twentieth Century* (London and New York: I.B. Tauris, 2014 [1996]), 649.

6. Andreas Aust, 'From "Eurokeynesianism" to the "Third Way": The Party of European Socialists (PES) and European employment policies', in *Social Democratic Party Policies in Contemporary Europe*, ed. Giuliano Bonolli and Martin Powell (London and New York: Routledge, 2005), 182.

7. Gerassimos Moschonas, 'Reformism in a "Conservative" System: The European Union and Social Democratic Identity', in *In Search of Social Democracy*, ed. John Callaghan, Nina Fishman, Ben Jackson and Martin McIvor (Manchester: Manchester University Press, 2009), 170.

8. Simon Hix, 'Parties at the European Level and the Legitimacy of EU Socio-Economic Policy', *JCMS: Journal of Common Market Studies* 33, no. 4 (1995); Robert Ladrech, 'Political Parties and the Problem of Legitimacy in the European union', in *Legitimacy and the European Union: The Contested Polity*, ed. Thomas Banchoff and Mitchell Smith (London: Routledge, 1999).

9. Knut Heidar, 'Parties and Cleavages in the European Political Space', ARENA working papers, WP 03/7, 2003, p. 3, https://www.sv.uio.no/arena/english/research/publications/arena-working-papers/2001-2010/2003/wp03_7.pdf [accessed 28 July 2021].

10. The Centre for History at Sciences Po Paris possesses a digital copy of these sources, the originals of which are preserved by the European University Institute in Florence.

11. Frode Forfang, 'Annual meeting of SAMAK, 21–22 January 1993', Oslo, 30 November 1992, 1 p., CAS-FJJ, PS 50 RI PSE. Formally founded in 1932, SAMAK is a joint committee including the autonomous islands of Greenland, Faroe Islands and Aland.

12. For a presentation of this argument see Ashley Lavelle, 'Explanations for the Neo-liberal Direction of Social Democracy: Germany, Sweden and Australia Compared', in *In Search of Social Democracy*, ed. Callaghan et al.

13. Daniel Rodgers, 'The Uses and Abuses of "Neoliberalism"', *Dissent*, Winter 2018, https://www.dissentmagazine.org/article/uses-and-abuses-neoliberalism-debate [accessed 25 July 2021]. Pierre Rosanvallon, *Notre histoire intellectuelle et politique 1968–2018* (Paris: Seuil, 2018), 277.

14. Mathieu Fulla, 'Quand Pierre Mauroy résistait avec rigueur au "néolibéralisme"', *Vingtième siècle. Revue d'histoire* 138, no. 2 (2018).

15. Mario Soares, Meeting of the Socialist Heads of state and government, 'Les acteurs du changement', handwritten report, 18 May 1983, CAS-FJJ, Archives of Lionel Jospin, First Secretary of the French Socialist Party, 2 PS 455.

16. Antony Burlaud, '"Faire rentrer la justice sociale dans la balance des paiements". La politique macro-économique de Michel Rocard', in *Michel Rocard Premier ministre: La deuxième gauche et le pouvoir (1988–1991)*, ed. Alain Bergounioux and Mathieu Fulla (Paris: Presses de Sciences Po, 2020).

17. J. Magnus Ryner, 'Neo-Liberalization of Social Democracy: The Swedish Case', *Comparative European Politics* 2 (2004), 101. Jenny Andersson and Kjell Östberg, 'The Swedish Social Democrats, Reform Socialism and the State after the Golden Era', in *European Socialists and the State in the Twentieth and Twenty-First Centuries*, ed. Mathieu Fulla and Marc Lazar (Basingstoke: Palgrave Macmillan, 2020), 336–9.

18. Cornel Ban, *Ruling Ideas: How Global Neoliberalism Goes Local* (Oxford: Oxford University Press, 2016), 34.

19. Geoff Eley, *Forging Democracy. The History of the Left in Europe, 1850–2000* (Oxford: Oxford University Press, 2002), 408.

20. CSPEC, 'Final Manifesto of the Confederation of the Socialist Parties of the European Community', 9 March 1984, 5, CAS-FJJ, 50 RI UPSCE 1984.

21. Laurent Warlouzet, *Governing Europe in a Globalising World: Neoliberalism and its Alternatives following the 1973 Oil Crisis* (London and New York: Routledge, 2018), 37–56.

22. Mathieu Fulla, 'Partager une culture économique sans le savoir. Les experts socialistes français et britanniques des années soixante-dix', *Ventunesimo Secolo* 44 (2019).

23. On the AES, see Mark Wickham-Jones, *Economic Strategy and the Labour Party* (London: Macmillan Press, 1996). On the *Programme commun de gouvernement* of the French Left, see Danielle Tartakowsky and Alain Bergounioux, eds., *L'union sans unité: le programme commun de la gauche, 1963–1978* (Rennes: Presses universitaires de Rennes, 2012).

24. Fulla, 'Partager une culture économique'.

25. Handwritten minutes of the dinner of socialist leaders held during the informal meeting of socialist leaders in Paris, 25 May 1984, 1–2, CAS-FJJ, Archives of the CSPEC, 50 RI UPSCE Elections eur. 84.

26. Jean-Pierre Cot, 'Projet de procès-verbal du bureau de l'union 14 et 15 mai à Strasbourg', Brussels, 2 June 1992, 5, CAS-FJJ, Archives of the CSPEC, 50 RI UPSCE 1990–nov. 1992.

27. SGEP, 'Provisional Conclusions of the Socialist Group on the Architecture of the New Europe adopted in Vilamoura on 4 June 1992', 1, SLMAL, Archives of SAMAK, 1213/F/1/2.

28. Allan Larsson, speech at the meeting of the Socialist Group of the European Parliament, 2–3 July 1992; Alan Larsson, 'En havstang till arbete', 21 April 1992, SLMAL, Archives of SAMAK, 1213/F/1/5.

29. SAMAKS Europagruppe, list of members, August 1992, SLMAL, Archives of SAMAK, 1213/F/1/5.

30. Axel Hanisch, 'Note à l'attention des membres du Bureau et des membres du groupe de travail "Larsson"', 3 December 1993, CAS-FJJ, Archives of the PES, PS 50 RI PSE 1993.

31. For a detailed account of the reasons that led PES leaders to consult the SAP although it was not yet a member party, see Mathieu Fulla, 'Put (Southern) Europe to work. The Nordic Turn of European Socialists in the Early 1990s', in *Rethinking European Social Democracy and Socialism: The History of the Centre-Left in Northern and Southern Europe in the Late 20th Century*, ed. Alan Granadino, Stefan Nygård and Peter Stadius (London and New York: Routledge, 2022).

32. 'Exposé d'Edgard Pisani au bureau de l'UPSCE des 3 et 4 février 1983', 8, CAS-FJJ, Archives of the CSPEC, 50 RI UPSCE 1983–1984. The French original refers to the British as *'autres'*, suggesting extreme difference, 'otherness'; Pisani also refers to the British as 'méchant', translated here as 'nasty', and which also suggests a mean, or spiteful disposition.

33. Bureau of the CSPEC, 'Projet de compte rendu de la réunion à Bruxelles le 13 février 1987', 24 February 1987, 3, CAS-FJJ, Archives of the CSPEC, 50 RI UPSCE 1986–1987.

34. Bureau of the CSPEC, 'Projet de compte rendu de la réunion du bureau du 8 avril à Madrid', 22 April 1985, 2, CAS-FJJ, Archives of the CSPEC, 50 RI UPSCE 1985.

35. Lionel Jospin, 'Intervention de Lionel Jospin, le 8 avril 1985 à Madrid, au bureau de l'UPSCE', 1, CAS-FJJ, Archives of the CSPEC, 50 RI UPSCE 1985.

36. Lionel Jospin, 'Intervention de Lionel Jospin, le 8 avril 1985 à Madrid', 3.

37. On the failure of European Socialism to promote the cause of 'Social Europe' from the late 1960s to the early 1980s, see Aurélie Dianara Andry, *Social Europe, The Road not Taken: The Left and European Integration in the Long 1970s* (Oxford: Oxford University Press, 2022).

38. Gerassimos Moschonas, 'The Party of European Socialists', in *Encyclopedia of European Elections*, ed. Yves Deloye and Michael Bruter (Basingstoke: Palgrave MacMillan, 2007).

39. Helen Drake, *Jacques Delors: Perspectives on a European leader* (London and New York: Routledge, 2000), 115.

40. PES, Axel Hanisch, Letter to Jacques Delors, 12 November 1993, and the third version of the Larsson report attached, Historical Archives of the European Commission (Brussels, hereafter HAEC), Forward Studies Unit/346.

41. James Sloam, *The European Policy of the German Social Democrats: Interpreting a Changing World* (Basingstoke: Palgrave Macmillan, 2005), 112.

42. Stuart Holland, *Out of Crisis: A Project for European Recovery* (Nottingham: Spokesman, 1983), 13.

43. Stuart Holland, 'Not an intellectual abdication of the Left. A response to Dani Rodrik', Polanyi Centre Publications, Advanced Research on the Global Economy, I.2017/WP01, 7.

44. Francis Cripps, Wynne Godley, 'A Formal Analysis of the Cambridge Policy Group Model', *Economica*, New Series 43, no. 172 (1976).

45. On Kaldor's critical analysis of the economic mechanisms of EEC, see Michael A. Landesmann, 'Nicholas Kaldor and Kazimierz Laski on the Pitfalls of the European Integration Process', *European Journal of Economics and Economic Policies: Intervention* 16, no. 3 (2019).

46. Penti Vaanen (general secretary of the SI), to Bureau members, Bureau circular No. B9/83, July 1, 1983, 'Work of the Socialist International Committee on Economic Policies', CAS-FJJ, Archives of the Socialist International, 60 RI (WB) 220.

47. 'Socialist International Economic Committee: Review of Work and Proposals for Future Action', Sheffield, 20 June 1984, 5, CAS-FJJ, Archives of the Socialist International, 60 RI (WB) 220.

48. On the Brandt Commission, see Bo Stråth, *The Brandt Commission and the Multinationals: Planetary Perspectives* (London and New York: Routledge, 2023).

49. There is an important body of literature dealing with the NIEO. See for instance, Mark Mazower, *Governing the World: The History of an Idea* (London: Penguin Press, 2013 [2012]); Giuliano Garavini, *After Empires: European Integration, Decolonization,*

and the Challenge from the Global South 1957–1986 (Oxford: Oxford University Press, 2012), 215–30; Vanessa Ogle, 'State Rights against Private Capital: The "New International Economic Order" and the Struggle over Aid, Trade, and Foreign Investment, 1962–1981', *Humanity. An International Journal of Human Rights, Humanitarianism, and Development* 5, no. 2 (2014); and the special issue edited by Nils Gilman, 'Toward a History of the New International Economic Order', *Humanity. An International Journal of Human Rights, Humanitarianism, and Development* 6, no. 1 (2015).

50. Michael Manley, *Global Challenge from Crisis to Cooperation: Breaking the North-South Stalemate*, report of the Socialist International Committee on Economic Policy (London: Pan Books, 1985).

51. Michael Manley and Willy Brandt, 'Breaking the North-South Stalemate', introduction to *Global Challenge* reproduced in *Socialist Affairs* 85, no. 4, 9.

52. 'Minutes of the meeting of the Socialist International Committee on Economic Policy, SICEP, Kingston, Jamaica – January 31–February 1, 1985', 8 March 1985, 4, CAS-FJJ, Archives of the Socialist International, 60 RI (WB) 220.

53. CSPEC, 'Une solution européenne à la crise. Contribution du groupe de travail au manifeste de l'UPSCE en vue des élections européennes', Luxemburg, 8–9 March 1984, 4, 14, CAS-FJJ, 50 RI UPSCE Elections Eur. 84.

54. Peter Haas, 'Introduction: Epistemic Communities and International Policy Coordination', *International Organization* 46, no. 1 (1992).

55. Georges Debunne, 'Flexibilité et réduction du temps de travail', July 1986, CAS-FJJ, Archives of the CSPEC, 50 RI UPSCE 1986–1987.

56. Ludo Cuyvers, 'Macroeconomic Effects of Expansionist Economic Policies: The Case for a Coordinated, Selected and Diversified Reflation in the EEC', July 1986 (revised and updated version), 28 July 1986, 4, CAS-FJJ, Archives of the CSPEC, 50 RI UPSCE 1986–1987.

57. CSPEC, 'More Jobs for Europe', 8.

58. For a striking example of this inaudibility, see 'The Appeal of Amsterdam', 19 May 1984, CAS-FJJ, Archives of the CSPEC, 50 RI UPSCE Elections eur. 84.

59. PES, 'Projet de procès-verbal du Bureau. Edimbourg le 9 décembre 1992', CAS-FJJ, PS 50 RI – PSE.

60. Warlouzet, *Governing Europe*, 123–5.

61. PES, 'Huit pistes essentielles pour l'emploi. Projet de rapport du groupe économique du PSE présenté par Gérard Fuchs', 5 August 1993, CAS-FJJ, Archives of the PES, PS 50 RI – PSE.

62. 'Compte rendu de la réunion du groupe de travail "Économique et social" du 29 mai 1993 à Strasbourg, 12 juillet 1993', 2, CAS-FJJ, Archives of the PES, PS 50 RI – PSE.

63. Bureau of the CSPEC, 'Projet de compte-rendu de la réunion du bureau du 6 décembre 1984', 'Intervention de Jacques Delors devant le bureau de l'Union des Partis socialistes de la Communauté européenne, le jeudi 6 décembre 1984 (annexe IV)', 10 December 1984, CAS-FJJ, Archives of the CSPEC, 50 RI UPSCE 1983–1984.

64. Bureau of the CSPEC, 'Projet de compte-rendu de la réunion du bureau du 2 décembre 1985 à Bruxelles', 3 December 1985, 10–11, CAS-FJJ, Archives of the CSPEC, 50 RI UPSCE 1985.

65. Interview with Christine Verger by Filippa Chatzistavrou, 22 June 2021, 15, Oral history programmes of the EU, https://archives.eui.eu/en/oral_history/INT302 [accessed 29 July 2021].

66. Christine Verger, 'Note pour P. Lamy. Objet: Congrès de l'Union des PS, Lisbonne, 4–5 mai 1987', 5 May 1987, Centre for history at Sciences Po (below CHSP), Jacques Delors Archives, JD 59 (91–93). Christine Verger, 'Note à l'attention du président. Objet: Congrès de l'Union CHSP des PS (dîner du 9.2 et réunion du 10.2) et votre entretien ce jour avec M. Spitaels', 8 February 1989, CHSP, Jacques Delors Archives, JD 512 (124–127).

67. Verger, 'Note à l'attention du président', 2.

68. CSPEC, 'Projet de compte rendu de la réunion du bureau', 6 November 1987, 6, CAS-FJJ, Archives of the CSPEC, 50 RI UPSCE 1987.

69. Moschonas, 'Reformism', 187.

70. Kenneth Dyson and Kevin Featherstone, *The Road to Maastricht: Negotiating Economic and Monetary Union* (Oxford: Oxford University Press, 1999), 691–745.

71. British Labour Party, 'Note sur le document de Jacques Delors intitulé: "Compétitivité perdue. Compétitivité retrouvée: l'approche européenne", rédigé par The Labour Party', 24 February 1986, 6, CAS-FJJ, Archives of the CSPEC, 50 RI UPSCE 1986–1987. This document is a translation of the original version written in English, which was not held in these archives. The Bureau of the CSPEC used to translate most circulars and working papers in the main languages of the EEC, namely German and French (and sometimes in Italian and Spanish).

72. Alessandra Bitumi, '"An uplifting tale of Europe". Jacques Delors and the Contradictory Quest for a European Social Model in the Age of Reagan', *Journal of Transatlantic Studies* 16, no. 3 (2018), 212.

73. Jacques Delors, '1992: the Social Dimension', address by the president of the Commission of the European Communities to the Trades Union Congress, Bournemouth, 8 September 1988, CHSP, Jacques Delors Archives, JD-74.

74. Patricia Hewitt quoted in Colm Murphy, *Futures of Socialism: 'Modernisation', the Labour Party, and the British Left, 1973–1997* (Cambridge: Cambridge University Press, 2023), 68.

75. Chris Boyd, 'Note to the file' about his trip to Stockholm, 14–15 October 1993, 1, HAEC, Forward Studies Unit/351.

76. Jérôme Vignon, 'Quelques commentaires sur "Yes, Europe can afford to work"', 4 November 1993, CAS-FJJ, PS 50 RI – PSE.

77. See for instance Pascal Lamy, 'Note pour le président', Objet: croissance-compétitivité-emploi – projet de Luigi Colajanni, 8 September 1993, 1, HAEC, Forward Studies Unit/351.

78. 'Documentation Livre Blanc', Fall 1993, HAEC, Forward Studies Unit/346.

79. Larsson, 'Put Europe to Work', 20.

80. George Ross, *Jacques Delors and European Integration* (Polity Press, 1995), quoted in Andreas Aust, 'From "Eurokeynesianism"', 184.

81. Andreas Aust, 'From "Eurokeynesianism"', 188.

82. Rutger Claasen et al., 'Rethinking the European Social Market Economy: Introduction to the Special Issue', *JCMS: Journal of Common Market Studies* 57, no. 1 (2019), 6.

83. Johansson, 'Tracing the Employment Title', 94.

Bibliography

Andersson, Jenny and Kjell Östberg. 'The Swedish Social Democrats, Reform Socialism and the State after the Golden Era'. In *European Socialists and the State in the Twentieth and Twenty-First Centuries*, edited by Mathieu Fulla and Marc Lazar, 323–43. Basingstoke: Palgrave Macmillan, 2020.

Aust, Andreas. 'From "Eurokeynesianism" to the "Third Way": The Party of European Socialists (PES) and European Employment Policies'. In *Social Democratic Party Policies in Contemporary Europe*, edited by Giuliano Bonolli and Martin Powell, 180–96. London and New York: Routledge, 2005.

Ban, Cornel. *Ruling Ideas: How Global Neoliberalism Goes Local*. Oxford: Oxford University Press, 2016.

Bitumi, Alessandra. '"An uplifting tale of Europe". Jacques Delors and the Contradictory Quest for a European Social Model in the Age of Reagan', *Journal of Transatlantic Studies* 16, no. 3 (2018): 203–21.

Burlaud, Antony. '"Faire rentrer la justice sociale dans la balance des paiements". La politique macro-économique de Michel Rocard'. In *Michel Rocard Premier ministre. La deuxième gauche et le pouvoir (1988–1991)*, edited by Alain Bergounioux and Mathieu Fulla, 243–63. Paris: Presses de Sciences Po, 2020.

Claasen, Rutger et al. 'Rethinking the European Social Market Economy: Introduction to the Special Issue', *JCMS: Journal of Common Market Studies* 57, no. 1 (2019): 3–12.

Cripps, Francis and Wynne Godley. 'A Formal Analysis of the Cambridge Policy Group Model', *Economica*, New Series 43, no. 172 (1976): 335–48.

Dianara Andry, Aurélie. *Social Europe, The Road not Taken: The Left and European Integration in the Long 1970s*. Oxford: Oxford University Press, 2022.

Drake, Helen. *Jacques Delors: Perspectives on a European leader*. London and New York: Routledge, 2000.

Dyson, Kenneth and Kevin Featherstone. *The Road to Maastricht: Negotiating Economic and Monetary Union*. Oxford: Oxford University Press, 1999.

Eley, Geoff. *Forging Democracy. The History of the Left in Europe, 1850–2000*. Oxford: Oxford University Press, 2002.

Fulla, Mathieu. 'Quand Pierre Mauroy résistait avec rigueur au "néo-libéralisme"', *Vingtième siècle. Revue d'histoire* 138, no. 2 (2018) : 49–63.

Fulla, Mathieu. 'Partager une culture économique sans le savoir. Les experts socialistes français et britanniques des années soixante-dix', *Ventunesimo Secolo* 44 (2019): 63–87.

Fulla, Mathieu. 'Put (Southern) Europe to Work. The Nordic Turn of European Socialists in the Early 1990s'. In *Rethinking European Social Democracy and Socialism: The History of the Centre-Left in Northern and Southern Europe in the Late 20th Century*, edited by Alan Granadino, Stefan Nygård and Peter Stadius, 48–66. London and New York: Routledge, 2022.

Garavini, Giuliano. *After Empires: European Integration, Decolonization, and the Challenge from the Global South 1957–1986*. Oxford: Oxford University Press, 2012.

Gilman, Nils, ed. 'Special Issue: Toward a History of the New International Economic Order', *Humanity. An International Journal of Human Rights, Humanitarianism, and Development* 6, no. 1 (2015): 1–16.

Haas, Peter. 'Introduction: Epistemic Communities and International Policy Coordination', *International Organization* 46, no. 1 (1992): 1–35.

Heidar, Knut. 'Parties and Cleavages in the European Political Space'. ARENA working papers, WP 03/7, 2003. https://www.sv.uio.no/arena/english/research/publications/arena-working-papers/2001-2010/2003/wp03_7.pdf [accessed 28 July 2021].

Hix, Simon. 'Parties at the European Level and the Legitimacy of EU Socio-Economic Policy', *JCMS: Journal of Common Market Studies* 33, no. 4 (1995): 527–54.

Holland, Stuart. *Out of Crisis: A Project for European Recovery*. Nottingham: Spokesman, 1983.

Johansson, Karl Magnus. 'Tracing the Employment Title in the Amsterdam Treaty: Uncovering Transnational Coalitions', *Journal of European Public Policy* 6, no. 1 (1999): 85–101.

Ladrech, Robert. 'Political Parties and the Problem of Legitimacy in the European Union'. In *Legitimacy and the European Union: The Contested Polity*, edited by Thomas Banchoff and Mitchell Smith, 94–114. London: Routledge, 1999.

Landesmann, Michael A. 'Nicholas Kaldor and Kazimierz Laski on the Pitfalls of the European Integration Process', *European Journal of Economics and Economic Policies: Intervention* 16, no. 3 (2019): 344–69.

Lavelle, Ashley. 'Explanations for the Neo-liberal Direction of Social Democracy: Germany, Sweden and Australia Compared'. In *In Search of Social Democracy: Responses to Crisis and Modernisation*, edited by John Callaghan, Nina Fishman, Ben Jackson and Martin McIvor, 9–28. Manchester: Manchester University Press, 2009.

Mazower, Mark. *Governing the World: The History of an Idea*. London: Penguin Press, 2013 [2012].

Moschonas, Gerassimos. 'The Party of European Socialists'. In *Encylopedia of European Elections*, edited by Yves Deloye and Michael Bruter. Basingstoke: Palgrave Macmillan, 2007.

Moschonas, Gerassimos. 'Reformism in a "Conservative" System: The European Union and Social Democratic Identity'. In *In Search of Social Democracy: Responses to Crisis and Modernisation*, edited by John Callaghan, Nina Fishman, Ben Jackson and Martin McIvor, 168–92. Manchester: Manchester University Press, 2009.

Murphy, Colm. *Futures of Socialism: 'Modernisation', the Labour Party, and the British Left, 1973–1997*. Cambridge: Cambridge University Press, 2023.

Ogle, Vanessa. 'State Rights against Private Capital: The "New International Economic Order" and the Struggle over Aid, Trade, and Foreign Investment, 1962–1981', *Humanity. An International Journal of Human Rights, Humanitarianism, and Development* 5, no. 2 (2014): 211–34.

Rodgers, Daniel. 'The Uses and Abuses of "Neoliberalism"', *Dissent*, Winter 2018, https://www.dissentmagazine.org/article/uses-and-abuses-neoliberalism-debate [accessed 25 July 2021].

Rosanvallon, Pierre. *Notre histoire intellectuelle et politique 1968–2018*. Paris: Seuil, 2018.

Ryner, J. Magnus. 'Neo-Liberalization of Social Democracy: The Swedish Case', *Comparative European Politics* 2 (2004): 97–119.

Sassoon, Donald. *One Hundred Years of Socialism: The West European Left in the Twentieth Century*. London and New York: I.B. Tauris, 2014 [1996].

Sloam, James. *The European Policy of the German Social Democrats: Interpreting a Changing World*. Basingstoke: Palgrave Macmillan, 2005.

Stråth, Bo. *The Brandt Commission and the Multinationals: Planetary Perspectives*. London and New York: Routledge, 2023.

Tartakowsky, Danielle and Alain Bergounioux, eds. *L'union sans unité: le programme commun de la gauche, 1963–1978*. Rennes: Presses universitaires de Rennes, 2012.

Warlouzet, Laurent. *Governing Europe in a Globalising World: Neoliberalism and its Alternatives following the 1973 Oil Crisis*. London and New York: Routledge, 2018.

Wickham-Jones, Mark. *Economic Strategy and the Labour Party*. London: Macmillan Press, 1996.

Index

A
Abbott, Diane, 206
Abrahams, Peter, 64
Adler, Emmanuel, 43
aid
   in Africa, 108, 128, 144–6
   to Europe, 66–7
   and limits of decolonisation, 128, 141
   in Vietnam, 161, 166
Algeria, 2, 5
   and British left chapter 3 *passim*
   and British media, 93–4, 97–105, 109, 111, 114
   comparison with British empire, 97–8, 105, 108, 112
   and de Gaulle, 104–5, 108, 111–12
   and EEC, 92, 112, 115
   Front de Libération National (FLN), 92, 98, 102–4, 108
   and Indochina, 97, 106–7
   and MCF, 94, 96–7, 99–101, 106, 114
   Organisation armée secrète (OAS), 92
   and Quakers, 106–9, 113
   post-independence, 5
   and Second World War, 41
   and SFIO, 6, 93, 98–101
   and Suez crisis, 97–8
   torture, 9, 91, 94, 99, 107, 114
   and transnationalising networks, 2, 13–14, chapter 3 *passim*
Alphand, Hervé, 46
American Socialist Party, 61–2
Amos, Valerie, 210, 218
Anderson, Perry, 110, 112
Andrade, Mario Pinto de, 132, 136, 140
Angola, 2, 127–8, 132, 138–9, 141
anti-fascism, 2
   and British democracy, 44
   European solidarity, 2, 10, 13, 129
   fascist regimes, 14, 129, 134
   and fascist risks, 95, 104–5
   organisations, 61–2, 143
antiracism chapter 7 *passim*
   Black Manifesto for Europe, 209
   British Black Caucus, 206
   contacts outside EU, 206, 212–13
   EU support, 211
   organising. See BWEN; SCORE
   response to British and EU legislation, 203–5, 207–8, 210
   role of women, 202, 209–13. See also BWEN; OWAAD
   and social justice, 16, 201–2, 207, 212, 214
Arafat, Yasser, 16, 187, 189, 192–6
Ashwood Garvey, Amy, 61
Assises du socialisme, 191
Association de Solidarité Franco-Arabe (ASFA), 192, 198
Atlantic Charter, 35, 39–40, 47–8
Attlee, Clement, 36, 44, 49, 96
Auriol, Vincent, 37, 41, 43, 48–9
Avenol, Joseph, 36
Avnery, Uri, 187

B
Baker, Eric, 106
Bandung Conference, 5, 109, 111
Bangura, Alfredo, 136
Baran, Paul, 228
Belkacem, Krim, 104
Beloff, Nora, 93, 103
Ben Barka, Mehdi, 113, 192
Ben Bella, Ahmed, 92, 108
Benn, Tony, 100, 109, 111, 113, 136
Bérégovoy, Pierre, 227
Bernal, John Desmond, 130, 137
Bevan, Aneurin, 95–8, 101–3, 105, 109
Beveridge, William, 38, 45–8, 94
Beveridge Report, 34, 46
Bevin, Ernest, 50, 95
Black Women and Europe Network (BWEN), 202–3, 210–13
Blatchford, Robert, 34
Blum, Léon, 34–8
Boateng, Paul, 206
Boavida, Américo, 136
Boris, Georges, 43–4, 46, 48
Bouhired, Djamila, 103
Boumendjel, Ali, 99
Bourdet, Claude
   and Algerian war of independence chapter 3 *passim*
   and anticolonial networks, 13–14, 18, chapter 3 *passim*
   arrest, 93–4
   and CND, 110–11
   dispute with Labour, 101–3, 109
   France-Observateur and Labour Left, 97–102, 104–5, 109, 114
   and French resistance, 91
   and Quakers, 93, 106–9, 113
   relations with British new left, 99–101, 104, 106, 110–13

Bourdet, Claude (*continued*)
  and socialist Europe, 63, 94–6, 99, 102, 111–15
  speaking/writing for British media, 91, 94, 96, 98, 106, 111
  support for Bevan, 95–6, 98, 105, 114
  visits to Britain, 94, 100–102, 105, 110–11
Bourguiba, Habib, 103, 106
Brandt, Willy, 145
  'Brandt Commission', 193, 233–4
  and Israel-Palestine conflict, 16, 186, 193, 195
  and Locarno-era thinking, 72
  and 'New International Economic Order', 7–8
  relations with Palme, 18, 162–4, 166, 169, 171
  and Socialist International, 193, 195, 234
  and Third-Worldism, 145
  and Vietnam war, 163–6, 168–9
  and wartime experiences, 15, 162, 166
Brezhnev, Leonid, 163
Britain
  and Anglo-Portuguese alliance, 14,143
  and antiracism chapter 7 *passim*
  and 'Atlanticism', 66, 95
  and 'Brexit', 17
  British Black Caucus, 206–7
  British Nationality Acts, 203–4
  Challenge to Britain, 136
  and Cold War surveillance, 94, 130–31
  economic policy, 3, 48, 69, 240
  and empire, 14, 105–6, 112, 128, 133, 136, 146
  and European Free Trade Association (EFTA), 112, 138, 143
  and European project, 12, 19, 48–9, chapter 2 *passim*. See also London Bureau, 91, 112–13
  France and Britain, 44
  impact of EU on migration chapter 7 *passim*
  importance for French left, 95–6, 98, 101
  and internationalism, 1, 8, 92, 104
  and Israel/Palestine, 15, 185
  and liberation of Portuguese empire in Africa chapter 4 *passim*
  new left, 99–100, 109–13, 141
  as place of anticolonial mobilisation chapters 3 and 4 *passim*
  as post-war economic model, 8
  and post-war reconstruction, 39, 48–50, 140
  and racism chapter 7 *passim*
  and Second World War chapter 1 *passim*, 59–60, 62, 129
  and SFIO in exile, 12, chapter 1 *passim*
  and 'Special Relationship', 39–40
  union with France, 40
  and United Nations, 46, 50, 106, 113, 133, 144, 146
  and Vietnam War chapter 5 *passim*
  and war of Algerian independence chapter 3 *passim*
  and Windrush scandal, 16
British Broadcasting Corporation (BBC), 93–4, 104, 111
Brockway, Fenner
  and Bourdet, 18, 93–4, 96, 99, 113–14
  Independent Labour Party, 13
  and Israel, 99
  and London Bureau, 61–3
  and Movement for Colonial Freedom, 108
  and MUSSE, 67
  and Portuguese colonies, 136, 145
  and Spain, 61
  and Vietnam, 113–14
Brouckère, Louis de, 35
Bullitt, William, 38
Butler, 'Rab', 3

C

Cabral, Amílcar, 132–3, 142
Cabral, João, 136
Caetano, Marcelo, 143–4
Calder, Ritchie, 94, 111
Callaghan, James, 136
Campaign for Nuclear Disarmament (CND), 110, 113
Carlsson, Bernt, 193, 195–6
Carlsson, Ingvar, 229, 239
Castle, Barbara, 99, 102–3, 108
Centre d'études, de recherches et d'éducation socialiste (CERES), 188–92
Cépède, Michel, 69
Chenal, Alain, 192
Chevènement, Jean-Pierre, 188, 190, 192
Cheysson, Claude, 196
China, 96, 138
Churchill, Winston, 12, 36, 42, 65, 68
Claes, Willy, 223
  'Claes Group', 224–32, 235, 240
  and Delors, 229, 235
  'Euro-Keynesian' approach to economics and employment, 226, 232
  influence of Kaldor and Cambridge Economic Policy Group, 233, 235
  updated Keynesian policies of 1970s, 228–9
Cold War

and attitudes to US, 13, 170
emergence of neoliberal policies in Europe, 17
end of, 17, 171, 223–4
and European unity, 59
and independence struggles, 128–30, 135, 145
informants and surveillance, 62, 129–30
intellectual cooperation, 6, 10, 12, 111
party divisions, 14, 65
studies, 6
and Vietnam chapter 5 *passim*
See also NATO; Soviet Union; United States
Cole, G. D. H., 100
Collins, Revd. John, 111
Comintern (Communist International), 13, 60–61
Commission for Racial Equality (UK), 18, 205–6, 208
Committee for the Freedom in Mozambique, Angola and Guinea (CFMAG), 141–4
Commonwealth, 16, 69
and EEC membership, 112–14
and European Single market/Single European Act, 203–4, 214
Confederation of the Socialist Parties of the European Community (CSPEC)
activities of, 17, 225, 227–8
and Delors, 238
disagreements among members, 230–31
and *Global Challenge*, 234
'More Jobs for Europe', 223–5, 228–9, 232
structural weakness, 225–9, 231, 237–8, 240
succeeded by Party of European Socialists (PES), 223
Congo (Belgian), 131, 135
Congress of the Peoples Against Imperialism, 92
Cot, Jean-Pierre, 229
Cot, Pierre, 42
Cross-Cultural Black Women's Studies Institute, 210
Crossman, Richard, 66, 95, 97

D

Dalton, Hugh, 41, 50
Davidson, Basil, 14–15
African Awakening, 131–3
as Africanist historian, 110, 128, 130–31, 133, 139–40, 145
and Algeria, 98–101, 108

Angola, 1961, 134–5
and British new left, 141
and Brockway, Fenner, 136
and CFMAG, 142–3
friendship with African leaders, 132–3, 136, 138–9, 145
In the Eye of the Storm: Angola's People, 140–41
journalist, 129–32
and Labour Party, 129, 135–7, 142, 145
The Liberation of Guinea, 139
and Lusophone Africa, 114, chapter 4 *passim*
and neutral belt in Europe, 99
and Portuguese left, 136–7
and Présence Africaine, 132, 137
surveillance, 130–31, 143, 146
and UDC, 130, 133–5
visits to Africa, 131, 133, 139, 146
wartime background of, 129–30
decolonisation
and British 'official mind', 146
and French new left, 92–3, 102, 112, 114, 185
and European integration, 4–5, 11, 14, 104
and socialism in Europe, 1, 4–7, 11, 13–14, 72, 104–5
and Cold War, 10, 128
post-independence aid, 144
resistance to, 65, 92, 132, 143
study of, 4–5, 10
unfinished, 19–20, 137, 140–41
De Gaulle, Charles
and Algeria, 104–5, 108, 111
and Britain, 38–9, 91, 111–12
and British Labour, 41–3, 49, 104–5
and French left, 3, 12, 41–5, 49, 105, 108, 111–12, 186
in London, 12, 37–9
and Soviet Union, 4, 49, 158
and United States, 37–40, 158, 167
and Vietnam, 158–9
Delors, Jacques
and Claes/Larsson proposals, 226, 231–2, 237–240
and CSPEC, 237–240
and 'Forward Studies Unit' (*Cellule de Prospective*), 225
Head of European Commission, 224
and 'new architecture of Europe', 239–40
and 'offshoring', 17
Depreux, Edouard, 93
Dong, Pham Van, 162, 167–8
Dos Santos, Marcelino, 132, 143
Douglas-Hume, Alec, 157

Dumas, Roland, 196
Dummett, Ann, 203

E

Economic and Monetary Union (EMU), 226–7, 236–8
Eden, Anthony, 36, 38–9, 41
Edwards, Bob, 61–4, 67–8
Egypt, 16, 97, 184, 186–7, 189
epistemic communities, 10, 234–5
Erhard, Ludwig, 157, 166
Estier, Claude, 98, 186–7, 189–90
'Euro-Keynesianism', 232, 235, 240
European Defence Community (EDC), 95–6
European Economic Community (EEC)
  and Britain, 19, 92, 110, 112–13, 203
  and CSPEC, 225, 231
  and migration, 19, 203, 212
  and MSEUE, 13
  and policy making, 7, 193, 223, 227–8, 234–5, 237
  and Portugal, 144
  and Schengen agreement, 205
  and Single Market, 16, 203, 214
  and Treaty of Rome, 73, 92, 205, 209, 214
  and TREVI Group, 205
European Employment Initiative (EEI), 223–4, 231, 239
European Free Trade Association (EFTA), 112, 138, 143
European integration
  and Britain, 19
  and conflict, 12, 59, 72
  and decolonisation, 4, 7
  and Europeanisation, 10, 73, 207–8
  and 'polity-making', 10
  and rights, 20, 201–2, 208
  and Schuman Plan, 69
  'Third Force', 64–9, 96, 99
  and transnationalism, 9, 12, 16, 19–20, 70, 208
Europeanisation, 9–10, 19, 201–2, 207–8, 212–4
European Movement (EM), 59, 65, 68–9, 71
'European-ness', 2
European Recovery Program. *See* Marshall Plan
European Single Market, 16, 203–5, 214, 229
European Society of Culture, 6
European Union
  Amsterdam Treaty, 17, 214, 224
  and borders, 3–4, 16, 19, 209, 214
  budget, 236
  and decolonisation, 4–5, 19
  Maastricht Treaty, 208, 211, 223, 226–7, 229, 239–40
  and socialist structures, 7, 225, 239
  transnational networks, 203, 214

F

Fabians, 44–5, 135
federalism, 12, 49, 59, 64, 68–9, 70–71
Figueiredo, António, 137
Foot, Michael
  on Algeria, 100–101, 114, 95
  and Bourdet, 93, 95–6, 98, 100–102, 109, 114
  and discussion of European defence, 95–6, 102
  in Labour Party, 93, 98, 102, 232
  and Suez, 98
Foot, Paul, 143
'Fortress Europe', 16, 201, 203, 208, 212, 214
France
  and Amnesty International, 137
  and antiracism, 208, 212–14
  and bombing of French embassy in Hanoi 1972, 160–62, 167–9
  British correspondents in, 95, 103–4
  British Labour views of, 44–6, 50, 94, 102, 104–5
  and empire, 14, 96–7, 104, 133. *See also* Algeria; Indochina
  and ILP, 63–4, 66
  and Israel/Palestine chapter 6 *passim*
  and liberation of Portuguese Africa, 142
  Mouvement contre l'armement atomique, 113
  and NATO, 111–12, 158, 167–8
  'New Left', 18, 91, 92
  and PLO, 16, 192–4, 196
  and racism, 204
  and Second World War, 3, 7, 12, chapter 1 *passim*, 65, 185
  socialists and economic policy, 66, 226–7, 231
  and Suez crisis, 15–16, 92, 98, 185
  and Treaty of Rome, 92
  and Vietnam War, 158, 167–8
France Observateur, 13, chapter 3 *passim*, 187
Frenay, Henri, 64, 68
French Communist Party. *See Parti Communiste Français*
French Socialist Party. *See* SFIO; *Parti socialiste*

Frente de Libertação de Moçambique (FRELIMO), 132, 138–9, 141, 143–4
Front de libération nationale (FLN), 92, 98, 102–4, 108

G

Gaitskell, Hugh, 3, 96, 98, 136
Gauche Européenne, 70
Gaza, 15–16, 189, 191, 194
Gillies, William, 43–4, 50
Globalisation, 4–5, 7, 10, 17, 19, 92, 228
Gouvernement Provisoire de la République Française (GPRF), 49
Grant, Bernie, 16–17, 202, 205–7, 209–11
Greece, 64, 67–8, 130, 208, 212, 226, 231
  Archeio-Marxist Party, 61, 63
  Pan-Hellenic Socialist Movement (PASOK), 236
Groupe de Recherche et d'Action pour le règlement du Problème Palestinien (GRAPP), 192–8
Groupe Jean Jaurès, 12, 33, 42–45
Guinea-Bissau, 127–8, 137–9

H

Hall, Stuart, 99, 101, 109–14
Halliday, Fred, 143
Hart, Judith, 144
Hauck, Henri, 43–4, 46
Hayek, Friedrich, 3
Heydorn, Heinz-Joachim, 63–4, 67
Hobsbawm, Eric, 100
Hodgkin, Thomas, 130, 135, 141
Hungary, 14, 129, 131
Huysmans, Camille, 35, 43
Huxley, Julian, 137

I

imagined communities, 8
Independent Labour Party (ILP)
  conflict with Labour Party, 64, 66
  decline, 65–6, 68, 70
  and London Bureau, 60, 62–3
  and Pivert, 64
India, 94, 96, 106, 113, 133–4, 205
Indochina, 61, 91, 96–97, 106–7, 139, 158, 167
internationalism, 8–9
  Black internationalism, 202
  and decolonisation, 7–9, 100, 114
  and regional integration, 7–8, 18
  and socialism, 7–9, 34, 60, 72, 113
  study of, 7–9, 92
International Union against Racism, 64
Israel chapter 6 *passim*
  and Brandt diplomacy, 16, 186, 193
  and Brockway, 99
  Convention des Institutions Républicaines (CIR), 186–7
  and European socialism, 15, 183–86
  Israeli Far Left Party (*Mifleget HaPoalim HaMeuhedet*, MAPAM), 18, 187
  Israeli Labour Party (*Mifléguet Poalei Eretz Israel*, MAPAÏ), 18, 183
  Israeli left, 184, 186–7, 193
  and Lebanon, 195
  and Mitterrand, 187–8, 192–4
  and Mollet, 183
  secret service, 192
  Shoah, 185–6
  Six Day War, 184–5
  and Socialist International, 163, 193, 195
  Suez crisis, 183
  Yom Kippur War, 190
Italian Socialist Party. See *Partido socialista italiano*
Italy
  and British left, 111, 113
  Catholicism, 109
  and EU socialist networks, 231, 235
  and independent Algeria, 5
  and London Bureau, 61
  and Nenni, 111, 185
  and rights, 104, 111, 137
  and SCORE, 208
  in Second World War, 129, 164

J

Jamaica, 7, 101, 233–4
James, C. L. R, 61
Jarret, Cynthia, 206, 211
Johnson, Lyndon Baines, 138, 157
Jospin, Lionel
  and criticism of the CSPEC, 231
  and EEC, 230–31
  support for Palestinian cause, 188, 192, 196
Jospin, Robert, 64
Jowitt, William, 46

K

Kaldor, Nicholas, 233, 235
Kellou, Mohamed, 102, 106
Kennedy, John Fitzgerald, 138, 158
Kenya, 61, 97–8, 105, 113–14, 131
Kenyatta, Jomo, 61
Keynes, John Maynard, 3, 46, 226–7, 240, chapter 8 *passim*
Khan, Naseem, 210
Kinnock, Neil, 229, 238
Kissinger, Henry, 161, 166, 168, 170

Kreisky, Bruno
  friendship with Willi Brandt and Olof Plame, 15, 18, 162–3, 171
  and Israel/Palestine, 15, 163, 193
  and Socialist International, 163, 171
  and Vietnam war, 162–3, 168–9
  wartime experiences, 15, 162, 168

L

Labour and Socialist International, 35, 61
Labour Party, British
  and Atlantic alliance, 13, 66, 96, 229
  Black leaders, 202–3, 205–7, 211, 214
  and Bourdet, 94–6, 98–9, 101–3, 109, 112, 114
  and British empire, 97–8, 105–6
  and de Gaulle, 38–9, 41–2, 104–5
  and economy, 3, 34, 69, 228–38
  and EEC/EU institutions, 230–36
  enduring Euroscepticism within, 230, 237–9
  and European defence, 95–6, 98–9, 130, 229
  and French exiles in Second World War, 33–9, 41–5, 49–50
  and Independent Labour Party (ILP), 13, 64, 66, 68
  and Israel, 16, 185–6
  'Keep Left', 95
  and immigration legislation, 17, 203
  and Lusophone Africa, 14, 128, 132, 135–7, 141, 143–6
  and 'More Jobs for Europe', 230, 232–3
  National Association of Labour Student Organisations (NALSO), 111
  post-war plans and SFIO, 46–49
  and racial equality, 205–7
  and Socialist International, 94–5
  and Suez crisis, 97–8
  and Third Force Europe, 14, 65–6, 68, 91, 99
  and Vietnam War, 157, 167
  and war of Algerian independence, 93, 100–101, 103–6, 114
  and welfare, 34, 68
  world government, 94
Laird, Melvin, 161
Lara, Lúcio, 132
Larsson, Allan
  and Delors, 226, 239
  and influence, 229–32, 235–6, 239–40
  'Larsson group', 224–6, 230–32, 224–6, 239–40
  and need for compatibility with EMU, 237, 239
  and 'New Deal for Europe', 224–6
League of Nations, 36, 38, 42

Lebanon, 194–5
Lee, Jenny, 95
Legum, Colin, 109
Lessing, Doris, 100, 137
Lester, Joan, 143–4
Liberalism
  liberalisation, 48, 73, 204
  limits of, soft politics, 42, 107, 134, 207, 212
  and socialism, 3, 35, 94
  and welfare, 46
London Bureau, 13, 59–64, 70, 72

M

Macmillan, Harold, 92, 135
Major, John, 209
Mandel, Ernest, 111
Manley, Michael, 7, 233–35, 240
Marshall Plan (European Recovery Program), 65, 67
Martin, Kingsley, 130–31, 134
Marx, Karl/Marxism, 93, 112
  and British left, 34, 60–62, 93, 111, 141
  disagreement about by socialists, 70–71
  and London Bureau, 60–63
  and Lusophone Africa, 138–9, 141, 146
  neo-Marxism, 228
  and *The Socialist Register*, 141
Mauroy, Pierre, 188, 196, 226
Mayer, Daniel
  and Britain in postwar Europe, 49
  French resistance, 37, 43, 45
  and Israel, 185, 193
Mayole, Matthew, 136
Maxton, James, 66
McNair, John, 61, 63, 65, 67
Meir, Golda, 184–5
Mendès France, Pierre, 96
Mendl, Wolf, 107–8, 113
Mikardo, Ian, 95, 101, 103, 108, 112
Miliband, Ralph, 141
Mitterrand, François, 16, 186–9, 191–4, 196
Mollet, Guy
  and British media, 97–102
  and socialist Europe, 64
  and Suez Crisis, 15, 97–9, 183–4
  and war in Algeria, 92, 97–102
Mondlane, Eduardo, 132, 139, 141, 143
Monnet, Jean, 40, 42, 46
Moore, Henry, 137
Morocco, 41, 106, 113, 192
Moulin, Léo, 71–2
Mouvement Socialiste pour les États-Unis d'Europe (MSEUE)
  and American Socialist Party, 61–2
  as bridge, 12–13, 18

early Movement for the United
   Socialist States of Europe (MUSSE),
   12, 60, 68, 72
and empire, 61, 65
and European Movement, 59, 65, 68-9,
   71
and federalism, 59, 64, 68-9, 71
Frankfurt Congress, 70-71
Gauche européenne, 70
and ILP, 60, 62-6, 68
International Socialist States of
   Europe, 63
Montrouge Conference, 65-8
structure. *See* London Bureau
Third Force, 60, 64-6
Trotskyism, 60, 62-3
United States of Europe, 62-4, 70
Movement for Colonial Freedom (MCF)
   and Bourdet, 94, 96, 99-101, 106, 114
   membership, 135, 141
   and repression in British empire, 97
   and torture in Algeria, 94, 99-100
*Movimento Popular de Libertação de
   Angola* (MPLA), 132, 135-8, 140,
   144
Mozambique, 127-8, 136-42, 144
Myrdal, Gunnar, 6, 162, 164

N

Nasser, Gamal Abdel, 184, 187. *See also*
   Egypt; Suez Crisis
National Peace Council, 106
Nehru, Jawaharlal, 94
Nenni, Pietro, 111, 185
neo-colonialism, 14-15, 140-41, 158
neoliberalism, 3-4, 17, 223, 226-7, 233
Netherlands
   and anticolonial networks, 142
   and antiracist networks, 202, 204, 208,
      212-13
   Dutch Labour Party, 19, 227
   Revolutionair Socialistische Partij, 63
Neto, Agostinho, 132, 135, 139-40, 144
New Leader, 63
New Left Review, 109-11, 113-14, 138
New Statesman and Nation, 14, 45, 95, 97,
   130-32, 134
Nidal, Abu (aka Sabri al-Banna), 196
Nigeria, 108, 131, 206, 211
Nixon, Richard, 157
Noel-Baker, Philip, 38, 41-42, 50
'normative Europe' and norms, 4,
   10, 15
North Atlantic Treaty Organisation
   (NATO)
   and British new left, 110-11
   and France, 167-8

and Portugal, 14, 128, 135, 138, 143-5
and Vietnam war, 163, 167, 170
Norway, 36, 108, 162, 169, 212

O

Öberg, Jean-Christophe, 160-61, 165, 167
Ocloo, Josephine, 208-9
Organisation armée secrète (OAS), 92
Organisation for Women of African and
   African/Asian Descent (OWAAD), 211
Orwell, George, 75, 130
Osamor, Martha, 16-17, 202, 210-11

P

Padley, Walter, 63
Padmore, George, 61-2
Palestine chapter 6 *passim*
   and Brandt diplomacy, 186, 193
   *Centre d'études, de recherches et
      d'éducation socialiste* (CERES), 188,
      190-92
   and Christian left, 191-2
   *Convention des Institutions
      Républicaines* (CIR), 186-7
   greater support within PS, 15-16,
      189-196
   and Mitterrand, 187-8, 192-4
   and Socialist International, 163, 193,
      195
Palestinian Liberation Organisation
   (PLO), 187, 189-96
Palme, Olof
   change in economic policy in 1980s,
      226-7
   and early opposition to Vietnam War,
      15, 57, 159
   friendship with Kreisky and Brandt,
      15-16, 18, 162-4, 166, 168, 171
   and Palestine, 193
   Palme Commission, 233
   and Pham Van Dong, 167
   and Second World War, 16, 168-9
   socialism of, 18, 171
   and US bombing of Hanoi, 160-62,
      164-6, 170
   and US sympathies, 162-4, 170
pan-Africanism, 61, 64, 109
Pannikar, K. M., 96
Parti Communiste Français (PCF), 3,
   35-6, 47, 188, 228
*Partido Africano da Independência da
   Guiné e Cabo Verde* (PAIGC), 127-8,
   132, 136, 138-9, 142
Partido italiano socialista (PSI), 111, 185,
   235
Partido Obrero de Unificación Marxista
   (POUM), 61

Parti socialiste (PS)
  Assises du socialisme, 191
  Centre d'études, de recherches et d'éducation socialiste (CERES), 188
  and Christian left, 191–2
  Convention des Institutions Républicaines (CIR), 186–7
  and CSPEC/PES, 229–31, 235
  and economic policy in Europe, 226–8, 229–32, 235
  Épinay Congress, 187–8, 191
  influence of Mitterrand, 186–7, 189, 192
  and Israel/Palestine, 16, chapter 6 *passim*
  Programme commun de gouvernement, 188, 228
Parti socialiste unifié (PSU), 18, 109, 111, 185, 191
Party of European Socialists (PES), 223, 225–6, 229, 231
  'Eight Recommendations for Growth and Employment', 235
Pétain, Philippe, 36–7
Peyrega, Jacques, 99
Philip, André
  and de Gaulle, 12, 43
  and distinctions within European socialism, 70, 109
  in London, 13, 18, 44
  and MSEUE, 69–72
  and MUSSE, 64
  and war in Algeria, 93
Phillips, Morgan, 98
Pineau, Christian, 185
Pisani, Edgard, 230
Pitt, David, 203, 206
Pivert, Marceau, 61–5, 93, 96, 99
planning
  contested, 4
  and EU policy thinking, 232
  in France, 3, 12, 44, 228
  'planism', 71
  Post-War Planning, 33, 40, 47–9
  pre- and post-war continuities, 3, 9, 12, 18, 44–6
  supranational, 65–70
Pleven, René, 37
Polish Socialist Party, 61, 67
Polydefkis, Henry, 64
Pompidou, Georges, 164, 167–8
Pontillon, Robert, 16, 184, 189
Portugal
  and antiracist networks, 207–8
  and British Left chapter 4 *passim*
  and colonial rule, 133–4, 138–9, 143–4
  criticism of Salazar's regime, 2, 14, 112
  and EFTA, 112, 138
  and EU economic discussions, 226–9, 231
  and Lusophone Africa chapter 4 *passim*
  and NATO, 14, 128, 135, 138, 144–6
  and Socialist International, 196
  and UN, 136
  war in Angola, 134
Portuguese Communist Party, 136
Présence Africaine, 101, 132, 142

Q

Quakers/Society of Friends, 14, 106–107

R

racial issues
  See also antiracism
  apartheid, 14, 105, 127, 130, 140, 146
  Commission for Racial Equality, 18, 206, 208
  and empire, 62, 105, 108, 136–7, 142
  Institute of Race Relations, 214
  International Union against Racism, 63–4
  race as construct, 15, 202
  Race Relations Act, 205
  racialisation processes, 9, 16–17, 20, 110, 203
  structural racism, 206–7
  Women under Racism, 210
Reagan, Ronald, 4, 233–4, 237
Resistance (Second World War)
  and French politics, 3–4, 13, 36–7, 49, 69, 91
  Comité national français (CNF), 33, 41, 44
  Commission pour l'étude des problèmes d'après-guerre, 46
  Conseil National de la Résistance, 63, 91
  in London (*Groupe Jean Jaurès*), 12, 33, 42–5
  place in debates on empire and foreign affairs, 111, 185
  and SOE, 41
  and support for alternative Europe, 64, 69, 91
  transnational, 11, 129
Rhodesias, 105, 114, 130, 132, 137–8, 144
Richardson, Josephine, 95, 111
Ridley, Francis, 61–3, 65–7
Robin, Jacques, 63, 67
Rocard, Michel, 191, 235
Rogers, Douglas, 97
Rogers, William, 161
Roosevelt, Franklin Delano, 4, 37–8, 40, 48

Roth, Andrew, 96–8, 102, 109, 112, 114
Rous, Jean, 96–7

S
Salazar, Antonio de Oliveira, 14, 133–4, 137–8, 143, 227
Samuel, Raphael, 99, 100–101, 110–12
Sartawi, Issam, 193, 196
Savary, Alain, 187
Scott, Michael, 99, 105
Section française de l'internationale ouvrière (SFIO)
  and Algeria, 6, 93, 98, 107, 185
  and British Labour in exile, 12, 37–8, 41–6, 49–50
  comparison with Labour, 34–6
  divisions, 12, 96–8, 101
  and 'Europeanism', 7
  in French politics, 34–6, 43, 45, 47
  and Middle East, 97–9, 184–5
  and planning, 45–6, 69, 71
  and socialist Europe, 61, 63
  and Socialist International, 109
  tension with British Labour over Algerian war, 97–103
  tensions with British Labour on Europe, 64, 66
  and world order, 47
Segal, Ronald, 106, 140
Séguillon, Pierre-Luc, 192
Senegal, 61, 139
Single European Act
  and Europeanisation, 204, 207
  and limits to freedom of movement, 204, 210–11, 214
  pro-market, 227
  and transnational antiracism, 16–17, 204, 210–211, 214
Slovo, Joe, 143
Smuts, Jan, 49
Soares, Mario, 195, 226–7, 229
Socialist International
  and EU economic debates of 1990s, 227, 232–5, 240
  and Franco-British tensions, 98, 109
  Global Challenge, 234
  and Israel/Palestine, 163, 171, 193, 195–6
  leadership, 171, 193
  membership, 18, 109
  Socialist International Committee on Economic Policy/Manley Group, 233–4, 240
  transnational left socialism, dilemmas of, 18, 60–61, 64, 70
South Africa
  anticolonial militants, 64, 105–6, 130, 140, 143

British relations with, 49, 131
  criticism of apartheid, 14, 105, 108, 114, 146
  Sharpeville, 164
  withdrawal from Commonwealth, 112
Sozialdemokratische Partei Deutschlands (SPD), 7, 63, 145, 186, 238
Spaak, Paul-Henri, 72
Spain
  anti-racism, 208, 212
  Civil War, 10–11, 13, 61–2
  colonies, 11
  and European economic policy, 226–7, 231
  political repression in, 2, 68, 130, 137
Stalin, Josef, 4, 13, 49, 59–60, 62, 95
Stalinism, 13, 60, 65
Standing Conference for Racial Equality in Europe (SCORE)
  and 'Black Manifesto for Europe', 209
  Black Women Sub-Committee, 209–12
  creation, 203, 205, 213
  leadership, 202, 206–7, 209
  and postcolonial Europe, 207, 213
  relations with EU institutions, 208–9
  transnational, 202, 207–9, 214
Suez Crisis, 15, 92, 97–99, 110, 183
Susini, Pierre, 160–61
Sweden
  antiracist networks, 204
  British links, 112
  and economic policy, 226–7, 229, 236, 239–40. *See also* Larsson
  and European leadership, 16, 162, 164, 166, 168
  interests in Africa, 145
  neutrality of, 18, 145, 159, 163, 170–71
  and Palestine, 193
  and postwar geopolitics, 6
  and Second World War, 15, 162
  and Swedish Labour Movement's Archives and Library, 164, 225
  and Vietnam war, 15, 18, chapter 5 *passim*
Swedish Social Democratic Party (SAP), 15, 162, 229
Sweezy, Paul, 228

T
Tazdaït, Djida, 18, 207, 211–12
Thatcher, Margaret, 3, 206, 233
Third World
  and anticolonial organising, 128–9
  and de Gaulle, 158
  and socialist thinking, 7, 145, 171, 191–2
Third-Worldism, 7, 127, 188
Thompson, E. P., 100, 110–11

Trades Union Congress (British TUC), 205, 208, 238
Tribune, 44–5, 94–102, 104–5, 111, 114, 137
Trudeau, Pierre, 165
Tunisia, 92, 103

U

Unemployment
  European policies, 17, 224, 227–9 (and chapter 8 *passim*)
  and international system, 39, 65
União Nacional para a Independência Total de Angola (UNITA), 140
Union de la gauche socialiste (UGS), 103, 109
Union Européenne des Fédéralistes (UEF), 68
Union of Democratic Control (UDC)
  creation, 130, 135
  and Portuguese empire in Africa, 133–5
  surveillance of, 94, 130
  and war of Algerian independence, 94, 99–100, 105, 114
Union of Soviet Socialist Republics (USSR)
  appeal to European communists, 3–4, 35–6
  British links, 35, 113, 130
  British visits, 62
  and colonial liberation, 4, 6, 131, 144
  and de Gaulle, 4, 158
  dissolution, 170–71
  and international system, 44, 48–50, 64, 66, 130, 166
  and Marshall Plan, 67
  and Middle East, 185
  and MUSSE/MSEUE, 65
  repression in, 14, 131
  and Second World War, 34, 40, 165
  and Vietnam, 163, 170
United Kingdom. *See* Britain
United Nations
  and Arafat, 195
  Charter of Economic Rights and Duties for States, 233
  creation, 46, 50
  Economic and Social Council of the United Nations, 48
  G-77 dominance, 233
  and liberation in Portuguese Africa, 127–8, 133, 138, 144–6
  New International Economic Order, 233
  United Nations Economic Commission for Europe, 6

United Nations Educational, Scientific and Cultural Organisation, 108, 146
United Nations Relief and Rehabilitation Administration, 47
  and Vietnam War, 160
  and war of Algerian independence, 106, 113
United States
  American left, 61–2, 96
  and British antiracist networks, 204, 206
  and British Labour, 36
  economic policy, 4, 47–8, 158–9
  and 'Fortress Europe', 201
  good offices, 103
  peace organisations, 93–4, 106–8, 130
  and Portuguese Empire, 128, 131, 135, 138
  and Second World War, 3–4, 34, 37–40, 45, 168–9
  in socialist economic policy in Europe, 226, 236
  in socialist plans for Europe, 13, 48–50, 63–4, 66–7, 70–71
  and Vietnam War, 15, 127, 138, 157–70
  and Ukraine, 170–71
  withdrawal from Germany, 158–9
Universities and Left Review (ULR), 99–102, 105–6, 110, 114
Uyl, Joop den, 227, 229–31, 237

V

Vaz, Keith, 206–7
Vichy Government. *See also* France
Viet Minh. *See also* Indochina; Vietnam
Vietnam War
  and Britain, 15, 114, 143, 157, 167
  and de Gaulle, 158
  escalation, 157–8
  and international reverberations, 2, 127, 138, 191
  and NATO, 163, 167, 170
  North Vietnam leaders, 18, 161–2, 167
  Operation Linebacker II/'Christmas Bombings', 160–62, 164–8
  and Palme. *See* Palme, Olof
  and Palme-Brandt-Kreisky intervention, 162–4, 166, 168
  and Quakers, 113–14
  self-determination, 159
  and Western differences, 165–8
Vignon, Jérôme, 239

W

Weil, Simone, 37
Weitz, Lucien, 95, 97–8, 101

Welfare
  and anti-racism, 208, 214
  and decolonisation, 8, 18
  British welfare state, 34, 46
  competing models, 8, 11–12, 72
  in EU policy, 236
Wilson, Harold
  and economic strategy, 232
  Israel, 16, 185
  and Lusophone Africa, 138, 141, 144
  and Vietnam War, 15, 157, 167
Wilson, Woodrow, 38
World Council of Churches, 18, 206, 210

Y

Yugoslavia, 111–13, 129

Z

Zaidi, Nora, 207
Zaremba, Zygmunt, 67
Zilliacus, Konni, 95, 110–12